Issues in Management Accounting

♦

Issues in Management Accounting

Second edition

Edited by
DAVID ASHTON
Professor of Accounting and Finance, University of Bristol
TREVOR HOPPER
KPMG Peat Marwick Professor of Management Accounting, University of Manchester
ROBERT W. SCAPENS
Professor of Accounting, University of Manchester

PRENTICE HALL

LONDON • NEW YORK • TORONTO • SYDNEY • TOKYO • SINGAPORE •
MADRID • MEXICO CITY • MUNICH

First published 1991

This second edition first published 1995 by
Prentice Hall International (UK) Limited
Campus 400, Maylands Avenue
Hemel Hempstead
Hertfordshire HP2 7EZ
A division of
Simon & Schuster International Group

Typeset in 9½/12 pt Palatino by Photoprint, Torquay, Devon

Printed and bound in Great Britain by Redwood Books,
Trowbridge, Wiltshire

Library of Congress Cataloging-in-Publication Data

Ashton, David.
    Issues in management accounting / David Ashton,
Trevor Hopper, Robert Sapens. — 2nd ed
        p.   cm.
    Includes bibliographical references and index.
    ISBN 0-13-189250-9 (pbk).
    1. Managerial accounting. I. Hopper, Trevor, 1946–.
II. Scapens, Robert William. III. Title.
HF5657.4.A84 1995
658.15'11—dc20   94–45025
                                                      CIP

British Library Cataloguing in Publication Data

A catalogue record for this book is available from
the British Library

ISBN 0-13-189250-9

---

    2 3 4 5   99 98 97 96 95

Contents

◆

List of Contributors

♦

DAVID ASHTON is Professor of Accounting and Finance at the University of Bristol. His research interests are mainly in the area of finance. He is currently working on differential information in markets, performance appraisal and financing decisions and estimates of costs of equity funding.

JOHN K. CHRISTIANSEN is Associate Professor at Copenhagen Business School. He has been a visiting Professor at New York University. His research interests are concerned with the organisational implications of management accounting and information systems. He is currently engaged in research on the organisational implications of quality control systems and the implementation of control systems.

WENDY CURRIE is a Senior Lecturer in the School of Management at the University of Stirling. Her research interests include the international management of information technology. She has written three books on this subject and several articles. Her current project looks at the management of IT projects in the public sector, manufacturing industry and financial services, and is funded by the Scottish Higher Education Funding Council (SHEFC).

DAVID DUGDALE holds the post of Associate Dean in the Bristol Business School, a faculty of the University of the West of England, Bristol. After reading for a degree in Physics and a PhD in Operational Research, he became CIMA qualified and spent sixteen years in industry working as a management accountant. Together with Colwyn Jones he jointly holds a CIMA research grant to study 'Throughput Accounting'.

MAHMOUD EZZAMEL is the Price Waterhouse Professor of Accounting and Finance at the University of Manchester Institute of Science and Technology (UMIST). His main research interests are the interface between management accounting and organisational behaviour with particular emphasis on divisionalised organisations, financial statement analysis, and accounting systems in not-for-profit organisations.

MILES GIETZMANN is a Lecturer in Accounting at the London School of Economics. His major research interests reside in exploring the interface between economic theory and management accounting.

TREVOR HOPPER is the KPMG Peat Marwick Professor of Management Accounting in the Department of Accounting and Finance at the University of Manchester where he is currently Head of Department. He has held visiting positions at the University of Michigan, USA; Queen's University, Canada; and the Universities of Kyushu and Fukuoka, Japan. His major research interests lie in the areas of management accounting and control, especially from organisational perspectives.

CHRISTOPHER HUMPHREY is a Senior Lecturer in Accounting at the School of Business and Economic Studies, University of Leeds. His research interests include international auditing practices and expectations, public sector accountable management systems and issues in accounting education.

JOHN INNES is Professor of Accountancy at the University of Dundee. In 1993 he was a Canon Foundation Visiting Fellow in Japan. His current research interests are cost management, change in management accounting and new management accounting practices including activity-based cost management and Japanese practices such as cost tables and functional cost analysis.

T. COLWYN JONES is Principal Lecturer in the School of Sociology, and Research Fellow in the Centre for Social and Economic Research (CESER) at the University of the West of England, Bristol. Since 1975 he has been teaching sociology to accounting undergraduates. He is the author of an undergraduate text, *Accounting and the Enterprise: A Social Analysis* (Routledge, 1995) and a number of papers (many with David Dugdale) on accounting rationality, accounting and technology, investment appraisal and change in costing systems.

ANNE LOFT, PhD is Associate Professor of Accounting at the Copenhagen Business School. A native of Britain, she has lived for the last eight years in Denmark and is one of the editors of the journal *European Accounting Review*. Her research interests are in the history of the accounting profession in the UK from 1860 to 1930, the recent history of the relationship between the accounting profession and the state in Denmark, and the current internationalisation of the accounting profession.

STEPHEN LYNE is a Lecturer in Accounting at the University of Bristol where he teaches management accounting to undergraduate, MBA and doctoral students. His main research interests are concerned with the organisational implications of management accounting, particularly budgeting systems and activity-based techniques.

JIM MACKEY is a Professor of Accounting at California State University, Sacramento. His current research interests include activity-based management in manufacturing and service industries, field research in the Theory of Constraints management and excess capacity measurement, and economic value analysis (EVA). His prior teaching positions were at York University, and the Universities of Wisconsin and Michigan.

FALCONER MITCHELL is Professor of Management Accounting at the University of Edinburgh. He has been researching activity-based costing for the last six years and is working in other areas of cost management, including Japanese practices and public sector applications.

JAN MOURITSEN is Professor of Management Accounting at Copenhagen Business School. His research interests include studying the social and political effects of accounting systems in the public sector and the private sector, especially with respect to the internationalisation of business.

OLOV OLSON is Professor of Public Administration at the School of Public Administration, University of Gothenburg, Sweden. His main research interests are in areas such as the new public sector, reforms of accounting systems and use of accounting systems.

DAVID OTLEY is the KPMG Peat Marwick Professor of Accounting at the Lancaster University Management School. He is General Editor of the *British Journal of Management*, and has held visiting positions at Michigan State University, Virginia Tech and Wirtschaftsuniversität, Vienna. His main research interests are in the design and operation of management control systems, with particular emphasis on their links with corporate strategy and performance-related pay systems.

ALISTAIR PRESTON is an Associate Professor at the University of New Mexico. His research interests are concerned with the origins and impacts of accounting practices in organisations and the development of qualitative research methods. He is currently working on exploring the use of photographic and graphic images in corporate annual reports.

ROBIN ROSLENDER is a Lecturer in Accountancy at the University of Stirling. Originally trained in sociology, he is also a graduate of the Chartered Association of Certified Accountants. His current research interests include the changing conditions of accounting labour, the development of accounting for strategic positioning, the reconstitution of management accounting in Russia and the diffusion of critical perspectives in accounting research.

ROBERT W. SCAPENS is Professor of Accounting and Director of the Centre for Interdisciplinary Research in Accounting at the University of Manchester. He is the Editor of *Management Accounting Research* and his publications include books on management accounting and on research methodology. He has extensive experience of research into various aspects of management accounting theory and practice.

MIKE THOMAS is an Assistant Professor of Accounting at the University of Nevada, Reno. His research and consulting involve empirical, field and normative studies in activity-based costing and management, total quality management and transfer pricing. He has previously taught at San Jose State University, California Polytechnic University, Oklahoma State University and the University of Wisconsin.

RICHARD M.S WILSON is Professor of Business Administration and Financial Management at Loughborough University Business School. He is founding editor of *Accounting Education: An International Journal*, Chairman of the Accounting Education Research Centre (based at Sheffield Hallam University), and Convenor of the British Accounting Association's Special Interest Group on Accounting Education. His main research interests focus on determinants of early career success in accounting and accounting for marketing/strategic control.

Preface

Management accounting textbooks tend to neglect a series of important theoretical and practical developments in the subject area. Conversely, much of the literature covering these developments is not easily accessible to either students or practitioners. The purpose of this book is to help reduce this schism. Active researchers in emergent areas have been invited to write about them in a manner appropriate to both students and practitioners of management accounting.

As in the previous edition, the chapters seek to explain in a straightforward fashion areas of research which directly impinge on management accounting practice. These include management control, microeconomics – especially agency theory, organisational behaviour, and history. Insights from theory and new practices that are explored include new methods of operations management, new computing and manufacturing technologies, strategy, investment appraisal, activity-based costing, transfer pricing, performance appraisal and rewards, creativity and environmental adaptation, and accountability in the public sector.

All of the chapters were specially commissioned for this second edition. Most of the chapters are new and all of the remainder have been substantially revised. Space precluded coverage of all the topics in the first edition, which remains, in our view, a substantive text in its own right. The second edition has incorporated three major new themes: cross-national studies of accounting practice and the internationalisation of business; new insights into management control, including more critical work; and the rise of allegedly new accounting methods stemming from new manufacturing cost management philosophies, including activity-based costing.

The aim of the book is to supplement, rather than to replace, existing second- and third-year undergraduate, advanced professional and postgraduate texts in management accounting. It is also intended that accounting practitioners interested in accessible expositions of contemporary research in management accounting will find the book useful. The favourable response to the first edition stimulated our decision to prepare this second edition. We are indebted to the many people who advised us how best to do this. However, only the reader can judge whether the book is effective in achieving our original intentions. We hope that it is.

DAVID ASHTON
TREVOR HOPPER
ROBERT W. SCAPENS

Acknowledgements

Figure 8.4 reprinted from L.A. Gordon, D.F. Larcker, and F.D. Tuggle, 'Strategic Decision Processes and the Design of Accounting Information Systems: Conceptual Linkages', *Accounting, Organizations and Society*, vol. 3, no. 3/4, p. 207. Copyright 1978, with kind permission from Elsevier Science Limited, The Boulevard, Langford Lane, Kidlington OX5 1GB.

Figure 8.8 reprinted with the permission of the American Accounting Association, and Professor R.A. Capettini.

Figure 8.13 reprinted with the permission of The Free Press, an imprint of Simon and Schuster, from *Competitive Advantage: Creating and Sustaining Superior Performance* by Michael E. Porter. Copyright 1985 by Michael E. Porter.

Figure 8.14 reprinted with permission from the *Journal of Cost Management*, vol. 5, no. 4. Copyright 1992 Warren Gorham Lamont, 31 St James Avenue, Boston, MA 02116. All rights reserved.

Figure 8.16 reprinted by permission from p. 120 of *Analysis for Strategic Marketing Decisions* by George S. Day. Copyright 1986 by West Publishing Company. All rights reserved.

Figure 8.17 reprinted with the permission of The Free Press, an imprint of Simon and Schuster, from *The PIMS Principles: Linking Strategy to Performance* by Robert D. Buzzell and Bradley T. Gale. Copyright 1987 by The Free Press.

Figure 8.18 reprinted with the kind permission of Professor Michael Bromwich.

Figure 8.19 reprinted from R. Simons, 'The Role of Management Control Systems in Creating Competitive Advantage: New Perspectives', *Accounting, Organizations and Society*, vol. 15, no. 1/2, p. 138. Copyright 1990, with kind permission from Elsevier Science Limited, The Boulevard, Langford Lane, Kidlington OX5 1GB.

CHAPTER ONE

The Changing Nature of Issues in Management Accounting

David Ashton, Trevor Hopper and Robert W. Scapens

The last few years have seen a renaissance in the theory and practice of management accounting. Management accounting has been forced out of the moribund state in which it largely addressed the problems of the technology of the nineteenth century and into a new era in which it has become increasingly conscious of the changing technological and organisational context of its operation. The impetus for this change has come mainly from practitioners who have recognised the inadequacies of existing costing and control systems and from academics aware of this failure. These changes have been accelerated by the increasing globalisation of product and capital markets and by changing production and information technologies. This has led to a re-examination of the process of costing and cost management and of its contribution to the management and control of organisations. In this book the changing nature of the issues in management accounting is explored. However, to understand why these changes were necessary, it is important to trace the development of management accounting.

Management Accounting in Retrospect

In the 1950s and 1960s Western industrialised countries, especially North America and Britain, held strong positions in international markets. Their products were highly regarded, they could be sold relatively easily, and competition on the basis of price or quality was relatively low. The assumption of benign and sometimes protected markets had several consequences for management control within companies. Management was concerned primarily with internal matters, especially production capacity. This focus on production meant that management controls were oriented towards manufacturing and internal administration rather than strategic and environmental considerations.

This manufacturing and internal emphasis was reflected by management styles within companies. Authority stemming from experience and position rather than professional expertise and qualifications tended to predominate. The emphasis lay on line hierarchies, with staff functions playing a secondary, supportive role. Management decision-making was assumed to be highly structured and formal, with readily identifiable objectives and decision alternatives. There was little innovation in products or production processes. Existing products sold well, and existing production processes were well understood.

Paradoxically, given the inwardness and cost orientation of control systems then prevalent, relative efficiency was not high. There was little incentive for firms to minimise manufacturing costs, as increased costs could often be passed on to customers. Also, in growing mass markets, unit cost reductions often flowed from economies of scale within mass production. Consequently, inefficient and poor management practices were common in many industries.

Despite the pioneering work of British engineers and accountants in devising cost accounting systems at the turn of the century, the application of such systems had been slow in Britain, compared, say, to North America. After the Second World War, as a consequence of Productivity Council visits to the United States and the advice offered by important management consultants, many companies adopted management accounting practices prevalent in the USA, for example divisionalisation, budgetary control and capital budgeting.

However, even where cost accounting systems were used, the dissemination of cost information tended to be slight, and its use for management decision-making poorly exploited. In general, cost accounting systems were only loosely integrated with management planning and control systems. Given that the latter were often very rudimentary, this is not surprising. Management accounting systems tended to be reactive, identifying problems and actions only when deviations from the business plan took place. Such systems reflected and reproduced mechanistic rather than innovative styles of management. Nevertheless, in the USA and especially Britain, such management accounting systems were, and may still be, the cornerstone of management control in corporations. While it would be unfair to attribute the blame for poor marketing, product development and technological innovation to the cost accounting systems, the focus on routine historical events and the neglect of prospective planning may have contributed to the financial conservatism of British industry and its alleged emphasis, like its American counterparts, on the short run and the status quo.

Pressures for change

The 1970s brought a considerable decline in the fortunes of British and American industry, although, in the case of Britain, closer examination shows this to be an acceleration of a trend of relative decline exhibited throughout this century. A world-wide recession, following the oil price shock of 1973, threatened established markets. This was compounded by a decline in protected markets and increased global competition particularly from Europe and newly emerging industrial nations, especially in the Far East. Accompanying and underpinning this increased competition was rapid technological development. Japan, for instance, was rapidly becoming one of the world's leaders in the use of robotics and computer-controlled processors. The new technologies reduced costs and improved quality, in many cases with far less labour. This had significant implications for employment and gave rise to social as well as economic consequences.

Technological change not only had an impact on manufacturing processes but it also had substantial effects on information processing within organisations. Developments in computers, especially the emergence of the personal computer, markedly changed the amount of data which can be accessed by managers. Managers can be informed to a far greater extent than ever before about all aspects of their company's operations. The design, maintenance and interpretation of information systems is now of considerable importance for effective management.

Thus the deployment of technology became crucial for industrial success. As well as its effects on internal operations and controls, increased scientific knowledge has created significant new markets, for example in electronics, and has given added importance to product innovation and development. This in turn requires companies to employ organisation structures and styles of management that are flexible and responsive to change. Unfortunately the initial response of British and American companies to these technological changes was disappointing. The reasons are complex; in the case of Britain especially, they include factors such as poor education and training, low rates of industrial research and development and, significantly for this text, styles and methods of management that do not foster competitive innovation.

During the 1980s there was a major decline in the absolute size of Britain's and the relative size of the USA's manufacturing industry. Some companies failed to meet the new competition and went out of business, while others modernised and became more cost-effective through the use of new technologies. The latter companies are, in general, now more competitive and technologically advanced than their predecessors, but automation alone was not a panacea. Selective investment in technology needed to be married, in many instances, to forms and philosophies of management distinctively different from their predecessors.

Alongside the decline in manufacturing industry, there has been an increase in the non-manufacturing sector. For example, there has been a continuing growth in the commercial and financial sectors of most economies, with major increases in the size of industries such as leisure and tourism. Also, the service and overhead activity within manufacturing firms has tended to increase in absolute and relative terms. In addition, in many countries, there has been a major transformation in the role and structure of the public sector, with an emphasis upon competition and commercialisation. As a result, conventional cost accounting with its origins in production and manufacturing is being found wanting for the effective management and control of these sectors and activities.

Through a process of growth and mergers, many companies are now much larger and more international. The increase in size, coupled with the need to employ more professional specialists, has led to highly differentiated organisations, with more specialist jobs and departments. However, the need to co-ordinate these differentiated activities in order to meet environmental challenges has placed a premium on integration and adaptation. The pressures created by the need simultaneously to cope with this and to adapt to increasingly competitive and differentiated markets with shortened product life-cycles have required newer and more sophisticated forms of management.

Many companies are meeting the challenge of global competition by introducing new management and production techniques, and at the same time controlling costs, often through reducing labour costs. 'Down-sizing' has become the phrase used by public relations officers to describe the process of removing layers of management and reducing the size of the labour force. Such a process emphasises the importance of controlling costs and operations with less managerial input. Also, many organisations talk about 'empowering' their employees. This means providing employees at all levels with the information they need to be able to take decisions themselves. In this environment there is a great need for management information to be diffused throughout the organisation, and the challenge for management accountants is to ensure that they are the primary providers of this information.

The 1980s have seen a rise in importance of transnational trading blocs. For example, in the 1990s the increasing size and influence of the European Union (formerly the European Community) has created both threats and challenges for industry. In addition the rise of South-East Asian economies represents major threats and opportunities. The effects need not be entirely negative. For example, Britain has been relatively successful in attracting foreign (outside the European Union) investment from companies who want to set up productive operations within the European Union. Just as earlier American investment in Britain infused new technologies and methods into British firms, the European and Asian trading partners of today may do likewise.

Curiously, and for better or worse, American cost accounting methods and the use of the English language have tended to dominate research, teaching and possibly accounting practice internationally. For example, it has been rare to find a leading textbook in English that paid any attention to material outside the USA or Britain. However, this is beginning to change for a variety of reasons. First, as organisations and trading become more transnational, planning and control systems need to pay attention to different cultures and traditions. Second, the relative economic success of non-English-speaking countries, such as Germany and Japan, where cost accounting practices and powers are significantly different, has meant that American and British managers and academics have had to fundamentally re-examine the effectiveness of previously uncontested assumptions about their costing methods. In some quarters it is asserted that traditional Anglo-American methods are the problem in attaining international competitiveness, rather than the key to success as previously presumed. For example, the greater power and influence of engineers within German and Japanese companies – including within their cost management systems – has raised a question mark over the dominance of accountants within American and especially British companies. Third, the globalisation of trade is beginning to be accompanied by an internationalisation of accounting knowledge. For example, leading research forums are tending to attract members from a wide variety of countries, whereas previously these tended to be primarily from a single nation. Although this is still at an early stage, it is making cost innovations and philosophies outside Britain and America better known.

To summarise, in the 1990s industry world-wide continues to face considerable uncertainty in both home and international markets, and unprecedented advances in manufacturing and information-processing technologies. In addition, organisation structures are tending to be flatter and information flows are needed at all levels of the organisation. It is important to recognise that service industries (including industries in the commercial sector) are forming a major and growing part of many economies, whereas the manufacturing sector has often declined very significantly. In addition, accounting is playing an increasing role in the restructuring, privatisation and commercialisation of the public sector in many parts of the globe. Given such economic and social turbulence and the implication of accounting in such trans-formations, it is perhaps unsurprising that accounting academics and practitioners are fundamentally re-examining its knowledge and methods.

Management Accounting Knowledge and Practice

In its early days management accounting was essentially concerned with such cost accounting issues as the determination of product costs. Production technology was relatively simple, with products going through a series of distinct manufacturing processes. At each stage it was fairly easy to identify labour and material costs. The speed of the manufacturing process was frequently governed by the speed of manual operations. Hence, direct labour provided a natural basis for assigning indirect costs to individual products. It was this manufacturing technology which gave rise to the cost accounting systems which are described in management accounting textbooks even today. During the 1930s the focus on product costs was supplemented by work on budgets and responsibility accounting, and extended to divisional performance measurement and transfer pricing in the 1950s. Such developments stemmed primarily from practical innovations by managers and engineers and were relatively uninformed by academic research.

It is interesting to note that researchers such as Johnson and Kaplan (1987), who are trying to address contemporary Western management accounting problems, lay great stress on the need to re-examine the history of management accounting. Such researchers believe that accounting research has become divorced from practice and, because of its domination of managerial education and training, it has frustrated rather than facilitated solutions to new problems. Chapter 5 of this book, by Mackey and Thomas, is illustrative of how new methods in operations management require approaches to management accounting control systems radically different from those outlined in traditional texts. However, as Chapters 2 and 4, by Loft and Roslender respectively, indicate, the theorisation and explanations of these historical accounts have been challenged for their managerial orientation and assumptions of economic determinism wrought by markets.

In contrast to the paucity of academic management accounting research in previous periods, it is probably fair to say that the late 1950s to the mid-1970s were the heyday of management accounting research. Academics believed that they had solutions to the problems faced by practitioners. Numerous papers were published in academic journals, many of which found their way into the professional accounting literature. Much of today's textbook material is derived from research undertaken in that period. This research largely entailed the application of neoclassical economic theory to the problems of business decision-making and control. The models and techniques were attempts to 'programme' the decision-making and control processes. It was assumed that the objective of management decision-making is to maximise the wealth of shareholders and that there is little uncertainty about either the decision alternatives or the decision outcomes.

By the early 1970s researchers were extending the models developed in the 1960s, primarily to deal with uncertain outcomes and the costs of providing information. There were linear programming models, cost variance investigation models, transfer pricing models, performance evaluation models, opportunity cost models, to name but a few. All these models were extensively researched and the associated decision procedures clearly defined. The objective of this research was to provide managers with a set of decision tools which would help them in their day-to-day work and provide optimal solutions to what were perceived as the key managerial decisions.

Despite pioneering work by Argyris and Simon, and their colleagues, in the 1950s, organisational and behavioural research into management accounting did not begin to flourish until the late 1960s. The 1970s witnessed a considerable amount of research into motivational aspects of management accounting systems. This was followed by contingency theory research, which tried to relate the design of accounting control systems to such organisational factors as size, technology and management styles, and to the type of environment in which they operate. Chapter 3 by Otley on management control, organisational design and accounting information systems and Chapter 11 by Lyne on accounting measures, motivation and performance appraisal illustrate the issues raised by this research. The essential message is that accounting systems cannot be designed independently of the characteristics and environmental context of the firm and of motivational factors and performance appraisal systems. This point is reinforced in several other chapters, especially in Currie's investigation of Japanese cost management systems in Chapter 15.

During the early 1980s rather less management accounting research appeared in the academic journals, and there were few major contributions in the professional press. In general, management accounting researchers became increasingly critical of the existing state of management accounting knowledge. Furthermore, it became apparent that there was a significant gap between the 'theoretical' material contained in management accounting textbooks and the methods used by management accountants in practice. During this period some researchers interested in management accounting began to look to social theories to provide a social critique of management accounting practice. Chapter 4 by Roslender reviews this 'critical' management accounting research.

A feature of the 1990s has been the impact which a small group of researchers in North America – principally Kaplan and his colleagues – has had on the concerns of managers and the emphasis given to issues of cost management. Research by academics, consultants and practitioners has attracted considerable attention in the professional press, but rather less attention in the academic press, although there are an increasing number of academics interested in assessing the impact of such developments on current managerial practices. This is reflected in the rise of specialist management accounting journals such as the *Journal of Cost Management*, the *Journal of Management Accounting Research* and *Management Accounting Research*. In Chapter 6, Innes and Mitchell describe the development of activity-based costing (ABC) and activity-based management (ABM), which have been the focus of much recent cost management research. They point out that only a minority of organisations have adopted ABC or ABM, although expressions of interest remain high.

Although a gap between theory and practice was recognised in the 1980s, not all researchers agree upon whether it constitutes a problem. Nevertheless, since the early 1980s management accounting research has become increasingly fragmented and has moved away from the trends which had emerged in previous research. Some of the more significant changes are described below.

Economic-based management accounting research has become less normative and more descriptive in an attempt more realistically to model and interpret managerial behaviour and the role of control systems. Agency theory, which is discussed by Gietzmann in Chapter 12, became a particularly important theoretical tool, as it permits researchers to explore conflicts over control and the contribution of rewards and information. Previously, economic theorists had tended to ignore internal organisational control problems, regarding the firm as essentially a single economic actor. Agency theory, by opening up what was previously regarded as a 'black box', offered the prospect of significant new insights into managerial control within firms. The importance of considering the behavioural and motivational consequences of economic systems is also noted in Chapter 7, by Ezzamel, on transfer pricing.

Other researchers have continued to use insights gained from behavioural science and organisation theory to look more closely at the nature of management accounting practices within the 'black box' of the firm. This research has attempted to study management accounting practices in the various organisational and environmental contexts in which it operates. Yet other researchers have become increasingly concerned about the social context of management accounting. These different approaches are reviewed in Chapters 3 and 4, by Otley and Roslender respectively, and they inform many of the other chapters including those by Dugdale and Jones, Humphrey and Olson, Loft, and Christiansen and Mouritsen.

There has been a significant revival of research examining contemporary accounting problems, for example the introduction of new methods of operations management, such as just-in-time manufacturing (JIT) and material requirements planning (MRP), and new systems for the control of overheads, such as activity-based costing. The new methods of operations management are reviewed in Chapter 5, by Mackey and Thomas; activity-based costing is evaluated by Innes and Mitchell in Chapter 6; and Currie in Chapter 15 and Dugdale and Jones in Chapter 9 both examine the problems of evaluating capital investments in advanced manufacturing technology. In addition there has been a growing interest in the link between management accounting and management information systems and the impact of advanced computer technology on accounting systems. These issues are examined by Christiansen and Mouritsen in Chapter 10.

The difficulties of adapting to environmental change have become another important research theme which is addressed in several chapters, albeit in different ways. In Chapter 8, Wilson is concerned with more general strategic and marketing issues and with how management accounting might become more proactive and externally oriented. A contrasting approach is adopted by Preston in Chapter 13, in which he examines how decision-making is related to managerial cultures and creativity. In so doing, he questions whether conventional 'rational' depictions of decision-making are appropriate, a theme which is pursued also in Currie's Chapter 15.

There has also been an increase in the variety of research methods used. This has led to a major methodological debate amongst accounting researchers regarding how research should be conducted and the philosophical basis which underpins it. The variety in current research methods is illustrated in various chapters: for instance, the mathematical economics approach of Gietzmann (Chapter 12), the behavioural analysis of Lyne (Chapter 11), the critical perspectives of Roslender (Chapter 4) and Loft (Chapter 2), the anthropological emphasis of Preston (Chapter 13) and the managerial pragmatism of Wilson (Chapter 8). Underpinning these various research methods are some fundamental methodological differences about the role and purpose of research. Although these methodological differences remain unresolved, common to all the methods is a significant change brought about by the increased emphasis upon fieldwork and descriptive research. Current research is now more directed to understanding practice, whereas previous research was more concerned with prescribing managerial behaviour and developing normative models.

There has been a growing interest in the international dimensions of management accounting and comparative studies of practice in different countries. As mentioned earlier, the 1990s have seen increasing globalisation of businesses and now any discussion of management accounting would be incomplete without a review of the implications of this international dimension. Many companies now operate in global product and capital markets and their managers need accounting systems to enable them to manage such diverse organisations. The impact of this on the management accounting systems of international firms is explored in Chapter 14 by Mouritsen. In addition, management accountants in various parts of the world have been looking at the practices used in other countries. The management and accounting practices of Japanese companies, especially within JIT and target costing, and German and Japanese firms in respect to the influence of engineers and operations management in cost management, have proved to be very interesting to Anglo-Saxon managers and accountants soul-searching about their existing practices and seeking ideas from successful competitors. This is a theme of Chapter 15 by Currie. Comparative studies across nation-states on how accounting shapes and is shaped by transformations in the public sector have been rare, which is surprising given its significance internationally, not least in previously communist countries. Chapter 16 by Humphrey and Olson, which compares the Swedish experience with that of Britain, is an exploratory attempt to try and open up such a debate.

Finally, there has been a significant evolution of research *on* management accounting, as opposed to research *in* management accounting. The revival of historical research as described by Loft in Chapter 2 is a notable example. In part, such research may be due to a genuine puzzlement about differences between textbook prescriptions and practice. In addition, there is an increasing interest in the social role of accounting. This has led to a growing number of critical studies seeking to understand the social and political context of management accounting – see Roslender, Chapter 4. Chapter 16, by Humphrey and Olson, on accounting in the public sector, is also in this vein. It questions the rhetoric and long-established assumptions of policy-makers about the effectiveness of accounting controls currently advocated in the public sector and notes that the effects of accounting change are not merely technical, acting upon efficiency considerations, but embrace fundamental issues regarding the nature of democracy and accountability within society.

These various changes in management accounting research are explored in greater detail below.

Recent Developments in Management Accounting Research: Addressing the Gap?

Developments in economic approaches

Academic concern over the perceived gap between theory and practice has led to major changes in economic-based management accounting research and to the development of other theoretical approaches. In general, there has been a drift away from normative economic research to more varied descriptive approaches that seek to model the complexities of management control and the internal organisation of firms in economic, organisational and social terms. The normative economic research had resulted in a series of decision models, such as discounted cash flow models and linear programming, which were intended to help managers make optimal decisions. Optimality was taken as synonymous with the maximisation of the wealth of the owners or shareholders, and it was tacitly assumed that once appropriate decision rules were identified, the employees would unquestioningly and unselfishly implement them. Any necessary control mechanisms were assumed to be provided through the discipline of market forces. If entrepreneurs and their employees were not wholly efficient, new firms would enter the industry and price-cutting would ensure that inefficient producers were forced out.

In practice, there are many social and economic barriers to perfect competition. Even the briefest acquaintance with industrial and commercial organisations suggests considerable slackness and apparent inefficiency. In principal-agent (PA) analysis, it is accepted that employees are motivated by self-interest rather than altruism and are more likely to pursue personal rather than organisational goals. Moreover, it is impossible to monitor continually the behaviour and actions of employees to prevent them from pursuing their own self-interests. What prevents the organisation, in such circumstances, from degenerating into anarchy is a series of binding agreements or contracts between the owners and their employees. These contracts specify the actions to be undertaken by employees as well as designating the rewards that will accrue to them. Thus, in PA analysis the economist is abandoning the view of the firm as an entity with the single purpose of maximising owners' wealth in favour of a view of the firm as a collection of interlinked contracts. The consequences of these assumptions are explored in Chapter 12 by Gietzmann.

The chapter by Ezzamel (Chapter 7) also examines economic models for setting transfer prices within divisionalised businesses to charge for goods and services exchanged internally. Transfer prices can have a major influence on the allocation of resources between divisions, and on the assessment of the performance of individual divisions and their managers. A transfer price which is 'high' will – other things being equal – result in the selling division appearing to be 'more' profitable and the buying division appearing to be 'less' profitable. This can lead to major shifts in the resources allocated to both divisions, with the apparently more profitable division gaining greater access to corporate resources relative to the apparently less profitable division. The success of a transfer pricing system in co-ordinating and guiding the activities of a divisionalised business depends on its ability to capture the relevant organisational and economic factors. Ezzamel illustrates the variety of factors which have to be considered in setting transfer prices. He also points out that many of the theoretical models which have been developed give undue attention to economic factors and fail to capture important organisational and behavioural factors.

Chapter 9, by Dugdale and Jones, which examines technical and organisational problems with investment appraisal techniques such as discounted cash flow (DCF), typifies some of the more recent research related to economic approaches. After an outline of the technical issues which have tended to dominate the finance literature, they raise more fundamental doubts stemming from empirical studies of practice. They note how Japanese firms tend not to place great reliance on such methods and that Western managers often persist in using techniques such as payback or accounting rate of return which are presumed to be deficient within an economic approach. However, they argue that, given the restricted assumptions of economic approaches, such 'deviancies' may be understandable. An uncritical reliance on DCF may lead to inferior decisions as it fails to embrace a series of organisational, strategic and operational factors. This is especially relevant to decisions involving investment in advanced manufacturing technology. Like Ezzamel, Dugdale and Jones do not advocate a complete abandonment of economic-based accounting techniques but instead they emphasise the need to better understand accounting in its organisational context. The attempt to do just this is the motivation behind much of the accounting research described in this volume.

Development of other theoretical approaches

While principal–agent analysis allows economic-based accounting theory to explore some issues in motivation and control, the model of motivation adopted is still that of the 'rational economic man' – motivated by self-interest and trading-off his greed against his dislike of work. This is a very simplistic and limiting view of motivation. Many management accounting researchers have turned to other disciplines in the social sciences to provide ideas, theories and research methodologies. The behavioural sciences offer management accounting researchers a much richer set of paradigms in which to study the motivational impact and consequences of budgeting and accounting-based performance measurement systems. Lyne reviews some of this research in Chapter 11.

In Chapter 3, Otley reviews the ideas from organisation theory which have come into the management accounting arena through the management control literature. He describes the contingency theory of organisational design and assesses the implications for a contingency theory of management accounting, highlighting the problem of using organisational performance as a measure of the effectiveness of a particular control systems design. Research suggests that performance is itself a contingent variable and therefore a fundamental circularity is involved in using it to measure effectiveness. Otley then discusses various approaches to measuring organisational performance and concludes that although accounting information has an important role to play in organisational control systems, it is an imperfect control tool which must be used alongside other information systems.

Preston in Chapter 13 takes this a step further, arguing that contingency approaches are insufficient for capturing the complexity of control and decision-making processes within organisations as they ignore vital aspects of behaviour, such as hunch, intuition, habit and culture. Whilst not dismissing contingency approaches entirely, he argues for a more anthropological, culture-based approach to studying accounting controls.

Roslender in Chapter 4 argues that the move to critical management accounting can be seen as a logical progression from the earlier use of behavioural science and organisation theory in management accounting research. He describes how critical management accounting explores the non-technical aspects of accounting for management using a broad range of social science perspectives and argues that, although this multi-perspective approach may seem confusing and even disconcerting to readers more familiar with the singular (uncritical) approach of conventional management accounting research, it has the potential to generate a genuinely social scientific approach to management accounting research which embraces a fuller range of significant factors, such as the role of the state, changes in the nature of capitalism and corporate governance and accountability – all of which are issues emerging, albeit in a different form, in the more pragmatic, managerially oriented debate over the relevance of conventional management accounting methods.

Developments in management techniques

A recurring theme in several chapters is how developments in computers, especially the availability of cheap personal computers and spreadsheet software, are having a major impact on how managers can conduct their analysis. Proponents of spreadsheets argue that their greatest strength lies in their facility for rapidly exploring alternative scenarios. This enables management to cope with uncertainty in decision inputs. These issues are explored in more depth in Chapter 10 by Christiansen and Mouritsen. They trace the impact of the revolution in computer technology on information and decision systems within the firm. They argue that while the new technology has facilitated the work of the management accountant, it also changes the role of the accountant within the organisation. Computers have automated much of the data-gathering and recording activities and in many firms data-gathering has been subsumed within production activities. New software such as spreadsheets has facilitated the analysis of financial planning, while the ease with which data are collected as part of the firm's activities has facilitated the generation of information for control purposes. However, the integration of management accounting systems and management information systems means that information is more widely dispersed within the organisation. This challenges the accountants' traditional monopoly position as suppliers of information. The authors draw a parallel between the design of management information systems (MIS) and that of accounting systems. They argue that management accountants are in a favourable position to continue to play a key role in the development, and the use, of the information technology, provided they accept the challenge. Moreover, they are trained in the key areas of model-building and the structuring and analysis of information. Also, unlike many computer specialists, they receive training in, and are therefore aware of, the organisational context in which they operate.

One of the major new management accounting techniques in recent years has been activity-based costing (ABC). As Innes and Mitchell discuss in Chapter 6, the idea of activity-based costing has existed for several decades, but it has gained prominence recently through the work of Kaplan and Cooper, following Johnson and Kaplan's book *Relevance Lost: The rise and fall of management accounting* (1987). Instead of allocating indirect costs using traditional volume-related measures of output such as direct labour hours, ABC identifies suitable cost pools for indirect cost and then uses appropriate cost drivers to relate the expenditure in the cost pools to the activities of the business. Although ABC has proved very popular, with seminars on the subject being greatly oversubscribed, the number of companies actually using the technique remains relatively modest, but expressions of interest and intent remain quite high.

One of the problems addressed by the advocates of ABC has been the capital appraisal of investments in new technology. They claim that activity-based measures are likely to prove more suitable for assessing the impact of introducing advanced production technology. In that ABC should more clearly identify cost drivers and hence cost savings, this would seem to be a plausible theory. However, it finds only limited support in the chapter on new manufacturing technology by Mackey and Thomas (Chapter 5) and those by Dugdale and Jones on the appraisal of new technology (Chapter 9) and by Currie (Chapter 15) who examines how Anglo-American companies use management accounting compared to their counterparts in Germany and Japan. All of these authors emphasise the strategic nature of the reasons for the adoption of advanced manufacturing processes. A detailed analysis of the costs and benefits of new technology does not necessarily provide the reason for its adoption, though it may well provide the justification.

A recurring theme of critics of ABC, which has recently been picked up by Johnson in *Relevance Regained* (1992), is that rather than being the revolution in costing it claims to be, it represents a continuation of failed Western techniques of management-by-numbers. Some of our contributors, such as Dugdale and Jones, Preston, and Currie argue that the most effective new techniques reside not in new product costings or more refined methods of capital appraisal, but rather in improving the decision-making processes associated with cost management. They argue that merely improving methods of investment appraisal, however laudable in itself, will not transform industry. What is needed is a greater understanding of technological issues by accountants, increased involvement in financial issues by engineers and managers and closer teamwork between these groups. This is strongly influenced by Japanese methods which often use simple, unsophisticated accounting data, but emphasise their integration into strategy through target costing, operations management through JIT and cost reduction teams. Currie (in Chapter 15) notes that Japanese and German companies use a larger battery of operational indices than their Anglo-American counterparts who instead stress financial indicators. If the afore-mentioned authors are correct, then their analysis suggests that advancement of methods may not necessarily be achieved through refined calculative techniques but through greater incorporation of motivational and group factors, employee influence and revised organisational structures that give greater power to engineers at the expense of accountants.

New technology and environmental adaptation

It can be argued that too often budgets represent the past carried forward, and the emphasis on monitoring performance by the feedback of actuals against budget leads to an over-concern with internal rather than external matters and past rather than future events (see Chapters 8 and 13 by Wilson and Preston respectively). It may be that this is the only role for management accounting as we know it. But this is not the view held by many of the contributors to this book. In Chapter 8 Wilson seeks to demonstrate how accounting practice can be integrated with strategy formulation and marketing. Wilson argues that cost accounting systems tend to be directed at the operational level, whereas studies of strategy suggest that key success factors lie in strategic choices and monitoring business performance relative to competitors. Hence, strategic management accounting systems need to look at the organisation holistically and to examine its competitive position. Such systems should look outwards and forwards, and examine, *inter alia*, the relative market share of existing products, their position in the product life-cycle, market prospects, the portfolio of products produced, and incorporate costings based on experience curves. The analysis should not be based solely on the individual organisation but on its competitive advantages relative to competitors. In addition, it should analyse competitors' past and future costs and their market performance and strategic options.

Earlier in this introduction it was argued that cost accounting systems described in textbooks assume relatively simple, labour-intensive production processes, whereas modern production technologies are highly automated, with much continuous processing. The speed of processing is no longer determined by the labour input. This change has profound implications for management accounting, as is discussed in Chapter 5 by Mackey and Thomas. They trace how manufacturing processes have changed following the adoption of materials requirements planning (MRP), just-in-time manufacturing (JIT) and automated manufacturing. They argue that traditional approaches to control and responsibility accounting are unsuitable in the new environment of operations management and that this new environment will require fundamental changes to the design of accounting control systems.

Traditional manufacturing processes use inventories to buffer individual departments against the uncertainties of supply from preceding departments and raw materials suppliers. Such buffering permits departments to be controlled as relatively independent entities through responsibility accounting systems, while co-ordination is achieved through master production schedules. Accounting systems focus on materials and labour costs, with overheads recovered by a system of overhead allocation. In such a system, inventories are accepted as a necessary 'evil'. MRP often produces significant reductions in inventories, but in so doing renders departments far more interdependent. Thus, performance measures emphasise meeting due dates, rather than the budget, as individual departments have much less autonomy.

MRP can be seen as an extension of traditional manufacturing methods, whereas JIT represents a very different philosophy. JIT presents a series of challenges to conventional cost accounting systems. For example, its climate of continual improvement means that standards are constantly changing. Also, adverse variances may not represent 'failures' but rather experiments directed at securing improvements. The performance emphasis switches from maximising fixed capacity to meeting short-term demand and quality. It is argued that this requires new accounting measures of effectiveness, including measures that reflect a longer time perspective than traditional efficiency measures. Given the team approach, with its flexibility and change, static negotiated budgets become less meaningful. Furthermore, JIT moves many of the traditional overhead functions, such as maintenance, work design and quality control, into the work cell; thereby making them direct costs and susceptible to more direct forms of control. Nevertheless, certain indirect costs remain as overheads; hence there continues to be an interest in overhead allocation bases and activity costing.

JIT may be a precursor to automated manufacturing systems. Mackey and Thomas trace how such systems call for increased discipline in submitting data and for accountants to be more involved in production scheduling. In addition, the increased proportion of fixed costs to variable costs makes pricing more difficult. Automation makes strategic planning and cost reduction at the design stage much more important. Target costing is commended but, like several other authors, Mackey and Thomas raise doubts about the effectiveness of financial appraisal methods such as discounted cash flow (DCF) for evaluating investments in advanced manufacturing technology.

Currie's Chapter 15 on comparative studies of management accounting is complementary to that by Mackey and Thomas for it traces how Japanese systems emphasise integration of functions and cost reduction within the firm from the initial stages of product design through to all phases of manufacture. Currie argues that management accounting and financial management in British and US firms play more central roles than in Japan and Germany. In the latter two countries firms tend to emphasise longer-run, broader strategic considerations, engineering and operational matters and use different methods of cost management and control than their counterparts in the USA and the UK. This raises major issues for British and US firms, especially as they tend to control through financial measures based on individual accountability and relatively loosely connected management functions. However, as Currie points out, application of German and Japanese methods to Anglo-American corporations may be difficult given different capital markets, corporate cultures and institutional relationships, not least with the state.

Social behaviour, control and creativity

Reports of Japanese methods of management accounting reinforce the relevance of behavioural research, for it raises a series of issues regarding how social factors such as groups, cultures and reward systems affect performance. Whilst economic-based researchers have acknowledged the need to model control systems and to incorporate payment systems into their analysis, emphasis upon monetary rewards as the major motivating factor means that their approach is still relatively simplistic.

Psychological theories of motivation more complex than economic ones are explored in Chapter 11 by Lyne. He examines how accounting controls are related to the systems of performance appraisal and rewards. Accounting systems are frequently integral to performance appraisal as they help define roles and expected levels of performance, and they report achievement to higher levels of management. Lyne examines several complementary theories of motivation: need satisfying theory, achievement theories, motivation-hygiene theory, equity theory and expectancy theory. He argues that the design of accounting systems is integrally connected to issues of organisational design, motivation and performance evaluation. He traces, through a review of pertinent research, how participation in setting accounting measures affects individual performance and how this is mediated by cultures, personality characteristics and task uncertainty.

These ideas are echoed in Chapter 13 by Preston, who argues that the conventional wisdom of budgeting is premised upon a rational model of organisational reality. This rationalist model has become so pervasive in management accounting theory and textbooks that it is taken for granted and rarely questioned. Preston argues that if we wish to understand more about budgeting and how it operates in organisations, it is necessary to explore and critically evaluate the philosophical underpinnings of the traditional budgeting model. He argues that 'rational' models assume that everything, including environments, organisations, organisational process and individual behaviour, belong to a presumed natural order, characterised as an objective, knowable system of variables and rules governing their relationship. Preston's concern is that this rational model of budgeting neglects the role of human beings. If human behaviour is seen as entirely determined by organisational structures and processes, then there is no room for the self-determining actions and creative expression of individuals. Prescriptions for improving creativity in organisations are relatively rare in the literature. This is due, in part at least, to a failure to recognise that budgets mean different things to different people and that organisations evolve different cultures. Thus, it is not possible, nor is it desirable, to construct general prescriptions for budgeting in all organisations. Rather, the designers of budgetary systems should consider the meanings that people attach to budgets and the way in which they may be integrated into, and give shape to, the culture of the organisation. Such a process involves the active participation of the organisational members and must allow ample room for improvisation and new ideas. It is suggested that alternative forms of budgeting should create an atmosphere of organised anarchy and promote playful and experimental behaviour. It should be recognised that creative potential is evident in organisations, and may be observed in the informal processes through which managers meet and discuss problems and future events. Within traditional management accounting, these informal processes are positively discouraged, thereby stifling any creative potential which may already exist.

Critique and policy

One of the offshoots of the perceived gap between theory and practice and the inadequacies of management accounting, especially with respect to new manufacturing technologies, has been an increased interest in management accounting history, which until recently has been relatively neglected. To understand the present it appears that we need to better understand the past, and it is argued that the resolution of current theoretical controversies may be helped through historical studies.

Chapter 2, by Loft, examines recent controversies in management accounting history which have emerged partly because of the arguments in Johnson and Kaplan's book, *Relevance Lost*. Their argument is that the management accounting systems which developed in the United States in the late nineteenth and early twentieth centuries have lost their relevance due to an over-emphasis on financial accounting and the excessive influence of academics in business schools. The early systems, they maintain, were crucial to the development of large firms, as they provided essential systems for internal co-ordination. However, there have been few developments since the 1930s, they argue, and the effects of obsolete and inappropriate systems are now becoming apparent, particularly with the advent of Japanese competition.

However, as Loft's chapter explains, Johnson and Kaplan's interpretation of history has been challenged, especially by 'critical' accounting researchers. These researchers challenge Johnson and Kaplan's assumptions that the cost accounting systems and associated technological and economic developments were inevitable or necessarily represented a form of social progress. Instead they argue that cost accounting was implicated in the domination and disciplining of labour in the early stages of capitalism and that the emergence of cost accounting was socially governed by the systems of thought then prevalent, the actions of the state and the results of inter-professional disputes between such groups as engineers and accountants. The debate continues and it may never be conclusive. Nevertheless, it is important in that it illustrates how accounting techniques are related to social factors and how accounting did not merely reflect society but also helped shape it.

These and related historical debates have more than academic significance for they are essential to understanding contemporary debates on the effectiveness or otherwise of conventional cost accounting techniques. Any assessment of their economic and social effects must reside in a clear understanding of why and how they evolved as they did. In the long run such historical work may provide insights into why Anglo-Saxon countries appear to lay greater stress on accounting techniques than new competitor countries such as Japan. It may also help to explain why expertise claimed by professional accountants in the Anglo-Saxon countries is demonstrated elsewhere by engineers or business economists. The value of historical work is that it can help us question long-maintained assumptions about the role and nature of management accounting, and thereby broaden our view of how controls might be reformed, not only from a corporate perspective but also from public-interest perspectives.

Such concerns are central to contemporary debates over the introduction of management accounting techniques and philosophies into the public sector. Humphrey and Olson, in Chapter 16, express concern, *inter alia*, that the methods being promulgated in the public sector are a simplistic caricature of private-sector practice. They show how accounting measures of efficiency can lower overall effectiveness and they argue that the individualistic enterprise culture grounded in a market-based philosophy can reduce the strengths of public-sector organisations by weakening commitments to service and collegial relations.

The new accounting methods used in the public sector may be technically deficient – for example, the emphasis on financial efficiency measures related to inputs rather than outputs may not complement desired effectiveness criteria and thereby produce dysfunctional behaviour. In addition, performance assessment based on the costs of individual units may be unreliable due to major interdependencies between units, which in turn may hinder integration in policy formulation and action. Nevertheless, the need to control service costs remains. It may be that the solution lies in improved and/or reformed accounting methods rather than the rejection of accounting *per se*. Humphrey and Olson question whether the assumptions and methods of control implied in conventional management accounting systems are appropriate to public-sector organisations with their ethos of public service, their conflicting and complex goals, and their modes of decision-making which stress the accommodation of conflict and the achievement of multiple goals. Above all, they raise the issue of whether democracy and public accountability are well served and reconcilable with the new management techniques.

In this context it is interesting to note that many of the other contributors express public-interest concerns about the effects of conventional management accounting systems in the private sector. For example, in Chapter 14, Mouritsen argues that transfer pricing systems of global corporations are inevitably connected to distributional issues. Small Third World companies may be so dependent upon large corporations that they lack the power to resist many of their demands and their involvement in domestic politics.

It is increasingly being recognised that management accounting systems cannot be value-free and neutral and that accounting systems have been central to a number of very contentious political programmes. For example, accounting is implicated in issues concerning the provision of public services by private-sector organisations. In this sense the accounting profession with its professed expertise in consulting does not merely follow policy but also helps shape it. In so doing, accounting systems and accountants affect the distribution of power and resources not only within organisations but within society more generally. Thus, it is perhaps unsurprising that an increasing volume of management accounting research, especially the critical approaches reviewed by Roslender in Chapter 4, is questioning the role of accounting in broader socio-economic contexts and examining whether there are alternatives outside the realm of traditional accounting expertise.

International considerations

A growing feature of contemporary management accounting research has focused on international comparative studies of practice and the effects of the increasing globalisation of business. In the USA and Britain this has been due partly to the fundamental re-examination of conventional accounting wisdom on the part of academics and managers provoked by a perceived failure of their firms to respond adequately to the new competitive pressures.

Chapter 15, by Currie, provides a detailed comparative analysis of management accounting practice in Japan, Germany, the UK and the USA. The differences she notes raise major questions about the relative effectiveness of Anglo-American methods and how the cost management function is conducted and organised. For example, in Japan and West Germany cost accounting knowledge and jurisdiction is much more the province of engineers rather than externally qualified accountants. However, as Currie indicates, any analysis and reform must take into account the ways in which socio-economic factors impinge on current practices and limit the scope for reform. International competition is unlikely to result in a homogenisation of practice.

This is also a lesson of Chapter 14 by Mouritsen on management accounting in global firms. He describes the variety of organisational designs which international firms use, each of which results in different cost system designs and roles. Whereas global corporations are highly integrated, with accounting playing a central part in integrating scattered segments through line budgets and plans, multidomestic conglomerate firms devolve detailed responsibilities and strategies to relatively independent segments and use portfolio management and return on investment (ROI) measures to control them. However, in both instances, internationalisation brings an increased need for accounting to be involved with new methods of currency management and political risk.

Chapter 16 by Humphrey and Olson is also an important corrective to over-generalised theories of international convergence of accounting practices. This chapter compares and contrasts how accounting has been implicated in programmes of public-sector reform in the UK and Sweden. The political aims and motivations in each country were very different, for example decentralisation to local government in Sweden, and centralisation and the diminution of the public sector in the UK. However, Humphrey and Olson argue that rhetorics of efficiency were justifications for accounting reform in each case and the methods adopted bear some similarities to one another. They go on to raise severe doubts about the ability of accounting to deliver the effects promised and, more fundamentally, they question the desirability of its effects upon democratic accountability. Despite widespread adoption of cost accounting techniques world-wide in programmes of public-sector reform, it is a neglected area of study. Researchers and policy-makers tend to see their own national changes as embedded in unique national socio-economic settings. However, whilst not wishing to deny the significance of national differences, the similarities of public-sector accounting change cross-nationally warrants greater study and explanation, as Humphrey and Olson point out.

As many of the contributions to this book suggest, the teasing out of common patterns of response by public- and private-sector organisations to global capitalism and how choices over strategies and controls are made in the face of variegated cultures and socio-economic pressures presents research and practice with an agenda that has barely been commenced.

Concluding Comments

There has been a recent growth and fragmentation of management accounting research. Despite the variety of topics and methodologies pursued, they tend to share a common recognition that the use of accounting by managers and others in organisations, and its role and social significance, is often more subtle and complex than seems to be appreciated in most current textbooks. Approaches to management accounting research, informed by economics, behavioural sciences, organisation theory or sociology, might appear to be mutually exclusive due to fundamental differences in the philosophies of the social sciences. However, there are some signs of a synthesis as researchers pull together theoretically divergent researches on similar topics, but it would be premature and perhaps naïve to believe that a single theoretical approach or set of theoretical prescriptions can be preferred. Indeed, the variety of research methodologies and topics is continuing to raise new issues and reinterpretations of management accounting theory and practice. Where this will culminate is unclear. However, it is evident that contemporary research is highlighting the complexity of understanding accounting knowledge and practices and the rapid changes they are undergoing. We now invite the reader to examine the approaches set out in the following chapters and to consider the issues raised.

References .

Johnson, T. and R.S. Kaplan (1987) *Relevance Lost: The rise and fall of management accounting,* Boston, Mass.: Harvard Business School Press.
Johnson, T. (1992) *Relevance Regained,* New York: Free Press.

CHAPTER TWO

The History of Management Accounting: Relevance Found

Anne Loft

The historian E.H. Carr writes, 'we can fully understand the present only in the light of the past'. However, until recently management accountants have shown little awareness of the relevance of historical understanding to current issues. In Carr's terms, the past was seen as completely irrelevant to the present. If considered at all, the history of management accounting tended to be seen as being concerned with how management accounting progressed from meagre beginnings in nineteenth-century factories to an important role in the running of twentieth-century business enterprises. Because the past was viewed as merely the imperfect prelude to the present, then the history was seen as a 'dusty' specialist subject of no relevance to current theory and practice. During the past decade or so this attitude has begun to change, and a growth in interest in the history of management accounting has accompanied a growth in understanding of its relevance.

Some Methodological Problems

Before looking into this 'relevance found' it is important to consider the methodological problem of how we should study the history of management accounting. This is not nearly such a simple matter as it might seem at first glance. If we are interested in the history of management accounting as practised in industrial enterprises, then clearly we are entirely dependent on what records remain for posterity. Are those that remain in some sense typical? Or have they been kept precisely because they were so atypical? The cost accounting system operated at Boulton and Watt's Soho Works in Birmingham in the late eighteenth and early nineteenth centuries is a case in point. It was almost certainly not typical – the organisational and production arrangements as a whole were clearly far more sophisticated than those usual at the time. So what significance does it have? Even if it is solely twentieth-century developments we are discussing then there are still difficulties: even at a particular point in time it may not have been clear to what extent cost accounting systems existed. Speaking in 1919, one of the leading experts in costing commented that 'there is a question as to the extent to which costs systems are being used in this country. That is a question which it is difficult to answer, because it would require more knowledge of what is going on in the country than I have got' (*The Accountant*, 12 July 1919, p. 40) – and he had just made a tour of the UK to study costing and Scientific Management!

Even if a historian has the original cost accounting records, it may still not be obvious from them how, and if, they were actually used. Samuel Seymour, a now retired management accountant whom I interviewed about a job he held between the wars as cost accountant, remarked: 'if the business was making a profit they weren't concerned with all my records. . . . in my time, I gathered a lot of statistics which have never been used'. If they *were* used then it may not be clear if they were used primarily as a basis for pricing items produced, or as a means to control labour costs and hence labour itself.

Many historians of management accounting have relied upon the descriptions of systems in manuals on cost accounting for manufacturers, or textbooks, or articles in engineering and accounting journals. These may describe the state of the art in theory, but how they relate to systems in practice is a question not easily answered.

Given all these difficulties, it is not surprising that there exist conflicting theories and interpretations of management accounting history. There is no simple, single, history of management accounting which can honestly claim to be *the* history. All histories are inevitably partial, and crucially dependent on the assumptions and theories of the author. This presents a problem for someone like myself, asked to write a brief history of management accounting.

Rather than just present one version of the history, I will attempt to deal with this by presenting some of the main schools of thought in the area. I will begin with the traditional view, and the revisions which have been made to it over the last decade by 'neoclassicists' (approach 1). Following this, I will move on to a discussion of the more controversial ideas which have emerged in the last decade or so. This begins with a discussion of Johnson and Kaplan's analysis presented in the book *Relevance Lost: The rise and fall of management accounting* (1987). They argue that efficient accounting systems for managerial decision-making and control developed in the nineteenth and early twentieth centuries, but have since been distorted and misused and this problem has led to the current inadequacy of American corporate management accounting systems in the face of competition in the modern world. Cost and management accounting has, quite simply, 'lost' its 'relevance' (hence their title). Here the history of cost and management accounting is brought firmly out of the dusty antiquarian corner of academic life it formerly inhabited, being used in an almost evangelical way to argue for change in the present (approach 2).

The third, and more radical, approach comes from a group of labour process scholars (in particular as represented by Hopper and Armstrong, 1991). They criticise Johnson and Kaplan's interpretation of history, arguing that the development of management accounting has far more to do with controlling labour than economic efficiency, presenting an alternative interpretation of the events described in *Relevance Lost*. Lastly, the radical history of cost and management accounting inspired by the ideas of Michel Foucault is explored (approach 4). These writers argue that the history of management accounting is properly seen in its social and organisational context as the history of a disciplinary technique which makes the worker into a 'governable person'.

In various ways all of these new ideas have made the history of management accounting relevant in a way not previously seen.

Traditional History and its Revision by Neoclassicists

According to traditional historians of management accounting, most of the costing procedures advanced before the late nineteenth century were very crude. Early cost 'systems' tended to be rather unsystematic, and rarely was any attempt made to co-ordinate them with the financial or commercial books. They were prime cost systems, that is they costed the finished product on the basis of the cost of direct labour and raw materials. The problem of overheads was scarcely considered.

The breakthrough in cost accounting came in Britain in the latter part of the nineteenth century. The emergence of cost accounting at this time was closely connected with the Great Depression (1873–96) where a drastic slackening of demand for engineering products and machinery led to intense competition and price-cutting. Suddenly it became crucial to the survival of a business to be able to calculate what its products cost to make.

S. Paul Garner, one of the most respected of the 'traditional' historians of cost accounting, places the turning point in its development at around 1885. In his book, *Evolution of Cost Accounting to 1925* (1954), he describes in great detail the rapid progress after this date. Overheads, as well as labour and materials, began to be allocated and apportioned to the various products in a systematic manner. Further, the costing records began to be integrated with the financial records within an enlarged double-entry bookkeeping system.

The first book to describe systematic methods for doing this was *Factory Accounts* by the British authors, Emile Garcke and J.M. Fells. Garner describes its publication in 1887 as 'probably having more to do with the advancement of cost accounting practices than any single book ever published' (p. 217). It ran through four editions by 1893, each edition containing refinements to the system and discussions of the latest methods for collecting cost figures and running a costing office effectively.

This early lead which the British had in developing cost accounting was quickly taken over by the United States after 1900, where pioneers such as A. Hamilton Church and John Whitmore began to further develop and elaborate methods for more reliable and accurate costing. As the importance of allocating all the miscellaneous manufacturing expenditures to products began to be emphasised, a great deal of effort and energy was spent on the vexed question of how to account for overheads. By the second decade of the twentieth century the issue of how to account for waste and scrap was being energetically tackled, and in the 1920s methods for standard costing were perfected. Garner's account of the 'evolution of cost accounting' ends in 1925, after which time, he argues, very few contributions of an original nature were made to cost accounting.

In the conclusion of his book Garner summarises his view on the history of cost accounting as follows:

> Cost theories and procedures have evolved as a natural corollary of their industrial environment. The expansion of the factory system during the last hundred years, the immense improvement in manufacturing methods and techniques, and the keener competition brought on by widening markets all combined to cause the manufacturer to appreciate more fully the necessity for adequate information as to his cost of production. Cost accounting as a managerial instrument was the most significant method of obtaining desired results. (p. 348).

In this view cost accounting is simply a tool for the manufacturer which has evolved in line with the evolution of the manufacturing enterprise. The need for cost accounting and the development of cost accounting systems have proceeded harmoniously hand-in-hand with each other.

Garner's study of the history of cost accounting is very thorough; however, it is limited in the sources it uses. It focuses on the development of systems as described in manuals for manufacturers, articles in professional journals and other publications. It is not based on archival research of costing systems 'in action'.

Recently a 'neoclassical' approach to cost accounting history has emerged, amongst the most active writers being Richard Fleischman, Lee Parker and Thomas Tyson. They follow the traditional line of thinking as expressed in Garner's quotation above, but argue that cost accounts were used as a direct aid to management much earlier than the late nineteenth century. The crucial difference between their work and that of the traditional historians such as Garner, is that they focus on detailed case studies of cost accounting systems in operation in factories. An example is the cost accounting system introduced at Boulton and Watt's Soho Works in Birmingham. At the Soho Foundry, which commenced production of steam engines in 1795, operations were organised on a far more rational basis than hitherto, parts and products were standardised as far as was possible, and the whole production process was carefully planned. Records were made which enabled control of stock and the accurate costing of materials and labour processes. Fleishman and Parker (1992) argue that in the four crucial areas of cost accounting – cost control, overhead accounting, decision-making and standard costing – Boulton and Watt were very advanced.

Through this, and other case studies, it is argued that cost accounting practices and techniques comparable to those of the modern period, including cost control and overhead allocation, had been developed much earlier than previously thought. These techniques were able to assist entrepreneurs with reducing costs, maximising profits and defending against competition.

The placing by the 'neoclassicists' of the origins of cost accounting as much earlier than the traditional historians maintain is linked to the different historical sources that they use. Traditional histories used as their main source published materials, whereas neoclassicists have based their conclusions on research in business archives. This leads them to different conclusions because the authors are examining very different things. Examining business archives, neoclassicists are enabled to place an early cost accounting system in its context in the organization being studied, and thus identify ways in which it could be used by management. Focusing on published material, the traditionalists have a tendency only to identify a development in cost accounting as having occurred when a technique has been standardised and formalised in such a way that it can be written up as a 'general knowledge' which can be applied to a variety of manufacturing situations.

Although they bring in more of the organisational context to their study of accounting than the traditionalists, neoclassicists share with them a rather passive view of cost and management accounting as a set of techniques serving the goals of the organisation and adapting as necessary to serve changing business needs. Accounting is seen as progressing in an evolutionary way, becoming constantly better over time. In various ways the following approaches break down these assumptions. They bring the wider economic and social context into their explanations of accounting's development, and examine how cost and management accounting might have played an active role in shaping organisations themselves.

Johnson and Kaplan's Approach

An important stimulus to the development of new ideas concerning the history of management accounting, and in particular to Johnson and Kaplan, was the work of the business historian Alfred D. Chandler. Chandler became famous in the area of business history for his books *Strategy and Structure: Chapters in the history of the industrial enterprise* (1962) and *The Visible Hand: The managerial revolution in American business* (1977).

It was not the main aim of his work, but unintentionally Chandler revealed the paucity of the traditional history of cost and management accounting. It was revealed not to be wrong as such, but overly narrow in its approach. He brought to the fore the importance of management accounting to the development of the giant firm, and vice versa. Chandler concluded that modern cost accounting arose in the United States during the mid-nineteenth century with the advent of the railroads, and a little later in the chemical, steel and metal-working industries. It arose because of a coupling of the growing size of organisations and the complexity of production processes, with oligopolistic markets consisting of a few large producers. These producers needed cost information in order to determine prices, to assess how the different parts of the business were performing, and generally to try to outwit their rivals. As giant, vertically integrated (and later multidivisional) corporations developed in the first decades of this century, management accounting became a key factor in the co-ordination of the wide range of activities taking place over a large geographical area.

Chandler's ideas inspired accounting researchers, amongst them H. Thomas Johnson. In his study of cost accounting at the Lyman Mills Corporation, a cotton textile firm operating in New England in the mid-nineteenth century, Johnson discovered a sophisticated cost accounting system in operation. At Lyman Mills cost accounting appeared to be in use primarily to solve organisational difficulties through acting as a means of internal control over activities. Johnson writes that:

> All the evidence examined points to the conclusion that Lyman used its elaborate cost system to facilitate control of internal plant operations: for example, to assess the physical productivity of mill operatives; to assess the impact on operations of changes in plant layout; and to control the receipt and use of raw cotton. (1972, p. 474)

Other work by Johnson, and by Willard Stone, seemed to confirm this idea. It was this work, coupled with inspiration from Oliver Williamson's transaction cost theory (1975), and Kaplan's insights on the lack of relevance of modern management accounting, which were merged to form the perspective presented in *Relevance Lost: The rise and fall of management accounting* (1987).

Johnson and Kaplan argue that it was the rise of the factory which was crucial to the development of cost accounting. In itself this is not at all controversial, but the reasons that they give for this are. As this work was inspired by the ideas of Williamson, it is helpful at this point to make a short excursus into his work.

Williamson is interested in explaining the origins and evolution of large corporations. This he does through comparing and contrasting the corporate form with the market system, viewing them as alternative ways of ordering the whole process of production and distribution. He argues that corporate management structures, such as management accounting systems, exist because their costs as a means of co-ordinating operations are lower than the alternative of market co-ordination. Imagine a situation where all the employees of IBM were not 'collectivised' under one corporate form, but were instead independent operators who were continually contracting through the market with their present colleagues, consumers and producers of the various services. Such a market-based structure of organisation might eventually produce a computer, but the total costs of doing so would most certainly outweigh the costs of the bureaucracy needed to replace the market. These costs of co-ordination (the costs of the bureaucracy and dealing in markets) have become known as 'transaction costs', and the whole approach has become known as 'transaction cost theory'.

Johnson and Kaplan apply these ideas to the development of cost and management accounting. In the market economy of Western Europe, which developed from around AD 1000, the information that the merchant needed to conduct business – to decide what to sell, and at what price – was provided by market prices. The double-entry bookkeeping which developed was merely a way of keeping records of money owing and owed. It did not act as an aid to decision-making and control. The rise of the factory changed all this. Market prices stopped supplying all conceivable information for decision-making and control when merchant-entrepreneurs contrived to administer the work of labourers by gathering them together into a centralised workplace. A prime example of this was the textile industry of Northern England (often regarded as representing the birth of industrial capitalism). Here merchants changed from making contracts with workers who made cloth in their homes, to a factory system where employers took over the organisation of production for the artisans. Instead of a piece-rate set by the market, where workers were paid for what they produced, there was a wage contract where the employee was paid for his or her time. If there was a piece-rate system in the factory it was the employer who set this rate.

However, there was a problem: no automatic market signals existed to allow the organisers of the factories to evaluate internal intermediate output, that is products which would be processed further. The question of 'how efficient was their production?', required an answer. An especially important cost was wages. The market wage for factory workers only contained partial information about the cost of the intermediate output produced by the worker. The missing information was the workers' productivity during the time they earned their wage. Cost accounting, hypothesise Johnson and Kaplan, was devised by these merchants as an ingenious means of replicating that information. Double-entry cost accounts held the potential to provide information about labour and other conversion costs per unit of output. It is noted how early textile cost accounts match the wages paid to workers with output produced. Comparing this with the cost of outwork gives a simple way of evaluating how efficient the factory is.

More complex cost accounting systems developed as businesses became larger and machinery more complex. The cost of processes could no longer simply be compared with rates outside the factory. Johnson's work on the cost accounts of the Lyman Mills illustrates these points. The conclusion reached is that, in the new large organisations that emerged in the nineteenth century,

> management accounting practices in manufacturing, rail transportation, and distribution firms had one common purpose: to evaluate a company's internal processes. . . . In all cases this new accounting information focused on the efficiency with which single-activity firms used resources in their internally managed processes. (Johnson and Kaplan, 1987, p. 42)

The existence of such systems leads Johnson and Kaplan to locate the origins of cost and management accounting at an earlier point than traditional histories. In this they agree with the neoclassicists but, differing from them, they focus very strongly on the internal control and efficiency functions of these systems. Now we come to the most important point in Johnson and Kaplan's argument, namely that the development of management accounting was important in actually *facilitating* the growth of large enterprises. Management accounting did not develop merely as a by-product of the growth in size of enterprises – it was an important factor in enabling this growth to occur. It focused attention on the advantages derived from internally organising production of parts rather than purchasing them in the market.

Further advances in management accounting systems were associated with the scientific management movement, whose most famous advocate was Frederick

Taylor. Started in the USA by engineer-managers (not accountants) during the last two decades of the nineteenth century, the movement's aim was to improve the efficiency of production processes by standardising jobs and processes as much as possible. By the early twentieth century the increased standardisation which the movement had brought to many aspects of factory life had proved very facilitative to the development of more sophisticated cost and management accounting techniques. Once jobs and processes had been standardised and norms set for how much labour time and raw material they should take, the actual labour time and raw material used could be compared on a systematic basis with this standard. Engineers and accountants used the information for three purposes:

1. To analyse the potential efficiency of tasks or processes (this developed directly from Taylor's work).
2. To compare the actual efficiency with this potential (an innovation credited to the management consultants Harrington Emerson and G. Charter Harrison). This was the forerunner of flexible budgeting systems.

Thus cost and management accountants were no longer just concerned with records of past expenditure, but could compare this to a pre-set standard. From these two usages a new purpose for cost accounting developed: to evaluate the *overall profitability of the entire enterprise*. In other words, the newly efficient parts should add up to a profitable whole, and deviations in profitability in practice should be traced back to their sources.

In addition to these uses, financial accountants discovered that standard cost information could be used for another purpose:

3. To simplify the task of valuing stock and work-in-progress for the yearly financial report.

According to Johnson and Kaplan, usages 1 and 2 were the crucial drive behind the setting up of cost accounting systems, while usage 3 was merely a by-product.

A merger wave in the United States around the turn of the century created huge vertically integrated firms. The most successful of these firms developed the unitary, or centralised, form of organisation, where the firm's overall operations were broken down into separate departments each with highly specialised activities. Each department was run by its own manager, leaving top management free to co-ordinate activities and to direct strategy and policy. This marked the birth of many of the mammoth US firms we know today: for example, General Electric, American Tobacco, National Biscuit, General Motors and Du Pont. Johnson and Kaplan discuss in detail the management accounting systems developed by Du Pont and General Motors between about 1900 and 1925, systems which bear many resemblances to those presently used in large and complex business organisations.

Following Williamson's transaction cost approach, Johnson and Kaplan claim that these firms were created because their owners perceived that there were opportunities to make higher profits in a large, well-managed hierarchy, rather than in using market exchange. Management accounting played an important role in ensuring that the costs of administrating the firm did not exceed the gains to be made from its existence; for the very complexity of the organisation could lead an integrated firm to sink into a morass of bureaucratic inefficiency, losing all the potential gains. The use of management accounting to control the transaction costs was of crucial importance to the firms.

Two new management accounting techniques were developed to assist this process: budgets (to co-ordinate and balance the internal flow of resources from raw materials to the final consumer); and return on investment (ROI). ROI, invented by Du Pont, was an important breakthrough because it provided a single figure which summarised performance. Du Pont was a huge enterprise consisting of vertically integrated business units. Calculating ROI for different parts of the enterprise enabled top management to measure the success of each part in using capital, and thus to allocate capital to the most profitable activities. It focused the attention of top management, for the first time, on the productivity and performance of *capital itself*. Nineteenth-century single-activity firms had tended to ignore how well capital was being used once it had been purchased. Now the efficient management of capital became a driving force in the firm; just as the calculation through cost accounting systems of such figures as cost per labour-hour drove the search for labour-saving efficiencies, so the calculation of ROI drove a search for more productive opportunities to use capital. An important object of management accounting systems became the assessment of overall profitability in these firms.

When, after the First World War, some of these vertically integrated firms became 'multidivisional', management accounting again played an important role, in this case in keeping the divisions acting together while working towards goals set by top management. Management accounting systems provided data to evaluate the performance of each of the divisions, to evaluate company-wide performance and to decide on future company policy. While in vertically integrated firms it was primarily top management who used the ROI figures to evaluate performance, in the pioneering multidivisional giant, General Motors, ROI was used to delegate to division managers the responsibility for using capital efficiently. Divisional managers could be controlled using these data, be refused more capital, or even be dismissed if they did not perform effectively. This was an important facility in situations where managers could pursue their own goals instead of those of the owners.

Johnson and Kaplan argue that by 1925 virtually all of the management accounting practices used today had been developed. The period after 1925 was characterised by a lack of progress, the reason for this being that after this period managers came to rely more and more on these *financial numbers themselves* as their basic information source. Not only did 'management by numbers' become the norm, but these numbers became more and more directed towards the function of valuing inventory in financial statements (the third use of costs according to the schema given above). Johnson and Kaplan express this in terms of manufacturing firms shifting from *'cost management'*, where an attempt was made to trace each product's consumption of resources for the purposes of managing costs, to a far less relevant *'cost accounting'*, which did not attempt to do this and was directed at the need to value inventory in financial statements. This is the crux of the problem of the 'lost relevance' of management accounting: the cost information that apparently aids financial reporting is misleading and irrelevant for strategic product decisions. What is needed is a return to the early aim of cost management which was accurate product costs – an aim which was difficult to meet then because of the high costs of information processing, but which could be met now with modern computer systems.

Johnson and Kaplan's history is written with a clear message: management accounting had a golden age from the late nineteenth century to the early twentieth, but now it has lost its relevance, it must change if American corporations are to survive in competitive world markets. It is hardly surprising that the content and message of *Relevance Lost* have proved controversial. Its thesis that existing management accounting systems are less than relevant has understandably been provocative to the proponents of such systems. Among accounting historians its use of an explanatory framework derived from economics and 'broad-brush' approach to history have raised debate. Provocative it may be, but it brings accounting history into a central position both in terms of the research agenda and in terms of practical business management.

Johnson and Kaplan have been criticized by accounting historians for their theoretical approach, their historical analysis and for the conclusions which they draw from it. In the next section the critique and alternative account which labour process theory can provide will be discussed (Hopper and Armstrong, 1991). However, first it is useful to examine some of the basic assumptions underlying Johnson and Kaplan's analysis of management accounting history.

As discussed earlier, underlying the traditional and neoclassical understanding was a rather simple evolutionary model of accounting as a set of techniques serving the goals of the organisation and being adapted as necessary to serve changing business needs. Johnson and Kaplan have a more complex model. The organisation is seen to exist in a wider environment which includes factors such as market conditions, degree of stability of the conditions of trade and fluctuations in exchange rates. Hence the discussion in *Relevance Lost* of the growth of multidivisional firms in an 'environment' characterised by oligopoly. The problem of controlling the organisation so that costs are minimised and profits maximised is seen as being solved through the *matching* of the characteristics of the environment to those of the control system (management accounting being an essential part of the control system). In this perspective practices tend to appear as inevitable, and to be the 'best' because they have survived. Multidivisional companies became dominant because the transaction costs of the organisational bureaucracy (including therein the cost and management accounting system) were less than the costs of using the market. It is argued that the recent problems faced by large American corporations have occurred because they are now out of step with the international competitive environment. If they do not adapt to the new global competition they will 'die out'. Part of this necessary adaptation process is the development of 'new and more flexible approaches to the design of effective cost accounting, management control, and performance measurement systems' (p. 224).

This form of reasoning can be described as 'Social Darwinist' – it assumes that organisations are like animals, they die out if they do not adapt to their environment. But organisations are fundamentally associations of sentient human beings and not animals. Historically, Johnson and Kaplan follow Chandler's line of causation: that the environment caused large companies to follow certain strategies, which in turn 'caused' the multidivisional company which survived because it was well adapted. Being well adapted meant having an appropriate management accounting system. However, an opposite line of causation may be just as valid, namely that the large companies' strategy of trying to dominate the market by driving competitors out, or swallowing them up, led to monopoly and oligopoly and this lead in turn to bureaucracy and wastefulness. Accounting systems were part of this wasteful bureaucracy.

The Labour Process Approach

Labour process theorists start from the perspective that organisational control systems are *not* neutral mechanisms for making production more efficient. Rather, they are practical means through which capital exploits labour on a day-to-day basis. The emphasis in the labour process approach is on detailed study of the ways in which workers are controlled in different organisational settings.

One of the founders of this approach was Harry Braverman, in his book *Labour and Monopoly Capital*, published in 1974. He writes that:

> when the capitalist buys buildings, materials, tools, machinery, etc., he can evaluate with precision their place in the labour process. He knows that a certain proportion of his outlay will be transferred to each unit of production and his accounting practices allocate these in the form of costs or depreciation. But when he buys labour time, the outcome is far from being either so certain or so definite that it can be recognised in this way, with precision and in advance. . . . It thus becomes essential for the capitalist that control over the labour process pass from the hands of the worker into his own. This transition presents itself in history as the *progressive alienation of the process of production* from the worker; to the capitalist it presents itself as the problem of *management*. Braverman, 1974, pp. 57–8; original emphasis)

This perspective, by focusing on how management activity, including accounting, routinely expresses and furthers the priorities of capital, brings questions of power and control to the fore. In Hopper and Armstrong (1991) the evolution of accounting systems is analysed as an aspect of overall changes in the pattern of control of the labour process. Rather than seeing the emergence and development of particular types of cost and management accounting as being explained by the search for economic efficiency, they argue that the development (or, indeed, abandonment) of particular types of cost and management accounting is better explained by the changes in controls over labour processes which changing phases of capitalism invoked.

Johnson and Kaplan use the accounting system of the Lyman Mills in the mid-nineteenth century to illustrate their point that the main role of cost accounting at this period was to monitor the performance of workers with the object of increasing the efficiency of the factory. Hopper and Armstrong cite studies which show that much of the gain in profitability from the early factory organisation of production came from the ability of owners/entrepreneurs to intensify labour through close disciplinary control and through extending the working day. Lyman Mills were part of the New England textile industry and other studies of the area in this time period show that at least *some* of the accounting information was used in the process of intensifying the exploitation of labour rather than making production more efficient (pp. 413–15).

Many developments in cost and management accounting occurred in the late nineteenth and early twentieth centuries. Johnson and Kaplan identify the purpose of these accounting systems to be to discover how efficiently tasks were being carried out, and to use the standards for potential efficiency provided by Scientific Management as a basis for comparison. Hopper and Armstrong challenge this interpretation, arguing that changes in control systems in the period were directed at the power of labour rather than at improving efficiency.

The period of the late nineteenth and early twentieth centuries was one in which work in American factories was reorganised and restructured in such a way that more semi-skilled, as opposed to skilled, labour could be used. This reorganisation enabled workers to become more easily substituted for each other – in other words, 'homogenised'. The homogenisation of labour was aided by mechanisation, reorganisation and the keeping of elaborate records in order to get information on what aspects of the work could be speeded up. Knowledge about production was no longer the domain of skilled workers, those who actually did the producing; instead it became more and more part of management knowledge. This was an important factor in subordinating and disciplining labour. The rapid development of cost and management accounting in this period was both a result of these processes (which made costs easier to measure) and a factor enabling their intensification. Knowledge about costs was something which was firmly and squarely in the hands of management, not workers; it was a useful tool in the control of labour.

Kaplan and Johnson describe how management accounting innovations, in particular ROI and budgeting, played an important role in the large, vertically integrated firms such as Du Pont. They enabled the firms to ensure that the costs of administrating such a large firm did not exceed the gains to be made from its existence. Hopper and Armstrong argue that this ignores important developments in the organisation of work at this period, namely that at the same time as Du Pont and General Motors were making pathbreaking accounting developments, the so-called 'drive system' of employment was being consolidated. The drive system was characterised by the reorganisation of work, a process facilitated by more mechanisation, job restructuring and increased plant size. This increased the impersonality of work and enabled the continuing expansion of the foreman's role. For the workers this meant a further de-skilling of their jobs. Their locally specialised skills became even more redundant than they had done under the earlier process of homogenisation. ROI and budgeting provided a way for top management to manage local managers to ensure that they used every method possible to remove slack and inefficiency at all levels. Fluctuations in demand led to periodic lay-offs of workers, despite the subsequent social hardship.

Management accounting controls such as budgets and ROI are thus argued to have arisen from the intensification of corporate controls over *managerial labour processes*. Bureaucracies were not sought by capitalists because they were more efficient than market co-ordination (Johnson and Kaplan), but were a cost which they suffered because they needed to control labour processes as completely as possible. The use of budgets and ROI was a means of gaining yet more knowledge, and thus power, over managerial labour processes.

The labour process approach thus reinterprets the events described by Johnson and Kaplan; rather than being due to a continual search for economic efficiency, Hopper and Armstrong view the development of cost and management accounting as being fundamentally associated with the struggle to control labour processes in the factory.

Management accounting is only one of a range of techniques which can be used to control labour processes. Viewing management accounting in this way helps to explain the phenomenon of the manufacturing success of countries such as Japan where firms do a lot less management accounting than in Anglo-Saxon countries. In earlier work in the labour process tradition Armstrong argues that in order to understand the dominance of *accounting* solutions to the problem of control in Anglo-Saxon environments, then it is necessary to examine the processes through which *accountants* have come to have so much power. He examines the historical process through which accountants, rather than members of competing management 'professions' such as engineering and personnel management, came to dominate.

In the United States during the period up to the turn of the century it was the engineering profession which held a dominant position in controlling work in factories (either as owners or as managers). However, in the increasingly large and bureaucratic factories of the turn of the century the engineers were gradually losing control to general managers. The engineers were aware of this problem and, through what we can call an 'ideology of engineering', they began to claim that scientific management was the answer to the difficulty of controlling labour, and engineers themselves should be in charge. Unfortunately for the engineers this knowledge of job timing, planning and organising could easily be appropriated by other groups of management workers. Engineers gradually lost control, they did not become the key managers in the huge corporations – accountants and financial managers did.

The origins of the success of accountants and financial managers lay in the response to the economic crises of 1920–2. Prior to this date corporations tended to be run by operational managers in a pyramid structure, in which accountants were amongst the staff advising these managers. After the multidivisional structure pioneered by General Motors became popular it tended to be financial staff and accountants who sat at the top of the organisation: for it was they who possessed the tools necessary for making decisions allocating capital between divisions. The growth of large corporations is not by itself enough to explain the growing power of financial staff. What was critical was that they were *already* represented in the management hierarchies, as they were in the United States (and the United Kingdom). One of the reasons for their presence was the audit requirements imposed by the securities market. This idea of the importance of the audit requirement seems to be confirmed by the observation that in Germany (where capital was supplied by banks) or Japan (where the government was a major source), such audit requirements were not imposed and accountants have never achieved the same power.

Armstrong's account relates the growth of management accounting to the growth in the influence and numbers of the professional group which practised it. In traditional management accounting history there is a simple line of causation, namely that top management of large corporations realised what a valuable technique management accounting was, with the resultant growth in the numbers of accountants. Armstrong emphasises the positive role of accountants in creating work for themselves. Having obtained a role in the hierarchy early on, they were able to move into powerful positions as the multidivisional form was introduced, subsuming under their authority the techniques of cost accounting developed by engineers.

This notion that accounting and other controls are substitutable, and the extent of use of accounting control systems depends on social and historical factors, involves considering accountants as well as accounting. Traditional historians consider accountants only when they make an appearance as pioneers of one or other technique; the other approaches we have considered do not go much further. This consideration of the link between the spread of the techniques and the status and role of the people who actually do the task is an important extension to the type of issues considered by management accounting historians. It naturally involves extending the type of historical source material considered to the study of management *accountants* as well as management *accounting*.

Foucault in Accounting History

Michel Foucault has inspired a rather different line of thinking in the history of management accounting. This is represented in the works of Miller and O'Leary (e.g. 1994), Loft (e.g. 1994), Hoskin and Macve (e.g. 1994) and the review article by Stewart (1992). Whilst Foucault does not write directly about the history of management accounting (nor indeed at any length about the factory), his ideas can be applied to it in a fascinating way, for he emphasises the importance in the development of modern society of techniques aimed at watching and controlling what individuals do – an importance which, he notes, has been previously overlooked by scholars.

In his book *Discipline and Punish: The birth of the prison* Foucault uses the history of prisons as an exemplar of a society-wide phenomenon occurring from the late eighteenth century onwards: the growth of 'disciplinary institutions'. Prisons, armies, hospitals, schools, mental institutions and factories all have in common the point that within them people are arranged and grouped into different categories – for instance, in the school according to their age and ability, in the hospital according to type of illness, and in the factory according to function. Even more importantly, they are arranged so that they can be watched and punished if they do not obey the rules – hence the phrase 'disciplinary institutions', in which 'disciplinary techniques' are practised. The term 'disciplinary techniques' covers a wide variety of methods of watching and controlling, including the recording of people's work, the progression of their illness and also the architecture of buildings themselves, which gives a clear space in which everything can be seen.

Disciplinary techniques grew in accuracy, extent and importance during the nineteenth century in armies, hospitals, schools, factories and other institutions. In the case of manufacturing, 'great manufacturing spaces' (to quote a contemporary source) were created where production could be organised on a more systematic basis than when conducted by outworkers, or in cramped and dark workshops. In such spaces individual workers could be assigned positions arranged to facilitate their surveillance and the creation of records about their work. These records in turn could enable the comparison of workers and the detailed assessment of their use to the business, i.e. control.

Loft writes how cost and management accounting can be seen as one of the techniques of surveillance and control of individuals in a business organisation. Its peculiar characteristic is that it replicates the production processes and makes them 'visible' on paper (or inside a computer) and in monetary terms. Through this *monetarisation* the virtual 'encirclement' of the activity of work by financial measures is achieved. Consider an item being physically produced on an assembly line; the adding to it of brackets, the painting of it, and so on, are procedures which have already been planned in the office and their consequences assessed through financial procedures. After the physical processes are over, the record of the events is again translated into financial terms to be compared with the budget. The line itself, the factory building and the watching supervisor are all disciplinary technologies. The discipline of accounting itself tends to operate further up the organisational hierarchy, enabling the 'managing of managers' (to use Hopper and Armstrong's phrase). However, management accounting is far more than a petty little control over managers. The effects of its discipline are felt from the very bottom of the organisation to the uttermost top – the accounting system 're-creates' the activity of the organisation in financial terms, enabling its control.

In making certain things visible, other things become 'invisible' – such as pollution of the environment and the physical and emotional effects on the employees who have to do repetitive boring jobs. Accounting is the disciplinary technology which enables the prioritising of the financial above all other considerations. The importance of Foucault's perspective is that it brings into the open and analyses the importance of the 'small' techniques of discipline, such as management accounting, which scholars have tended to ignore. The history of management accounting must be seen as the history of one of the central disciplinary techniques in industrial society.

Foucault was a professor of the history of systems of thought. He was concerned with explaining how what we think of as 'true' and our present 'systems of thought' came to have this status. He concentrated on what he called 'the human sciences', the intellectual disciplines concerned with the creation and application of knowledge about humanity. Thus he worked on such subjects as the changing concepts of madness and its distinction from reason over the last five centuries, and on the emergence of modern medicine. It is through the operation of the disciplinary controls that knowledge is created which adds to the knowledge base of the human sciences. Thus it is through the systematic observation of patients in hospital that medical knowledge has been created. It is through the regular observation of work and workers that 'scientific management', 'the social psychology of industry' and so on have been created. Knowledge and power are closely linked – knowledge enables power, and power enables knowledge to be created. Accounting knowledge is a 'truth' about work created through the monetarisation of measurements of the process of work. The process of the measuring of work, which is at the basis of accounting, involves the exercise of power; the legitimate knowledge of work is that in the record, not that in the worker's memory. The knowledge of costs, of variances and so on, is used in the process of disciplining managers (and possibly back through them to workers), and also in the process of creating the budget which forms the norm for the next period. Knowledge and power are thus tightly linked together.

Foucault aims to help us understand how the world is today by reminding us of how the things we take for granted, and our ways of speaking about them, came into being in the first place (this he calls the 'genealogical' question). It involves challenging the assumptions, the 'truth' of our time, by going back into history and examining the details of the emergence of this 'truth'; not to look for *the* single origin, but the whole complex of dispersed origins. Thus from this view, in order to understand the current power of management accounting, we should seek the diverse origins of the system of thought called 'management accounting' and of its practice. The question of how it relates to other practices and ways of thought must be addressed.

Hoskin and Macve have written of the origins of management accounting from a Foucauldian viewpoint, tracing its links back to the development of double-entry bookkeeping. They ask two central questions of the history of accounting. First, why is it that accounting first developed in Europe in the thirteenth and fourteenth centuries? Second, why was it only sporadically used before the nineteenth century?

Most accountants have a vague idea that an Italian called Pacioli invented double-entry bookkeeping in 1494. Hoskin and Macve remind us that accounting history scholars have demonstrated that Pacioli was only publicising what was already done in practice. They hypothesise that accounting was born out of the reading, writing and examining initiated in the medieval universities. This new knowledge formed through processing texts gave power to the learned 'masters' and 'graduates' of the universities. This was connected with the spread of an 'arithmetic mentality' and the growth in the analysis and rewriting in various forms of what had already been written (e.g. commentaries and indexes to the Bible). Whilst in Johnson and Kaplan's view the introduction of double-entry bookkeeping was a rational means of keeping track of what was owing and what was owed in an increasingly complex market economy, Hoskin and Macve see it as a more complex process connected with social movements at the time. It is no mere accident that new systems of accounting coincided with the idea of purgatory where God becomes the great examiner in the sky to whom all are 'accountable' for their actions.

Although by 1400 Italian merchants were using accounting as a tool of management and control, for many centuries the use of accounting hardly spread and there was little technical development. Hoskin and Macve attribute this to there being no 'power–knowledge framework' in which the techniques 'could discover their modern applications'. Crudely put, the world was not yet in such a state that such a development could occur. Accounting tended to be a sporadically updated record of the past; it was not concerned with the future – in other words the coherent network, in time, of disciplinary techniques which surround work in our society: planning and budgeting before work was carried out, measurement during the processes and checking afterwards, were absent. According to Hoskin and Macve, it was only after the development of the giving of 'marks' in educational institutions that the power of education, and thereby accounting, was transformed. In the late eighteenth and early nineteenth centuries a new kind of mathematisation was taking place on many fronts, tending toward the *quantification* of human qualities, of which the giving of marks for performance is the most crucial. Constant examination and constant marking together create a way of tracing and predicting an individual's performance. This 'marking' fed back into accounting practice through a very specific event: the creation in 1817, at the United States Military Academy at West Point, of a sophisticated system of marking, surveillance and discipline. Pupils of the system were later crucial to the introduction of the techniques of management and accounting which were to spread throughout American industry.

Hoskin and Macve discuss in detail the West Point/Springfield Armory link. The key person in this link was Daniel Tyler, who as a pupil at West Point experienced an educational system which combined a hierarchical organised structure which gave precise times and places for each individual's work, and a dynamic system of testing and evaluating done by numbers and applied to every element of cadet life. It was the examination at Springfield that brought together the hierarchical structure and judgement with reference to a standard. Tyler introduced at Springfield between 1832 and 1842 systems of human accountability, where it was discovered that accounting knowledge was a powerful technique for harnessing human performance. It could provide a link between the whole financial system and the disciplining of work in general. The West Point system had an impact on US industry: first in the US armories at Springfield and Harper's Ferry; and second, through the organisation of the first forms of corporate managerialism on the railroads – developments which Chandler has shown to be of crucial significance to the emergence of modern management accounting.

In their examination of the origins of modern management accounting Miller and O'Leary focus on the first three decades of the twentieth century, the period when standard costing and budgeting emerged in their modern form. Looking at this development from a Foucauldian standpoint, they see it as a small, but important, part in the growth of disciplinary power generally. The individual became subject to new forms of discipline within the factory (e.g. through accounting) and outside (e.g. having 'intelligence' and 'healthiness' measured). At the end of the nineteenth century a new impersonal 'scientific management' was beginning to spread in American industry (as noted earlier). Instead of the personal supervision of the boss, there were norms and standards for work, including how it was to be done. Even mundane tasks, such as shovelling coal, became subject to this discipline. Workers were observed shovelling, measurements made, and this knowledge used to instruct precisely *how* they should shovel in order to be most efficient. After detailed norms and standards were created, the boss needed, theoretically, only to step in when these were not maintained. Through planning, recording and checking work through records, discipline came to be seen to reside not in the will of the boss, but in the economic machine, the anonymous demands of efficiency. Standard costing and budgeting, an important element in the range of new disciplinary techniques, measured the work of the individual on a daily basis, enabling the 'governing' of their activity. These accounting techniques provided a way of expressing in money terms the contribution of individuals to the collective efficiency of the enterprise. Beyond the factory disciplinary power spread. This was a time when efficiency was much debated, the idea being that if all the citizens were more efficient, the nation as a whole would be more efficient. The notion emerged that government should ensure this efficiency through programmes directed at improving the mental and physical health of the population. Programmes put into action included intelligence testing (which would enable individuals to be 'scientifically' allocated to suitable education or work) and sterilising the mentally retarded to stop them breeding more of their own 'inefficient' kind. Miller and O'Leary discuss the development of management accounting in the context of what they call the construction of 'the governable person'. This refers to the idea of the person as having certain attributes which could be measured and through which they could be controlled or 'governed'. In the enterprise management accounting – along with the scientific management out of which it grew and the nascent industrial psychology – helped to make the person 'governable'.

Looking at the same period as Miller and O'Leary, but from a slightly different standpoint, Loft examines the history of cost accounting in the United Kingdom during the turbulent period of the First World War and the years immediately following, when the practice of cost accounting spread rapidly. An important part in this appears to have been played by an unforseen consequence of certain actions of the government. From small beginnings in 1914, the scale of the war grew. Five million men entered the armed forces and the power of the state over individual citizens and business increased tremendously. The scale of war production was enormous. By the end of the war the Ministry of Munitions controlled over 3.5 million workers and it was claimed to be the biggest buying, importing, selling, manufacturing and distributing business in the world. Some factories were taken over by the government, but in most cases it did not fire the existing management and take-over the running of the factory itself. Rather, it allowed the original owners to run the business whilst controlling in detail what went on. The problem was, what should manufacturers be paid for the items which the government directed them to make, and for which there was no normal market price? It was solved through a regulation which laid down that the price should be what it *cost* to make plus a margin for profit. Suddenly the measurement of costs became far more important, manufacturers were forced to look more closely at their costing systems and the government set in process procedures for checking and analysing costs.

Costing techniques do not spread independently of knowledgeable individuals. Chartered and Incorporated accountants working from their professional offices were employed by the government to administer this new law. From being almost entirely occupied with bankruptcy, auditing and financial accounting, professional accountants' expertise came to include cost accounting.

The emphasis on costing gave clerks involved with it a new importance. In the reorganisation of job categories in the first population census after the war, one of the new additions was 'costing and estimating clerks'. After the war some of these higher-ranking clerks who had become involved with cost accounting formed an association called the 'Institute of Cost and Works Accountants', the forerunner of the 'Chartered Institute of Management Accountants'. Their aims were, first, to be accepted as 'professional' accountants like the members of the Chartered and Incorporated bodies from which they were excluded; and second, to further the spread of 'scientific' costing techniques in British industry. Thus here the diverse 'origins' of management accounting are illustrated – origins that include the unintended consequences of the uneasy course which the wartime British government steered between 'business as usual' and a totalitarian command economy. This shows how the spread of the discipline (including both the knowledge and the disciplinary technique) of accounting in the twentieth century is not simply to be found in Johnson and Kaplan's rational economic necessity. As discussed by Armstrong in the American case, it has much more complex origins which cannot be separated from the fortunes of the occupational group(s) who carry out the work and who 'market' the techniques to manufacturers.

The last piece of work to be examined is a case study (Bougen, 1994). Inspired by both Foucauldian and labour process studies of accounting, he examines in detail a case study of the use of accounting in industrial relations in the 1920s. He examines closely how a particular UK company, Hans Renold and Co. Ltd, used accounting as an important tool in a strategic management initiative to improve worker–management relations and corporate performance. Renold (the firm was family owned) introduced a complex profit-sharing scheme in 1921 where bonus payments were to be linked to increased efficiency in production. The idea was that it should not be just a simple 'carrot' to get workers to be more efficient, but would also be a way of 'educating' employees in the harsh realities of the commercial world. To this end a committee of management and employee representatives was set up to monitor the scheme.

Renold was probably surprised when employees began to challenge the technical details of the profit-sharing scheme, especially an item called 'wages on capital'. As time went by labour became more and more dissatisfied, for the scheme failed to generate bonus payments from mid-1921 to early 1923. The savings which labour made seemingly went only to safeguard the 'wages of capital', there being nothing left for them. There was tension, for management continued to attempt to educate employees about the realities of business life through discussing the company's problems and priorities within the accounting framework provided by the profit-sharing scheme. Suspicion grew, and as the employees gained a growing grasp of the framework's intricate mechanics, they began to challenge management decisions, arguing, for example, that work done by outside concerns could be done more easily and cheaply within the firm. They also began to argue in a sophisticated manner over the descriptive ability of accounting, and its reconciliation with their own perceptions of factory activities. They recognised the capacity that management had to manipulate data for their own purposes: by mid-1926, the firm was making good profits, but management reformulated the profit-sharing scheme to their own advantage. Eventually the scheme was terminated after a merger of the company in 1930.

Bougen writes that this case demonstrates how personal objectives and expectation, organisational structures and environmental circumstances all influence the emergence of systems of accounting; they do not emerge in an organisational and environmental vacuum. In this case the use of accounting was not simply the result of a single rational line of thought, but of a variety of organisational processes, including the *idea* of its use as an educational tool. In practice it was used to create the agenda and script for management–labour discussions and to attempt to enhance managerial control over workshop activities. As labour challenged the scheme, so management changed the accounting. The development of accounting systems cannot be divorced from the underlying power structure of the organisation; the scheme was initiated, designed (and changed) by management. Accounting was 'injected' into the core of the management–labour relations in the factory and became a focal point for the articulation of disagreements and challenges by labour of management's authority. In methodological terms we have moved a long way from the traditional 'innovations of the great men' perspective. Traditional historians of accounting would not have interested themselves in this case – it has little or nothing to do with technical progress in accounting – no new innovation such as a new form of overhead allocation emerged from it. However, it shows how an appreciation of the emergence, roles and consequences of accounting is impossible without study of the social, economic and political relationships of its context. Many of these issues have only come to light in 'the new accounting history', as Miller *et al.* call it (1991).

Conclusion

This chapter was subtitled 'Relevance Found': from being a dusty, seemingly irrelevant subject, the history of management accounting has become the object of much wider interest and debate over the last decade or so. The 'new' management accounting history spans a range of methodologies and different theoretical approaches. In this chapter I have dealt with the main schools of thought, dividing them into four main categories. Dividing them up like this is naturally something of an oversimplification, for example, writers using different approaches may be inspired by each other, but it forms a useful way of beginning to analyse the wide variety of approaches.

Traditional historians of management accounting focused on the development of management accounting techniques. They showed how modern management accounting slowly but surely evolved from primitive nineteenth-century cost accounting through the efforts of pioneers such as Garcke and Fells. Their main source of evidence for this was descriptions in handbooks for manufacturers and articles in trade journals. While the methodologies used by the new historians vary, they have in common that they use a wider variety of historical evidence than did the traditionalists – from business archives to social conditions. Documents and other evidence which would not have been considered interesting under the traditional approach become so if, for example, the perspective is changed from being one which focuses on choice of method of calculation of overhead rates to how measurement of costs was used to manage labour.

The first school which was examined here, the neoclassicists, concentrate, like the traditionalists, on the development of management accounting techniques. However, they focus on business archives from the late seventeenth and early eighteenth centuries, rather than on published material such as handbooks. Their detailed research of these archives leads them to believe that the forerunners of modern management accounting systems are to be found much earlier than previously thought. Whether the systems identified were widespread, or (as seems more likely) specific to particular manufacturers who were before their time in many respects, is an interesting question. The almost total lack of handbooks and trade journals dealing with costing in this earlier period suggests that most systems were specific to a particular manufacturer, or to a group of manufacturers in a particular area.

Strongly influenced by theories of transaction costs coming from the discipline of economics, Johnson and Kaplan cover a wide sweep of history from the distant past to the (apparently) problematic present. Viewing management accounting through these economic spectacles leads them to identify the growth of management accounting as intimately connected to the strategy and structure of large business enterprises such as Du Pont. Indeed, the reason that these businesses could develop in the way in which they did was because the new accounting techniques such as return on investment (ROI) enabled top management to run them efficiently. Their wide generalisations and cover of a huge sweep of history are impressive, but questions can be raised about the validity of their historical explanations which rely on assumptions of underlying economic rationalities.

In Johnson and Kaplan's world view, employees of the firm are 'merely' a factor of production with a cost to be minimised, they are not sentient beings but economic ciphers controlled by the wage contract. Critics say that this explanation helps to mystify the origins of management accounting, which, like many other management techniques, acts primarily as a means of controlling labour. The labour process approach focuses on studying in detail how management accounting developed as a way of controlling labour. Social and political aspects of the introduction of management accounting are brought to the fore. Like Johnson and Kaplan, Hopper and Armstrong have a grand sweep to their history, but it brings in different forms of evidence, in particular material concerning the de-skilling and reorganisation of work to facilitate managerial control – a managerial control which extends down from top management through all the layers of the business hierarchy. Accounting is only one of a range of techniques used to control labour. Armstrong discusses how the culturally disproportionate – compared for example to Japan – importance of accounting in the USA and UK is connected with the rise of a powerful accounting profession, thus bringing into the discussion of the development of management accounting the importance of the rise of a group of professionals whose aim was to promote the use of accounting techniques and act to realise their implementation in organisations.

The fourth approach which was discussed was that of the scholars influenced by the ideas of Michel Foucault. This is a more diverse group; a fact which reflects, amongst other things, that Foucault himself never wrote about accounting, and several different themes have been adopted by accounting scholars from his work to throw light on its development. One important concept is that of accounting as a disciplinary technique, another the linkage of power and knowledge, in this case power in the enterprise to the knowledge created through accounting systems. Unlike the labour process approach, this is not expressed in terms of capital's exploitation of labour. Rather, the introduction of accounting systems is seen in terms of the creation of 'governable persons' who are held in a disciplinary web of control wherever they find themselves in the organisation. Foucault's method for doing historical research involves the detailed study of archives. In this there are some commonalities with the neoclassical approach, but whilst the neoclassicists emphasise the development of techniques to measure product costs, Foucauldians emphasise the development of techniques for measuring human performance – the origins of accounting as a disciplinary technique. Foucault emphasises the importance of looking for the diverse and non-obvious origins of disciplinary techniques, for the accidents of history. This has been reflected in accounting in studies of the importance of particular historical events at first sight a long way from the factory floor, for example wars.

The history of management accounting has become relevant in two distinctive ways during the last decade or so. First, it has been shown to have relevance to our understanding of accounting in the present. Second, management accounting history has been placed in its more general historical context. It is no longer *just* the history of management accounting, but it is part of the history of business enterprise, the history of labour, and in general of the creation of the modern world. As part of this wider history management accounting is shown to do more than just *reflect* social movements and contexts; it is also shown to be *constitutive*, creating in organisations a 'reality' of costs and profits which shapes actions and events far beyond its immediate surroundings.

Bibliography

The references in this chapter have deliberately been kept to a minimum. They give some ideas for further reading. For the reader who wishes to go further, the citations in these books and articles give a wealth of possibilities.

The traditional approach

Garner, S. Paul (1954) *Evolution of Cost Accounting to 1925*, Alabama: University of Alabama Press (reprinted 1976).

The neoclassical approach

Fleischman, R.K. and L.D. Parker (1992) 'The cost accounting environment in the British Industrial Revolution iron industry', *Accounting, Business and Financial History*, vol. 2, No. 2, pp. 141–60.

The Johnson and Kaplan approach

Johnson, H.T. (1972) 'Early Cost Accounting for Internal Management Control: Lyman Mills in the 1850s', *Business History Review, Winter*, vol. 46, pp. 466–74.
Johnson, H.T. and R.S. Kaplan (1987) *Relevance Lost: The rise and fall of management Accounting*, Boston, Mass.: Harvard University Press.

The labour process approach

Braverman, H. (1974) *Labour and Monopoly Capital: The degredation of work in the Twentieth Century*, New York: Monthly Review Press.
Hopper, T. and P. Armstrong (1991) 'Cost accounting, controlling labour and the rise of conglomerates'. *Accounting, Organisations and Society*, vol. 16, No. 5/6, pp. 405–38.

The Foucauldian approach

Bougen, P. (1994) 'Accounting and labour: integrations and disintegrations', in Hopwood and Miller, 1994, pp. 138–67.
Foucault, M. (1977) *Discipline and Punish: The birth of the prison*, Penguin.
Hopwood, A.G. and P. Miller (1994) *Accounting as Social and Institutional Practice*, Cambridge: Cambridge University Press.

Hoskin, K. and R. Macve (1994) 'Writing, examining, disciplining: the genesis of accounting's modern power', in Hopwood and Miller, 1994, pp. 67–97.

Loft, A. (1994) 'Accountancy and the First World War', in Hopwood and Miller, 1994, pp. 116–37.

Miller, P. and T. O'Leary (1994) 'Governing the calculable person', in Hopwood and Miller, 1994, pp. 98–115.

Useful review articles

Ezzamel, M., K. Hoskin and R. Macve (1990) 'Managing it all by numbers: A review of Johnson & Kaplan's "Relevance Lost" ', *Accounting and Business Research*, pp. 153–66.

Miller, P., T. Hopper and R. Laughin (1991) 'The new accounting history: an introduction', *Accounting, Organisations and Society*, pp. 395–404.

Stewart, R.E. (1992) 'Pluralizing our past: Foucault in accounting history', *Accounting, Auditing and Accountability Journal*, pp. 57–73.

CHAPTER THREE

Management Control, Organisational Design and Accounting Information Systems

David Otley

A modern business enterprise is a complex entity. Its survival depends upon its ability to match the needs of a large number of people including customers, suppliers, employees, providers of finance and national governments. It employs people with a variety of different skills, often in widely scattered locations. Raw materials and other goods and services are obtained on a world-wide basis, often from other equally complex organisations. The products it manufactures (or, increasingly, the services it provides) are often of considerable technological sophistication, and are sold in a global market-place. People, money and machines are combined together to produce goods and services on a scale that is unique to the present age.

We often take the existence of such organisations for granted, and complain when they fail to meet our expectations, but what is remarkable is that such complex systems generally do work satisfactorily and provide the basis on which our standard of living depends. Admittedly not all organisations succeed: many small firms fail to develop into larger ones, and frequently fail to survive at all. Even well-established organisations can fail to adapt to changes in technology or consumer taste and be forced to withdraw from whole areas of activity, with the consequent repercussions on their employees, suppliers and customers. Yet, even when faced with problems on a massive scale, organisations tend to survive, albeit in a more or less drastically amended form.

How is it that organisations are able to control such a complex web of activities in such a way as to satisfy the requirements of all interested parties? What are the control mechanisms that are used to enable them to survive in a rapidly changing environment? How do their aims and objectives become translated into the myriad of related actions necessary for their achievement? Such is the subject-matter of management control, which is fundamentally concerned with the achievement of organisations's goals and purposes by the co-ordination of the work of managers within organisations. In this chapter we will examine some aspects of the design and operation of systems of management control and their relationship with accounting information systems. Accounting is an important tool of control, but it is only one tool amongst many and, although it may occupy a central position in a control structure, it must be supplemented in a variety of ways.

Information has been aptly described as the cement that binds an organisation together. Without a regular supply of appropriate information, the organisation would indeed fall apart. Much of this information is obtained informally and sometimes accidentally; some is speculative and qualitative in nature. But the central core of management information is provided by management information systems, of which the management accounting system is an important component. The most noticeable feature of the management accounting system is that the information it conveys is expressed in terms of money. This focus on the financial dimension of organisational activity is often misunderstood. It does not occur because the main purpose of the organisation may be to make money, although it must certainly be admitted that the generation of surplus funds is a condition for long-term survival. Rather, money provides a common language in which the results of a wide range of disparate activities can be expressed and aggregated. Money is the language of business because it provides a unique means of measuring the results of dissimilar activities in common terms. Thus management control systems rely to a considerable extent upon management accounting information systems. The art of using accounting information for effective control is still not fully understood, but we will be exploring several of its aspects in this chapter.

Management Control

This use of the term 'management control' dates from the pioneering work of Robert Anthony, who was for many years Professor of Accounting at the Harvard Business School. Anthony's (1965) classic definition of management control was 'the process by which managers assure that resources are obtained and used effectively and efficiently in the accomplishment of the organization's objectives' (p. 17). He saw management control as being sandwiched between the processes of strategic planning and operational control, which can also be superimposed upon an organisational hierarchy, as shown in Figure 3.1.

Strategic planning is concerned with setting goals and objectives for the whole organisation over the long term. By contrast, operational control is concerned with the down-to-earth activity of ensuring that immediate tasks are carried out. Management control is the process that links the two. Global goals have to be broken down into sub-goals for parts of the organisation; vague statements of future intent have to be given more substantive content; long-term goals have to be solidified into shorter-term goals. The process of management control is designed to ensure that the day-to-day tasks performed by all those involved in the organisation come together in a co-ordinated set of actions which assist overall goal attainment. This can be seen primarily as the planning and co-ordination function of management control. The other side of the management control coin is its monitoring and feedback function. Regular observations and reports on actual achievement are necessary to ensure that planned actions are indeed achieving desired results. Thus hourly, daily, weekly, monthly, quarterly and annual feedback cycles are necessary to enable timely corrective action to be taken when things do not go to plan.

This point of view is reflected in a more comprehensive definition of a management control system put forward by Lowe (1971):

> A system of organizational information seeking and gathering, accountability and feedback designed to ensure that the enterprise adapts to changes in its substantive environment and that the work behaviour of its employees is measured by reference to a set of operational sub-goals (which conform with overall objectives) so that the discrepancy between the two can be reconciled and corrected for. (p. 5)

Figure 3.1   The position of management control within an organisational hierarchy.

This general definition stresses the role of a management control system (MCS) as a set of control mechanisms designed to assist organisations to regulate themselves, whereas Anthony's definition is more specific and limited to a narrower subset of control activities. Indeed, it may be argued that Anthony's approach is too restrictive in that it assumes away two important problems. The first of these is concerned with the procedures organisations go through in attempting to define their strategies, goals and objectives. Such procedures are typically complex and ill-defined, with strategies being produced as much by accident as by design. The processes involved in corporate strategy will be considered in more detail later. The second problem concerns the methods used to control the production (or service delivery) process, which are highly dependent upon the technology in use, and which differ markedly from one type of organisation to the next. Anthony conveniently relegates these control issues to the realm of operational control!

Anthony's approach can be seen as a preliminary ground-clearing exercise, whereby he limits the extent of the problem he sets out to study. In such a complex field as management control, this is a very sensible first step. But it must be recognised that it constructs a set of blinkers which cause only a part of the overall issue to be seen. Anthony focuses on the role of management accounting as the centrepiece of the MCS, and tends to neglect other controls that exist in the business enterprise. Although he clearly states that he believes that social psychology rather than economics forms the basic discipline upon which the study of MCS rests, most of his work is in fact concerned only with accounting control systems.

In summary, a useful MCS cannot confine itself solely to accounting measures of performance, important as these undoubtedly are. Some activities are controlled by physical counts of production and technical measures of performance. The MCS has also to be concerned with those areas of performance that cannot be measured in precise, quantitative terms according to a precise schedule. For example, market share and competitive position, employee commitment and morale, and the progress of research and development work are all vitally important to the continued well-being of the enterprise, but they cannot be captured in accounting terms alone. Even when accounting information is relevant, it is the response of individuals to that information that is crucial to its effectiveness in bringing about overall organisational control. Management control is therefore as much about motivating and influencing human behaviour as it is about the technical design of information systems.

Basic Issues in Management Control

In designing a management control system there are three fundamental questions that need to be addressed. Interestingly, these three questions seem to remain the same whereas the answers are continually being updated in the light of new circumstances that affect the organisation. (As an aside, it is pertinent to remember the external examiner who commented upon the fact that the questions in an economics examination appeared to be the same as those set in the previous year. He was assured that this posed no problem, as the answers were different this year!) The operation of an MCS can be seen as the continual development of new solutions to the same underlying issues. The three questions are as follows:

1. What are the performance measures that will represent good performance, both for the total organisation and for its parts?
2. What are the appropriate standards of performance and how are these to be set for each part of the organisation?
3. What are the rewards that will attach to the successful attainment of these targets? Or conversely, what are the penalties that will occur if the targets are not achieved?

Performance measures

The first question is the most fundamental and the most difficult to answer. There is rarely a single objective that subsumes all others. Even profitability has to be assessed in terms of its short-term and long-term components, and in relation to growth, capital structure and liquidity. More crucially, how to obtain high profitability in a complex, competitive and uncertain environment is not, and probably can never be, a well-understood process. There are trade-offs to be made between competing demands on resources, and there are also the desires of influential and powerful participants to be considered. Deciding on corporate strategy is as much a matter of politics as it is one of rational decision-making.

Once some overall objectives or plans have been established, these general, overall goals have to be broken down into subsidiary goals that relate to different matters such as product range, quality, market segmentation, customer service and so on. Further goals need to be developed for parts of the organisation and for the different business functions such as production, marketing and personnel. The development of all of these sub-goals requires choice and creative input; they do not follow inexorably from the overall goals.

Finally, although some aspects of good performance can be quantified, many other aspects cannot. Even when a goal is quantifiable, the means of achieving it may not be well understood. Thus decisions on programmes of action designed to achieve goals may well be open to discussion concerning their likely effectiveness. Further, discussion of means to an end (such as plans, budgets and action programmes) is likely to be used as a way of amending ends, even when these are not ostensibly under consideration.

Thus the question of how good performance is to be defined is one which is open to continual debate, choice and amendment within the organisation. At any one time the dimensions being emphasised are likely to be multiple, partially conflicting and often ambiguous. To the extent that means–end relationships are not fully understood, plans designed to achieve these ends are also debatable in terms of their likely effectiveness. The definition of appropriate performance measures that can be used to

transmit a sense of purpose and direction through the organisation hierarchy is a
major function of the MCS.

② Setting performance standards

Once a performance measure has been defined, the next issue to be settled is the level
of attainment that is required. Here there is usually an immediate conflict between
what is desirable and what is currently attainable, with both being subject to
considerable ambiguity. In addition, the people in the best position to make such
judgements about the feasibility of standards are often the very managers who will
be held accountable for attaining them. Because they have a vested interest in the
outcome of the standard-setting process, they may bias and manipulate both the
standard set and the reported results concerning its attainment. These issues impinge
directly upon the budget-setting and budgetary control processes that take place
within organisations and upon which there is an extensive academic literature which
is discussed in other chapters.

   This conflict between the attainable and the desirable reverberates up and down
the organisation, with senior managers tending to emphasise overall desirability and
their subordinates being more concerned with feasibility. It affects matters such as
planning procedures (top-down vs bottom-up), decision-making (participation,
consultation or neither) and organisational design (span of control vs number of
hierarchical levels). The whole question of performance measurement and control
will be considered in more detail later.

③ Linking rewards to performance

The final issue that needs to be addressed is the connection of rewards (and/or
penalties) with results. It is all very well to set quantitative performance targets for
managers, but they will be effective only to the extent that the manager is motivated
to achieve the target set. This requires the establishment of links between target
achievement and valued (although not necessarily financial) rewards. These mechanisms can take a variety of forms, ranging from the encouragement of cohesive peer
groups where members assist and encourage each other in achieving targets
(characteristic of Japanese styles of management) to the explicit linking of substantial
monetary rewards to target achievement (most prevalent at senior management
levels in the USA, but also inherent in all incentive payment schemes).

   There is no doubt that incentives can be devised that will encourage managers to
achieve – or at least report – a high degree of target attainment, but the means used
are not always those intended or desired. Such schemes may promote competition
between managers where co-operation would have been preferable, and may
encourage the manipulation of actions and reports so that senior managers become
increasingly misinformed about what is actually happening whilst being lulled into a
false sense of security that all is well.

Contingent Approaches

As a management control system continues in use, the tentative answers initially given to these three questions tend to be changed in the light of experience and changing circumstances. Different organisations are likely to develop different answers in different circumstances. The recognition of these inherent differences has led to the development of contingency theories of organisational design and of management accounting. The fundamental basis of contingency theory is that there is no universally best answer to such questions; rather, the MCS needs to be specifically tailored to the needs and specific circumstances of the organisation for which it is intended. In this section we will review these contingency theories and seek to outline their impact on MCS design and use.

The contingency theory of organisational design

One of the most fundamental ways in which an organisation controls its activities is the way that it structures those activities, by assigning authority and responsibility for different tasks to different managers and groups of employees. But although organisational structure is a powerful mechanism to ensure that defined tasks are consistently performed, it can also create difficulties by restricting managers' attention solely to their own sub-area and neglecting necessary tasks which require co-ordination across departmental boundaries.

Much of the basis of accounting control rests on the definition of responsibility centres, be they cost centres, profit centres or investment centres (or, occasionally, revenue centres). The manager of a responsibility centre can be given clear targets relating to the defined area of responsibility, and be held accountable for those aspects of performance which can be controlled. Indeed, there is empirical evidence to suggest that managers are held more broadly accountable for many activities within their defined area of responsibility, even where they can exercise little effective control. Many accounting procedures, such as transfer pricing mechanisms, have had to be invented in order to preserve the fiction of self-contained, independent responsibility centres for which an overall measure of profitability can be constructed.

Thus, the central aspect of formal organisational structure is the segmentation of activities into subsets that can be handled by individual managers. This process has been termed *differentiation*, and refers to the tendency for organisational sub-units to develop their own ways of working to cope with their own specific circumstances and tasks. The complementary process of *integration* is necessary to co-ordinate the activities of the different sub-units, and the management accounting system often plays a key role in this process. This approach to viewing the design of formal organisational structure has been formalised under the banner of contingency theory.

The contingency theory of organisational structure can be traced to the pioneering work of Burns and Stalker (1961) and Woodward (1958), who were forced to adopt contingent explanations in order to account for the empirical data they had collected on organisational functioning. It was codified into a formal theory, most notably by Thompson (1967), and by 1970 could be described as being the dominant approach in organisation theory. The most coherent body of empirical research conducted within the paradigm is probably that of the Aston School. The thrust of this work was to identify various *contingencies* which were believed to have an important influence on how organisations chose to structure themselves. The major contingent variables were found to be organisational size, production technology and various features of the external environment such as its competitiveness and inherent uncertainty. In short, by the early 1970s there was a strong tradition of empirical work that was based on the premise that the appropriate structure for an organisation was strongly affected by the characteristics of its external environment, and by features of its internal technology, although there was still some scope for managerial choice. However, by and large, this work failed to demonstrate strong and consistent relationships between context, structure and organisational performance.

The reason for this apparent lack of progress in identifying the situational determinants of organisational structure is probably rooted in the incompleteness of the model under consideration. As organisational design is concerned with both structure and social processes, it seems that there is no single most appropriate structural response to a particular type of environment, but rather that there is a range of possible responses involving both structure and process. This may account for the disparities in reported empirical results, which concentrate almost entirely on issues of structure to the neglect of process. But the contingency theory of organisational structure is important in the design of control systems both because structure is itself an important control mechanism, and because it was the precursor of the contingency theory of management accounting.

The contingency theory of management accounting

The contingency theory of management accounting represents an attempt to identify the most appropriate (accounting-based) control system for a given set of circumstances. In principle, such an idea is not new, as practising management accountants have always tried to adapt their systems to be more useful in a particular set of circumstances. But what was new was the attempt to identify the most important contingent variables and to assess their impact upon control systems design. However, it has to be said that the theory was more successful in identifying contingent variables than in analysing their impact. Part of the reason for this deficiency lies in the fact that the theory tends to focus exclusively on management accounting controls, rather than the much broader package of overall controls used by organisations. Nevertheless, it is instructive to consider the major classes of contingent variable that were identified.

Contingent variables

Environment

It is perhaps self-evident that the nature of an MCS will be affected by the external environment in which it operates, as the purpose of a control system is to assist an organisation to adapt to the environment that it faces. However, it must be emphasised that formal accounting control systems comprise only one of many potential controls that can be adopted. For example, the sophistication of accounting controls is influenced by the intensity of competition faced by the firm, but two other environmental characteristics have been shown to affect control systems design, namely dynamism (rate of change) and heterogeneity (number of different product markets served). Each of these characteristics is associated with an emphasis on different aspects of accounting control. Other authors have identified the degree of structural complexity of an enterprise and the degree of turbulence in its environment as exerting a major influence on control systems design. Whereas increasing structural complexity leads to the addition of new accounting tools to those already in use, environmental discontinuity will often require the replacement of tools which have become obsolete by new ones.

Environmental stress, restrictiveness and aggressiveness have also been referenced by researchers. All of these aspects of an organisation's environment involve factors such as the availability of opportunities and the extent to which the firm is influenced by other organisations. It can be argued that the existence of powerful interest groups increases the level of uncertainty faced by the organisation. Similarly, a high degree of internal complexity may also increase uncertainty at the centre, if only through inadequacies in information processing. Thus, the major underlying factor appears to be environmental unpredictability in all its guises. However, the considerable body of work on the effects of unpredictability on information and control systems design has yet to be fully incorporated into MCS research.

Technology

One of the longest-established relationships between a contingent variable and control systems design has been that associated with production technology. Woodward's work which linked different structural arrangements with particular workflow patterns has been paralleled by MCS design. It has long been recognised by accountants that the nature of the production process determines the amount of cost tracing (rather than cost apportionment) that can take place. The level of accuracy possible in job-costing cannot be carried over into process production because the bulk of costs are incurred jointly by a range of final products. There is thus a technological constraint on the design of accounting controls due to product interdependence.

Technology was specifically introduced as a major variable in early contingency studies. Two dimensions of technology were studied (the number of exceptions that arise in the production process and the search procedures used to resolve such exceptions) and were shown to be highly correlated with measures of information systems style (i.e. the amount, focus and use made of data). More recent work has indicated a positive association between the degree of automation in the production process and the formality of budget systems use. Other work has suggested that managerial functions can best be understood by focusing on environmental variables, whereas the structure and processes used by operating units will be more directly related to technological variables.

Size

Organisational size is an important factor affecting both structure and other control arrangements. As an organisation grows, it will tend to organise initially on a functional basis. However, increased growth by means of diversification and the consequent exposure to more diverse product-market environments prompts the reorganisation of activities into semi-autonomous divisions where accounting-based performance measures dominate the control system. Further evidence of the impact of size on control techniques was found in studies of the role of management accounting systems following merger or take-over. Differences in control practices that exist prior to a merger almost entirely disappear afterwards as the new subsidiary is required to conform to the practices laid down by the acquiring company. It may be that pressures for conformity to corporate control systems limit the ability of subsidiary companies to design and operate the control systems most suited to their individual circumstances. If so, attention needs to be paid to the alternative control procedures that are put into place to supplement them. With the tendency towards corporatism in many areas of economic activity, where ownership is concentrated in the hands of a few global corporations, more complex information-handling systems will be needed to cope with the increased levels of complexity and diversity.

Strategy

Consideration of corporate strategy has, rather surprisingly, not been prominent in studies of control systems design despite arguments that differences in corporate strategy should lead to differences in planning and control systems design. Chandler (1962) demonstrated a link between corporate strategy and organisational structure, but this has not been carried through into the design of other control mechanisms until recently.

Most of the limited empirical research that has examined the relationship between strategy and MCS design uses different typologies. Examples of these include defenders, prospectors, adaptors and reactors; cost leadership, differentiation and focus; and build, hold and harvest. However, the use of different strategic typologies creates difficulties in integrating the research evidence, and only recently have there been attempts to reconcile these different variables.

A study which examined the relationship between business strategy, style of evaluation and effectiveness found that when greater reliance is placed on long-run criteria of evaluation and managerial bonuses are determined by subjective (non-formula) methods, effectiveness is enhanced for 'build' strategies but diminished for 'harvest' strategies. By contrast, another study found that spending decisions in conditions of rapid growth were more constrained by short-run criteria such as monthly profit targets. Such a relationship seems highly plausible, as resources are often in very short supply during periods of rapid growth, and the studies may not be in conflict. It may be quite possible to attempt to manage resources carefully during rapid growth whilst at the same time attempting to increase market share in a competitive environment; for example, significant differences have been found between the control systems of 'prospectors' and 'defenders'.

It is perhaps surprising that such a fundamental factor as corporate strategy has been relatively neglected until recently. If a control system is concerned with ensuring the attainment of objectives, then attention must surely be paid to the nature of those objectives, which are codified in corporate strategy. Further, in any contingency theory, the appropriate matching of controls to circumstances requires the assessment of effectiveness, which again can only be assessed by reference to objectives.

The issue of effectiveness

This raises a fundamental issue which concerns all contingency formulations. The idea of an *appropriate* match between control systems design and the characteristics of an organisation and its environment requires the measurement of effectiveness. This can only be assessed in terms of the purposes of the organisation, which may be codified in its corporate strategy. It is a fundamental weakness of much contingency theory that adequate consideration has not been given to the specification of appropriate measures of organisational effectiveness, and simple short-term accounting measures of performance have been used (and in many cases no measure of performance, or only managerial self-assessment, has been used). In addition, there is a further complicating factor in that it is highly likely that effectiveness is itself a contingent variable.

The case for effectiveness as a contingent variable is straightforward. The controls used by an organisation are highly likely to be influenced by how successful it is. Highly successful organisations are likely to have surplus resources and not to require strict formal controls. Indeed, it may even be argued that such controls would stifle the creativity upon which their success is seen to rest. By contrast, less successful organizations are likely to be less well endowed with resources and have to manage carefully those limited resources they do possess, thus requiring an emphasis on strict formal accountability and financial controls. There is a parallel from the capital budgeting literature where an inverse relationship has been found between the adoption of sophisticated capital investment appraisal techniques (i.e. DCF methods) and firm performance. This is difficult to explain if performance is viewed as the dependent variable, but becomes much more obvious if it is regarded as the independent variable. That is, firms which are currently performing poorly are more likely to adopt more sophisticated capital investment appraisal techniques; those that are performing well do not need them as urgently.

This exposes a fundamental circularity in most formulations of contingency theories. We cannot use performance as a criterion for demonstrating a good matching of control practices with circumstances if performance is itself an important contingent variable. In practice, there are likely to be virtuous and non-virtuous circles. Good performance can be associated with appropriate control practices which result in improved performance in the future. Poor performance may well be associated with dysfunctional control systems which will fall further into decline over time. There is no easy answer to these problems; however, they do illustrate the necessity for studies of control systems which are longitudinal (which study the operation of the system over a period of time) rather than cross-sectional (which take a snapshot at only one point in time). Some richer accounts of control systems in action are now being published, and it is likely that this type of study will lead to greater insights into the complex area of control systems design and use.

Performance Measurement and Appraisal

Performance appraisal is the cornerstone upon which effective management control rests. Managers who know that they will be held accountable for their performance at some future date will be constantly concerned with the consequences of their current actions. The expectation of future accountability has an immediate and continuing effect: all actions will be evaluated in terms of their impact on future appraisal.

But how is 'performance' to be defined? We have seen that it is multi-faceted and cannot be reduced to simple, quantitative measures. Indeed, an excellent aid to clarity in thinking in this area is to attempt to replace the term 'performance' with a more precise concept whenever it occurs. The conflict is well illustrated by two polar approaches towards paying for performance. At one end of the spectrum we have reward systems based on the attainment of precisely defined, quantitative (often accounting-based) performance measures. The inherent unfairness of such systems is often commented upon in that the performance measures are inevitably short-term and narrowly based, so that wider aspects of performance are ignored; also the standards of performance that are set may become less valid with the passage of time and the changing competitive environment. At the opposite end of the spectrum are totally subjective methods of performance appraisal that are dependent upon the judgement of a manager's superior. Although such methods can take a wide range of contextual factors into account, they can also be subject to bias (both deliberate and unintended) and require the existence of a high level of trust to be seen as fair.

Some of the major issues that need to be resolved in the construction of a practical set of performance indicators are as follows:

1. Organisational purposes are complex and cannot easily be reduced to a single,

integrated measure of overall performance, although profitability is often used in this role.

2. When multiple performance measures are used, some idea of their relative importance or ranking needs to be communicated.
3. Some tasks require the co-operation of managers of different sub-units; a performance measure for a single sub-unit is inevitably inadequate, despite attempts that may be made to incorporate interactions within the system (e.g. by systems of transfer pricing).
4. Some aspects of performance cannot be measured quantitatively; these may often be very important, but there is a tendency for quantitative measures to dominate more qualitative assessments.
5. The essence of managerial work is such that required results often cannot be specified in advance; assessment of performance inevitably becomes subjective.
6. Managerial performance may have to be distinguished from the economic performance of the unit for which the manager is responsible; however, the distinction between what is 'controllable' and what is 'uncontrollable' is not clear-cut.
7. Management takes place in a complex and uncertain environment; it may be inappropriate only to reward achievement, as effort may also be deserving of recognition.

Performance measurement

The difficulties involved in specifying and rewarding managerial behaviour have led to a concentration on monitoring and rewarding performance, despite the issues outlined above. The measures of performance most often used involve accounting information, and use budgets as the standard against which results are compared. Thus, there are further issues in defining the appropriate standard against which performance should be monitored, especially in industries subject to rapid environmental change.

There are a number of sources of information that can be used in setting appropriate standards of performance; none is sufficient in itself, but collectively they can give substantial guidance:

1. The performance of the same unit in previous time periods.
2. The performance of similar units elsewhere (either within the organisation or outside it – this is the exercise of 'benchmarking', extensively recommended in the modern management literature).
3. The performance necessary to achieve desired goals.

It is important that standards of performance relate closely to plans which are designed to lead to the achievement of those standards. Nothing is more insidious than the 'planless' budget which often results from top-down budget cuts. It gives a false sense of security to senior managers, who may believe an underlying plan exists, and it is profoundly de-motivating to their subordinates, who know it does not.

Using accounting information in performance appraisal

The most direct impact of accounting information on managerial behaviour occurs when it is used for performance evaluation. That is, if managers believe that their performance will be evaluated on the basis of accounting numbers then they will attempt to influence those numbers so as to present themselves in the most favourable light. Although such behaviour may frequently be in the best interests of the organisation, it may sometimes induce a whole range of harmful side-effects, many of which have been documented in the accounting literature. The way in which accounting information is used by superior managers in performance evaluation is crucial.

The inappropriate use of accounting information in performance appraisal often results in unexpected and inappropriate behaviour, and the size of the unintended negative consequences can be alarming. Much research has focused on the operation of budgetary control systems as these have been recognised as having a pervasive influence in a wide range of organisations, both public and private. When budgets are used as standards against which performance is subsequently evaluated, rewards become directly connected with budget achievement. Managers wishing to obtain a good evaluation will clearly be motivated to ensure that they achieve their budget targets. A major part of designing and operating an effective system of budgetary control largely devolves into the construction of a set of performance measures which, if achieved, will result in the desired overall performance of the organization. There is usually little difficulty in motivating managers to achieve the specified results; what *is* difficult is ensuring that the results are achieved in an appropriate manner, rather than in ways detrimental to the organization.

The difficulties in specifying and rewarding appropriate managerial behaviour have led to a concentration on the monitoring and rewarding of results. The most commonly used measures of performance involve accounting measures of results and use budgets as the standard against which performance is assessed. Thus, the budget standard itself will come under considerable pressure and the measures of actual performance may be manipulated to give the impression of satisfactory performance when it does not exist. Finally, and most seriously, actual behaviour may be modified so that desired results appear to be obtained although the reported results may have been brought about in an undesirable manner.

One reported example of such manipulation was in the area of repair and maintenance budgets. A particular company set its repair and maintenance budgets on a flexible basis (i.e. the greater the production level, the more was allocated to repairing and maintaining the production facilities). On an annual basis this was sensible, but month by month it was more sensible to maintain machinery in slack, rather than busy, periods. Thus, managers behaving in a sensible manner would overspend in low production months and underspend in high production months. However, if their superiors held them strictly responsible for keeping within their cost budgets, they would report spending exactly in line with budget. However, in the high production months they were not able to spend the full amount on repairs and maintenance; they maintained their reported spending by categorising other expenditure as repairs and maintenance. The overall result was that too little in total was spent on repairs and maintenance, with consequent problems in the medium term.

Despite these problems, accounting measurement procedures are recognised to be of value in a wide variety of organizations, and budgetary control is all but ubiquitous. Some of the problems associated with the use of accounting performance measures appear to be avoided by managers using the imperfect accounting information in more complex ways than is suggested in the technical accounting literature.

Style of accounting information use

An important study distinguished between a rigid (budget-constrained) and a flexible (profit-conscious) style of budget use. The rigid style involved senior managers holding their subordinates strictly accountable for meeting their cost budgets; any variance was regarded as inappropriate. By contrast, the more flexible style still attached considerable importance to meeting the budget, but the senior manager would be prepared to accept a reasonable explanation for overspending. For example, if a machine had broken down, a works manager may have to choose between a quick repair that would result in a further malfunction in the near future, or a more expensive repair that would give continued benefit. The latter may result in current overspending, but be preferable in the long term. In the example reported in the previous section, managers controlled in a rigid manner tended not to report overspending, whereas those evaluated in a flexible manner overspent in 'slack' periods, but balanced this by underspending in 'busy' periods.

Where accounting information is an imperfect indicator of actual performance, the use of a rigid style is inappropriate and leads to high levels of stress and anxiety amongst managers, poor relationships with both colleagues and subordinates, and a variety of other dysfunctional consequences, such as the manipulation of accounting data. However, the more flexible style avoids many of these harmful side-effects whilst still emphasising the importance of firm cost control.

A subsequent study deliberately chose to observe a situation where budgetary and accounting information represented a more adequate basis for performance evaluation. It found that, in these circumstances, the rigid style of evaluation did not lead to the harmful consequences previously observed. However, budgetary manipulation was observed, but was connected with the performance of the units being managed, with poor performing units showing the greatest budgetary bias. More recently, these results have been placed in a wider context by noting that accounting standards of performance will be a less complete description of adequate job performance in conditions of high uncertainty, and that a more flexible use is appropriate. A later study has also suggested that managers should be evaluated in a more subjective manner if their unit faces a high degree of uncertainty. Much of this work is surveyed in an excellent review article by Briers and Hirst (1990).

The central findings of these studies relevant to the impact of accounting control are twofold. First, it is the way in which accounting information is used by senior managers and the rewards that are made contingent upon budget attainment that are critical in determining the impact of the accounting information system. Second, the effect of placing a high reliance upon accounting measures of performance is contingent upon such circumstances as the degree of knowledge we have about how managerial behaviour contributes towards successful performance (often low) and also the uncertainty that exists in the external environment. When faced with internal and external uncertainties of this sort, what may be required is a reward system that is supportive of innovation and that avoids penalising the occasional failure, for only then will managers feel able to devote their efforts towards achieving success rather than avoiding failure.

An Example

A practical example of the conflicts that can arise when the performance measures produced by the accounting system imperfectly reflect the underlying economic reality is given below. Although perhaps somewhat extreme, it clearly illustrates some of the problems that can arise in practice. Readers are encouraged to work through the data given and to analyse the optimum price both from the perspective of the overall company and from the perspective of the impact the choice of such a price will have on the reported profits of the product department.

Perkins Pumps

Perkins Ltd manufactures industrial pumps and associated products in a single factory. One of their range, the Perfecta pump, is a specialist precision item which is made on a unique machine having no alternative use. This machine is operated in a small dust-free room in a corner of the main factory building, and Perfecta pumps are assembled and packaged for distribution here. The management of Perkins Ltd do not think that the pump is a very profitable item, but wish to keep it in production because it enables them to offer a more complete range of products to their customers, which they believe gives them a competitive advantage. The pump is priced relatively highly at £1250 and about 250 pumps a year are sold.

Recently Perkins Ltd has appointed a new marketing manager who has conducted market research which leads her to believe that sales could be increased to 400 pumps a year if the price were to be reduced to £1000, and to 750 pumps a year at a price of

£800. Such a price reduction would incur no extra selling and administrative costs as these sales would be made to existing customers using the present salaried salesforce. The general manager of the Perfecta department, which operates as a profit centre, sees little virtue in such a change because he believes it will reduce the already slim profit margin. He is particularly concerned that he will become ineligible to participate in the firm's profit-sharing scheme, which allocates a percentage of total company profits to be distributed amongst those departmental managers whose departments have been in profit during the financial year.

At present the costs incurred in producing 250 pumps are budgeted to be as follows:

	£
Direct materials	52,500
Direct labour	22,500
Other variable costs	15,000
Departmental fixed costs	108,000
Total departmental costs	198,000
Factory overheads (allocated at 100 per cent of direct labour cost)	22,500
Total factory cost	220,500
Selling and administration (allocated at 40 per cent of total factory cost)	88,200
Total cost	308,700

Perkins's total factory overhead costs and selling and administrative costs are fixed irrespective of changes in the production level of the Perfecta pump.

Commentary

It should be clear that the lowest price suggested (i.e. £800) yields the greatest contribution to the company if variable costs are direct materials, direct labour and variable departmental overheads. However, the cost allocation methods adopted make costs which are truly fixed appear to be variable to the department. Thus, moving from a high price to a low price (and thus from a low volume to a high volume) moves the department from a reported profit to a reported loss, and the departmental manager's concern is justifiable. The difference between the calculated increase in company contribution and the decrease in departmental profit will appear in the over-recovery of overhead costs, or in less overhead costs being charged to other departments.

There may be a case for adopting more sophisticated methods of charging out overhead costs (e.g. the use of activity-based costing and the identification of appropriate 'cost drivers'). This is likely to be a medium-term solution. In the short term it suggests the use of budget targets, agreed with a senior manager, that will form the basis of subsequent performance evaluation.

Conclusion

Management control is a vital function in a modern business enterprise, and it is usually reliant upon accounting information systems and budgetary controls. But although accounting information has an important role to play, any such information is an imperfect control tool and has to be used in a way which takes account of its limitations, and which is appropriate to the circumstances in which it is used. Further, it is possible that the lack of use of accounting information is as serious a problem as its misuse, particularly at junior levels. Line managers will ignore formally produced accounting information unless it can be shown to be of value to them, and may develop alternative and informal information systems alongside the official system. The responsibility lies with the accounting information systems designer to develop a deeper understanding of the information requirements of specific tasks so as to be able to provide more relevant information.

Bibliography

A fuller account of the role of accounting information in management control is provided by a textbook:

Emmanuel, C.R., D.T. Otley and K. Merchant (1990) *Accounting for Management Control* (2nd edn), London: Chapman and Hall.

A more economic orientation to many of the same issues can be found in:

Ezzamel, M. and H. Hart (1987) *Advanced Management Accounting: An organisational emphasis*, London: Cassell.

A shorter and more readable account of many of the organisational and social dimensions of accounting, which covers the full range of accounting activity in organisations, is:

Parker, L.D., K.R. Ferris and D.T. Otley (1989) *Accounting for the Human Factor*, Sydney: Prentice Hall.

A similar book, but one which reviews the research literature in more detail, is:

Macintosh, N. (1985) *The Social Software of Accounting Information Systems*, London: Wiley.

Readers wishing to dip into some of the early studies upon which this chapter is based are especially recommended to read the following:

Anthony, R.N. (1965) *Planning and Control Systems: A framework for analysis*, Boston: Harvard Graduate School of Business.
Burns, T. and G.M. Stalker (1961) *The Management of Innovation*, London: Tavistock.
Chandler, A. (1962) *Strategy and Structure*, Cambridge, Mass.: MIT Press.
Lowe, E.A. (1971) 'On the idea of a management control system', *Journal of Management Studies*, vol. 8, issue 1, pp. 1–12.

Thompson, J.D. (1967) *Organizations in Action*, New York: McGraw-Hill.
Woodward, J. (1958) *Management and Technology*, London: HMSO.

Finally, a most useful review article which summarises much previous research on the impact of style of accounting information use on managerial behaviour, is:

Briers, M. and M. Hirst (1990) 'The role of budgetary information in performance evaluation', *Accounting, Organizations and Society*, vol. 15, issue 4, pp. 373–98.

CHAPTER FOUR

Critical Management Accounting

Robin Roslender

Critical management accounting is best described as a way of conceptualising management accounting which explicitly focuses on the non-technical aspects of this branch of accounting. As a necessary complement to the conventional wisdom which presents management accounting as a collection of techniques, the aim of critical management accounting (CMA) is to promote a greater level of self-awareness among management accountants. Ultimately, the objective of CMA is to contribute to the development of an improved or enhanced form of management accounting, one which is more balanced in emphasis and insightful in nature. CMA breaks with the economics underpinning which characterises much of accounting. In so doing, it firmly distances itself from management accounting's traditional commitment to the natural scientific, objectivistic, quasi-experimental paradigm sometimes termed *positivism*. Instead CMA explores the non-technical aspects of accounting to management using a broad range of social scientific perspectives.

The move to CMA can in some part be understood as a logical progression from management accounting's earlier interests in behavioural accounting and organisational analysis. Behavioural accounting dates back to the early 1950s and the work of Argyris in the field of budgeting. During the following decade the emergence of a neo-human relations tradition in organisational psychology provided the behavioural accounting researchers of the 1960s and early 1970s with a powerful literature to exploit. Organisational analysis, and in particular the systems and contingency perspectives, made rapid strides in the later 1960s and was enthusiastically integrated into management accounting research in the mid-1970s. The discipline base of organisational analysis was sociology rather than psychology, although a form of sociology which was still very skewed towards the positivistic paradigm (Burrell and Morgan, 1979). Further explorations within sociology were to become a defining feature of CMA when it emerged in the early 1980s (Roslender, 1992). Interestingly, *Accounting, Organizations and Society*, the journal which has served as the principal vehicle for most of the early papers in CMA, refers in its subtitle to the behavioural, organisational and social aspects of accounting, capturing perfectly the progression evident in the move to critical management accounting.

At the time of writing it is increasingly possible to talk of a critical accounting project or movement which spans the discipline of accounting. In this way CMA might be viewed as simply one aspect of the broader project. This would be a misconception, since to a very large extent management accounting researchers have been in the vanguard of the project, with the other branches of accounting having only recently begun to catch them up. There are a number of reasons why management accounting took the lead: the subject-matter of management accounting which has consistently lent itself to study from many different perspectives and standpoints; the comparatively undefined nature of management accounting, i.e. accounting to meet the information needs of management; the varied experiences and expertise of people who have become associated with management accounting, particularly within the academy. As arguably the most 'open' branch of accounting, it is well suited to be its most progressive.

It should not be imagined that critical accounting is in the process of becoming a further branch of accounting, parallel to financial reporting, management accounting, auditing, financial management, taxation, etc. Critical accounting exists to provide a critical perspective on accounting. More correctly, we should talk of critical perspectives on accounting, for critical accounting features an array of such perspectives. These will be outlined and discussed in the following pages, principally in the context of management accounting. One final introductory point: in this chapter the term 'critical' will be applied to a range of perspectives designed to increase management accounting's self-awareness. What defines all of these as critical is their rejection of the paradigm of positivism. This is a contentious position to embrace since one of the perspectives to be considered below, Critical Theory, is sometimes presented as being the only truly critical perspective, on accounting or society in general. At the end of the chapter the reader will, hopefully, be in a position to debate this view at some length.

Interpretive Sociology

Management accounting's initial critical perspective emerged in the early 1980s. Interpretive sociology entailed a clear departure from the positivism which character-ised both behavioural accounting and organisational analysis. In its place interpretive sociology substituted a *hermeneutic* emphasis. The focus for enquiry was meaning, the objective of enquiry being to understand the meanings which individuals have within the social order. It was Max Weber at the turn of the twentieth century who argued most powerfully that sociology, as a genuinely *social* science, must embrace a methodology, i.e. a mode of enquiry, significantly different from the natural sciences. He championed the use of *verstehen* as the means of achieving the *interpretive understanding* of the meanings, actions, intentions, etc., of the individuals who contributed to the social order. A positivistic methodology was not able to provide the same purchase on understanding meanings and for this reason was inherently unsuitable for advancing sociological insight. Weber's contention was effectively to remain the minority position for the next sixty years as sociology developed as a strongly positivistic science. When the discipline eventually rejected this approach in the mid-1960s, Weber's *verstehen* sociology, together with a number of cognate perspectives, was embraced by a generation of younger sociologists who quickly developed its hermeneutic foundations to create an interpretive sociology. In this enhanced contemporary form, the focus on actions, meanings and interactions was extended to include actors, their actions and intentions, the making, unmaking and remaking of the social and the meanings, intentions, objectives, etc., which underpin the processes this entails.

The promise of an interpretive sociology perspective for management accounting research was first outlined by Colville (1981). He levelled his critique of positivistic social scientific enquiries at the development of behavioural perspectives in accounting which in his view had contributed very little accounting knowledge in the previous twenty years. Colville argues that the principal explanation for this was behavioural accounting's lack of methodological awareness. Whether in the guise of social psychology, organisational psychology or organisation theory, including contingency theory, the predominantly positivistic methodology was incapable of providing significant insights. The alternative proposed by Colville draws on the work of Weber, together with a number of other sociologists who were key figures in the anti-positivism debates of the 1960s, particularly Glaser and Strauss. Colville argues that Glaser and Strauss offer a means of operationalising interpretive sociology in the form of *grounded theory*. In such 'theory' understanding emerges from the data in an inductive manner. Rather than imposing theory on the data, thereby fitting them into pre-existing categories, the aim of grounded theory is to generate understanding directly from the data. Verification does not assume the same significance which it has in positivistic enquiries, being replaced in grounded theory enquiries by a heightened need for sensitivity on the part of the researcher to what the data are indicating. Turning to the question of what benefits this offers for the study of organisations, Colville argues that an interpretive perspective provides a focus on organisational processes, in particular on how the reality of organisations is produced and reproduced by actors, i.e. the social construction of (organisational) reality. For all of these reasons Colville concludes that behavioural accounting must be reconstructed as interpretive sociology and thereby moved on from its behavioural emphases and their positivistic underpinnings.

Although never specifically mentioned by Colville, it is the case study method which is best suited to provide the data from which interpretive sociology's grounded theory emerges. Colville himself was subsequently to publish papers which successfully employed the case study method. However, the most insightful example of management accounting research from this perspective remains the National Coal Board (NCB) case study of Berry, Capps, Cooper, Ferguson, Hopper and Lowe (1985). The authors describe their work as an attempt to understand management control systems in practice and, in particular, the ways in which control

operated in one area of the NCB. The interpretive foundations of the study are
further exemplified by the adoption of a perspective which explores the rationales for
practice offered by those involved, rather than a 'conventional' approach which
focuses on organisational pathology and deviations from some idealistic theoretical
position. At all times the authors are conscious of the partiality of their resultant
understanding but take confidence from soundings which suggest that their account
is viewed by participants as a reasonable representation of the area in question.

The main finding of the research is that traditionally two quite separate control
systems coexisted. At the level of the Area and individual collieries, control was
based on output and production targets. This reflected a 'coal-getting' culture which
had existed for many generations, being embraced by management and workforce
alike, and which served as the basis for the constructed reality of successful
coalmining. At the national and regional levels there was evidence of a control
structure which involved a sophisticated system of financial planning and controls.
Traditionally the two systems were only loosely coupled, an arrangement which
served all of the interested parties – including successive governments – well, but at
some considerable cost. At the time of their research the authors were aware that the
Conservative administration was intent on promoting the operation of market forces
across all industries, a change which inevitably threatened the prevailing negotiated
order of the NCB at the local level. History has demonstrated that the costs of the
continuation of the coal-getting culture have been borne by the industry's workforce,
so much so that the industry is now expected to contract to as few as a dozen
collieries by the end of the century.

Case studies such as this one offer a means of generating the sort of understanding
that genuinely social scientific explanations require. However, their ultimate value,
like that of interpretive sociology in general, is open to some debate. First, they
furnish depth and detail but often do so in a very bland way. This blandness is
typified in the conclusion to the Berry *et al.* study which describes the NCB as
providing a 'fascinating arena' for studying the different philosophies which can co-
exist in an organisation. The adoption of a hermeneutic methodology does not
involve any political engagement, and in this way it is viewed as offering little real
advance on positivistic enquiries. This criticism was not lost on several of the
researchers involved. They were subsequently to offer a number of more provocative
interpretations of their data. Second, even consciously rejecting the need to embrace
a politically informed position does not overcome the problem of generating partial
understandings. The idea of theory emerging from the data is a very powerful image
to be deployed in demonstrating the limitations of positivistic sociology. However, it
is necessary to recall that as observers we already carry around a range of
interpretations of what it is that we see, and so all that we are able to provide by way
of interpretive understanding is *our* interpretive understanding. Third, and finally,
the focus on process which interpretive sociology provides should not be confused
with an inherent capacity to offer a measure of detailed historical insight. Interpretive
sociology is principally concerned with the present, i.e. the here and now, and only to
a much lesser extent with the immediate past and the very near future. Where history

is included in case studies, it is normally for contextualising purposes and is usually essentially descriptive in nature. In this respect interpretive sociology is an ahistorical perspective.

Marxist Perspectives

In an attempt to overcome the limitations of an interpretive sociology perspective, a number of critical management accounting writers turned to the legacy of Marxist theory. This had also been the experience of those sociologists who, in the 1960s, were seeking a more radical form of sociology than the Weberian alternative offered to the dominant structural-functionalist perspective. Critical accounting was fortunate in being able to take advantage from two decades of development of Marxist theory, both within sociology and beyond. During this time there had been a massive expansion in the volume and interpretation of the extant literature. However, by the later 1970s it was possible to begin to map the complex terrain of Marxist theory in insightful ways. Among these was the distinction between what Burrell and Morgan (1979) termed *radical structuralism* and *radical humanism*. Radical structuralist perspectives were based on Marx's later, more materialist writings, while radical humanist perspectives were based on his earlier, more idealist thought which afforded greater significance to the notion that individuals create the world in which they live.

Within the Marxist tradition of management accounting research it is possible to identify three different perspectives. Two of these, political economy and the labour process perspective, are more structuralist in emphasis, while the third, Critical Theory, is more humanistic. All three, however, are explicitly informed by the imperative of producing understanding for the purpose of promoting socially desirable change. Each will be considered in turn below.

Political economy

This perspective is most evident in the work of Cooper and Tinker and a number of their associates. Cooper and Sherer (1984) provide a clear statement of the characteristics of a political economy of accounting. They begin by arguing for a recognition of the existence of power and conflict in society. For this reason it is necessary to scrutinise the effects which accounting reports have on the distribution of income, power and wealth in society. Consequently, the contested nature of value forms a major theme in such enquiries. Attention is also to be paid to the specific historical and institutional environments in which accounting occurs, together with the roles played by multinational business enterprises, the state and any other interested parties. A concern with the potential of people is necessary at all times, as is the issue of their emancipation. This is to be complemented by an exploration of the manner in which the practice of accounting can contribute to this emancipatory objective.

Overall, a political economy perspective on accounting is based on the belief that accounting is not something neutral, nor that it simply responds to the needs of society. Instead, it is to be viewed as shaping society and in this respect it can be captured and used to reshape society in a more emancipatory way. Cooper and Sherer offer three imperatives for anyone who wishes to employ a political economy perspective: be *normative*, i.e. make your value judgements explicit; be *descriptive*, i.e. interpret the behaviour of accounting and accountants in the context of the society in which they are located; and be *critical*, i.e. consider which kinds of accounting are worthwhile outside of their existing environment. In their concluding comments, Cooper and Sherer argue that the market for accounting research is unlikely to promote a satisfactory level of research of a political economy nature. For this reason it is crucial that accounting researchers concerned with the interests of other groups in society act upon these concerns.

The political economy perspective is employed in Neimark and Tinker's (1986) paper on the origins and social consequences of General Motors' management control systems. The paper, which is in three parts, begins by considering the limitations of a number of influential management accounting theories which collectively inform the orthodox control model, the model usually found in textbooks. Among these are agency theory, transaction cost theory, contingency theory and the inducement contribution model of the firm. The first limitation identified by Neimark and Tinker is a lack of concern with the socio-historical context of management control systems, in particular the structural relations and institutional forms which characterise contemporary capitalism. This lack of concern is compounded by a failure to recognise how the organisation and its environment are interrelated, in particular how the environment permeates the internal structure and social relations of an organisation. In those cases where there is concern with the environment (for instance, in contingency theory), it is generally inadequately conceptualised. There is a failure to recognise the political, economic and cultural factors which determine the nature and distribution of individuals' skills, the social value of such skills and the character and distribution of life-chances. Further concern is expressed about the conception of organisational performance which characterises the orthodox control model; the desirability of the organisation's survival is taken for granted at the expense of a concern for the social costs involved, e.g. unemployment, skill obsolescence, community decay, environmental degradation, etc.

In the second part of the paper, in place of the orthodox model Neimark and Tinker propose an alternative 'dialectical approach to control'. This involves four elements: viewing control systems as evolving totalities; identifying the roles played by contradictions in the process of change, particularly those which result from the existence of unequal and antagonistic social relations, i.e. classes; a concern with the relationship between the organisation and its environment, viewing both as parts of a totality in which they are each the product and determinant of the other; and finally, the role which self-awareness plays in promoting social change. From this perspective the driving force for social change in capitalist societies is the development and displacement of the contradictions which are inherent in the structure of society itself and the institutions which constitute it. The third part of the paper considers the strategy of internationalisation of production and distribution adopted by General Motors in the sixty-year period to 1976. Neimark and Tinker use their alternative control model to highlight the interplay of resolutions and impediments to the problem of capital accumulation and the way in which this acts as a force for change in both the organisation and the broader society. In this way the social origins and consequences of control systems are revealed in a way which is inconceivable within the orthodox control model.

Neimark and Tinker's macro-level analysis exemplifies rather clearly what the term 'structuralism' means in the description of political economy as radical structuralism. Although the authors reject a positivistic methodology in the course of their paper, and indeed talk of the social construction of management control systems, there is no evidence to indicate that they are seeking to understand General Motors' management control systems from the point of view of either the workforce or the management. What is on offer in their paper is a re-interpretation of existing insights, using a heavily politically infused framework. This amounts to quite the opposite of the notion of grounded theory as embraced by interpretive sociology. Indeed, there is a sense of the analytical framework completely overshadowing the case material, a characteristic which political economy shares with a good deal of research carried out from a Marxist perspective. These observations have to be balanced against the generation of a form of knowledge which is claimed to be capable of hastening the emancipation of the mass of those who live their lives within the constraints imposed by capitalist society.

The labour process perspective

In contrast to political economy, the labour process perspective focuses on a specific element of the social order, the labour process. Marx viewed the labour process, and the distorted forms which it takes under capitalism, as a crucial focus for enquiry. This is understandable given that he viewed the labour process as the means of securing the material base of human existence, the site on which labour is engaged in the creation of value. Under capitalism, Marx argued, human creativity is systematically corrupted in the pursuit of ever-increasing exchange values. In the hundred years after he discussed the labour process in the first volume of *Capital*, comparatively little attention was paid to it by most of those who embraced his broader project. However, in the 1970s this situation changed dramatically. The publication of Braverman's *Labour and Monopoly Capital* (1974) rapidly gave rise to a deluge of labour process analyses which in turn provided the foundations for the labour process perspective. Among the central concerns of the labour process perspective are the divorce of conception from execution within the capitalist labour process, the attendant deskilling of the mass of the workforce and the reproduction of management control within the capitalist mode of production. Much, although not all, of the work which has been carried out from a labour process perspective has been concerned with the objective or structural, rather than subjective or humanistic, aspects of class relations and class struggle. For this reason it shares the radical structuralist designation with political economy.

Within management accounting research the case for adopting a labour process perspective was first presented in a 1987 paper by Hopper, Storey and Willmott. They argued that while an interpretive perspective offers a significant advance on the traditional approaches to management accounting research, it is not able adequately to theorise accounting as a social practice, i.e. as a set of practices which are both the medium and outcome of the political and economic context in which they are embedded. The labour process perspective promises to address the problems and silences which are associated with interpretive sociology. It views organisational goals as the goals of vested interests, namely capital. Management accounting techniques are, therefore, devices designed to secure the reproduction of those interests, and are unconcerned with questions regarding the distributional conflicts which accompany the capitalist labour process. Instead they exist to institutionalise the subordination of labour and to ensure that management's control strategies are realised. Organisations are viewed in the labour process perspective as structured by and reflective of the external pattern of class relations, rather than as some form of negotiated order. In this way the organisation is a site of class struggle, an unequal struggle in which the techniques of management accounting serve to increase the power and control of management who are the agents of capital.

The labour process perspective views the logic of efficiency as a mystificatory device intended to conceal the pursuit of control by management. The very language of management accounting serves to legitimate sectional interests and in this way is wholly ideological. As ideology, this language represents the imaginary relationship of individuals to the real conditions of their existence. As a historically aware perspective, the labour process perspective demonstrates that management accounting is not simply a supportive, politically neutral recording function. Management accounting is a means of disciplining and controlling the workforce which has successfully served the interests of capital and its managerial agents. Nevertheless, management accounting also illustrates the ambiguous role which managers and supervisors play in the capitalist labour process. Managers and supervisors are in fact only materially privileged labour, simultaneously the victims as well as agents of control, and in this way they are potentially an important force in the struggle for control by labour over capital. Finally, the labour process perspective views the deviant behaviour of workers as evidence of their capacity for resistance. Such resistance is viewed as a reaction to the inequities and contradictions which characterise the existing social organisation of work, and is something which is to be supported.

In the final sections of their paper, Hopper *et al.* argue that the most fruitful way forward is with a labour process perspective which is more conscious of the role played by human agents, i.e. both managers and workforce, than is evident in Braverman's own work (a gesture in the direction of interpretive sociology), and which is informed by concepts such as totality and contradiction (from political economy). They term this enhanced labour process perspective a 'dialectical framework', one in which there is analytical space for both an appreciation of the inter-subjective character of production relations, and a grasp of their structure as a medium and outcome of the interplay between political, ideological and economic forces. Perhaps the best example of such an analysis is to be found in the 1986 reinterpretation of the NCB case study material by Hopper, Cooper, Lowe, Capps and Mouritsen. However, a more conventional labour process paper is Hopper and Armstrong's (1991) critique of Johnson and Kaplan's history of cost and management accounting, *Relevance Lost*.

Hopper and Armstrong believe Johnson and Kaplan's account to be flawed on both theoretical and empirical grounds, while some of their prescriptions for the rejuvenation of management accounting are ill-founded. Their principal criticism is that Johnson and Kaplan focus on the issue of efficiency rather than exploring the relationship between management accounting and the pursuit of greater effort by workforces. On the theoretical front, Hopper and Armstrong argue that Johnson and Kaplan inherit a number of problems by basing their thesis on transaction cost theory. The difficulties involved in defining the nature of transaction costs are a fundamental weakness. Similarly, the assumption of perfectly competitive markets has little historical support. Transaction cost theory commonly confuses gains from efficiency with those from increased effort because the employment contract normally provides employers with the right to direct labour rather than access to a certain quantity of labour. This effectively legalises the practice of exploiting labour. Transaction cost theory assumes rationality in management decision-making, whereas a focus on the control of labour, with an emphasis on results, problematises such assumptions. Finally, Johnson and Kaplan's explanation for the stagnation of management accounting after 1925 involves a departure from transaction cost theory as they place the blame on the failings of financial accountants and academics. Hopper and Armstrong are unconvinced by this movement away from transaction cost theory. In their view, it raises the question of whether the cost accounting systems which have supposedly failed American business have persisted because they offer management a form of advantage (over labour) which transaction cost theory is unable to conceptualise.

Turning to Johnson and Kaplan's detailed historical analysis, Hopper and Armstrong offer an alternative based on the labour process. They argue that during the period 1820–70 it was the intensification of labour and the lengthening of the working day, rather than the emergence of cost accounting techniques, which were responsible for gains in productivity. Where skilled labour continued to be employed, the internal contracting system, initially developed to provide benefits for the employers, increasingly proved to work in the interests of employees. Employers resented the profits which accrued to their employees and for this reason decided to begin to pay more of their employees directly. This necessitated maintaining detailed accounting records, resulting in increased costs in the short term, not gains in efficiency. The same records, however, provided an increased visibility of the labour to be intensified (and if necessary disciplined), and where returns were available for creaming off – in other words, gains in control rather than efficiency.

The period 1870–1930 is viewed by Johnson and Kaplan as one in which efficiency gains accrued as a consequence of the development of vertically integrated companies. Hopper and Armstrong consider the role played by Scientific Management in the creation of deskilled and fragmented workforces, thus extending labour's subordination to capital. This was also the era of the development of standard costing which is viewed by Hopper and Armstrong as a means to achieve control over craft labour. Whereas previously historical costs were based on the practical experience and expertise of such workers, standard costs were the preserve of management who used them to extend their control and the process of labour intensification. In the 1920s budgetary control and return on investment techniques were developed to control increasingly complex organisations. Taken together, such techniques constituted a comprehensive 'drive system' of employment and anti-union campaigns designed to ensure management control.

Hopper and Armstrong argue that the lost relevance perceived by Johnson and Kaplan from 1925 onwards is better understood in terms of a refocusing of accounting emphasis. In the primary sector, i.e. that sector of the labour market characterised by employment stability, relatively high rewards, relatively skilled work and career structures, a new labour–capital accord meant that budgets were now used for planning rather than cost control purposes, while cost information was used for pricing purposes. By increasing sales, management recognised that they would be in a better position to reward and retain their existing workforces, and to increase market share and profitability. In this context, an appreciation of the full costs of products was desirable, hence the significance of absorption cost techniques (with their financial reporting underpinnings), which promised to provide accurate and reliable information for competitive pricing. In this way the capture of cost and management accounting by financial accounting can be viewed as a beneficial development rather than a detrimental episode.

Hopper and Armstrong conclude their analysis by offering an alternative view of the future for management accounting. Its restored relevance is due to the end of the labour–capital accord attendant upon the increased level of global competition. New means of controlling the labour process are now required, hence the appeal to activity accounting with its emphasis on cost management. Agency theory is also relevant to real-life issues, argue Hopper and Armstrong, particularly if linked to managerial reward initiatives. Conversely, there may be a further increase in the influence of financial reporting on management accounting as the international capital market becomes the major determinant of the allocation of capital, and corporations are able to transfer the costs of increased international competition from their own balance sheets to the national balance of payments.

Given the basic similarity of the labour process and political economy perspectives, it is important to establish what benefits the former offers over the latter. Being a more focused perspective, it is easier to relate labour process thinking to accounting practice. This is particularly so in the case of management accounting since both are closely associated with work and organisations. In this way the labour process perspective provides an appealing and insightful way of producing a radical critique of management accounting. This more concrete focus also means that the labour process perspective is readily employed in conjunction with a case study methodology. The labour process concept itself provides the 'theory' for verification in the course of enquiry. However, those who argue for the employment of the labour process perspective make no claims to objectivity. This is a politically informed and directed perspective which sets out to present a particular understanding of the world which it is seeking to change, and for this reason it is not to be embraced lightly.

Critical Theory

Critial Theory (CT) is the third Marxist perspective which has informed management accounting research. Unlike both political economy and the labour process perspective, CT is a radical humanistic perspective. It began as a project initiated in the 1920s by the members of the Institute for Social Research at Frankfurt – the Frankfurt School. Their objective was to explain the underlying nature of capitalist society in a way quite different to that of the prevailing Marxist orthodoxy, and thereby to contribute to the creation of a revolutionary proletarian consciousness. However, much of the output of the Frankfurt School was to take the form of philosophical treatises which were rather abstract in nature and extremely difficult to understand. One consequence of this situation is that CT has rarely had a significant political impact, a consideration which must always be borne in mind when debating the claim that CT, as the embodiment of the philosophy of praxis, is the only true critical perspective.

For the past thirty years the tradition of CT has been most closely identified with the work of Jurgen Habermas, now established as the most eminent living social theorist. During this time his writing has been subjected to extensive analysis and criticism. Few would deny that in the early period Habermas' work had an overtly radical political tone. Subsequently, his politics have become increasingly submerged in a meta-theory of social evolution which is couched in heavily systemic terms and draws on an impressive range of social scientific and humanities insights. However, Habermas' passionate commitment to the production of a thoroughgoing critique of those contemporary social theories associated with postmodernism which repudiate the ideal of progress, i.e. the transformation to a better social order, continues to identify him as a radical liberal thinker. In these endeavours he continues the traditions of CT, linking theory and practice in the pursuit of general human emancipation.

Laughlin (1987) argues that Habermas' CT perspective should be employed to study the interrelationship between the social roots of accounting and its more technical aspects. The argument is based on three key characteristics which CT exhibits. First, CT focuses on the dynamic link between theory and practice and is committed to change. Second, CT places emphasis upon developing a critique of the status quo, and the need for transformation to a better life with its ethical implications. For Laughlin these are important issues which have been overlooked in contemporary accounting research. Finally, CT views organisations in their historical and social context and seeks to identify hidden meanings, to go beyond the seen in order to reveal the forces which give rise to change. These characteristics were more prominent in Habermas' earlier work on the theory of knowledge-constitutive interests. In this work he rejected both sociological positivism and interpretive sociology and in their place he substituted a critical social scientific methodology committed to both understanding and emancipation. Laughlin also outlines a methodological approach specifically concerned with understanding and changing accounting systems. He presents a three-stage approach: first, researchers develop their (critical) theories about the systems they are studying; second, they discuss these theories with their subjects, the researched, the objective being to enlighten them and thereby establish a consensus; finally, based on this consensus, possible changes are suggested, evaluated and enacted in order to produce change, i.e. emancipation.

In the course of the paper Laughlin introduces Habermas' concerns with evolution and communicative action, together with a number of his key concepts. Among these concepts are *lifeworld*, a type of cultural space which gives meaning and nature to societal life; *systems*, which are the tangible, technical elements giving expression to the cultural lifeworld; and *steering mechanisms*, the means of guiding the behaviour of systems. In addition Habermas uses the concept *inner colonisation* to identify the debilitating process whereby the technical sphere (systems) overpowers the social sphere (lifeworld). Laughlin argues that although Habermas does not discuss the role of accounting phenomena, they are crucially associated with the inner colonisation process and would benefit from critical scientific enquiry. In Laughlin's view, if Habermas' theory is sound it is language itself which has created the division between the social and the technical aspects of accounting, and thus it is language which can produce change, i.e. what is needed is a change in the *discourse* of accounting. In his evaluation of Habermas' CT perspective, Laughlin recognises that it potentially presents a number of difficulties, including its applicability at a micro-level. However, in general he commends it as an attractive alternative to other emergent methodologies.

Broadbent, Laughlin and Read (1991) use a CT perspective to evaluate a number of recent financial and administrative changes in the National Health Service (NHS). The manner in which the authors develop an evaluatory model is conceded to involve some moulding of Habermas' work and a less prevalent concern with change. However, the paper is argued to be fully informed by Habermas' theory of social evolution. The link between the lifeworld, steering media (*sic*) and systems is reasserted, with the lifeworld now being discussed in its culture, society and personality dimensions. The orderly progression of evolution by way of improved communication processes is described together with its consequences for steering media and systems. Internal colonisation occurs when steering media 'get out of hand', disturbing the equilibrium and resulting in a loss of meaning in the lifeworld accompanied by disorder and the emergence of psychopathologies. One significant example of steering media getting out of hand is that of *juridification*. Where juridification occurs, law becomes increasingly constitutive, i.e. freedom-reducing, rather than regulative, i.e. freedom-guaranteeing, in nature. As a result the steering media can only be legitimated through procedure rather than substantive justification.

Broadbent *et al.* propose three refinements of Habermas' model which they claim result in a less abstract theory which is capable of operationalisation in an evaluatory form. First, it is necessary to conceive of both steering media and systems as having their own micro-lifeworlds, steering media and systems. In this way societal steering media can be seen to constitute a range of governmental, professional and financial institutions which guide the behaviour of societal systems through a range of steering mechanisms. This reflects the level of differentiation in contemporary society. Second, rather than talk of only regulative and constitutive steering mechanisms, it is necessary to recognise that it is only possible to evaluate specific mechanisms for specific periods of time and that it is not possible to guarantee the occurrence of intended behaviour within the organisation system. Finally, as it is not possible to discuss with every member of society the question of the positioning of the organisational system *vis-à-vis* the lifeworld and its operation, it is necessary to communicate with only active organisational participants.

By making these refinements to Habermas' model it is possible to consider the relationship between the steering mechanisms which the Department of Health as an institutional steering medium has employed in respect of the NHS as a societal organisation system in recent years, from the viewpoint of the NHS and with particular reference to accounting as a steering mechanism. The remainder of the paper is taken up with their empirical analysis, which first focuses on the colonising effects of broad accounting-related initiatives such as value for money, management information systems, management budgeting and resource management. Next Broadbent *et al.* turn to the processes of steering, which they find to be increasingly patterned, constitutive and which promote colonisation. Juridification is argued to have become more prominent, with greater reliance on rules and regulations to promote accountability within the service. The end result has been the creation of a managerialist philosophy within an NHS increasingly staffed by externally trained managers on short-term contracts who are often partly rewarded with performance-related pay. To Broadbent *et al.* this has constituted an enforcement of the Department of Health's (political) will on a reluctant NHS, something which they are unable to conclude is not a good thing from the point of view of society, at least not given the current state of development of their evaluatory model.

Such a conclusion is highly symptomatic of the value of a CT perspective. By comparison with either political economy or the labour process perspective, the results of the application of the critical theoretic are often coded, subsequently obscuring the political insights which the project was fashioned to provide. It is tempting to conclude that Habermasian CT is the intellectual equivalent of 'designer socialism', i.e. radical in name but eminently respectable in nature. However, there can be no doubting Habermas' own commitment to the struggle against the implications of postmodern philosophy and the need to keep a focus on the emancipation of the mass and the betterment of humanity's collective being. An equally fundamental problem with CT is the loss of its defining humanistic dimension. Habermas' writing has become increasingly characterised by its systems theoretic emphasis which provides little or no place for the individual. The systemic qualities and characteristics of Laughlin's variant of CT are self-evident, particularly in the refinement of Habermas' model. The logic of the argument for a movement from a lifeworld, steering media and systems emphasis to one of systems and steering mechanisms, i.e. organisations and institutions, leaves little or no room for a concern with either history or the active construction of organisational reality by those involved at the lower level. Attempting to make the methodology more applicable at the micro-level simply serves to draw attention to the lack of any humanistic dimension. Consequently, a perspective which promises to integrate radical political commitment and methodological self-awareness has developed in such a way as to offer little or no advance on the conventional wisdom of management accounting. At best it exists as a fine blend of idealism and systems thinking, based in an appealing, if impractical, research methodology. And exceedingly difficult to understand.

Postmodern Perspectives

Habermas' defence of modernism against the threat of postmodernism has already been mentioned. Now it is appropriate to consider those critical perspectives which are closely associated with postmodernism. Whereas modernism entails a belief that humanity has the capacity to progress, to better itself and to do so on the basis of rational thought, postmodernism rejects such notions. For postmodernists, there are no higher states, no better worlds, no such thing as progress or the control of nature. These are only traits of the modernist faith which need to be constantly re-evaluated through radical critique. Modernism as a purposeful project is rejected together with its meta-theories and grand narratives, particularly Marxism in all its forms and its progressive axioms. Postmodernists firmly reject the accusation that they are neo-conservative thinkers (Neimark, 1990), arguing that in place of the totalising politics characteristic of modernism it is more important to engage in politics at a lower or localised level.

As a philosophical movement postmodernism is not concerned with the individual as the human agent who stands at the centre of rational control and understanding. Postmodernism's anti-humanism does not give rise to an elaborate return to some form of structuralism, however, for in place of the active human agent, *process* emerges as the principal focus for enquiry. But not process in the usual sense of becoming, since this would re-admit the notions of improvement and progress. Postmodernism focuses on process in the sense of what is happening, the events which are occurring out there and which require to be investigated in relevant ways. Postmodernists argue that it is *discourse*, i.e. information, knowledge and communication, which is of particular significance, and for this reason it is necessary to develop a methodology that reflects this. The methodologies of positivism, hermeneutics and critical social science are rejected in favour of a new approach to the project of discourse analysis. Conventional modernist marks of rigour are also exchanged for a radical intellectualism involving iconoclasm, consciously obscure and convoluted narratives, suggestions and a good measure of purposeful internal inconsistency. There is no claim to completeness nor closure, only the wish to provoke debate. At the extreme it has been suggested that it is impossible to be 'wrong' from a postmodern perspective, because to be 'right' would ultimately support the modernist project. In this respect what has been offered in this and the previous paragraph is only one path through the postmodern project; much the same goes for the rest of this section.

Postmodern thought is most evident in contemporary French philosophy and derives from the writings of the nineteenth-century German philosopher Friedrich Nietzsche. To date Michel Foucault and Jacques Derrida have been the most influential postmodern writers in the context of accounting research, with additional insights provided by researchers informed by the work of Latour, Ricoeur and Baudrillard. One of the interesting features of postmodern accounting research is that it has appeared in the literature in a much more diffused way than was the case with interpretive sociology or the Marxist perspectives. As a result, the critical accounting project has rapidly expanded to embrace a fuller range of topics including the role of rhetoric in accounting, accounting conceived of as inscription, the standard-setting process and the gendered nature of accounting.

The Foucauldian perspective

To date Foucault has made as great a contribution to the development of critical management accounting as any thinker. Although his work was known and employed in the early 1980s, it came to prominence in parallel to both the labour process perspective and CT in the later 1980s. Foucault was not a social theorist who set out to construct an all-embracing scheme of knowledge. As a historian of the present he developed an alternative, distinctly postmodern approach to historical analysis. This entailed a pair of analytical techniques known as the *archaeological* and the *genealogical* methods. The former is prevalent in his earlier work on psychiatry, medicine and the human sciences and their relationship with society, health and knowledge respectively. Focusing on discourse, the aim of the archaeological method is to establish discursive series, i.e. systems of discourse, and to determine where these begin and end. An axiom of this method is that there are discrete systems of discourse which are independent of the conscious speaker. In an attempt to demonstrate how history is discontinuous, Foucault employs the term *episteme* to identify different periods of thought featuring different discursive practices. The active human agent is irrelevant since it is not a question of who speaks the discourse, but what discourse is spoken. Foucault also sought common features in a variety of discourses and the rules which regulate and govern discursive practices. In this way Foucault borrows from his own earlier, structuralist leanings, having at one time been a student of the leading French structural Marxist, Louis Althusser (Burrell, 1988).

In his later writing on power and sexuality it is the genealogical method which is to the fore. In common with his archaeological work, Foucault rejects any totalising vision of history, again focusing on discontinuity and the ruptures in social change. He remains concerned to decentre the subject and questions the ideas of human enlightenment and progress. Foucault's objective in utilising the genealogical method is to locate the present in the past, rather than seeking to reconstruct the past as in traditional history. There is no search for underlying laws and finalities, no concern with depth. Genealogical enquiry focuses on the superficial and the unexpected, reflecting the view that reality is as it appears to be. It is the genealogical method which also gives rise to Foucault's substantive concern with *power-knowledge*, his thesis on the interdependence of bodies of knowledge and relations of power. In *Discipline and Punish* he distinguishes two modes of domination in Western history: the traditional, which is characterised by extremes of violence, and the disciplinary, which is characterised by subtle forms of correction and training. The latter mode of domination replaced the former in the eighteenth century and as a result a wide range of organisations, including hospitals, factories, housing estates and schools, increasingly adopted the (disciplinary) character of the prison, which for Foucault was the site of the move from a traditional to a disciplinary mode of power. In Foucault's view Bentham's design for the Panopticon was *the* metaphor for the disciplinary mode. It provided a means of observation and close surveillance of inmates without them being able to observe their observers. The eighteenth century also saw the human body become an object or target for manipulation and training, thereby losing its mystery. This in turn gave way to the emergence of a crucial normalising function which was performed by professional groups such as ana-tomists, doctors, health workers, etc., henceforth to be recognised as the judges of normality. In the nineteenth century the disciplinary mode spread to sexuality with further extensions of the normalising function and the proliferation of power-knowledge.

For Foucault most existing explanations of power are fundamentally flawed. Power does not reside in things but in a network of relationships. As power-knowledge is an ever-present feature of such relationships, it is misleading to conceive of power as residing in the state and somehow filtering down through the various levels of society. Power is located in the micro-physics of social life, in the depths of society. As a result we are all imprisoned within power-knowledge, we experience it in some form at every moment of our lives and in this way it is not something of which we can rid ourselves with any ease. This formulation might seem to suggest that progress in the modernist sense is possible, if difficult. However, this is a position which Foucault clearly rejects, although not to the extent of eschewing all forms of localised resistance.

Miller and O'Leary's (1987) paper on the construction of the governable person remains a seminal example of management accounting research from a Foucauldian perspective. They focus on the development of two major management accounting techniques – budgeting and standard costing – during the period 1900–30. Using a combination of both the archaeological and genealogical methods and a focus on the power-knowledge effects of budgeting and standard costing, Miller and O'Leary successfully avoid producing a reconstructive history. The authors identify four themes which inform their analysis: first, how accounting in conjunction with other practices served to construct a particular field of *visibility*; second, how this alighted on the individual by means of norms and standards which served as a source of discipline in the work lives of individuals in the early years of this century; third, how this related to a range of developments occurring at a societal level, and which resulted in an increased administration of social life; finally, how budgeting, standard costing and these related developments were articulated in the discursive pro-grammes of the period. Underlying Miller and O'Leary's analysis is the belief that accounting is not a neutral practice, and that it must be recognised as part of a network of power-knowledge relations built into the fabric of organisational and social life. Accounting is a significant constitutive element in the normalising socio-political management process intended to render visible all forms of individual activity in the pursuit of organisational efficiency.

Miller and O'Leary argue that budgeting and standard costing emerged as part of a range of discursive practices concerned with both the physical and mental health of individuals, discursive practices which were evident at both the micro-and macro-levels. Together with Scientific Management and industrial psychology, budgeting and standard costing operated on a particular site, that of the organisation, serving as facilitative technologies designed to promote the visibility and accountability of the individual. At the macro-level, a discourse of national efficiency was also evident, one underpinned by various philosophical and sociological theories on the advances promised by a rationally administered society. Eugenics and the movement for mental hygiene exemplify these discourses. Taken together, this set of discursive practices aimed to construct the governable person at both the organisational and the societal levels. In their final substantive section Miller and O'Leary turn their attention to behavioural accounting. They believe that this development seeks to continue the process of achieving governability in the accounting/organisation space, albeit by promoting a form of freedom by countenancing departures from rationality. The active engineering of the organisationally useful person, therefore, continues into the present, with accounting redefining its terms and objectives as a social practice to enhance its contribution to effective socio-political management.

It is possible to raise questions about just how faithful Miller and O'Leary are to the Foucauldian legacy, given that what they have produced has the quality of closure about it. Nevertheless, there can be no doubt that they offer an insightful and

provocative alternative history of these two techniques, one which clearly demonstrates the non-neutrality of a pair of key techniques of management accounting.
Linking budgeting and standard costing with a range of equally politicised
techniques such as Scientific Management and industrial psychology, and demonstrating their common intentionality, is a valuable exercise. However, Miller and
O'Leary's paper raises two important questions regarding the critical accounting
project of which it forms part. First, how valuable would this sort of work be if it
existed in isolation, except for textbook accounts of technical issues? The added value
of Foucauldian work is not in doubt, although its absolute value may be. Second,
there is the question of political engagement. Foucault argued consistently for
localised engagement with networks of power-knowledge. Where in most accounting
research from a Foucauldian perspective is this imperative realised (cf. Moore,
1991)?

Derrida and deconstruction

Discourse is also the focus of attention for Derrida, a second postmodern philosopher
whose work has been influential in recent critical accounting research. However,
while Foucault was concerned with history, Derrida's work focuses upon language,
meaning, texts, writing and communication. In his view, language is simply a
structure of material marks or sounds which are in themselve 'undecidable' (Cooper,
1989). Meaning and understanding are not naturally intrinsic to the world which in
itself is meaningless and chaotic. Consequently, it is we – human agents – who
introduce both meaning and structure into the world with the result that all
discourses have to be constructed. In order to achieve the objective of revealing the
ambivalences of discourses, i.e. their essential uncertainty which gives rise to self-
contradictions and double-binds, it is necessary to *deconstruct* discourses. By adopting
this technique it is possible to reverse the process of construction and to demonstrate
the artificiality of the ordinary, assumed structures of the social world. Deconstruction is consistent with Derrida's broader project to demonstrate the primacy of
process over structure. He argues that our traditional ways of thinking are so
structure-biased that we are unable to recognise the need to think in terms of
process.
    Deconstruction is performed on texts which themselves come into existence as a
consequence of the operation of writing. Writing for Derrida is the process by which
human agents inscribe organisation and order on their environments. Historically,
writing has been viewed as subordinate to speech. The spoken word is viewed as
being prior to the written word which performs the function of acting as a vehicle for
speech. The real significance of writing has been suppressed as speech has become
privileged. Derrida's concept of writing as the physical act of inscription is not reliant
on the existence of metaphysical entities which exist independently of human
intervention. Writing is not concerned with the meaning and content of messages. It
is simply a structure and organisation of representations. For Derrida nothing exists

beyond these marks. This is not to claim that nothing exists before any particular act of inscription, since Derrida recognises that we are written as we write. By this he means that the human agent is involved in the world in a process of reflection with the result that consciousness occurs on the rebound. This process of reflection is indirect in nature, being a relationship with what was previously inscribed. Later ideas always take precedence over what was initially there and in this way writing is no longer to be viewed as supplementing oral communication but necessarily pre-dates it. Writing is in fact the basis upon which speech is possible rather than being the vehicle for it.

Although writing (as inscription) is propelled to the fore in Derrida's analysis, the writer is not to be allowed any greater credibility in making sense of any text. In deconstructing a text, the reader's interpretation of the words on offer is as valid as that of its writer. In their introduction to deconstruction in accounting research, Arrington and Francis (1989) describe it as a challenge to an author's attempt to privilege a particular position as a superior way of arriving at closure around knowledge. Deconstruction holds nothing sacred, questions every assumption and interrogates all privilege in knowledge production. It is not an act of relativism, rather an attempt to bore into texts in order to demonstrate how the legitimacy of any claim to an external metaphysical grounding beyond the text is only linguistic and rhetorical, i.e. sophistry on the part of the author. Deconstruction subverts the attempt to achieve closure around knowledge production and to silence other voices by claiming to possess a superior awareness of truth. Deconstruction operates on the pretexts of texts in order to demonstrate their author's commitments to particular social and moral orders. In this way it is a political act, one designed to critique and dismantle intellectual elitism.

The text which Arrington and Francis select for deconstruction is Michael Jensen's paper 'Organisation theory and methodology'. This paper argues for privileging the positive accounting theory project, on the grounds that it offers a superior means of achieving closure around accounting knowledge. Arrington and Francis' deconstruction is performed in a series of nine rhetorical moves which involves taking what the author's text says quite literally, and revealing how the text dismantles itself as a result of violating its own rule system. Move 1 demonstrates how Jensen's assertion that before the emergence of positive theory any decisions can only be unpurposive contradicts the possibility of making a purposive decision to develop positive theory. Move 2 poses the question: how is it possible to develop a positive theory in a non-normative way? The next pair of moves illustrates how in supplementing his thesis by making reference to the survival of the fittest and the minimisation of agency costs, Jensen reveals a series of undesirable outcomes of positive theorising. Arrington and Francis' fifth move focuses on Jensen's difficulties with the value of logical positivism, a development which questioned whether observation was a privileged way of knowing, over the naïve positivism which he clearly wishes to embrace. Move 6 demonstrates how Jensen's text fails to mark a significant departure from the (normative) ASOBAT (A Statement of Basic Accounting Theory). Move 7 questions the advance offered by Jensen's focus on contracts rather than the notion of the behaviour of organisations. The final pair of moves questions the lack of empirical data in Jensen's paper and the significance which he accords to non-quantitative evidence in the context of positive accounting research.

In seeking to assess the contribution which deconstruction can make to extending the critical accounting project, it is instructive to turn to the closing paragraphs of Arrington and Francis' paper. Here we learn that deconstruction does not involve replacing one privileged theory with another. Deconstruction operates on all texts, and in particular on their pretexts, in order to dismantle their pretensions. Deconstruction involves embracing a humility in scholarship which precludes even offering people guidance on what is in their best interests. Instead, Arrington and Francis conclude that 'We must become the critical, self-reflective peddlars of questions rather than answers. Deconstruction is much more interested in the questions, in opening up rather than closing off discourse.'(p. 25)

Looking to the Future: greater insight from more perspectives

The six perspectives discussed in the preceding pages by no means exhaust the stock of critical perspectives available to researchers committed to advancing the critical management accounting project. Postmodernism also offers an alternative to the interpretive sociology perspective in the form of the sociology of science writings of Latour. Robson (1991, 1992, 1994) has explored Latour's perspective in the context of financial reporting while Preston, Cooper and Coombs (1992) have borrowed from Latour's work to understand the *fabrication* of budgets in the NHS. Latour's emphasis on process, discourse and rhetoric is evident in his *sociology of translation* which focuses on the discursive process by means of which equivalences are created between otherwise different entities. Echoing the Foucauldian notion of power-knowledge, Latour links translation with the objective of achieving *action at a distance*, a significant motive for parties, particularly governments, involved in the installation of new forms of control and calculation, e.g. management budgeting initiatives in the NHS.

The poststructural hermeneutics of Ricoeur are commended to accounting researchers by Arrington and Francis (1993). The distinction between speech and text is also central to Ricoeur's perspective. Rejecting the link between language and meaning, Ricoeur argues for a hermeneutics of discourse and discursive events. He identifies a number of elements which characterise such events and, in so doing, acknowledges that discourse exhibits two polar extremes in the form of speech and writing. These two extremes give rise to two hermeneutic horizons, a position which Arrington and Francis believe has significant consequences for what we recognise as accounting. After Ricoeur, Arrington and Francis argue that there is a necessity to re-imagine accounting as a cultural practice of giving economic accounts which have economic, moral and hermeneutical implications both for those who give and for those who receive them.

To date, Baudrillard's sociology of the postmodern, and its contribution to accounting research, remains relatively unexploited. Puxty (1993) is clearly captivated by the promise of Baudrillard judging by the way he announces that Baudrillard disrupts and challenges (practically) everything while causing us to wonder if only rhetoric (and not actuality) exists. In a recent lecture on Hyperreal America, Baudrillard (1993) compares the experimental microcosm Biosphere 2 with the leisure concept known to us as Disneyland. The former, he argues, is a fake experiment, the latter a fake imaginary. There is no longer a 'real' America for there is no difference between the imaginary or experimental model and the real or actual workings of American society.

The future will, hopefully, be marked by the emergence of even more perspectives for advancing the critical management accounting project. Although such a prospect may seem confusing, even disconcerting, to readers comfortable with the (uncritical) singular perspective of orthodox management accounting, this multi-perspective quality should be recognised as a measure of the comparative maturity of CMA. It is a source of strength and not a sign of weakness. It should not be viewed as indicative of CMA being in a pre-paradigmatic state from which a pre-eminent paradigm will eventually emerge. This would constitute a regressive step. For this reason the structuration theory perspective developed by Giddens, and deployed by Macintosh and Scapens (1990, 1991), provokes an ambivalent response from this author. Equally problematic is any tendency towards eclecticism, at least in its more unsophisticated forms. This is more likely to be a problem for those who would base themselves in some postmodern position and for whom a rejection of eclecticism is tantamount to closure and privilege. As far as possible we must encourage the proliferation of a multi-perspective approach to critical management accounting and, in so doing, generate a set of genuinely social scientific discourses which explore the space in which accounting to management is enacted.

References

Arrington, C.E. and J.R. Francis (1989) 'Letting the chat out of the bag: deconstruction, privilege and accounting research', *Accounting, Organizations and Society*, vol. 14/1, pp. 1–28.

Arrington, C.E. and J.R. Francis (1993) 'Giving economic accounts: accounting as cultural practice', *Accounting, Organizations and Society*, vol. 18/2/3, pp. 107–24.

Baudrillard, J. (1993) 'Hyperreal America', *Economy and Society*, vol. 22/2, pp. 243–52.

Berry, A.J., T. Capps, D. Cooper, P. Ferguson, T. Hopper and E.A. Lowe (1985) 'Management control in an area of the NCB: rationales of accounting practice in a public enterprise', *Accounting, Organizations and Society*, vol. 10/1, pp. 3–28.

Braverman, H. (1974) *Labour and Monopoly Capital: the Degradation of Work in the Twentieth Century*, New York: Monthly Review Press.

Broadbent, J., R. Laughlin and S. Read (1991) 'Recent financial and administrative changes in the NHS: a critical theory analysis', *Critical Perspectives on Accounting*, vol. 2/1, pp. 1–29.

Burrell, G. (1988) 'Modernism, postmodernism and organisational analysis 2: the contribution of Michel Foucault', *Organisation Studies*, vol. 9/2, pp. 221–35.

Burrell, G. and G. Morgan (1979) *Sociological Paradigms and Organisational Analysis*, London: HEB.

Colville, I. (1981) 'Reconstructing "behavioural accounting" ', *Accounting, Organizations and Society*, vol. 6/2, pp. 119–32.

Cooper, D. and M. Sherer (1984) 'The value of corporate accounting reports: arguments for a political economy of accounting', *Accounting, Organizations and Society*, vol. 9/3, pp. 207–232.

Cooper, R. (1989) 'Modernism, postmodernism and organisational analysis 3: the contribution of Jacques Derrida', *Organisation Studies*, vol. 10/4, pp. 479–502.

Cooper, R. and G. Burrell (1988) 'Modernism, postmodernism and organisational analysis: an introduction', *Organisation Studies*, vol. 9/1, pp. 91–112.

Foucault, M. (1977) *Discipline and Punish: the Birth of the Prison*, London: Allen Lane.

Hopper, T. and P. Armstrong (1991) 'Cost accounting, controlling labour and the rise of conglomerates', *Accounting, Organizations and Society*, vol. 16/5/6, pp. 405–38.

Hopper, T., J. Storey and H.C. Willmott (1987) 'Accounting for accounting: towards the development of a dialectical view', *Accounting, Organizations and Society*, vol. 12/5, pp. 437–56.

Hopper, T., D. Cooper, T. Lowe, T. Capps and J. Mouritsen (1986) 'Management control and worker resistance in the National Coal Board: financial controls in the labour process', in Knights, D. and H.C. Willmott (eds), *Managing the Labour Process*, London: Gower pp. 109–141.

Jensen, M.C. (1983) 'Organisation theory and methodology', *The Accounting Review*, vol. 58/2, pp. 319–39.

Laughlin, R. (1987) 'Accounting systems in organisational contexts: a case for critical theory', *Accounting, Organizations and Society*, vol. 12/5, pp. 479–502.

Macintosh, N.B. and R.W. Scapens (1990) 'Structuration theory in management accounting', *Accounting, Organizations and Society*, Vol 15/5, pp. 456–77.

Macintosh, N.B. and R.W. Scapens (1991) 'Management accounting and control systems: a structuration theory analysis', *Journal of Management Accounting Research*, vol. 3, pp. 131–58.

Miller, P. and T. O'Leary (1987) 'Accounting and the construction of the governable person', *Accounting, Organizations and Society*, vol. 12/3, pp. 235–261.

Moore, D.C. (1991) 'Accounting on trial: the critical legal studies movement and its lessons for radical accounting', *Accounting, Organizations and Society*, vol. 16/8, pp. 763–91.

Neimark, M. (1990) 'The king is dead: long live the king!', *Critical Perspectives on Accounting*, vol. 1/1, pp. 103–14.

Neimark, M.D. and A.M. Tinker (1986) 'The social construction of management control systems', *Accounting, Organizations and Society*, vol. 11/4, pp. 369–96.

Preston, A.M., D.J. Cooper and R.W. Coombs (1992) 'Fabricating budgets: a study of the production of management budgeting in the National Health Service', *Accounting, Organizations and Society*, vol. 17/6, pp. 561–93.

Puxty, A.G. (1993) *The Social and Organisational Context of Management Accounting*, London: Academic Press.

Robson, K. (1991) 'On the arenas of accounting change: the process of translation', *Accounting, Organizations and Society*, vol. 16/5/6, pp. 547–70.

Robson, K. (1992) 'Accounting numbers as "inscription": action at a distance and the development of accounting', *Accounting, Organizations and Society*, vol. 17/7, pp. 685–708.

Robson, K. (1994) 'Inflation accounting and action at a distance: the Sandilands episode', *Accounting, Organizations and Society*, vol. 19/1, pp. 45–82.

Roslender, R. (1992) *Sociological Perspectives on Modern Accountancy*, London: Routledge.

CHAPTER FIVE

Costing and the New Operations Management

Jim Mackey and Mike Thomas

This chapter traces how the evolution of manufacturing processes has impacted upon cost accounting systems (CAS). Four significant manufacturing environments are considered on this evolutionary continuum:

traditional;
materials requirements planning (MRP);
just-in-time (JIT);
automated.

Manufacturing technologies have evolved from artisan through traditional decoupled manufacturing to JIT and automated processes as improvements in machinery, materials and human abilities have progressed. The application and role of cost systems have evolved accordingly. Different cost systems are appropriate as manufacturing processes evolve. Consequently, management accountants must be familiar with many alternative techniques to determine which are appropriate for each situation. This chapter outlines the conditions that change with varying operating environments, and cost system responses to these changes.

Traditional Manufacturing Processes

Traditional manufacturing processes evolved from the break-up of craft production into a series of small, individual tasks. The objective was to increase productivity by reducing complex tasks to simpler ones that could be easily learned, analysed and improved. The economic trade-off was the additional investment in co-ordination costs. Consider, for example, the making of a musket. The craft approach employs one highly skilled artisan making or supervising several apprentices who produce a complete weapon from stock to barrel. The factory approach mechanised and divided this process into a series of relatively simple activities, each easily taught to less skilled labourers and controlled by a few knowledgeable managers or foremen. Similar machines were grouped together according to their functions (e.g. gunstock-making, barrel-making and assembly). These groups evolved into individual departments and usually formed the basis of cost centres. It is this technology that features so strongly in the education of management accountants.

The flow of materials through the plant affects the production technology. Two production extremes exist, a job shop and a flow shop. Most traditional manufacturing falls somewhere between these extremes. Understanding these two extremes is important because recent technological innovations have resulted in complex, costly job shops becoming more like flow processes.

Figure 5.1 compares material flows for these two extremes. Arrows represent flows of work-in-process (WIP), while each box is a cost centre. For example, in a job shop making muskets, production starts in the wood shop for stock-making (A), then to B for sanding, C to add the stock and fixtures, then back to B to sand and finish, and finally to D for testing.

Consider the manufacture of store fixtures. The job shop may make custom store fixtures, while the flow shop makes one standard fixture. Each square represents a machine group. The arrows illustrate the flow of WIP. In the job shop, each custom fixture may follow a unique path, spending different times in each centre. Job shops become flow shops when only standardised fixtures following the same flow path are manufactured. To get a better idea of how this flow approach allows us to classify products, examine Figure 5.2.

Figure 5.2 represents a product-process matrix. The vertical axis identifies the extremes of product flow, while the horizontal axis classifies products from unique to standardised. In general, job shops present a more difficult management challenge.

Table 5.1 illustrates some of the environmental differences between job and flow manufacturing in terms of products, markets and process characteristics. Characteristics commonly observed in JITs are also noted. The transition to JIT allows

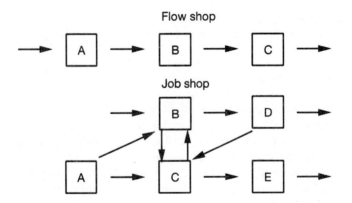

Figure 5.1   Comparison of WIP in job and flow shops.

production of custom products in a flow environment. Thus, JITs have been most economically applied in mid-range product variety industries (Figure 5.2). JIT illustrates how new management changes are moving from job to less costly flow shop environments. As environments change, the cost system must be adapted to maintain its accuracy and relevance. Without appropriate changes to the cost system, it will generate information ranging from misleading to useless and act as an impediment to change.

Traditional operations management

Figure 5.3 illustrates traditional manufacturing through the four key management areas: (a) raw materials; (b) cost/responsibility centres; (c) the overall production system; and (d) finished goods inventories and marketing.

Materials management

Traditional manufacturing uses inventories to decouple complex processes into manageable activities. Quality, delivery and cost create three uncertainties in

Table 5.1 Environments.

Comparison of product and market environments	
Custom products	Commodity products
Discrete units	Non-discrete units
High unit value	Low unit value
Many products	Few products
Consumer demand	Derived demand
Low sales volume	High sales volume
Marketing emphasis on product features	Marketing emphasis on product availability and price
Many product design changes	Few product design changes
Comparison of manufacturing environments	
Job shop	Flow shop
Process layout	Product layout
Low volume	High volume
Variable routeings	Fixed routeings
Flexible equipment	Specialised equipment
Labour intensive	Capital intensive
Skilled craftspersons who build the product	Highly specialised, trained operators who monitor and control process equipment
Jobs not overlapped between work centres	Job overlapping
Capacity is difficult to define	Capacity is well defined
Shorter lead time to increase capacity	Longer lead time to increase capacity

Source: adapted from Taylor *et al*., (1981).

materials management. Traditional manufacturing operates under considerable uncertainty with respect to delivery dates and quality. Inventories smooth production by creating a cushion, or buffer, so that the manufacturing process operates relatively

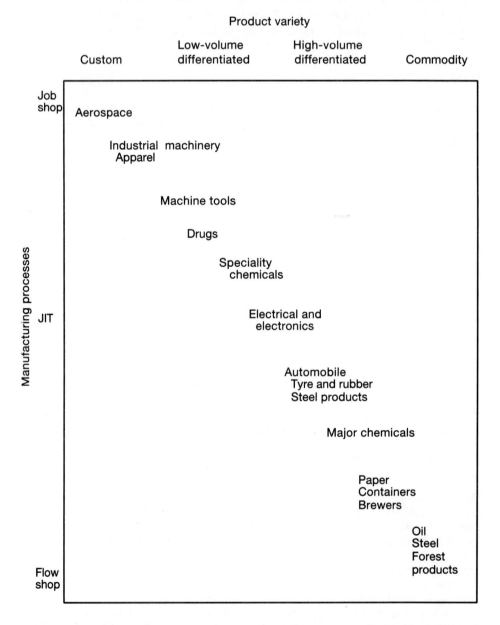

Figure 5.2 Traditional product-process continuum (adapted from Taylor *et al*,, 1981).

independent from these uncertainties. Large inventories provide insurance against missed deliveries and poor-quality materials. Consequently, traditional accounting measures have ignored delivery and quality problems, and emphasised the remaining controllable issue of purchasing budgets and price variances.

Cost centres management

Within cost centres, additional uncertainties regarding labour, machinery and scheduling must be considered. Through large WIP buffers, traditional manufacturing copes with environmental uncertainties associated with labour (e.g. low skills, low motivation and high absenteeism) and machinery (unreliability and inconsistent quality). Jobs queued up waiting to be worked on (i.e. WIP buffers) allow department managers to pick and choose among jobs to match men to machines, batch

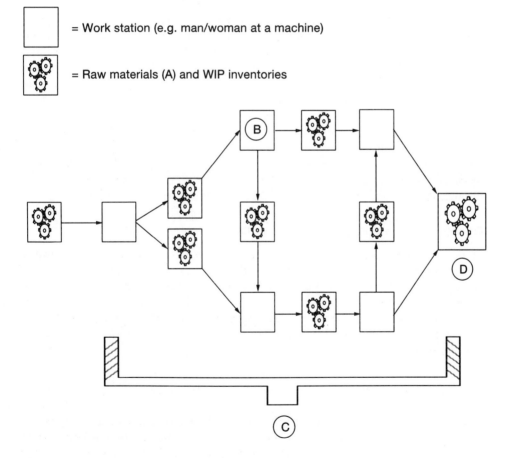

☐ = Work station (e.g. man/woman at a machine)

= Raw materials (A) and WIP inventories

Figure 5.3 Management of the traditional manufacturing process.

compatible job set-ups and defer less suitable jobs. Because set-ups can be costly and require skilled labour, batching similar jobs provides opportunities for cost savings. These potential savings motivate management to keep high levels of WIP. This strategy, however, creates problems with scheduling production because jobs tend to get lost or delayed, often forcing costly expediting.

Cost systems frequently evaluate shop-floor managers in terms of efficiency, based upon the relationship between inputs and outputs. Long production runs offset expensive set-ups and contribute to higher input/output efficiencies. Consequently, the misuse of efficiency variances can create situations where meeting production schedules is of secondary importance. Therefore, managers often ignore the efficient use of WIP because this is rarely evaluated at the shop-floor level. In fact, larger WIP levels make the management of cost centres easier.

Overall factory management

Scheduling is used to co-ordinate purchasing, manufacturing and sales. The nature of the production flow, however, leads to significantly different scheduling uncertainties. For example, flow shops possess sequentially linked machine centres and less varied production (see Figure 5.1), and are easier to schedule than job shops. For most flow shops, an easily identifiable fully loaded (bottleneck) department determines short-term scheduling capacity. Job shops, on the other hand, present a more difficult problem as they produce a variety of products. In these situations, bottlenecks float (i.e. move among departments) as the demand for products changes. The traditional solution – a push system – 'pushes' more jobs (WIP) on to the shop-floor to ensure that all work centres are busy. This strategy leads to many other problems, including long due dates and job expediting. As expedited jobs are pushed through the shop, economies that could be realised by batching are lost.

Finished goods inventory and marketing management

Marketing management deals with uncertain demand, quality and warranty problems, and long manufacturing lead times. These uncertainties can be lessened by large finished goods stocks, thereby allowing marketing to act independently of manufacturing. Push systems, coupled with this independence, support inflexible production schedules. Product mix thus cannot be changed in a timely manner as market demand fluctuates. This, in turn, results in obsolete inventories and lost profit opportunities.

Traditional cost system influences on operations management

Traditional cost systems were designed primarily for financial accounting needs. Consequently, the aggregate valuation of inventories for income statement reporting (cost of goods sold) and current asset reporting (balance sheet) was more important than providing relevant information needed to manage production uncertainties.

If financial accounting profits serve as a basis for factory manager evaluation, managers may feel compelled to increase production in spite of weak sales demand. The more units produced, the lower the fixed overhead allocated to each unit, and hence the lower the production cost per unit. Suppose the set-up cost is £100. A job lot of 100 units would bear a charge of £1 per unit while a job lot of 200 units would cut this cost per unit in half. Absorption costing motivates factory managers to fully utilise fixed capacity through long production runs. Both conditions lead to high inventory levels.

Since accountants usually apply all overhead costs using only one allocation base (e.g. direct labour hours) in traditional shops, many step costs that vary with production runs are classified as fixed. This creates a problem in the management of finished goods and marketing (i.e. pricing and product profitability) for short-run decisions. Set-up costs provide a good example since they vary with the number and similarity of jobs, but not with the number of units in a job. For accounting purposes, set-up costs can be treated as fixed or variable. Both treatments can be misleading for pricing, but they do not normally lead to material errors in the financial statements. To provide accurate pricing data, more than one cost basis must be employed as in activity-based costing (see Chapter 6). Further, the criteria for costing precision should be related to pricing requirements.

Behavioural problems can also arise with traditional cost systems when misused in performance evaluation. Since traditional cost systems are dominated by the materiality standards of financial statements, overhead costs remain less precise than direct costs. Traditional accounting defines fixed and variable costs by their response to changes in a specific activity base such as units of output for homogeneous products, or direct labour for heterogeneous products. Virtually any costs not varying directly with production volume will normally be classified as fixed overhead. Few companies demand detailed standards for overhead costs. While texts encourage the separation of variable and fixed overhead, few traditional manufacturers actually develop more than one total overhead application rate. This encourages managers to shift costs into overhead categories since these are less easily observable and hence less important in their performance evaluations. Activity-based management systems have evolved to make overhead costs more visible.

The separation of production activities can create hostility and internal competition as each manager is responsible for a theoretically distinct set of controllable costs considered by upper management to be independent from other work centres. New production economies, generated more by teamwork than individual effort – for example by a Total Quality Management (TQM) team – violate these conditions of unambiguously defined activities, to create a more holistic view of productivity and manufacturing success.

When shop-floor managers understand the process better than upper management, budget-based evaluation motivates lower-level managers to build in a budgetary cushion (slack). Since negotiated budgets serve as the basis for evaluation, shop-floor management has an interest in making the budgets easily attainable.

Another motivational problem relates to innovation and improvement. The original conditions under which standard costing evolved assumed that the industrial engineer (or management) understood the 'one best way' to do the job. This thought process can be regarded as 'innovation from above'. Implicit historical assumptions about quality (erratic), reliability (uncertain) and industrial relations (hostile) also existed. Consequently, while direct labour and shop-floor management may be able to innovate for improved efficiency (innovation from below), they may be discouraged by the budgetary consequences of their innovations, namely the subsequent tightening of cost standards.

Materials Requirements Planning (MRP)

MRP, first introduced by IBM in 1970, essentially substitutes better information systems for excessive inventories. MRP schedules production through the factory so that managers no longer require excessive WIP to compensate for scheduling problems between cost centres. MRP does not deviate from most of the previous underlying assumptions about co-ordinating machine centres. Instead, MRP co-ordinates the flow of materials by releasing work orders for parts to the factory based upon a master production schedule, and the current number and location of parts in the factory. Figure 5.4 presents an overview of the information base used by MRP.

Materials, WIP and scheduling management

Assume product C sales will average 100 units per week and optimal batch production size is 500 units. The Bill of Materials for product C is programmed into the computer. The hierarchy in Figure 5.4 represents the information included in a typical Bill of Materials.

The MRP program records the number of inventory components in each sub-assembly along with time standards for moving, waiting, setting-up and running each component. This information allows production to be time-phased, or co-ordinated, so that at the final assembly of C, sufficient CA, CB and CC components are available. In this example, each level of production is assumed to take the same amount of time (one week) and no surplus components are in WIP. While these assumptions are highly unlikely in practice, MRP can easily handle the variety that our illustration cannot.

Additionally, the need to hit the due dates for component arrivals in specified departments encourages shop-floor discipline. Because missed due dates result in idled departments, however, minimum WIP levels may still be maintained.

Contrast this with traditional manufacturing utilising various types of economic order quantity models to signal production or purchase of new components when a re-order point is reached. Statistical rules depending upon long-term forecasted demand rates establish the re-order point. Thus, the re-order of particular parts was separated from short-term changes in demand for finished or higher-level components. A key innovation of MRP as an inventory management system lies in the concept of dependent demand. Finished products are assembled from families of components which may subdivide into families of sub-components, and thus work down the hierarchy in Figure 5.4. Cost centres using MRP for scheduling are more interdependent than those under the traditional manufacturing because of the dependent demand linkages built into the program. MRP only orders as needed by the production schedule.

Initially, the MRP system could generate only the first step in the planning process (parts ordering/manufacturing). The next problem is ensuring sufficient capacity in each cost centre. MRP II incorporates the MRP schedule into a capacity planning system, and outputs integrated production, purchasing and machine usage schedules. Later versions of MRP (MRP III) further expand this system by integrating MRP with cost accounting, accounts payable, sales ordering and other related activities. Most MRP systems are far from perfect, but significant improvements in shop-floor discipline reduce uncertainty. It should be clear, however, that MRP does not change the production philosophy. It merely reduces WIP through improved information flows. MRP thus substitutes information for high WIP levels.

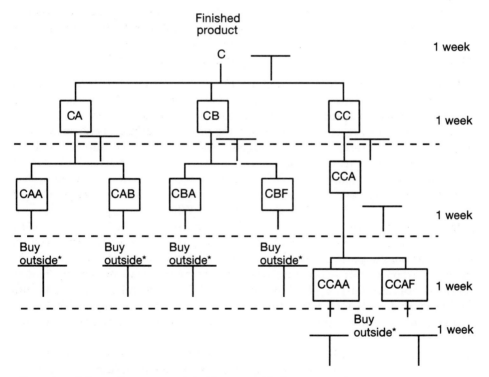

*Inventory information accumulated in general ledger accounts

Figure 5.4 The information base of MRP.

MRP's impact on cost accounting systems

The impact of MRP systems upon cost accounting, however, remains quite subtle and perhaps not fully understood. All manufacturers have scheduling systems of varying degrees of sophistication, whether labelled MRP or not. Irrespective of these differences, MRPs have some common features:

1. Significant decreases in inventories render previously separate functions more interdependent. With the elimination of WIP buffers, cost variances appearing in a subsequent cost centre may be caused in previous centres and transported through the system. While this phenomenon also exists in traditional manufacturing, the independence of cost centres often results in a failure to recognise it.

2. MRP creates additional non-accounting performance criteria related to meeting due dates. Advanced systems can report these criteria through graphical analyses.

3. As due dates take priority over budgets, shop-floor managers lose some discretion. This redistribution of authority does not indicate a decline in the importance of cost management, but rather that due dates are at least equally as important.

4. Better data discipline also encourages better shop-floor discipline. Management now recognises WIP levels and product flows from real-time MRP output. In turn, cost system information must also be available in real time to provide input into the MRP program, and to supplement it in shop-floor process control.

MRP systems impact upon budgeting, control and short-run decisions. Depending upon the type of MRP used (I, II or III), accounting budgets may be more or less closely integrated with the MRP system. Planning tends to be more accurate and detailed. Consequently, building slack into the process is difficult because activities are more easily observed. Tighter budgets will more likely be implemented. As control shifts from a cost orientation to include due dates, machine and labour scheduling, and minimising inventory, the management process becomes less decentralised. Shop-floor managers exercise much less discretion over the selection of jobs because of scheduling priorities and reduced WIP levels.

In addition, managers are now responsible for timely, accurate data input. Unless incentives are changed to enforce schedules while providing accurate data to control costs, behavioural problems can occur. MRP systems fundamentally change the nature of responsibility accounting. Traditionally, after-the-fact accounting reports initiate control activities. Under MRP, this *output-driven* control is augmented with *data input* as a basis for control. Since the shop-floor is now responsible for the accuracy of the data input into the system, shop-floor discipline is further enhanced.

A major reason for MRP failures is data inaccuracy from the lack of shop-floor discipline. For example, in job shops (Figure 5.2) with unreliable data on set-ups and run times for unique products, MRP schedules will be misleading. As product variety decreases, and set-up and run times become more accurate, MRP is more useful. At the other end of the extreme, flow shops with commodity products and reliable schedules do not need the power of an MRP system. As was previously observed with JIT production systems, MRP scheduling software is more useful in mid-range product variety environments.

The role of accounting in decision-making has also changed. Make versus buy (outsourcing), capacity changes, and even overtime decisions, carry implications not limited to any one department. Because MRP requires more precise standards to function, accounting standards for pricing and inventory valuation should also be upgraded.

Just-in-time Manufacturing (JIT)

MRP systems introduce new information and more efficient management co-ordination, but they do not represent a radical change in manufacturing philosophy. JIT represents a different philosophy, and is changing the way we regard the role of inventory. In traditional manufacturing, WIP buffers allow independent respons-ibility centre management. Traditional scientific management solutions typically consider some optimal WIP levels, and trade-offs between spoilage and output, but system-wide effects are often ignored.

On the other hand, Japanese economies (where JIT was invented) did not develop along the same lines as traditional Western manufacturing economies. Significantly different environmental factors forced a radically new approach. Japan lacked raw materials, space and energy, and needed foreign credits to pay for scarce raw materials. However, Japan possessed a plentiful supply of motivated, skilled and relatively low-cost labour. The Eastern philosophy of the group over the individual, and teamwork over individual success, sharply contrasted with the assumptions about labour that drove traditional Western manufacturing.

Additionally, since transportation costs to export markets were high, high value-to-weight products were most suitable for foreign export. The distances between Japan and foreign markets also made warranty cost management critical. High quality became a marketing strategy and a method to reduce warranty costs. With little knowledge of foreign needs or markets, they developed short turn-round manu-facturing focused directly on consumer preferences. A customer-focused planning and operating system resulted, identifying activities by whether they added value to the customer.

These viciously competitive conditions motivated JIT manufacturing. JIT is an element of TQM and consists of a set of ideas and approaches that systematically introduce constant improvement. The JIT philosophy strives to remove non-value-adding co-ordinating activities (e.g. the substitution of WIP and expensive control systems with general manufacturing flexibility and quality improvements). These ideas simultaneously decrease the response time required to adapt to market changes and reduce costs.

Some authors consider JIT as a prerequisite for, or subset of, activity-based management and TQM because of the quality focus it engenders. Quality became important to the Japanese in two contexts:

1. Quality expectations of incoming materials require specifications and delivery dates to be met exactly. Improved quality removed the need for the excess raw materials inventories to buffer against scrap and delivery uncertainties.

2. Quality expectations in manufacturing require process controls to minimise inspections, rework, spoilage and warranty costs.

Japan's motivated workforce, trained to be flexible in skills, working hours and salaries, can handle both production and cost flexibility. Bonuses based upon company profits can account for up to 50 per cent of a worker's annual income. Reduced company profits result in a reduced bonus. Besides the obvious motivational effects, this system directly improves the company's competitiveness. Labour costs change directly with profits, thus allowing price competition without renegotiating labour contracts.

Factory management under JIT

The major changes initiated by JIT are the management of factory environments and the restructuring of production departments into work cells. This philosophy searches for practical ways to eliminate the need for inventories. It regards inventories as a means of hiding problems rather than resolving them. The focus rests not on the decomposition of tasks, but rather upon the interaction of activities within the production process as a whole. Traditional manufacturing organises similar machines together to simplify tasks within cost centres. Refer back to Figure 5.4. WIP may return to the same centre again and again as they are combined into larger components. For example, parts CAA, CAB and CA may be returned to grinding after each is combined.

The JIT approach strives to create different work cells which may include a variety of different machines. A JIT cell produces a particular product or a family of components, rather than performing a set of specific functions (e.g. grinding, polishing or assembly). For example, JIT cells may produce component CA including the production and assembly of parts CAA and CAB. Ideally, any WIP will be in the process of conversion and never sits idle. A JIT cell, then, may be comprised of a mix of machinery, and requires cell workers to be flexible (performing a variety of tasks). This philosophy is the reverse of traditional manufacturing which reduces the complexity of tasks within the work centre, but produces a large variety of sub-components. JIT increases the variety and complexity of tasks within the work cell, and reduces the variety of components exiting the cell. Both produce the same number of final products.

Simplification is a key concept. One means to accomplish this is by using existing components in new products. For example, at Caterpillar Tractor, new products cannot include more than 30 per cent new parts. Further, by placing different activities within a cell, parts in a JIT shop only go to one cell for processing. This simplification reduces materials handling, routeings and WIP, and the production flow between cells is less complex, making co-ordination easier.

However, significantly more demands are made of labour, regarding both skills and task discipline. Emphasis falls on teamwork, and behavioural, cultural and/or system-wide controls, rather than through traditional bureaucratic controls that isolate cost centres. Workers must be motivated to make sacrifices for the whole. Slack exists in the form of machine and labour flexibility, not in inventories or long lead times. Normally, management sets production schedules so that a balanced mix of components can be produced in each cell. This organisation balances the flow of work through the shop. Once set, the production schedule requires absolute discipline in order to meet the planned production so that work is not unintentionally idled by the lack of components.

Factory management changes from the traditional *push* to a *pull* system. Because forecasts form the basis for the traditional system, orders are released (pushed) to the shop as determined by the master schedule. Long lead times necessitate this approach. For pull systems, individual components are not built until specifically requested (pulled) by the succeeding department, or by a sales order to initiate production in the last cell. The Toyota system operates as a pull system. Workers perform machine maintenance and other tasks until an order (*kanban*) is placed for their components. Traditional overhead costs, such as maintenance, are reduced, and become part of the cell's direct labour cost. This approach is a distinct contrast to the traditional accounting notion of efficiency, namely keeping workers and machines working constantly, eliminating idle time.

Of course, management still wishes to maximise the utilisation of cell capacity. For example, at Kyocera (a Japanese ceramics manufacturer) and Harley-Davidson, idle time, while not necessarily an evil as in traditional shops, is still a lost opportunity to enhance profits. Outsourcing (using idle cell capacity to meet other companies' needs) generates additional profits.

Minimising set-up times also enhances flexibility because it is easier to switch production to a different product. The time spent setting up a machine reduces the time available to run it, and consequently reduces production capacity. Reducing set-up time allows for smaller lot sizes that do not significantly increase per unit costs. It can also increase plant capacity despite the variety of products and demands. Thus, the need for high levels of finished goods is significantly reduced.

Other reasons for excessive inventories are unreliable vendor deliveries and vendor quality. JIT solves these uncertainties by forgoing the short-term benefits of competitive bidding in order to develop long-term vendor relationships. In exchange, the vendor's production schedule, deliveries and quality standards are synchronised with the plant. As suppliers must be dedicated to continuous improvements, they become a part of the manufacturer's competitive advantage. Consequently, they must be chosen and monitored (e.g. with ISO certification standards) very carefully. To accomplish such tight co-ordination, computer-based information technologies are often created as part of JIT conversions. At the California Nummi plant – a joint venture between Toyota and General Motors – the production schedule is linked with component manufacturers in Japan and local suppliers so that deliveries are made within a three-hour time period.

Innovation and improvement through kanbans

The ultimate JIT system responds exactly to demand with zero inventories. Although this ideal is virtually impossible to achieve, an important advantage of JIT lies in its superiority in identifying where improvement can be made. Process (built-in) quality control (versus end-of-the-line inspection) is extremely important if WIP is replaced with minimum-size kanban containers. At Toyota, each worker exercises constant quality control and can shut down the entire line if a defect is discovered. No WIP buffers exist to hide the problem. When lights and whistles go off indicating where the shutdown occurred, engineers and workers descend upon the station to solve the problem. Since the failure represents an opportunity to improve the system, it receives reverential attention. In this philosophy, no guilt-laden finger-pointing occurs.

JIT systems allow controllable incremental improvements where the benefit is greatest, in part through a strategy of causing failures. The steps involve systematic reduction of kanban container sizes until production flow problems occur. Upon tracing the problem to its cause, the removed units are replaced into the system until a solution can be implemented, so that no production is lost. This process is repeated until another failure signals an opportunity to improve the system elsewhere. A series of minute, usually low-cost, improvements and, more importantly, a culture of continuous improvement are the results.

With a severe problem, re-engineering and automation may be necessary. Many practitioners consider JIT to be a necessary prerequisite for the efficient introduction of automation. JIT facilitates three aspects of capital investment usually considered difficult under traditional systems:

accurate identification of potential candidates for improvement;
estimates of system-wide benefits to the organisation as a whole;
follow-up continual monitoring of the improvements through the JIT management process.

To facilitate re-engineering and cost reduction, JIT separates activities into value-added and non-value-added (the production and co-ordinating functions within traditional systems). Examples of non-value-added activities are moving, storage and various types of overhead that do not directly improve (add value to) the product. Further analysis extends this idea to the physical space and assets within the plant. Western manufacturers have extended these concepts by attaching costs to activities as part of activity-based management.

Innovation and improvement with the Theory of Constraints

Yet another approach to the transition from traditional manufacturing is the Theory of Constraints (TOC). TOC involves focusing on bottlenecks and unbalanced work centres. In many cases, this approach becomes more suitable as product variety increases (i.e. approaching the left tail of the continuum in Figure 5.2) by providing more flexibility and easing implementation. In other cases, further down the continuum, TOC may also be an effective bridge from traditional manufacturing to JIT.

TOC uses a management scheduling technique called 'drum-buffer-rope'. The bottleneck is the drum that sets the pace for releasing orders to the shop-floor. All non-bottleneck departments are designed to have sufficient capacity to adjust easily to production variety. Thus, they need not be managed in detail. Only the bottleneck can reduce or enhance the flow of products. It becomes the focus of attention. WIP is the buffer used to protect the bottleneck, assuring it is never idle or waiting for work. The rope is the time required to reach the bottleneck, and signals order releases.

Under this system, WIP is valued at the cost of materials, outsourcing and incremental overhead (like power). All other labour and support costs are treated as fixed period costs and are not assigned to inventories. TOC plants consider any market price in excess of materials to be acceptable. This allows management considerable strategic freedom. The 'death spiral' attributed to full cost-plus bidding, where unit costs increase with decreases in volume, is avoided. Competitive conflicts between responsibility centres also are avoided. The objective is to maximise throughput. As throughput values are market value or output based, TOC values are closer to exit values, rather than the traditional historical cost entry values. The drum-buffer-rope planning has been credited with increasing flexibility to the point that lead times rival JIT systems. Numerous companies have credited TOC systems for their successful operations.

TOC supports continuous improvement by identifying and eliminating constraints. Once removed, the next constraint becomes the focus for improvement. When applied correctly, it leads management to focus systematically on the activities that will provide the greatest short-term benefits. TOC's key competitive advantage is short range, i.e. market premiums from producing unique products in a timely manner.

The application of drum-buffer-rope, however, becomes economically suspect as the number of non-bottleneck departments increases. Drum-buffer-rope systems lack the accounting controls of traditional costing systems, or the visual controls of JIT systems. The lack of direct cost controls for non-bottleneck departments may make the realisation of long-run economies and capital budgeting difficult.

Mangement implications of JIT

Let us consider the changes to the four management functions of the purchase of raw materials, the production process, control of production and the marketing and distribution of finished goods (see Figure 5.3):

1. Purchasing departments (A) no longer manage raw materials nor continually shop for better prices, but monitor deliveries and quality by direct, close relationships with a few suppliers.

2. Production departments (B) change from a simple set of similar activities to the complex production of families of parts.

3. New information technologies, such as electronic data interchange (EDI), act as a co-ordinating mechanism linking entities. Management of the overall process (C) has been simplified through EDI and the advent of new production technologies such as JIT. Within entities, quality and JIT cell control eliminate most of the uncertainties that destroyed scheduling accuracy. Less information processing is required to achieve the same level of control. Quality control becomes a shop-floor responsibility where failures may be easily and immediately observed. Preventive and corrective process controls replace after-the-fact detective controls.

4. Production flexibility substitutes for excessive finished goods (D). Marketing and manufacturing are now closely coupled. Manufacturing is capable of producing a wide variety of products with competitively short lead times.

The concept of constant improvement creates difficulties for companies adapting to JIT. Japanese applications of cost-benefit analysis look at much longer paybacks, with JIT as a strategic decision and return on investments (ROI) playing a lesser role. Most Western companies, on the other hand, maintain complex capital budgeting systems. Once JIT has been accepted as a strategic decision, though, capital budgeting may become less significant. JIT operates as an incrementalist system, and generally progresses in a series of small, inexpensive improvements.

Consequently, a set capital budget, probably within the current spending limits of most plants, could provide sufficient funding for several improvements. When the plant-wide spending limits are met, however, some justification for further projects may be required. Justification is based upon system (plant-wide) performance. This is not justification 'before-the-fact', using numerous detailed measures, as is usually the case for traditional capital projects. In JITs, acceptance will be much more a function of personal judgement legitimised by a track record of improving performance.

Long-term scheduling becomes less crucial to production due to JIT's flexibility and shorter lead times. Since JITs are more vulnerable to short-term demand fluctuations, however, capacity measurement is very important because cell capacity cannot be changed easily to handle short-term demand surges.

In traditional environments, budgeting determines the feasibility of production and profit figures, and it establishes standards for performance. A number of problems can result:

1. Push systems with excessive inventories allow each cost centre to operate in relative independence.

2. If the production process is not well understood or not observable by higher management, shop-floor management will be motivated to protect against tight budgets through creating slack.

3. This often takes the form of negotiated budgets between top and bottom management.

4. If accounting systems use negotiated standards, it may be difficult to ensure that each cost centre is efficient.

5. Further, the incentive to communicate innovation from the shop-floor is also reduced by negotiated budgets.

Control systems utilising benchmarking and target costing create standards that eliminate negotiations by justifying the standards in terms of the best practices (benchmarks) or market constraints (target costs). Both benchmarking and target costing can reduce the risk of hidden slack built into standards by the shop-floor. To illustrate, line management may be more motivated to introduce slack when standards are believed to be imposed from the top (upper management or engineering). Conversely, line management may be more motivated to accept the same standards when they are justified in either of the following ways:

Benchmarking: 'We have to hit these standards because others are doing the activities this well. If we don't, this process will be outsourced. Then, where will our jobs be?'

Target costing: 'We have to hit these standards because our competition has set the sales price and we need this profit to stay in this line of business. If we drop the line, where will our jobs be?'

Once the shop-floor buys into these (ideal) standards, negotiation is no longer an issue. The standards are set competitively by the market-place, not by management and the shop-floor.

Control implications of JIT

Behavioural controls, based on the plant's culture and stressing team approaches, become important because of the emphasis on constant improvement and within-cell co-ordination. JIT shifts responsibility to the production floor and operational controls, and away from after-the-fact cost variance reporting. The control emphasis shifts from debating standards to the automatic consideration of each new cost improvement as the new standard.

The role of variances needs to change in a pull system because sales (instead of schedules) drive utilisation. If insufficient demand arises, workers perform other functions, such as maintenance. Further, long before variances are reported, workers have pinpointed and corrected problems. Learning and continuous improvement are stressed. Therefore, the motivational impact of cost variances must always be carefully considered.

Traditional cost variance systems are based on assumptions such as efficiency is promoted through maximising capacity utilisation. This is a strategy of reward based on cost minimisation (e.g. direct labour and direct materials usage variances) while JIT, driven by TQM, is a value-maximising strategy. Idle capacity adds value to the customer through reduced lead times and flexibility. Cost minimisation is still important in JITs, but it is secondary to value enhancement through customer satisfaction. Thus variances based on an activity-based costing (ABC) system will be most useful in focusing continuous improvement on the activities with the greatest financial impact, and recording the financial impact of continuous improvement activities. Western management and workers have a long tradition of using financial information to justify action ('managing by the numbers').

JIT applications simplify shop-floor management and reduce the number of support activities so that remaining activities may be measured in detail with less effort. Some authors suggest that plants, like service organisations, should keep detailed overhead records to control these costs, and identify where the greatest costs and potential savings exist. While JIT identifies non-value-added assets and activities as overhead, it does not provide a systematic identification of where cost savings will be greatest. As a result, new cost analysis techniques, such as ABC, identify these costs.

ABC's role in JITs may change as cells mature, however. In the early stages of JIT development, value analysis and activity chains (e.g. Ishikawa cause–effect diagrams) help identify non-value-added activities and costs. As JITs mature, stable work cells make overhead allocation easier. Many complex co-ordination and maintenance functions have been shifted to the cells, thereby reducing the need to co-ordinate activities, as well as the number of arbitrary allocations. Consequently, JIT makes the application of ABC easier.

Especially during initial development, when JIT benefits are suspect, ABC supports JIT by measuring successes (e.g. cost savings through reduced set-ups). At one Campbell Soup plant, *ad hoc* cost system analysis was necessary to support and legitimise JIT conversion. As one of its plant managers commented, 'Everybody here hates JIT. But we know we have to do it to survive.' On the other hand, in another JIT conversion at a manufacturer of trenching equipment, socio-technical systems analysis was used to design a formal ABC cost variance system prioritising activities for quality improvement and redesign. Regardless, cost analysis plays a significant role in the acceptance of new concepts by the shop-floor. After the shop-floor has bought into the JIT, however, the need for detailed cost information to justify it may be lessened.

Backflush cost systems

When JIT shop-floor control is high, backflush systems simplify accounting and significantly reduce its cost. Granting slight variations in practice, usually only two general ledger accounts are maintained: raw materials-in-process and conversion costs. Backflush costing breaks the factory into logical input-output points (called 'trigger points'), and measures the materials put in and the materials coming out. Inputs are valued at actual cost and outputs at standard cost. Detailed labour accounting and WIP valuation through work centres are eliminated. Due to JIT's process quality, WIP is reduced to constant-sized kanban containers. This eliminates the need for equivalent units calculations, further simplifying the cost accounting system.

Backflush systems are not designed to report detailed variances. While they will give indications of productivity changes for the areas between trigger points, backflush systems do not focus improvements on the most costly activities. Consequently, they may be most beneficial in well-established, re-engineered and behaviourally accepted JITs.

Activity-based management, just-in-time and cost system information

Cost data is only one element of organisational competitiveness. Another is short lead times (cycle time) as this also adds value to the customer. Cycle time must be measured, since shortened cycle times increase velocity, throughput and capacity.

Because of the specialised nature of JIT cells, increased machine flexibility and cross-training of labour are also very important. Measures to evaluate the ability of the system to handle variety and uncertainty are required and need to be developed. The cost of maintaining and increasing machine and labour flexibility should be important to JIT management, although many of the benefits cannot be measured with existing cost systems. The challenge for accountants lies in creating monetary measures for the management of these activities. While a long-term, non-financial, statement-driven strategy suits the Japanese, Western companies must consider the 'bottom line' due to the nature of their financial institutions. However, given the scepticism about the accuracy and usefulness of such measures, accounting control may shift from its current level of detail into more aggregated figures, such as in backflush systems.

Another issue on the horizon is how activity-based management (ABM) systems will evolve to improve value measurement. Current cost orientations do not measure value-added from the *customer's* perspective. Current entry-value costing may need to evolve to exit-value systems. This will change ABM's focus from the most costly activities (which may not be the easiest to improve) to the activities adding the greatest value.

Consider how value-adding (or exit-value) costing changes management's focus for different automobile markets. In markets with high petrol costs, different performance-enhancing options may be desired by customers. But in high-corrosion environments (the seashore), paint options may be more valuable to those customers. The current ABM focus ignores the different markets, focusing on engine options as these have a higher cost than paint options. In the coastal market, the greatest opportunity for increased sales is from paint enhancements. The failure of the current focus is that it stresses cost minimisation, not value maximisation. With non-value-added activities, cost minimisation and cycle time issues should be paramount. However, ABM will need to evolve into a focus on value-added (strategic, market-driven) activities.

Cost systems to support TQM

Since TQM eliminates one reason to have WIP, and makes the implementation of re-engineering and automation easier, quality performance needs to be monitored using both short-run and long-run measures. The current costs of quality (COQ) model measures prevention and appraisal costs, comparing them to internal and external failure costs. COQ should be able to demonstrate the value of TQM by showing savings from the reduction of failures that offset, and hopefully far exceed, investments in prevention and appraisal activities. This is a critical management accounting function to support new technologies. A Texas Instruments plant, for example, used COQ to justify implementing TQM. Once the plant's culture had changed, COQ measures were largely dropped.

This use of the COQ model is not surprising as it is an odd mixture of historical costs and subjective estimates. Three measurement problems with the model can also lead to misspecifying the value of the cashflows related to quality changes. First, only current costs are considered. This understates the savings that may last the life-cycle of the product. The second problem concerns valuing lost sales from external failures. For example, in a Motorola application, the portion of external failure costs related to lost sales was the bulk of the COQ savings. Because these estimates are so subjective, their credibility is crucial. Consistent calculation procedures must be maintained and disclosed. In addition to estimating the volume of lost sales, lost profit per unit valuation is problematic. Should it be based on lost contribution margin or lost revenues? Fortunately, despite these problems, COQ measures have proven useful in successfully introducing TQM.

The third problem involves the short-run emphasis on the relative COQ mix with respect to revenues. The JIT and TQM continuous improvement philosophy, along with target costing (discussed below), should enhance the accountant's motivation to measure instead the relative mix between COQ categories, and variances from the COQ budget.

Long-range attention also needs to evolve into a comparison of the changes in COQ category budgets over time. As accountants measure the evolution of JITs, attention should be focused on developing models of normative mixes for various evolutionary stages. These measures can then provide benchmarks for measuring continuous quality improvements and movement toward TQM objectives. More consistent with the JIT focus, emphasis will be placed on the zero defects model, while abandoning the cost minimisation model.

Automated Manufacturing

One of the strengths of JIT is that opportunities for automation are readily identified and can be efficiently analysed. The job-to-flow shop continuum, illustrated in Figure 5.5, identifies automation as a corollary of JIT. Computer-aided design and computer-aided manufacturing (CAD/CAM), and automatic storage/retrieval systems (AS/RS), represent significant expensive new developments in support systems. While JIT is not necessarily a prerequisite for automation, implementing JIT in non-automated or partially automated activities increases automation success in the following ways:

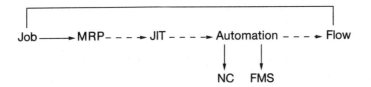

Figure 5.5 Functional design adaptations form the traditional job-flow continuum.

1. JIT optimises the human elements so that we know when automation is really necessary.
2. JIT is a learning system that therefore reduces the complexity and uncertainty surrounding automation.
3. JIT cell visibility facilitates effective evaluation of automation success.

Automated machinery comes in many forms with many different attributes. Compare numerically controlled machines (NC) to flexible manufacturing systems (FMS). NC machines produce components according to optimal run sizes, and usually require time-consuming manual set-ups, loading and unloading, and highly skilled employees. FMS, on the other end of the continuum, consists of wholly automated groups of self-set-up machines with automated material carriers that load and unload jobs; the entire process operating from a centralised computer. Ideally, support labour is only required for maintenance and occasionally to replace tools.

NC machines, often because of costly set-ups, are most economical with larger jobs. FMS, concentrating upon families of parts with similar characteristics, have the objective of using rapid set-ups to economically produce one part at a time. A complex set of mathematical models, utilising standards and detailed specifications, schedule and route the workflow to maximise the utilisation of each machine in the FMS cell. Economical production of small runs of customised parts in an FMS system is not possible without CAD/CAM systems. CAD is a computerised support system replacing the engineering graphics function. Once CAD combines with other software, production feasibility and routeing can be established.

AS/RS can yield significant material-handling advantages. AS/RS equipment brings inventory storage baskets containing needed components to workers (called 'pickers') and then returns them by conveyors to their storage positions. Components for small jobs or mixed-sales deliveries can be handled quickly despite their complexity, reducing delivery lead times and increasing the variety of parts per order at a lower incremental cost. The combination of this group of NC, FMS, CAD/CAM and AS/RS represents significant investments in technology to allow the efficient production of small jobs. Production typifies that of a job shop. In addition, other longer-linked, highly automated production machinery is used for commodity products. Consequently, automation can be applied to the manufacture of products traditionally made in either job or flow environments.

The following predominant characteristics become evident within automated plants:

1. Quality, in the sense of meeting specifications, is crucial, since automated processes tolerate little deviation from specifications.
2. Due to higher utilisation rates and low inventory levels, less slack is available for rejects, planning errors or machine breakdowns.
3. Consequently, preventive maintenance of key machinery is also very important.
4. Predictability befriends automated systems, uncertainty does not.
5. Simplification and standardisation dramatically reduce the software complexity required to run the system.
6. Data discipline becomes critical for all software.
7. Hence, TQM and JIT enhance automation success.

Automation's impact on planning and control systems

Capital budgeting decisions must take account of the level of uncertainty, both short and long term, as well as quantitative and qualitative factors. Uncertainty embraces the lack of understanding of current activities and future activities. This problem often creates more problems when automation evolves from an MRP or traditional manufacturing environment, as such enterprises tend to evaluate the decision to automate with respect to individual cost centres while ignoring system-wide influences. Automating from a JIT system often ensures a better understanding of the factors influencing the process.

Automation requires improved control over quality and better shop-floor discipline in order to generate savings; factors which are not easily quantified. Typically, inventory and lead times drop, less space is required, and delivery reliability improves after automating. The decision to automate, however, is generally not well serviced by traditional accounting measures such as discounting (NPV, IRR), ROI or payback measures. Instead, customers or the market-place often force the decision upon management. In other words, management perceives that they must increase automation or go out of business. The emphasis becomes one of identifying the optimal form of that investment, rather than its economic feasibility. The issue then becomes a debate as to how to finance it, and not whether the net present value is positive.

The nature of planning will also change since FMS allows shorter master production schedules. But the old job shop problem of balancing machine loadings against product mix still haunts these systems. The accountant as a team member will become more involved with mathematical models and simulations that can be used as effective means to balance machine utilisation. Opportunity costs will become the basis for bidding and costing jobs.

Pricing becomes a tricky issue. The popular response of accountants to the pricing issue lies in supporting absorption costing since the bulk of automated equipment costs are fixed and long-term. Some suggest that full costing be supported by identifying layers of fixed costs separated by their unique time-budget horizons. Separation by time horizons allows incremental pricing decisions to be linked to suitable strategic decisions.

An alternative argument can be presented for variable costing, however, since the bulk of the costs are fixed and provide long-term service. Strategic pricing promotes the need for variable costing, so that the short-term costs may be evaluated, especially when machines are under-utilised. When machining centres become bottlenecks, the measurement of opportunity costs (shadow prices and throughput) becomes important for short-run profit maximisation.

Increased machine reliability, tight quality specifications and the precise timing of workflows have substantially reduced most of the uncertainties viewed as traits of traditional job shops. With reduced uncertainty, discrete mathematical computer models can cope with a variety of products. Planning for capacity and flexibility then becomes more important, and operational control is regarded as a given. Operations rely less on annual plans, instead emphasising monthly scheduling, and annual budgeting bears less importance as a control device or an information source. Automated systems are very sensitive to data and specification errors, though. Internal control of computer systems will, of necessity, grow in importance for the management accountant. Necessary day-to-day feedback and mathematical control displaces much of accounting's traditional control and data-gathering roles. However, at least until superior models are developed, management still employs budgeting as a useful means to motivate the remaining employees. This, of course, diminishes in importance as automation replaces the direct labour workforce.

This shift in the relationship among labour, overhead and material costs affects cost classification as well. The relative percentages of variable versus fixed, and controllable versus non-controllable costs change. While indirect highly skilled labour costs increase, direct labour costs shrink. Overheads increase and can vary significantly among cost centres, as activities have different levels of automation with more or less costly equipment. Lower spoilage rates and the need for better quality influence material costs, which are now the largest variable cost.

Fixed costs become an increasingly significant part of overall costs and hence their control becomes an important cost system issue. The classification of controllable and non-controllable costs has also changed, as many of the controllable costs that remain were formerly lumped into fixed overhead costs. But now, because of their increased importance, specific overhead costs should be tracked to facilitate the new methods of shop-floor control. Again, the use of multiple overhead application rates (or ABC cost drivers) becomes more important.

Short-term decisions, such as make or buy, or add/drop a product, often become easier as more costs become fixed. However, costs previously classified as fixed (because measurement was difficult) are now shown to vary with different cost drivers in ABC systems. For example, some systems have been observed that measure the cost of material handling based upon cause and effect. Previously, these costs were simply lumped into fixed overhead because they did not represent a significant proportion of the variable costs. Traditional cost systems only consider costs that vary with production volume to be 'variable costs'. ABC systems, contrarily, attempt to reclassify traditionally labelled 'fixed costs' into costs that vary with some cost driver in a cause–effect relationship.

Regardless, accurate costing of automated processes will require separate cost pools rather than factory-wide cost pools. Different types and groups of equipment can vary significantly in cost. Therefore, separate cost pools linked to specific types of equipment are necessary for accurate costing. The classification of the machine operators as direct labour can also be difficult when one person operates several machines. Set-up specialists create further new costing problems, and rational cause– effect methods of allocating these costs must be designed.

Target Costing and New Operations Management

Target costing systems come into play from the beginning of the product's life-cycle. A target profit is subtracted from a target price derived from the characteristics of the product and projected sales volumes over its life-cycle. This determines the allowable cost. For example, the target price determined by marketing may be £200. This £200 less a target profit of £40 leaves an allowable cost of £160. However, the current cost to produce this design may be well in excess of the target cost. If calculated at £220, the target for cost reduction (through value engineering or kaizen costing) is £220 less £160, equalling £60. There are slight variations on this theme in practice, but this is essentially the calculation. Obviously an excessive drifting cost (i.e. the £220) could lead to rejection of a product very early in its development, thus leading to savings of many thousands (or millions) of pounds.

When projects go forward, target costs are benchmarks and become part of the new cost system monitoring continuous improvement. A new variance calculation identifies the spread between target and actual (drift) costs for every component, sub- component, and related activity. As target costs must be integrated into operating and capital budgets, accountants need to develop expertise in calculating them through benchmarking the best practices both within and outside the industry.

Additionally, there is a real cultural benefit from the implementation of target costing philosophies. The importance of target costing systems is the shift they cause to market-based efficiencies and planning focuses. Under these systems, the customer drives product development, and competition drives the definition of efficient manufacturing. Accountants are largely responsible for measuring these new uncertainties. The continuous updating of target costs in the accounting- manufacturing database, and the benchmarking of activities, will become primary job characteristics of modern management accountants. This trend is well established in Japanese companies and is currently becoming a critical component of other large international organisations engaged in re-engineering using value chain analysis.

Management accountants will have to learn to work in multi-disciplinary project teams. They will provide the costing expertise, and develop new market-based planning and monitoring systems. Multi-disciplinary project teams will require costing expertise in the application of such techniques as concurrent (or simultaneous) design, value engineering and target costing. These methodologies are most effective when used with ABC and standard costing systems.

Concurrent design involves the participation of marketing, research and design, manufacturing, and distribution management to simultaneously design and manage products. The management accountant is part of this team as a link to estimate the impact of design on manufacturing, distribution and warranty costs (e.g. life-cycle costing). For example, Caterpillar Tractor International uses a centralised seventeen-plant world-wide database. With this cost system, they can design new products using existing facilities to meet target costs.

Re-engineering based on target costs represents a radical restructuring of the enterprise, modelling it as a value chain of activities that provide value to the customer. By costing and benchmarking these activities, areas of critical competency and strategic advantage or disadvantage can be identified for exploitation, improvement or outsourcing. We believe this will become yet another role offering significant opportunities for the modern management accountant.

Conclusions

Management accountants must be aware of the influence of new technologies and changes in production management on the usefulness of various accounting techniques. Most of the issues are not new, but their significance changes under different sets of conditions.

Until very recently only one well-understood philosophy of manufacturing existed. A relatively narrow set of techniques was sufficient to meet management's needs. Many of the underlying assumptions about inventories, quality and labour management were simply taken for granted and not considered issues important enough to be discussed in accounting textbooks since the underlying philosophy of traditional manufacturing was relatively consistent from plant to plant. But now these assumptions are changing, some for the first time in almost one hundred years. Consequently, the role of the managerial accountant is also changing and becoming more management-oriented. For example, cost accountants must:

carefully analyse their environments;
be aware of production technology changes influencing the current costing system;
work with other professionals, like the production engineers, to ensure the implementation of appropriate changes to the cost system required to maintain its relevance as environmental uncertainties and management information needs evolve; and
develop the facility to deal with soft measures while still maintaining their objectivity and credibility.

In the future, cost (and profit) management systems will replace the more narrow traditional cost systems. These new systems will produce a variety of costing and profitability measures, and performance indicators (not always financial) with the emphasis on relevance, even if this entails some sacrifice of precision.

We envisage the future management accountant as, perhaps, not even maintaining an office. Rather, he/she will travel around the enterprise and its environment, laptop computer in hand, logging into an integrated, computer-based information system, downloading data and devising output (often graphical) formats to provide real-time, relevant information on demand. Analogously, we may evolve into the role of an informational ombudsman.

It would be remiss not to offer an opinion on where new operations management is going in the future. Is traditional manufacturing dead? Probably not – at least not in the short term. But different aspects of all traditional systems will be radically changed. A key point must be clear by now: since very few manufacturing environments can be uniquely classified as job, process, JIT or FMS systems, the great majority of situations will consist of a mix of these environments.

Even more difficult to cope with, most plants will be continually undergoing transitions. Thus, the accountants of the future will be unable to apply the relatively clear textbook prescriptions of the past to each new situation. We must be proactive and directly involved in management decisions in order for cost management systems to evolve in a form compatible with these new technologies. Environmental changes within and without the plant can influence the measurability, usefulness and the cost/benefits of accounting systems. As accountants, we need to understand the conditions in each unique environment influencing our product – management information. Future management accountants will resemble – if in fact we have not already become – more artisans than technicians, more Picassos than Taylors, and more generalists than specialists.

Bibliography

Background readings on new environments

Capettini, R. and D.K. Clancy (1987) *Cost Accounting, Robotics, and the New Manufacturing Environment*, Sarasota, Fla.: American Accounting Association.

Howell, R.A. and S. Soucy (1983) *Factory 2000+: Management Accounting's Changing Role*, Montvale, NJ: Institute of Management Accountants.

Lee, Y.L. (1987) *Management Accounting Changes for the 1990s*, Artesia, Calif.: McKay Business Systems.

Taylor, S.G., S.M. Seward and S.F. Bolander (1981) 'Why the process industries are different', *Production and Inventory Management*, no. 4, pp. 9–24.

Reviews of CAS methods used in new environments

Bennett, R.E., J.A. Hendricks, D.E. Keys and E.J. Rudnicki (1987) *Cost Accounting for Factory Automation*, Montvale, NJ: Institute of Management Accountants.

Cokins, G., A. Stratton and J. Helbling (1993) *An ABC Manager's Primer*, Montvale, NJ: Institute of Management Accountants.

Horvath, P. (1993) *Target Costing: A State-of-the-Art Review*, Kempston, Bedford: IFS International.

Howell, R.A., J.D. Brown, S. Soucy and A.H. Seed III (1987) *Management Accounting in the New Manufacturing Environment: Current cost management practice in automated (advanced) manufacturing environments*, Montvale, NJ: Institute of Management Accountants.

Mackey, J. and V. Hughes (1993) 'Decision-focused costing at Kenco', *Management Accounting*, May, pp. 22–6.

Implementation issues

Becker, S.W. (1993) 'TQM does work: ten reasons why misguided attempts fail', *Management Review*, May, pp. 30–3.

Keegan, D.P., R.G. Eiler and C.R. Jones (1989) 'Are your performance measures obsolete?', *Management Accounting*, June, pp. 45–50.

Thomas, M. and J. Mackey (1994) 'Activity-based cost variances for just-in-times', *Management Accounting*, April, pp. 49–54.

Yang, G.Y. and R.C. Yu (1993) 'Strategic costing and ABC', *Management Accounting*, May, pp. 33–7.

CHAPTER SIX

Activity-Based Costing

John Innes and Falconer Mitchell

♦

Costing outputs have been a core part of the service provided by management accountants for well over a century. Indeed the origins of the contemporary management accounting discipline lie in the costing practices which were developed more than a century ago. Costing is a function which links both financial and management accounting. Without product cost information a manufacturing, wholesale or retail organisation would be unable to segregate the cost of sold and unsold outputs and as a result could not obtain periodic measurements of its profitability or that of its individual divisions, market segments or products. Aside from this, product (or service) costs provide valuable information for management and are used in a range of managerial decisions, as a basis for generating cost control feedback and as performance measures.

Thus product costs can be used for a variety of purposes. Moreover, they can be computed in a variety of different ways. The utility of a given approach has therefore to be assessed against its relevance for any specific purposes. This chapter performs this assessment for one particular approach known as activity-based costing (ABC) which has become increasingly popular in practice in recent years. Both the product costing and cost management aspects of ABC are assessed. However, before this assessment is undertaken the origins and the mechanics of ABC are explored.

Origins

While the idea of ABC has existed for several decades, it was only in the latter half of the 1980s that it emerged as a popular form of costing in practice. Its rapid emergence is largely attributable to Professors Robin Cooper of the Claremont Graduate School and Robert Kaplan of the Harvard Business School who found the ABC concept being applied in a small number of large USA manufacturing businesses where some dissatisfaction with conventional approaches to costing was apparent. The experiences of these organisations were published as Harvard Case Studies and also initiated a series of articles which outlined and developed the application of ABC. Thus ABC owes its current status both to the practitioners who first designed and effected its practical implementation and then to the academics who translated this work into a more general framework and who contributed to its popularity and dissemination through their publications.

The attraction and the rapid rise of ABC have been due to a number of interrelated factors. First, the degree of change in many business organisations was very great during the 1980s. Computer-aided manufacture, flexible manufacturing systems, total quality management and just-in-time approaches were all common developments. All of these provided an environment of change within which management accounting had been conspicuous by its adherence to convention. Moreover, the efforts of manufacturers to provide a wider range of products, more customisation and flexibility, better quality and faster and more reliable response to customers were all developments which involved extra investment and resource acquisition and which led in many firms to changes in the structure of cost.

As many of the extra costs fell within the indirect category, production overhead became a more significant cost element and, where automation was also in evidence, its relative importance was often compounded by a reduction in direct labour. These contemporary developments in manufacturing tended to require more resource in four particular areas:

1. In the logistics of production where scheduling work became more complex and planning was more involved.
2. In the matching of resource availability to the production plans.
3. In the achievement of quality throughout the production process.
4. In the ability to cope with changes, for example in product range or specification, in technology and in customer requirements.

However, it should be noted that increased workload in each of these areas (and hence increased cost) was not simply related to corresponding increases in the volume of output. Rather, the resource requirements of these types of activity were dependent upon the increasing diversity, complexity, quality and flexibility of production output.

Realisation that production volumes were not the main driving force behind a substantial proportion of overhead raised questions about the validity of the traditional approaches to overhead costing. For the most part the traditional approach consisted of production centre overhead rates based on direct labour time, direct labour cost or machine time. All of these bases, however, were strongly influenced by the volume of production output. To use them in product costing for the types of overhead described above could lead to systematic miscostings. This problem was magnified in those sectors where direct labour had been reduced through automation. Indeed, with the growth in overheads, some firms were using overhead rates which were 2000 per cent or more of direct labour cost. Table 6.1 illustrates how the growth of overhead cost and the fall in direct labour combine to produce these high rates. Of course, where rates of this size are in use then the absence of a close relationship between the direct labour content of products and

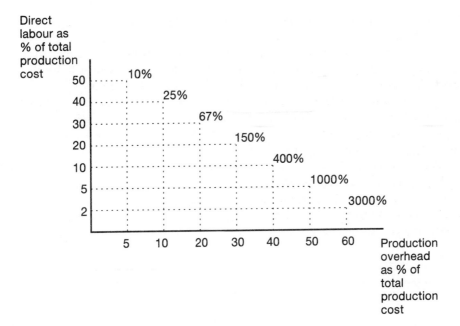

Table 6.1   The impact of falling direct labour and growing overhead on production overhead rates.

their consumption of overhead resource will quickly lead to serious miscostings. The example contained in the next section demonstrates how this occurs.

A similar problem can arise with non-production overheads (sales, marketing, distribution and administration) where a global rate perhaps based on production cost is used to attach these overheads to individual products. Again this will result in a single variable, such as production cost, determining each product's share of these overheads, often in circumstances where the actual cost relationships are considerably more complex. In these situations an ABC methodology results in a costing practice which is based on a more realistic tracking of resource consumption to products and other cost objects.

Mechanics

Overview

To gain an appreciation of the mechanics of ABC it is useful to start with an overview of the structure of a simple system. Figure 6.1 provides this by highlighting the flow of costs from inputs (resources acquired) to outputs (final products or services). Note that the system covers only those indirect costs not suitable for traditional costing.

Direct costs and volume-driven overheads can be dealt with competently by conventional means.

The system operates broadly on a two-stage basis. First, the indirect costs are allocated or apportioned to a number of cost pools, each of which is based on a particular activity. Once each activity has been costed, the second stage involves computing a costing rate for each activity cost pool. This is achieved by selecting an appropriate work volume measure (known as a 'cost driver') for each and dividing a period's activity cost by the period's cost driver volume. This rate is then applied to the firm's individual product lines. Consequently, the cost of each activity is attached to each product in proportion to the cost driver volumes associated with each product. The system is thus based on the two propositions that (a) activities consume resources and costs; and (b) products consume activities. Its two stages are akin to those of more traditional systems. The key difference lies in the elimination of production departments as the basis for cost pooling and the abandonment of

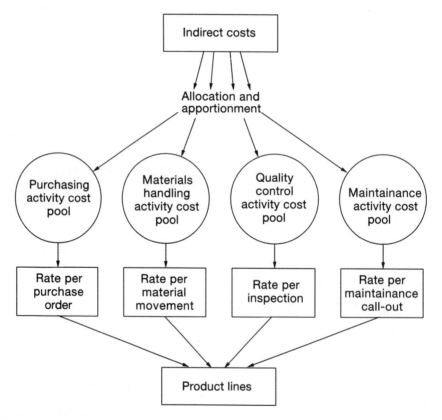

Figure 6.1 ABC system cost flows.

production volume characteristics (e.g. labour time and machine time) as the basis for attaching the overhead to products. Instead ABC uses activity cost pools and cost driver rates to attribute overhead costs to individual product lines.

Design steps

Designing an ABC system involves four key steps, each of which is now considered in turn.

Identify activities

This step requires the management accountant to acquire a familiarity with what is happening in the indirect areas of the organisation. This has to be done systematically and may involve examining physical plans of the workplace (to identify how all space is being used) and the payroll listings (to ensure all relevant personnel have been taken into account). This examination normally has to be supplemented by observation of work and particularly by a series of interviews with staff involved.

A number of criteria underlie the choice of activities. The activities should be at a reasonable level of aggregation. To break activities down into actions and tasks (e.g. filing an order, photocopying a document) is usually too detailed for product costing purposes. Such actions and tasks are normally combined into large purpose-oriented activities (see Figure 6.2 for some typical examples).

The final choice of activities will be judgemental in any organisation. In some of the earlier reported cases the activity cost pools ran into hundreds while more recent cases tend to suggest that around twenty or thirty cost pools have become more common. The choice is between information detail and the cost of setting up and operating the system. For example, an activity such as quality control could be subdivided into appraisal activity and prevention activity. The benefits of this would lie in the more detailed profile of cost reported to management and in a possible increase in the homogeneity of the costs in each activity cost pool. For example, the number of inspections might relate well to the cost homogeneity of the appraisal

Activity	Cost driver
Production schedule changes	Number of change orders
Customer liaison	Number of customers
Purchasing	Number of purchase orders
Production process set-up	Number of set-ups
Quality control	Number of inspections
Material handling	Number of material movements
Maintenance	Number of call-outs

Figure 6.2 Examples of activities.

activity but it may be that the prevention activity is better explained by the historical reject rate of products. In other words, instead of the one activity of quality control with one cost driver, namely the number of inspections, the identification of the two activities of appraisal and prevention led to two different cost drivers, namely the number of inspections and the reject rate.

Costing activities

After establishing the activity structure for the system it is necessary to identify the resources consumed by each individual activity during the relevant period. This provides a basis for identifying the level of cost in each pool. Both allocation (where particular individuals, suppliers or pieces of equipment are identified as having a full-time commitment to a specific activity) and apportionment (where labour or equipment resources are shared by two or more activities) will be involved at this stage. In the absence of time records, labour and equipment usage will have to be identified in broad terms by observation and interview. For other costs such as occupancy the most appropriate available measures of resource consumption (e.g. space occupied) should be used. Thus approximation and estimation are inherent in ABC systems.

The activity cost information generated in this way has value in its own right. It represents what is often a novel profiling of overhead cost for management. Rather than analysing cost in terms of input type (labour, supplies, equipment depreciation), it indicates how resources have been applied in the business. This provides another basis for assessing expenditure and identifying opportunities for cost reduction from the revealed pattern of expenditure and also from inter-plant and past period comparisons. Indeed some organisations have developed their ABC systems only to this stage, as their objective has been to aid cost control and cost reduction rather than to calculate new unit costs.

Identify cost drivers

In order to link the activity costs to product or service outputs a cost driver has to be identified for each cost pool. The cost driver is a quantitative measure associated with the workload of the activity. It normally reflects the output of the activity. It should give a good explanation of the behaviour of costs in the pool and should be identifiable with each product line for the final stage of product costing. As historical data are often not available to undertake statistical testing of the relationship between the cost driver and the behaviour of costs in the cost pool, the choice of cost driver may require the exercise of judgement. This should involve management with local and detailed knowledge of the activity for not only will they be best placed to make the judgement, but the credibility of the resultant system will to a large extent depend on their acceptance and use of it.

In practice four alternative types of cost driver are to be found:

1. *Pure volume cost drivers*. These are by far the most common and examples are given in Figure 6.2. Normally they are assumed to represent a reasonably homogeneous measure of the output of the activity concerned.

2. *Weighted volume cost drivers*. These exist where the output of the activity is clearly non-homogeneous. For example, if purchasing were an activity pool and purchase orders were made both domestically and overseas, the overseas orders might involve considerably more administrative work. Rather than split the purchasing pool into two parts (home and overseas purchasing) and have separate cost drivers for each (home purchase orders and overseas purchase orders), it may be more convenient to simply weight the overseas orders *vis-à-vis* the home orders. Thus, from an assessment of the work undertaken to make the respective orders it might be decided that each overseas order be weighted by 1.5 before determining the total weighted volume of cost driver to be used in calculating the appropriate rate.

3. *Situational cost drivers*. Occasionally, a situational characteristic of the activity can be important in determining its workload and thus hold credence as its cost driver. For example, the number of suppliers pertaining to a particular purchasing activity could be used as the cost driver. In other words, the number of suppliers is not an output measure of the activity but may be a convenient surrogate for a pure volume cost driver such as the number of purchase orders. Furthermore, some of the purchasing cost may relate to vetting and liaising with individual suppliers.

4. *Motivational cost drivers*. These tend to be used when the intention is to motivate cost-conscious behaviour, rather than produce product cost information in the most accurate manner. The cost driver may lack some of the qualities mentioned above but by its selection may give prominence to one particular aspect of operations and influence managerial behaviour in a desired manner. For example, in Japan the element of direct labour hours has remained a popular cost driver, despite its inherent flaws in a contemporary context, because it makes labour a costly resource and motivates designers to design labour out of the product.

Application of cost driver rates

To complete the operation of the system the cost driver rates are applied to the costing of product (or service) outputs. This costing requires two further conditions. First, the cost driver measure must be capable of association with specific products. Thus, for example, the number of material movements occurring during a period must be monitored, collected and related to the product output. Establishing this type of data-gathering is often one of the extra costs of ABC. Second, unless the exercise is being done in retrospect for a past period, the rates must be predetermined, i.e. based on estimated activity cost levels and cost driver volumes for the current period. Only on this basis can the system operate to cost output as it happens. To maintain the integrity of the system these estimates will need monitoring and, if necessary, adjusting regularly.

ABC Illustration

ABC Ltd manufactures two types of pewter tankard: a standard tankard with minimal embellishment and a decorated tankard customised on the basis of selected options. The costs incurred and other production and sales data for the last year are given in tables 6.2–6.5.

Data

Table 6.2 Direct costs and resource usage.

	Standard tankard	Customised tankard
Direct material	£5.00	£6.00
Direct labour	£6.00	£8.00
Direct labour hours	1.5	2
Machine hours	0.25	0.4

Table 6.3 Production overhead.

	£ 000s
Purchasing*	700
Material handling*	400
Quality control*	500
Machine maintenance**	300
Set-up**	400
	2,300

* Currently absorbed on a direct labour hours basis = £1.6m.
** Currently absorbed on a machine hours basis = £0.7m.

During the year production was carried out in batches of 1,000 (standard product) and 100 (customised product). A set-up and 10 quality inspections occurred for each batch. In addition, each batch of standard tankards required 10 material movements and each batch of customised tankards 30 movements. The standard tankards required 20,000 purchase orders and the customised orders 30,000. Finally there were 100 maintenance call-outs on both the standard and the customised production, making 200 maintenance calls in total.

Table 6.4 Non-production overhead.

	£000s
Sales	200
Delivery	280
Customer liaison	300
	780

These costs are currently absorbed on a production cost basis. During the year the standard tankards required 200 sales visits, 60,000 delivery miles and 200 customer liaison visits while the customised tankards required respectively 300 visits, 90,000 delivery miles and 400 visits.

Table 6.5 Production and sales.

	Standard tankard	Customised tankard
Production and sales	200,000 units	50,000 units
Unit selling price	£30.00	£40.00

Product costings

Table 6.6 Traditional costing.

	Standard tankard £	Customised tankard £
Direct material	5.00	6.00
Direct labour	6.00	8.00
Production overhead (see Note 1)	8.50	12.00
Non-production overhead (see Note 2)	2.93	3.90
FULL UNIT COST	22.43	29.90

Note 1

	Labour hours basis	Machine hours basis
(a) Production overhead rates $=$	$\dfrac{£1.6m}{(200,000 \times 1.5) + (50,000 \times 2)}$	$\dfrac{£0.7m}{(200,000 \times 0.25) + (50,000 \times 0.4)}$
$=$	$\dfrac{£1.6m}{4000,000 \text{ direct labour hours}} =$	$\dfrac{£0.7m}{70,000 \text{ machine hours}}$
$=$	£4 per direct labour hour	$=$ £10 per machine hour

	Standard tankard	Customised tankard
(b) Production overhead		
Labour hours basis $=$	£6.00 (1.5 hrs $\times$ £4)	£8.00 (2 hrs $\times$ £4)
Machine hours basis $=$	£2.50 (0.25 hrs $\times$ £10)	£4.00 (0.4 hrs $\times$ £10)
	£8.50	£12.00

Note 2

Overhead rate $=$ $\dfrac{\text{Total non-production overhead}}{\text{Total production cost*}}$ $=$ $\dfrac{£0.78m}{£5.2m}$

$=$ £0.15 per £ of production cost

* Direct material + direct labour + production overhead
($£1.3m + £1.6m + £2.3m$) $=$ £5.2m

Standard tankard	19.5 $\times$ £0.15	$=$ £2.93
Customised tankard	26.0 $\times$ £0.15	$=$ £3.90

Table 6.7 Activity-based costing.

	Standard tankard £	Customised tankard £
Direct material	5.00	6.00
Direct labour	6.00	8.00
Production overhead (see Note 3)	3.67	31.32
Non-production overhead (see Note 4)	1.46	9.76
FULL UNIT COST	16.13	55.08

Note 3 Cost driver rates

	Activity cost (£000s)	Cost driver volume	Cost driver rate	Standard tankard (£000s)	Customised tankard (£000s)
Purchasing	700	50,000	£14.00 per order	280.0 (20,000 × £14)	420.0 (30,000 × £14)
Material handling	400	17,000	£23.53 per movement	47.1 (2,000 × £23.53)	352.9 (15,000 × £23.53)
Quality control	500	7,000	£71.43 per inspection	142.8 (2,000 × £71.43)	357.2 (5,000 × £71.43)
Machine maintenance	300	200	£1,500 per call-out	150.0 (100 × £1,500)	150.0 (100 × £1,500)
Set-up	400	700	£571.43 per set-up	114.3 (200 × £571.43)	285.7 (500 × £571.43)
				734.2	1,565.8
Per unit				(÷ 200,000 units) = 3.67	(÷ 50,000 units) = 31.32

Note 4

	Activity cost (£000s)	Cost driver volume	Cost driver rate	Standard tankard (£000s)	Customised tankard (£000s)
Sales	200	500	£400 per visit	80 (200 × £400)	120 (300 × £400)
Delivery	280	150,000	£1.87 per mile	112 (60,000 × £1.87)	168 (90,000 × £1.87)
Customer liaison	300	600	£500 per visit	100 (200 × £500)	200 (400 × £500)
				292	488
Per unit				(÷ 200,000 units) = 1.46	(÷ 50,000 units) = 9.76

Discussion of Results

Table 6.8 summarises the costing results and puts them in the context of current selling prices. The traditional costing shows both products profitable and earning comparable profit margin percentages. However, ABC indicates that the standard product is almost twice as profitable as previously thought while the customised tankard is in fact a substantial loss-maker. ABC reflects the fact that small-batch customised production is considerably more costly than standard production because of the complexities which it introduces and its consequent heavier consumption of the various types of overhead resource. Traditional overhead costing has resulted in the standard tankard systematically cross-subsidising the customised product.

In effect ABC generates a different signal for management. It should trigger consideration of product pricing policies, of product line viability and of improving the cost management of the customised tankard. ABC can also provide some guidance on this last aspect by its detailed analysis of the range of factors which underlie the high customised product cost. For example, set-ups carry a high cost. Can production be organised so that fewer are necessary? Can set-up procedures be

Table 6.8 Product pofitability.

	Standard tankard £	Customised tankard £
Traditional costing		
Selling price per unit	30.00	40.00
Full unit cost	22.43	29.90
PROFIT PER UNIT	7.57	10.10
ABC		
Selling price per unit	30.00	40.00
Full unit cost	16.13	55.08
PROFIT/(LOSS) PER UNIT	13.87	(15.08)

modified such that each set-up costs less? In this way ABC directs management attention to areas which are often obscured by traditional costing.

Activity-Based Product Costs   *Disadvantages.*

Although, in an organisation of any complexity, determination of *the* cost of outputs is something of a mirage, the activity-based approach does provide a means of associating resource consumption with products which is more rigorous and sophisticated than the convenient conventional approaches. It is more defensible and experience has shown (as demonstrated in the above illustration) that in both manufacturing and service organisations it produces significantly different results which can raise a variety of issues for management. The extra detail and visibility that it gives to a large component of output costs can enhance managers' understanding of cost and behaviour and also provide an opportunity to exploit a range of cost management possibilities as outlined below.

However, as with any costing system, it is not without imperfections. There remains the arbitrariness of apportionments at the stage of activity cost pooling. It is doubtful if complete homogeneity within cost pools can be achieved and the application of cost driver rates assumes a linear relationship between activity cost and cost driver. The existence of activity costs which are fixed in relation to the selected cost driver would make the accuracy of any rate dependent on the underlying activity volume being achieved. Cost drivers may also lack homogeneity (inspections, purchase orders and set-ups may differ considerably) and may relate to more than one product output (e.g. where a purchase order involves acquiring material for several products). The latter point is akin to the joint cost problem, to which solutions have a high degree of arbitrariness.

The costs produced by an ABC system are full costs which some ABC advocates suggest are the long-run variable costs of the organisation. They are thus considered particularly appropriate for strategic product line decisions. However, some caution should be exercised in this respect as they do represent past costs and reflect conditions which have applied in a past period. For decision-making a future emphasis is necessary and costs should be reconstituted in the light of proposed changes in technology and operating conditions. Despite this historical emphasis, activity-based product cost information can certainly play an attention-directing role by indicating – more reliably than a traditional costing system – those products where resource consumption has been high relative to their revenue generation. This should then encourage a forward-looking analysis which will provide the basis for a variety of decisions, as is discussed further under the following section on cost management.

Cost Management

The above section on activity-based product costs has highlighted the limitations of ABC. A completely accurate unit product cost does not exist. However, the general finding from most ABC research projects to date is that managers believe that the unit product cost from ABC is closer to reality than that from traditional costing. For example, managers have a gut feeling that a traditional overhead costing system overcosts high-volume products and undercosts low-volume products by associating too much overhead cost with the former and too little overhead cost with the latter. Therefore, managers are generally more willing to use ABC information than traditional overhead cost information because, as the above example illustrated, an ABC system associates more overhead cost with low-volume products than does a traditional overhead costing system. The early ABC case studies in the second half of the 1980s concentrated on product costing but the potential for using activity-based cost information for cost management very quickly became apparent. Activity-based cost management (ABCM) will be discussed under the following headings of activity analysis, classification of activities, budgeting, use of ABCM information, performance measurement and problems.

ABCM

Activity analysis

Even in ABC product costing systems, managers are involved in the process of determining activities and cost drivers. Such a process raises questions about the management of such activities. Basically, ABCM gives a new visibility to overheads. The overhead costs are classified in a very different way, as illustrated in Table 6.9 with customer order processing of £300,000.

Table 6.9 illustrates the very different perspective on overheads which an activity-based analysis gives, compared with the traditional analysis. The total overheads, of course, remain the same but the ABC analysis will give rise to a very different set of

Table 6.9   Customer order processing.

	£000s
Traditional analysis	
Salaries	160
Travel	74
Depreciation of office equipment	36
Stationery	17
Telephone	13
	300
ABC analysis	
Taking customer orders	96
Giving quotations	48
Assessing credit worthiness of customers	43
Liaising with customers	41
Expediting	37
Resolving problems	35
	300

questions from the traditional analysis. For example, why were £37,000 spent on expediting and £35,000 on resolving problems? The traditional analysis of overheads did not provide such information.

For cost management purposes a major difference with ABCM is that the activities may cross existing departmental boundaries such as administration, credit, customer liaison and accounting. This can cause problems in terms of who is responsible for controlling such costs. Some organisations have attempted to solve this particular ABCM problem by making an individual responsible for those processes which cross departmental boundaries. Other organisations have adopted an even more radical solution by actually changing their organisational structure from the former departmental basis to one constructed around the new activities. Top managers in such organisations have been so convinced of the benefits of the activity-based approach that they have been willing to accept the costs and disruption involved in such a reorganisation.

It is important to realise that ABCM can take place without any activity-based product costing. Indeed many organisations use ABCM in this fashion. Such organisations, of course, must still identify and cost the various activities within their organisation, but they do not link the activity cost pools with their individual product lines. However, in addition to identifying activity cost pools such organisations usually identify the related cost drivers so that they have a better understanding of the behaviour of their overhead costs. Such activity-based information then forms the basis of the cost management system and the next step is usually the classification of the various activities.

Classification of activities

The activity analysis usually surprises managers who had not realised the amount being spent on certain activities. This leads to questions such as are all these activities really required and, if certain activities are required, can such activities be performed in different ways? Some organisations have taken such an informal questioning approach and found it helpful for cost management. Other organisations have adopted a more formal approach by classifying activities as value added or non-value added, while some have used a different classification of core, support and diversionary activities.

Value added or non-value added

The value-added approach takes the perspective of the customer. Does an activity add value to the product or service from the point of view of the customer? If the answer is no, this activity is classified as non-value added and efforts are made to eliminate such activities. The scope for cost management in the area of non-value-added activities is illustrated by Brimson's (1991) suggestion that most organisations incur between 20 and 40 per cent of their total expenditure through non-value-added activities. However, in practice most organisations have found it impossible to eliminate all non-value-added activities, but they have tried to reduce their expenditure on such activities.

For many organisations the non-value-added activities arise because mistakes have been made and have to be corrected. This is therefore one area where some organisations have established a link between ABCM and total quality management (TQM). With the TQM philosophy of doing everything 'right first time', many non-value-added activities can be eliminated. However, non-value-added activities include not only inefficient activities, but also ineffective activities. For example, delivering materials to the production line may involve activities such as receiving, unpacking, storing and issuing the materials. It can be argued that from the customers' point of view only receiving materials adds value. The other three activities of unpacking, storing and issuing materials could be eliminated if the suppliers deliver materials directly to the production line on a just-in-time basis so that these materials could go directly onto the production line. One of the criticisms of ABCM is that it is too inward-looking and ignores the external environment, but this example illustrates that ABCM can involve solutions outside the organisation.

Core, support or diversionary

Although the distinction between value-added and non-value-added activities is perhaps the most widely used basis of classification, another useful classification is into core, support and diversionary activities. For example, a core activity for a travelling salesperson is sitting with the customer and concluding a sale, while a support activity is travelling to the customer and a diversionary activity is sitting listening to the customer's complaints about the products received from a previous order. Bellis-Jones (1992) argues that core activities involve a special expertise which is part of the competitive advantage of the organisation and such activities provide a service to customers. Support activities are required to make the core activity possible. Diversionary activities involve time being diverted from the core and support activities and usually stem from deficiencies in the system.

Bellis-Jones suggests that such activity analyses have revealed that on average core, support and diversionary activities consume 30, 35 and 35 per cent of the time available, respectively. In other words, 70 per cent of the time in most organisations is not spent on core activities. It is perhaps salutary to apply this core, support and diversionary classification to the use of our own time. In the ABCM context the core, support and diversionary classification is applied to the activity analysis. One aim is obviously to try to eliminate as far as possible the diversionary activities. Again, experience has shown that it is usually impossible to eliminate all such diversionary activities, but the time and cost associated with such activities can generally be greatly reduced.

Very often the activity analysis helps to reduce diversionary activities because ABCM involves examining activities across various departments. For example, the problem for the above travelling salesperson may be the late delivery of the previous order to the customer. This problem may be traced back through the production department to the purchasing department and to suppliers who did not deliver the raw materials on the dates promised. Bellis-Jones claims that following a core, support and diversionary classification of activities and the resulting decisions and actions, on average it is possible for an organisation to increase the percentage of time spent on core activities from 35 to over 50 per cent. The core, support and diversionary classification of activities can be a useful cost management technique. Following such an analysis and classification of actual activities (whether by informal questioning, value-added and non-value-added or core, support and diversionary classification), some organisations have also applied this activity-based approach to their budgeting process.

Budgeting

In the traditional budgeting system the weaknesses of taking last year's actual expenditure and adjusting for a projected inflation rate and proposed new initiatives are well recognised. Activity-based budgeting (ABB) is one way of moving away from such a system. The visibility given to overheads by the activity-based approach has already been discussed. This visibility is the basis for ABB. The activity approach highlights not only the resource inputs (costs) but also the outputs in terms of the cost drivers. Usually these cost drivers are expressed in non-financial terms, such as the volume of purchase orders or the level of service provided.

ABB links the proposed resource inputs and the expected outputs for the forthcoming period. For example, if the activity volume is expected to fall (such as fewer purchase orders) then the resource input will also be budgeted to fall. ABB also recognises that some resources will be required for activity-sustaining (non-volume-related) as distinct from activity-variable resources. Activity sustaining might include the costs of managing the activity and of providing a minimum capacity for that overhead activity. In contrast, the activity-variable resources are driven directly by the level of output of that particular activity. Such an analysis of the behaviour of the cost of each activity helps the budget-setting process.

An activity-based approach means that resource inputs must be justified in relation to each activity. For example, if an activity has been identified as non-value added, but it has proved impossible to eliminate this activity in the short term, there would be no question of increasing the resources available for it. Indeed, one objective would be to reduce the resources devoted to such a non-value-added activity. This seems very much like common sense, but organisations which have adopted ABB have found that in previous years the resources devoted to non-value-added activities have usually been increasing rather than decreasing. This process of ABB not only links more directly the planned resource inputs and the expected level of outputs, but also helps to identify in advance any surplus capacity in individual activities. This allows managers to take the necessary corrective action, such as moving resources away from one activity to another activity.

ABB means that the resulting actual versus budget comparison can be more meaningful. One reason is the fact that ABB is based on activities which cross traditional departmental boundaries, rather than the traditional budgetary system based on departments. Another reason is that the actual cost driver volumes provide comparisons with budgeted volumes which can highlight, in non-financial terms, activities with major discrepancies from the budget. Managers frequently find such non-financial comparisons a more meaningful starting-point for investigating the reasons for such discrepancies than the simple financial comparisons of actual and budget. Some organisations have found that investigations of variances in cost driver volumes give a better indication of actions to be taken than their traditional budgeting system. This discussion of ABB has emphasised the importance of activities and cost driver volumes and these are also at the heart of the use of ABCM information. However, it is important to emphasise that many organisations use ABCM information without having ABB.

Use of ABCM information

When you read some of the ABCM literature it is easy to form the impression that ABCM can be equated with cost reduction. However, ABCM is really about cost management, which includes profit improvement and not just cost reduction. The identification of the value-added and core activities may mean increased expenditure on such activities. Existing ABCM case studies and research have revealed a number of uses of ABCM information. One of the most important of these has been the use of activity analysis as a common language within many organisations. Managers in different functional areas understand activities and cost drivers. Previously, managers did not believe the cost information based on traditional overhead absorption bases such as labour hours or machine hours, and did not use such information for cost management purposes. In contrast, these same managers are now using the activity information to simplify or combine activities and are managing the cost drivers.

Managers are using information about cost drivers in a variety of ways. For example, some managers have calculated the practical capacity of each activity, given existing resources (such as the number of purchase orders which can be processed), and therefore have an indication of the spare capacity for each activity, expressed in terms of its cost driver. These managers can then take decisions about managing such spare capacity. Other managers have attempted to reduce the volume of certain cost drivers in order to reduce costs. For example, in some organisations the number of material movements have been reduced with the result not only of a corresponding reduction in costs, but also of a saving in the production cycle time. In many sectors, the time element has become an important competitive advantage. ABCM has a part to play in such time competition.

To date one of the most important uses of ABCM information has been at the design stage of new products and services. Indeed some organisations such as Tektronix have provided designers with cost driver information to encourage them to use existing parts rather than new parts in new products. For example, the overhead cost for a low-volume component might be ten times its material cost, whereas the overhead cost of a high-volume component might be only one-third of its material cost. The aim is to encourage the use of more common parts in different products without adversely affecting the quality of the design of new products. Another example of using ABCM information to influence designers is that of Hewlett-Packard where the cost driver information helped designers to choose between alternative designs. The overhead cost of one alternative was approximately three times that of another. Before ABCM was introduced, the designers had no such detailed information about overheads and had to use the labour hours or machine hours overhead absorption rates. With approximately 80 per cent of all costs being committed before production begins in many manufacturing organisations, it is important that accountants provide relevant information for the design and pre-production stages of the product life-cycle. ABCM information has proved to be particularly useful during the design stage of new products.

However, to date the main uses of ABCM information have been during the production stage. For example, Gietzmann (1991), in his case study of the implementation of an ABC system in an engineering components manufacturer, found that the ABC information highlighted the importance of set-ups and this led to set-up times being reduced by approximately 25 per cent. In some organisations ABCM has also been used in make-or-buy decisions and has led to the sub-contracting of certain activities. In another engineering company the ABCM information on purchasing concentrated managers' attention on problems such as late deliveries, short deliveries and poor-quality raw materials. This information enabled this engineering company to identify twenty problem suppliers and take the necessary corrective action, which varied from changing some suppliers to working with others to overcome the existing problems.

At the other end of the value chain from suppliers are the customers, and ABCM has been increasingly used in relation to marketing activities and customer profitability. Some organisations have found that they did not know which customers caused or 'drove' which costs. Customer-driven costs include delivery, quality, after-sales service, administration, documentation, discounts and sales promotion. By identifying the customer – rather than the product – as the cost object, some organisations have used ABCM to identify for the first time their least profitable and loss-making customers. This has led to actions to try to improve the profitability of such customers. Indeed in some cases the customers have been shown the ABCM information, and prices and contracts have been renegotiated. ABCM and customer profitability have been used in both the manufacturing and service sectors.

To date most of the ABCM case studies and research have concentrated on the manufacturing sector, but an increasing number of service-sector organisations are now using ABCM. For example, financial-sector organisations such as banks and insurance companies have implemented both ABC and ABCM. In the financial sector ABCM has been used particularly to identify non-value-added activities. Education, hospital, retail and transport sectors are other service areas where ABCM has been used successfully. The use of ABCM information in both service and manufacturing organisations has led some of these to adopt activity-based performance measurement systems.

Performance measurement

One of the features of ABCM is that certain key activities are identified. Some organisations have therefore changed their performance measurement system to include or even to concentrate on such activities. Very often the cost drivers are the basis for the performance measures. These cost driver performance measures can be either non-financial or financial but, as with all performance measures, one of the main objectives is to influence behaviour. For example, a non-financial operational performance measure might be the number of engineering changes in a particular period. This could have the effect of reducing the number of such changes. As with all performance measures, activity-based measures must be used with care in order to avoid the dysfunctional effects, such as the performance measure becoming an end in itself rather than a means to an end. One advantage claimed for activity-based performance measures is that the activity-based approach helps to integrate non-financial and financial performance measures. One problem with all non-financial performance measures is their relationship with financial performance measures – particularly those used by groups outside the organisation to assess its performance. If the key activities have been correctly identified, monitoring the non-financial performance measures for such activities should be helpful in improving the overall financial performance of the organisation.

Many organisations which use activity-based performance measures try to monitor not only the efficiency of activities, but also other characteristics such as the time taken to complete activities and the quality of the activity output. For example, in the purchasing activity the performance measures might include not only the daily number of purchase orders, the number of purchase order errors and the cost per purchase order, but also the time taken to complete a purchase order and the number of purchase orders expedited. The quality of the purchasing activity might be measured in terms of service to the 'customer' within the organisation; for example, the time elapsed from the receipt of the purchase requisition to the placing of the purchase order, or the percentage of deliveries early, on schedule or late. It is important to determine the key performance measures and, obviously, not all these purchasing measures would be key for any one organisation. As with all performance measures when the internal or external environments of the organisation change, so the key activities may change and, therefore, the activity-based performance measures may also need to change.

Problems

ABCM, however, is not a panacea. Research by Cobb, Innes and Mitchell (1992) has revealed a number of problems experienced by organisations which have implemented ABCM. The amount of work involved in setting up the system and data collection were the two most common problems. Some organisations have replaced their traditional costing system with an ABC system but others have run the two systems in parallel. However, even where ABC is the only costing system, it is still time-consuming to identify the activities, gather the information about the activity cost pools and determine the most appropriate cost drivers. This process usually involves time-consuming interviews with managers and generally more than one interview with each manager. An ABCM system involves collecting data which have not previously been collected, such as the number of pallet deliveries. Furthermore, experience has shown that although now most organisations begin with fewer than twenty-five activities, the number of activities and cost drivers tends to increase as managers wish to refine the system. In addition, most organisations are constantly changing and this usually means changes for the ABCM system.

As well as these technical problems, there may also be organisational and behavioural consequences which stem from the adoption of ABCM. For example, the selected activity cost pools may not correspond to the formal structure of cost responsibilities within the organisation. Purchasing activity may be found in the purchasing, production, stores, administrative and finance departments and, therefore, clear 'ownership' of the activity and its costs may be problematic. Where the ABCM system is used as a basis for responsibility accounting, some reshaping of the organisation structure may be necessary. ABCM also introduces a whole set of new measurements in the form of cost driver rates. Where these are perceived as performance measures, some attention must be paid to their motivational impact. For example, the rate per set-up may be reduced by increasing the number of set-ups (the rate denominator), although this may raise total costs and cause disruption.

Another problem which is seldom mentioned in the literature, but which happens in practice, is that ABCM can become associated with redundancies. If this happens, it will be much more difficult to determine accurate data about activities, cost pools and cost drivers. However, other ABCM problems such as the lack of staff time, scarce computer resources and other priorities are not specifically activity-based problems but reflect the more general problem of making any changes to the management accounting system.

Conclusions

It is important to remember that ABC and ABCM have really only become popular since the late 1980s. To date only a minority of organisations have adopted ABC or ABCM, although interest still remains high as shown by the number of activity-based courses and publications and also by the number of firms offering activity-based consultancy services. However, it is still too early to know whether the activity-based approach will have long-lasting and fundamental effects on management accounting in the overhead area or whether it will be like many other new management accounting techniques of the past which have become less widely used as time passes.

However, there are some encouraging signs for ABC and, in particular, for the activity-based approach. One such sign is that in many organisations the activity-based approach is not viewed as an accounting technique but as a management tool. In many cases managers have been the driving force behind the implementation of ABCM. Usually the accountant is only one member of the ABCM team and the managerial interviews have been conducted by other managers. Another advantage for the activity-based approach is that managers from different functional backgrounds relate very easily to the language of activities and cost drivers. In the longer term the fact that managers throughout an organisation are using this common language of the activity-based approach may turn out to be one of its main advantages.

In summary the main benefits of ABC and ABCM are different product costings; greater visibility of overheads; emphasis on activities crossing departmental boundaries; improved understanding of overhead cost behaviour by managers; control and reduction of overhead costs by eliminating or reorganising activities; increased resources for core or value-added activities; new performance measures; and a common language across the organisation. Despite the problems and limitations associated with ABC and ABCM, the managers in most organisations that have implemented it are continuing to use it enthusiastically and are finding that its benefits outweigh its costs. It appears that the activity-based approach is worth considering for all organisations where overheads are a significant percentage of total costs.

Bibliography

Bellis-Jones, R. (1992) 'Activity-based cost management', in C. Drury (ed.) *Management Accounting Handbook*, Oxford: Butterworth–Heinemann and CIMA, pp. 100–27. This chapter gives some interesting practical examples of ABCM from the viewpoint of a consultant.

Berliner, C. and J.A. Brimson (1988) *Cost Management for Today's Advanced Manufacturing: The CAM-I conceptual design*, Boston: Harvard Business School Press. Despite being called a conceptual design this book has had a major influence in persuading practitioners to assess activity-based cost management. CAM-I is a non-profit-making organisation which is still at the forefront of activity-based management developments in practice.

Bhimani, A. and D. Pigott (1992) 'Implementing ABC: A case study of organisational and behavioural consequences', *Management Accounting Research*, June, pp. 119–32. This is a British case study written jointly by an academic and practitioner emphasising the organisational and behavioural consequences of ABC.

Brimson, J.A. (1991) *Activity Accounting*, New York: John Wiley and Sons. This book explores some of the practicalities of ABC from the viewpoint of a consultant.

Cobb, I., J. Innes and F. Mitchell (1992) *Activity-Based Costing: Problems in practice*, London: CIMA. This research monograph concentrates on the actual and perceived problems in practice with ABC and ABCM.

Cooper, R. and R.S. Kaplan (1991) *The Design of Cost Management Systems: Text, cases and readings*, Englewood Cliffs, NJ: Prentice Hall. This is a very useful source of both activity-based case studies and readings.

Cooper, R., R.S. Kaplan, L.S. Maisel, E. Morrissey and R.M. Oehm (1992) *Implementing Activity-Based Cost Management: Moving from analysis to action*, Montvale, NJ: Institute of Management Accountants. Already this book has helped to move the emphasis from product costing to cost management in the activity-based approach.

Gietzmann, M. (1991) 'Implementation issues associated with the construction of an ABC system in an engineering components manufacturer', *Management Accounting Research*, September, pp. 189–99. This is a British case study concentrating on the implementation issues of ABC.

Innes, J. and F. Mitchell (1990) *Activity-Based Costing: A review with case studies*, London: CIMA. This research monograph gives a review of the early product costing aspects of ABC and includes the first three published British case studies on ABC.

Journal of Cost Management. This American journal is not very well known at present in Europe but it very often includes the latest theoretical and practical developments in the activity-based area. The best articles have been reprinted in B.J. Brinker (ed.) (1993) *Emerging Practices in Cost Management*, Boston: Warren Gorham & Lamont.

Kaplan, R.S., J.K. Shank, C.T. Horngren, G. Boer, W.L. Ferrara and M.A. Robinson (1990) 'Contribution margin analysis: no longer relevant and strategic cost management: the new paradigm', *Journal of Management Accounting Research*, Fall, pp. 1–32. These are papers and discussions from a 1989 conference which expose some of the different attitudes about the early developments of ABC and ABCM.

Staubus, G. (1990) 'Activity costing: twenty years on', *Management Accounting Research*, December, pp. 249–64. This article provides an historical perspective to the ABC debate.

CHAPTER SEVEN

Transfer Pricing

Mahmoud Ezzamel

♦

Economic Theory and Transfer Pricing

The early work on transfer pricing was based on traditional economic theory which assumed that firms rely on the pricing mechanism to determine the optimal product mix which maximises profits. Three main assumptions are usually invoked in arriving at optimal transfer prices. First, the firm has two divisions: an intermediate division (I) which makes and sells an intermediate product, for example yarn, and a final division (F) which buys the intermediate product and transforms it into another product which is then sold in the outside market, for example lengths of textile. Second, the work technologies of both divisions are independent of each other as are demands for their products. Technological independence means that the operating costs of each division are not affected by the level of operations in the other division. Demand independence implies that additional external sales by either division do not affect the external demand for the products of the other division. Third, divisions have restricted autonomy in running their activities, with the maximisation of overall company profit being the overriding criterion to top management. Given these assumptions, optimal transfer prices can be derived under different market situations ranging from perfect competition, through imperfect competition and discriminating monopoly, to complete absence of external markets.

Perfect outside markets

If the intermediate product can be traded in a perfect external market, then the market price will be the optimal transfer price (see Hirshleifer 1956). In this case the market price is established through the interaction of supply and demand in a free and competitive market. Each division should be permitted maximum autonomy in relation to setting its activity level and as to whether it should transact with other divisions in the company or with external customers and suppliers. Acting as a selfish profit-maximiser, each division would determine its optimal activity level as the one at which its marginal cost (MC) equals its marginal revenue (MR). Quite simply, divisions would behave as if they all constitute one entity whose aim is to maximise global profit. Further, in this setting complete decentralisation leads to economies in information transmission, since knowledge of the market price obviates the need for vertical flow of detailed information. There are no advantages to be gained from vertical integration between divisions given the presumed absence of transactions costs in external trading.

Imperfect outside markets

In reality, markets exhibit various degrees of imperfection. For example, selling a product in external markets usually involves incurring various costs in the form of advertising, transport, credit terms and debt collection. Further, firms may prefer to rely on internal sources of product supply rather than being completely dependent upon more risky external suppliers. Moreover, there may not be a perfect substitute for the internal product in external markets. These, and similar, imperfections provide strong arguments in favour of internal trading between company divisions since this minimises the costs and uncertainties mentioned above.

Suppose, for example, that the external market exhibits only one type of imperfection in the form of transportation cost which has to be incurred by both seller and buyer. In this case the seller receives P_s (the market price *less* transportation cost) and the buyer pays P_b (the market price *plus* transportation cost) such that $P_b > P_s$. The question now is: what is the optimal transfer price? The following numerical example illustrates this problem and derives the optimal transfer price.

International Fabrics Plc produces textiles for a variety of household uses. Its intermediate division I transforms raw cotton into yarn, which can be sold externally or alternatively to the final division F. Division F turns the yarn into finished textile which is sold externally. The current market price for yarn is £550 per 1,000 lb. If either division transacts in the external market, it has to incur transportation cost of £50 per 1,000 lb. The detailed cost and revenue information for a typical week of operations, and the solution, are contained in Table 7.1.

The solution derived in Table 7.1 was first suggested by Gould (1964), who pointed out that the optimal transfer price depends on the precise relationship between P_b, P_s, and $\bar{P}$, where $\bar{P}$ is defined as the point at which MC_1 intersects NMR_F (£400 in the example). The curve NMR_F is the net marginal revenue of the final division (i.e. its marginal revenue less its marginal cost except the price for the intermediate product). The relationship between these terms can be one of: $P_b > P_s > \bar{P}; \bar{P} > P_b > P_s$ and $P_b > \bar{P} > P_s$.

The first relationship corresponds to the one represented by the example. The last case, which is discussed later, is similar to the situation where there is no external market for the intermediate product.

When $P_b > P_s > \bar{P}$, setting the transfer price $P^* = P_s$ maximises company profits, as is shown in Figure 7.1. In that figure the *effective* marginal cost curve for the firm is ABC, since beyond point B it would be cheaper for the firm to buy externally rather than make further quantities of the intermediate product. The *effective* net marginal revenue curve is JKL, since beyond point K it would be more profitable for the firm to sell further units of the intermediate product in the external market rather than to division F. The intersection of ABC and JKL determines $P^* = P_s$, and the optimal level of activity for division I at OQ_I. At $P^* = P_s$, division F handles the quantity OQ_F. Compared with outside trading, internal trading increases the profit of division F and of the overall company by the amount $P_s P_b SK$. In the case of International Fabrics Plc, this is reflected in an increased level of activity for the final division F from 2,000 lb to 3,000 lb. The quantity $OQ_I - OQ_F$ should be sold on the outside market at P_s. It is straightforward to establish that when $\bar{P} > P_b > P_s$, the transfer price should be set equal to the purchasing price ($P^* = P_b$).

Several important observations emerge from this analysis. First, once some form of intermediate market imperfection is assumed, the benefits to the parent company of

Table 7.1 International Fabrics Plc: revenue and cost data: slightly imperfect intermediate market

Quantity (lb)	Intermediate total cost (£)	Division I marginal cost (£)	Final division F[a] Net total revenue (£)	Net marginal revenue (£)
1,000	100	100	700	700
2,000	300	200	1,300	600
3,000	600	300	1,800	500
4,000	1,000	400	2,200	400
5,000	1,500	500	2,500	300
6,000	2,100	600	2,700	200
7,000	2,800	700	2,800	100

[a] This is a total revenue excluding the separable costs of the final division.

Solution: Given a market price of £550 and transportation cost of £50 per 1,000 lb, $P_b = £600$ and $P_s = £500$. The marginal cost of division I and the net marginal revenue of division F are listed above. International Fabrics should produce internally as long as the marginal cost of the intermediate division is below £600 per 1,000 lb; above this level it will be cheaper to buy externally. Similarly, the company should sell yarn internally as long as the net marginal revenue of the final division is greater than £500 per 1,000 lb; below that level it is more profitable to sell externally.

The optimal solution is determined by the intersection of the effective MC_I curve (that is the curve which takes into account the opportunities of purchasing externally when this is cheaper than producing internally) and the effective NMR_F curve (that is the curve which takes into account the opportunities of selling externally when this is more profitable than selling internally). This occurs at Q = 5,000 lb where MC_I = effective NMR_F = £500. This is the optimal transfer price. The intermediate division I should produce 5,000 lb of yarn; sell 3,000 lb to the final division F at £500 per 1,000 lb, and sell the remaining 2,000 lb in the external market at the same price.

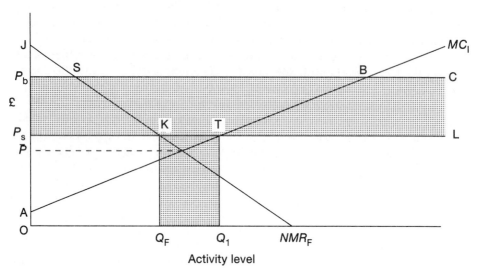

Figure 7.1 The optimal transfer price in a slightly imperfect market.

internal trading become obvious (an increased profit by the amount P_sP_bSK in Figure 7.1). Second, if the overall goal of the parent company is profit maximisation, divisions can no longer have complete autonomy in making their operating decisions. When $P_b > P_s > \bar{P}$, enforcement rules must be designed and applied by top management to ensure that division I sells the quantity OQ_F to division F at $P^* = P_s$. If division I exercises its monopolistic power over division F and charges $P^* = P_s$, the company will operate below its optimal activity level. A similar argument applies to division F when $\bar{p} > P_b > P_s$. Hence, in this analysis, some divisional discretion is sacrificed in favour of aiming to attain overall company optimality. Third, there are incentives for only one division to trade internally – only one division reaps all the benefits of internal trading. Either the selling price, P_s, or the buying price, P_b, is taken as the optimal price. For example, in the case of International Fabrics Plc it is the final division F which benefits from internal trading, by expanding its activity level by 1,000 lb. Fourth, divisional profit cannot be used to assess rationally divisional viability. For example, in Figure 7.1 if the intermediate division I is to be discontinued, the loss to the company as a whole will be more than apparent divisional profit (AP_s T less divisional fixed costs) by the amount P_sP_bSK.

Discriminating monopoly markets

The preceding situation involved only minor imperfections in outside markets. Frequently, the extent of market imperfections is much greater, thereby making internal trading even more advantageous. An example of this is the situation where the intermediate division I has monopolistic power sufficient to allow it to sell the intermediate product internally at a price lower than the one it receives from its external sales. Hirshleifer (1956) has shown that in this case the optimal transfer price, P^*, should be set equal to the marginal cost of the intermediate division (MC_I) at the output level which maximises company profit ($P^* = MC_I$). This is illustrated in Figure 7.2.

In Figure 7.2 the output OQ_1 of the intermediate division I is established by the intersection of MC_I and mr_t ($MR_I + NMR_F$) at point H, giving a price $P^* = OA$. The quantity to be sold to the final division F is OQ_2, where $P^* = NMR_F$. The quantity OQ_3 is to be sold in the outside market at $OB > P^*$. The above solution may be derived by the head office assuming that it has knowledge of the divisional demand and supply functions. Alternatively, the same solution can be derived by the divisions if either provides the other with its demand or supply function. Thus, if division F were to determine the optimal solution, it would need to obtain details of d (the demand curve facing the intermediate division I), MR_I and MC_I from division I. If instead division I were to derive the optimal solution, it would need to obtain information about NMR_F. In Figure 7.2 it is assumed that division I plays the dominant role in determining the transfer price after securing the demand function of division F, NMR_F. However, top management would need to impose enforcement rules in order to ensure that division I does not exercise its monopolistic power and charge division F a higher transfer price, which would be against overall company interest.

Once more, most of the limitations associated with imperfect competition are

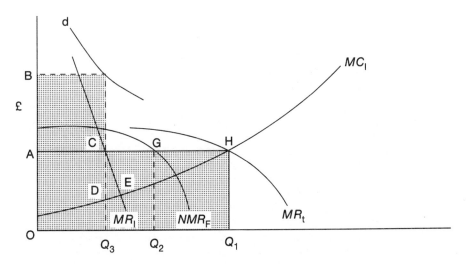

Figure 7.2 The optimal transfer price for a discriminating monopolist.

present here. First, apparent divisional profit does not reflect 'real' divisional contribution to company profit. Second, interference by central management greatly restricts divisional autonomy. Third, because of information asymmetry, even with central management interference, there is no guarantee that divisional managers will not manipulate cost and revenue functions to their advantage.

To illustrate this case refer back to International Fabrics Plc. Assume now that the intermediate division I can sell the yarn in an imperfect market where it faces a downward-sloping demand curve. Assume that the marginal revenue associated with that demand curve is as depicted in Table 7.2. As is shown in that table, the optimal solution for International Fabrics Plc is for the intermediate division I to

Table 7.2 International Fabrics Plc: revenue and cost data: highly imperfect market

Quantity (lb)	MC_I (£)	MR_I(£)	NMR_F (£)
1,000	100	950	700
2,000	200	850	600
3,000	300	750	500
4,000	400	650	400
5,000	500	550	300
6,000	600	450	200
7,000	700	350	100

Solution:
The general rule is to sell each batch in the most profitable market as long as the marginal revenue is higher than the marginal cost of production. This means that we have to compare the marginal cost of each batch with the marginal revenue in each market. Hence:

	MR_I	NMR_F
The first 1,000 lb go externally;	950 >	700
The next 1,000 lb go externally;	850 >	700
The next 1,000 lb go externally;	750 >	700
The next 1,000 lb go internally;	650 <	700
The next 1,000 lb go externally;	650 >	600
The next 1,000 lb go internally;	550 <	600

The intermediate division I should produce 6,000 lb, sell 4,000 lb externally at a price derived from the downward-sloping demand curve facing it in the external market, and sell the remaining 2,000 lb to the final division F at £600 per 1,000 lb (this is the level of MC_I at 6,000 lb of yarn). Production should stop at 6,000 lb because the marginal cost of the next 1,000 lb (£700) exceeds the net marginal revenue of the final division at 3,000 lb (£500), and the marginal revenue in the external market at 5,000 lb (£550).

produce 6,000 lb of yarn, to sell 4,000 lb in the external intermediate market and 2,000 lb to the final division F. The transfer price should be set equal to £600 for every 1,000 lb (this is the level of MC_I at which the optimal activity level for the whole company, 6,000 lb, is reached). The price charged by the intermediate division I to external buyers would be much higher, as determined by the demand curve facing that division.

The absence of outside intermediate markets

The same general rule of pricing at marginal cost extends to the case where the intermediate commodity has no outside market. If we assume that the company faces a competitive market for the final product, the best solution for the firm is to produce that level of output at which the company's overall marginal cost equals the price in the final market. Again, this optimal solution can be achieved either by top management or by individual divisions subject to central supervision. In the earlier case of an imperfect intermediate market, the intermediate division I played the dominant role in arriving at the optimal solution. To demonstrate that either division can play this role, division F is given the task of deriving the solution in the present case which is achieved as follows (Figure 7.3).

1. Division F obtains from division I its supply schedule showing how much it would produce at any transfer price P^* for the intermediate commodity. This should be the same as MC_I, if division I is to behave rationally and set its output level where $MC_I = P^*$.
2. Division F derives a curve showing the difference between the final market price and the transfer price for any level of output, $P - P^*$. Division F sets its output level where $MC_F = P - P^*$ at Q_1, establishes the transfer price $P^* = OR$, and then passes it on to division I.
3. Division I, given P^*, produces Q_1, since this is where $MC_I = P^*$. The profit of division I would be equal to the area DSR and that of division F would be equal to the area ABC. Top management, however, should ensure that division F does not sub-optimise to increase its profit at the expense of the company. If division F is left free, it can derive a 'quasi-marginal' revenue curve marginal to $P - P^*$, the one denoted mr, and set its output at Q_2 with the lower transfer price OM. At a joint output level of Q_2, the profit of division F will be greater than before, but overall company profit would be less at Q_2 than at Q_1.

Evaluation

Despite its valuable contribution towards a better understanding of some of the issues related to transfer pricing, the traditional economic theory model has several limitations.

First, it overemphasises the attainment of corporate optimality at the expense of maintaining divisional autonomy, and this is likely to result in adverse behavioural implications. The very idea of divisionalisation is frequently interpreted to imply significant delegation of decision-making power, and hence divisional managers are likely to feel alienated if top management imposes great constraints on the manner in which they run their divisions. The model also assumes that central management can induce divisional managers to act in a manner consistent with its interests, but this may not occur for the following reasons:

1. Top management is unlikely to know divisional cost and revenue functions and hence may not know which action is optimal.

2. Divisional managers may engage in sub-optimal strategies, for example changing the resource allocation pattern to their advantage, which are difficult to detect by central management.

3. Perceptions of risk by divisional managers and their attitudes towards risk may induce them to operate at levels different from those deemed optimal by top management. For example, they may extend their product range in order to smooth out divisional periodic profits and hence consolidate their positions as managers,

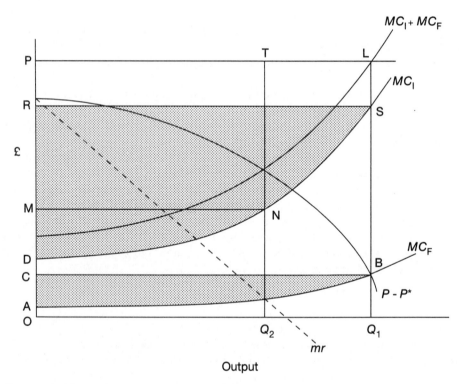

Figure 7.3 The optimal transfer price when there is no outside market.

even though the new product lines may be less appropriate from the company's point of view.

Second, marginal cost-based transfer prices reasonably reflect opportunity cost only when the market for the intermediate product is highly competitive, or if there exists one demanding division requiring the product. If there is more than one demanding division, the opportunity cost will be the highest of the marginal cost and the revenue forgone by diverting resources from alternative uses (see Dopuch and Drake, 1964). Further, accountants use variable cost (which is assumed constant per unit within the relevant range of output) as a proxy for marginal cost. To set the transfer price equal to variable cost would leave the intermediate division with a loss equal to its total fixed costs, and this implies that it cannot operate as a genuine profit centre. Finally, marginal cost pricing could result in obscuring true divisional profitability by passing on cost efficiencies/inefficiencies across divisions.

Third, the traditional model assumes that company divisions are independent of each other with regard to both production technology and demand. However, the prevalence of technological and demand interdependence in practice restricts the applicability of the model significantly.

Mathematical Programming Models

It has been suggested that some of the above limitations can be reduced if mathematical programming models are used to determine transfer prices. One such model is linear programming(LP), the optimal solution of which yields a set of prices known as 'shadow prices'. A shadow price is the opportunity cost of a unit of a scarce resource in terms of the amount of contribution that will be added to company profits if one more unit of that resource becomes available. Typically, the transfer price of a resource, P^*_i is set as

$$P^*_i = VC_i + W_i \tag{7.1}$$

where VC_i is the variable cost of resource (i), and W_i is the shadow price of resource (i). In order to investigate the implications of such a technique in the context of transfer pricing, let us refer back to International Fabrics Plc.

Let us assume now that International Fabrics Plc consists of three intermediate divisions, I_1, I_2 and I_3, and two final divisions, F_1 and F_2. Suppose also that:

I_1 has a capacity of 2,000 units of product X_1, the variable cost per unit is £5
I_1 has a capacity of 3,000 units of product X_2, the variable cost per unit is £3
I_3 has a capacity of 6,000 units of product X_3, the variable cost per unit is £3

Assume that each of the two final divisions produces one final product, Y_1 and Y_2 respectively, as in Table 7.3. The associated LP model would then be as follows:

Table 7.3   International Fabrics Plc: revenue and cost details:

	Selling price (£)	Variable cost (£)	X_1 (unit)	X_2 (unit)	X_3 (unit)	Net contribution margin (£)
		Input required of intermediates				
Y_1	65	9	4	3	4	15
Y_2	60	16	2	4	4	10

$$\text{maximise } Z = 15Y_1 + 10Y_2 \qquad \text{(total contribution)}$$

subject to
$$4Y_1 + 2Y_2 \le 2{,}000 \text{ (capacity of } I_1, X_1)$$
$$3Y_1 + 4Y_2 \le 3{,}000 \text{ (capacity of } I_2, X_2)$$
$$4Y_1 + 4Y_2 \le 6{,}000 \text{ (capacity of } I_3, X_3)$$
$$4Y_1 \text{ and } Y_2 \ge 0$$

The optimal solution for the firm is: $Z = £9{,}000$, $Y_1 = 200$ units, and $Y_2 = 600$ units. At this level of activity, all the productive capacities of intermediate divisions I_1 and I_2 are fully utilised, but intermediate division I_3 has a spare capacity equivalent to 2,800 units of product X_3. The shadow prices associated with the capacities of the intermediate divisions are $W_1 = £3$, $W_2 = £1$ and $W_3 = 0$.

Using equation 7.1, the transfer prices for X_1, X_2 and X_3 are:

	X_1 £	X_2 £	X_3 £
VC_i	5	3	3
W_i	3	1	0
	8	4	3

The net contributions of divisions F_1 and F_2 are shown in Table 7.4

Table 7.4   Net contribution of divisions F_1 and F_2.

	Division F_1		Division F_2	
Selling price	£65		£60	
Less cost of intermediate input	£		£	
	X_1 4 × £8 = 32		2 × £8 = 16	
	X_2 3 × £4 = 12		4 × £4 = 16	
	X_3 4 × £3 = 12		4 × £3 = 12	
Total cost of transfers	56		44	
+variable cost of final divisions	9		16	
Total variable cost	— £65		— £60	
Net contribution	—		—	

Linear programming thus permits the determination of the mix of products which is consistent with the optimal allocation of resources, and generates good proxies for opportunity cost in the form of shadow prices. However, in the context of transfer pricing this model has several limitations.

First, it assumes that cost and revenue functions are linear whereas in reality they tend to be non-linear.

Second, shadow prices are accurate measures of opportunity cost only if (a) the product mix does not change and (b) resources are utilised efficiently. These conditions do not always hold in practice. Changes in either of these conditions can result in changes in shadow prices and can thus render previously derived shadow prices inappropriate for transfer pricing. Moreover, shadow prices can be helpful to divisional managers only in so far as they guide them towards the selection of the optimal product *combination*, but not in deciding on the optimal *level* of activity. Given the assumptions of constant variable cost (marginal cost) and contribution margin (marginal revenue) per unit, the marginal cost curve and the marginal revenue curve will not intersect and hence divisional managers will be indifferent to production levels at the optimal transfer prices. (The reader should check the effect on the net contributions of Y_1 and Y_2 of the transfer prices just calculated.) Hence other mechanisms will have to be employed in order to motivate divisional managers to pursue optimal production policies.

Third, if the resources used in producing the intermediate product are non-binding (non-scarce) constraints in the optimal solution, the shadow price will be zero and the transfer price will equal the variable cost per unit. Hence, the division cannot operate as a profit centre. An example of this is the intermediate division I_3 of International Fabrics Plc, which in the optimal solution has a spare capacity of 2,800 units of X_3. Because the resources of this division are not scarce, the shadow price per unit is zero and the transfer price is set at £3, which is the variable cost per unit. Further, shadow prices may lead to sub-optimal decisions in the long term. For example, divisional managers may avoid acquiring excess plant capacity for future expansion since this would reduce their shadow prices and, hence, their transfer prices if plant capacity becomes non-binding in the short term.

Fourth, divisional autonomy is restricted under linear programming since the optimal solution for the company is usually derived by central management. Moreover, given this centralised structure, potential economies in processing and transmitting information usually associated with decentralised structures will be forgone.

To overcome some of these limitations the use of the decomposition model has been suggested (see Baumol and Fabian, 1964). This model, it has been argued, offers greater decision-making autonomy to divisional managers without adversely affecting the overall interests of the company. According to the decomposition model, the total programme is divided into the headquarters plan and the divisional plans/ programmes. The headquarters and the divisional managers will each solve their own programme independently but with relevant information being communicated in both directions.

To illustrate this idea, refer back to International Fabrics Plc. Assume now that in addition to the capacity constraints with which each of the intermediate divisions operates, division F_1 has available a maximum of 1,000 machine hours and division F_2 has a maximum of 1,800 man hours. Each unit of Y_1 requires 5 machine hours whereas each unit of Y_2 requires 3 man hours. The total programme for International Fabrics Plc will be:

$$\text{maximise } Z = 15Y_1 + 10Y_2$$

subject to	$4Y_1 + 2Y_2 \leq 2{,}000$ (capacity of I_1)	(7.2)
	$3Y_1 + 4Y_2 \leq 3{,}000$ (capacity of I_2)	(7.3)
	$4Y_1 + 4Y_2 \leq 6{,}000$ (capacity of I_3)	(7.4)
	$5Y_1 \leq 1{,}000$ (capacity of F_1)	(7.5)
	$3Y_2 \leq 1{,}800$ (capacity of F_2)	(7.6)
	all $X_i, Y_i \geq 0$	

The headquarters plan consists of the objective function plus constraints 7.2, 7.3 and 7.4; it is assumed to be unconcerned with the constraints 7.5 and 7.6 of the final divisions. Expressions 7.2, 7.3 and 7.4 represent the constraint sets of the intermediate divisions which are demanded by both final divisions. As such, they represent common corporate resources. The programme of each of the final divisions consists of its objective function which can be directly derived from the corporate objective function (e.g. maximise $15Y_1$ – the contribution from Y_1 for division F_1) and its own constraints, equation 7.5 for division F_1 and equation 7.6 for division F_2. Neither of the final divisions need concern itself with the corporate constraints represented by the capacities of the intermediate divisions. The mechanism of the decomposition algorithm operates as follows:

1. Given that the optimal transfer prices for the relevant commodities are not initially known, the headquarters announces a set of provisional transfer prices as a starting point.
2. Each division optimises its contribution subject to the prices announced and its own resource constraints, and submits the solution to the headquarters.
3. The headquarters compares divisional demands for each commodity resulting from step 2 with the supply of that commodity. Most likely, demand will not exactly match supply. The headquarters would then announce a revised set of transfer prices in an attempt to match supply with demand, by increasing the prices if demand was greater than supply or decreasing the prices if demand was below supply. These new prices are then communicated to divisions.
4. Steps 2 and 3 are repeated until the headquarters reaches an optimal solution, where supply and demand are exactly matched. Divisions are then informed of the optimal transfer prices, which they subsequently use to determine their activity levels.

To summarise, the decomposition model derives optimal values for scarce resources by treating the organisation as an internal market. It determines transfer prices for multi-product, multidivisional firms, and hence it is more realistic than the traditional economic theory model which usually deals with a two-division firm with only one intermediate product. It can also model explicitly divisional interdependencies, for example demand interdependence, in the constraint set of the relevant divisions. Finally, compared with the LP approach it attains significant economies in the cost of information transmission through division of information. Each division solves a problem which contains only its own technological coefficients and imputed prices, while the central management solves a problem which contains only the overall linking information, that is the objective function of corporate profits, corporate as opposed to divisional resource constraints and the divisional production levels.

Yet the decomposition model has some important limitations. First, divisional autonomy is restricted since final output decisions regarding both quantity and product mix are made by the central management rather than by divisional managers. Thus, even though divisional managers deal with their own parts of the plan, it is top management who decides when an optimal solution is reached and instructs divisional managers accordingly to accept the transfer prices determined. As with the traditional economic theory and LP models, attaining corporate optimality is the overriding priority even if that results in significant reductions in the levels of divisional autonomy. Second, as is the case with the previous models, there is no guarantee that the final solution will be optimal at corporate level because divisional managers have a vested interest in manipulating the data which they supply to their own advantage. This criticism is rooted in the fundamental notion that prices alone are not sufficient to ensure the making of optimal decentralised decisions, since a decision which is optimal for the company as a whole can be sub-optimal, and hence undesirable, at divisional level. Although several incentive schemes have been developed in order to induce truthful supply of information by divisional managers, such as the Groves (1973) scheme, they have had limited success in practice because they are based on many restrictive assumptions.

Organisational-based Transfer Pricing

Transfer pricing, differentiation and integration

The analysis of transfer pricing presented thus far has two main limitations: it oversimplifies economic reality and it ignores behavioural issues. Thus, in order to facilitate the analysis, most models abstract away from situations of complex interdependencies between divisions and reduce the transfer pricing problem to simply a microeconomic model or a mathematical programming exercise. This emphasis produces models of limited value. Moreover, in seeking to make decisions which are optimal at corporate level, the models allow for only limited measures of autonomy for divisional managers. The models have not explicitly linked transfer pricing to the organisational and behavioural contexts of the firm such as diversification strategy, organisation structure and intra-firm transactions (Spicer, 1988).

Explicit consideration of these contexts is needed for a more informed knowledge of transfer pricing techniques and implications. The transfer pricing problem is as much a behavioural and organisational issue as it is a purely economic issue.

One immediate organisational issue in transfer pricing systems is the extent to which they can contribute to the attainment of the requisite differentiation and integration of company divisions. *Differentiation* can be defined as the segmentation of the company into specialised sub-units and the differences in the behaviour of organisational members caused by this segmentation. *Integration* refers to the quality and extent of collaboration between sub-units in response to the extent of co-ordination and unity of effort imposed upon them by their environments.

The transfer pricing mechanism enhances differentiation in so far as it helps separate and illuminate responsibility for different stages of production. Further-more, if the transfer pricing mechanism is routine, as is the case when it is based on a well-defined formula such as cost-plus, it helps to achieve the required integration in situations of low to moderate complexity. In these situations, standard operating rules and procedures are relied upon frequently. Moreover, when designing a management accounting system, the requisite degree of differentiation should be considered carefully. Thus, if differentiation necessitates the segmentation of the organisation in a manner that is different from the one consistent with the accounting system, the segmentation based on differentiation should prevail. For example, it may be convenient from a reporting point of view to separate a number of highly dependent functions into divisions. Such temptation should be avoided because it is opposed to the notion of integration suggested above. In summary, the accounting system should not impose artificial profit centres on the organisational structure (Watson and Baumler, 1975).

Transfer pricing can thus be considered as an important mechanism for achieving integration and resolving conflict in organisations. In this respect, negotiated transfer prices offer a promising means for achieving effective integration by helping to resolve inter-divisional conflicts. Recent research based on simulation suggests that negotiations can be a particularly effective transfer pricing method if linked sensibly to the company's incentive system (Chalos and Haka, 1990; Ravenscroft, Haka and Chalos, 1993).

It is worth noting, however, that in the absence of a relevant outside market, the transfer price is likely to reflect the divisional manager's ability to negotiate rather than his ability to control economic variables. Moreover, negotiations between divisional managers may degenerate into personal conflicts, although the potential for this can be reduced for the following reasons. First, although organisational members could have different perceptions and working styles they may have many common attributes by virtue of being members of the same organisation, and hence agreement among them can frequently be attained. Second, the use of skilful mediators would help in maintaining the continuity of negotiations. Third, guidelines can be provided for conducting negotiations. Empirical evidence, however, indicates that in several cases agreement between negotiators is not automatically secured without central directives.

Bailey and Boe (1976) combined some of the behavioural analysis discussed above with mathematical modelling and developed a behaviourally orientated transfer pricing model. The model has the following characteristics: (a) it is dependent upon the organisational structure of the firm; (b) it uses multiple goals; and (c) divisional managers are not expected to subscribe to organisational goals. The model assumes that the firm's organisational structure consists of Corporate Management (CM), Division Management (DM) and Operating Management (OM). While remaining deterministic, the model specifically allows for the possible existence of alternative production characteristics at the operating level. The optimal solution to the problem is guided by derived shadow prices and is organisationally dependent; it is a satisficing rather than a global solution.

The model explicitly accounts for pooled, sequential and reciprocal inter-dependencies. *Pooled* interdependence means that two or more tasks can be performed independently of one another. *Sequential* interdependence refers to situations where tasks have to be performed according to strict ordering, say task 1 before task 2, task 2 before task 3 and so on. *Reciprocal* interdependence occurs when a constant input–output interrelationship has to be observed among several tasks, so that individuals involved in these tasks co-ordinate their efforts through frequent interactions.

In the Bailey and Boe model, pooled interdependence is represented at any of the three levels, CM, DM and OM. Sequential interdependence is represented along the lines: CM → DM → OM; this establishes the order of the tasks associated with the three organisational levels. This means that each higher organisational level is responsible for integrating the activities of lower sub-units. Direct contact between sub-units not sequentially linked is not permitted. Reciprocal interdependence is reflected in the formulations at the next-higher organisational level. Thus, if OM_1 and OM_2 were reciprocally dependent, this would be reflected in the formulations of the relevant DM (the one to which OM_1 and OM_2 belong). The model also allows for the existence of gaming, given the possibility that multiple and conflicting goals exist at each organisational level. Gaming is also likely to be problematic in the case of reciprocal interdependence, particularly when it is not uniquely known to the higher management level.

The Bailey and Boe model offers a good illustration of how some important organisational concepts can be combined with formal modelling to generate a plausible transfer pricing scheme. However, the model has many of the limitations associated with mathematical programming techniques described earlier.

Linking the transfer pricing process to organisation structure

A number of researchers, for example Swieringa and Waterhouse (1982) and Eccles (1983; 1985), have argued that the objectives of any transfer pricing system are strongly linked to the firm's organisation structure. For example, firms with low product diversification have higher levels of goods transfers between divisions compared with firms with high product diversification (Vancil, 1979), presumably because of the high levels of interdependence between divisions in firms with low diversification. Also, the firm's philosophy towards decentralisation impacts on the way its activities/products are assigned to individual divisions, thereby influencing the degree of divisional interdependence. Hence, intra-company transfers are likely to be determined by firm diversification strategy and organisation design.

Building on the work of Watson and Baumler (1975) on the behavioural context of transfer pricing and of Williamson (1975) on the economics of internal organisation, Spicer (1988) developed a theoretical framework that links transfer pricing to organisation structure. Spicer generated a number of hypotheses which focus on the transfer pricing process in organisations rather than on methods of determining transfer prices *per se*. The first of Spicer's hypotheses reaffirms the statement made above; namely that transfers of intermediate products within a firm are related to that firm's diversification strategy, its product design and its organisation structure for the reasons mentioned earlier. Spicer goes on to identify three factors which, he contends, have a strong impact on the nature of the transfer pricing process in an organisation. The first factor is the level of investment specifically earmarked for a particular transaction. The second factor is the frequency with which a particular transaction occurs and its volume. The third factor is the level of uncertainty or complexity associated with a particular intra-company transaction. When the level of each of these three factors is high, Spicer argues, a firm is likely to:

1. Have a strong incentive to control make-or-buy decisions centrally since this facilitates close co-ordination of activities and speedy response to emerging contingencies.

2. Develop well-specified procedures for arbitration to reduce or resolve the conflict that occurs between divisional managers involved in internal transfers of products. Such arbitration procedures are necessary in order to safeguard the interests of the parent company by promoting co-operation and adaptation between divisions.

3. Reduce emphasis on exclusive reliance upon profitability in assessing and rewarding the performance of divisional managers in favour of broader measures and incentives that promote co-operation and adaptation between divisional managers. Again, this is important for safeguarding overall company interest because excessive reliance on profitability can place divisional managers in competitive and adversarial positions that could endanger corporate survival.

Spicer then goes on to link the suitability of particular methods of transfer pricing to specific product and transaction characteristics. Thus, market-based transfer prices are most suited to situations where the intermediate product is of a standard type, which at the most requires minimal adjustment to suit customer needs. At the other extreme, transfer prices based on manufacturing costs are appropriate when the product is highly specialised and customised, since it would be difficult – perhaps even impossible – to find market prices of comparable products. In the intermediate situation where the product is of a moderate level of customisation (i.e. between the highly standardised and the highly customised) manufacturing cost of production will play an important role in the negotiations that take place between divisional managers in order to arrive at a transfer price.

Spicer's analysis provides an interesting set of theoretical hypotheses that explicitly focuses on the transfer pricing process and links that process explicitly to organisation structure and to the characteristics of the intermediate products and the transactions of concern. It has to be remembered, however, that as yet these hypotheses lack empirical validation. Future empirical research may therefore support or refine these hypotheses further.

Organisational Interpretations of Transfer Pricing

The above discussion indicates, to some extent, that underlying any transfer pricing system developed is a theory of the organisation. This particular notion has been elaborated by Swieringa and Waterhouse (1982). They argue that, in relation to issues like transfer pricing, different models of the organisation emphasise different events, lead to different definitions of the problem, raise different diagnostic questions and provide different answers to the questions. To illustrate their argument, they contrast five models of the organisation: (a) the traditional model (used predominantly in the literature on transfer pricing), (b) the Cyert and March behavioural model, (c) the Cohen and March garbage-can model, (d) the Weick organising model and (e) the markets and hierarchies model. They compare these models through the use of four dimensions, or what they call 'paradoxes': goals versus action-determinants, process versus outputs, adaptability versus stability, and simplicity versus complexity.

Goals versus action-determinants

The traditional model of the organisation is premised on the notion of well-defined, predetermined organisational goals. Goals are assumed to precede actions. The analysis typically focuses on identifying actions which are consistent with predetermined goals. Thus, from this perspective actions relating to transfer pricing are analysed in terms of their contributions to well-specified organisational goals. Optimal actions are assumed to be consistent with organisational goals. Whenever possible, central management interferes and modifies actions which threaten the supremacy of such goals.

The remaining four models of the organisation do not view goals and actions as following a specific order. Their main focus is on understanding factors that determine outcome. The Cyert and March behavioural theory views goals as fluid, being influenced by the nature of bargaining that takes place between organisational members, the composition of the coalition and the definition of organisational problems. Goals are viewed as emerging through experience. In this model, activities related to transfer pricing can be seen as reflecting long-term bargaining between divisional managers with the aim of arriving at an acceptable pricing rule. Such a rule can then be used to negotiate the internal environment in which managers operate and to contribute to the avoidance/reduction of uncertainty.

In the garbage-can model, goals are decoupled from actions: actions result from a context-dependent set of problems, solutions, participants and choice opportunities. Outcomes are not likely to appear closely related to goals. Choices are made when the combination of these elements makes action possible. In this context, the transfer pricing situation is viewed as a choice opportunity which can lead to specific actions. The problems brought to this choice opportunity could include, for example, the inability of divisions to exploit their external markets and the manoeuvring by divisions to exploit each other by attempting to arrive at favourable transfer prices. The solutions for these problems can include, for example, divisional bids and dual pricing schemes.

According to Weick's organising model, past histories are used to endow actions with plausibility and legitimacy. Actions are related to the reduction of uncertainty rather than to pre-specified goals. Thus the choice of a specific transfer pricing system can be seen as a means of explaining, or legitimising, past actions and making them appear consistent with highly valued organisational goals. For example, the use of negotiated transfer prices can be legitimised in terms of freedom of action and liberal managerial style. In contrast, transfer prices imposed by top management can be legitimised in the name of integration and subordination of individual interests to group interests.

Markets and hierarchies rely on the mechanisms of internal organisation and the norms of socialisation to curb the tendency towards opportunism in situations of small-numbers bargaining and asymmetric information. The argument that there exist various economies in mediating transactions does not have to be based on the existence of well-specified goals. This theory focuses on using transfer pricing mechanisms to settle disputes, to act as incentives which foster co-operative internal trading, and to economise and regulate the flow of information. Hence, the transfer pricing system is viewed as a means of minimising the costs of trading intra-company products.

Process versus outputs

The traditional model focuses on the development of transfer pricing systems and procedures which motivate divisional managers to act in a manner consistent with the interest of the company as a whole. Divisional interests are assumed to be subordinated to company interests. The remaining four models focus on the process of determining transfer prices, and related rules and procedures. The Cyert and March behavioural model views this process as an episode of ongoing, long-term bargaining between divisional managers. The garbage-can model treats it as a choice opportunity into which problems and solutions are dumped by divisional managers and the headquarters. Weick's organising model views this process in terms of enactment and legitimation of past actions. According to the markets and hierarchies theory, the process is viewed in terms of mediating transactions through markets or hierarchies and curbing tendencies towards opportunistic behaviour by divisional managers. These latter models then emphasise the process through which transfer prices are determined, rather than the prices *per se*.

The analysis of Swieringa and Waterhouse (1982) suggests that, by emphasising transfer pricing processes, shared beliefs and co-operative behaviour are promoted and thus different expectations held by various divisional managers can converge. Shared understandings of situations and agreements on future actions can be attained by exchanging information and fostering interactions between managers.

Adaptability versus stability

Viewing transfer pricing as a process through which structure and control evolve, this process can be subject to pressures for organisational adaptation and learning which may conflict with pressures for organisational stability and predictability. All four non-traditional models (the behavioural, the garbage-can, the organising and the markets and hierarchies) emphasise organisational learning and adaptation to cope with information asymmetry and uncertainty. They also show awareness of the presence of stabilising elements in organisations as reflected in programmed activities, rules, standard procedures and incremental changes in behaviour.

Swieringa and Waterhouse suggest that transfer pricing can contribute to both organisational stability and change. Thus, the transfer pricing system can act as a stabilising force if the pricing rules become part of the organisation's enacted reality. Such rules can also help to stabilise the organisational coalition by determining the basis for the distribution of rewards and by legitimising authority. To contribute to organisational learning and adaptation, transfer pricing rules can be coded with expiry dates. This is likely to introduce greater uncertainty and to stimulate search behaviour for new transfer pricing rules, and to encourage experimenting with them.

Simplicity versus complexity

Under the traditional model, the transfer pricing problem is greatly simplified because that model is based on the assumptions of economic rationality, existence of well-defined goals and antecedence of goals to actions. This also permits the abstraction of the transfer pricing process from its organisational context. Swieringa and Waterhouse note that such a situation requires little information. The locus of emphasis is simply on evaluating the degree of consistency of transfer pricing methods and procedures with the predetermined goals of the organisation.

The remaining models offer more complex views, in which the dimensions and the process of the transfer pricing choice situation are intertwined with many dynamic organisational features, so that it is not sensible to abstract them from their organisational context. For example, in the garbage-can model transfer prices are the outcome of context-dependent problems, solutions, participants and choice opportunities. Thus the nature of the problems facing internal trading influences transfer prices – and so also do the personalities of divisional and top managers involved in the transfer pricing process.

The insightful analysis of Swieringa and Waterhouse demonstrates the richness and complexity of transfer pricing in an organisational context. Their work also warns of the serious limitations of analysing transfer pricing through the lens of any one model of the organisation to the exclusion of others. Considered in combination, these models together offer a more comprehensive view of transfer pricing.

Summary

The main purpose of this chapter has been to provide a review of the literature on transfer pricing schemes which have been developed in order to facilitate the allocation of resources within a company and the evaluation of divisional performance. The success of the pricing system in performing these tasks depends largely on its ability to capture the relevant economic and organisational characteristics of the company. In essence, the divisionalised organisation is a dynamic and interactive web of interdependent divisions, which seek the attainment of some goal(s). Transfer pricing schemes employed by the company not only impact on the degrees of co-operation and integration that take place between divisions, but they also influence the extent of decision-making autonomy enjoyed by divisional managers.

The transfer pricing systems developed by economists and management scientists range from the less sophisticated traditional economic model of a two-division firm with no externalities, to the more sophisticated mathematical programming models dealing with multi-product, multidivisional firms with differing externalities. The development of the more sophisticated models has made the transfer pricing problem setting more realistic. However, these models share some underlying assumptions which reduce their validity.

First, these models assume goal consensus. The possibility of goal conflict, which is considered inevitable under modern organisation theory, is not explicitly entertained in these models (with the exception of the model developed by Bailey and Boe). Further, participants are assumed to submit complete and honest information either to each other, as under the traditional economic model, or to the central management, as under mathematical programming models. Thus, information manipulation by divisional managers is not assumed to occur. To the extent that both goal conflict and gaming occur in reality, control over the allocation of resources within the divisionalised organisation may be dictated by forces other than the pricing mechanism, for example personal power or specialised knowledge of divisional managers.

Second, underlying the above transfer pricing models is the common belief that the price mechanism is a theoretically sound tool for regulating economic activities. However, the price system may not always be useful. For example, when the activities of some divisions are highly interdependent, prices do not lead to an optimal solution unless they have been appropriately modified to motivate divisions to take cognisance of such interdependence. Even if these modifications were introduced, they typically lead to increased levels of centralised control.

Third, the problem of uncertainty is hardly, if ever, considered by transfer pricing models. Thus, under the traditional transfer pricing model uncertainty is generally assumed away, while under the decomposition model uncertainty is introduced but only in a very rudimentary fashion. Uncertainty is likely to affect greatly the determination of appropriate transfer prices. The divisionalised organisation can be viewed as an economic entity facing different sets of transfer prices, with each set corresponding to a particular state of the world. Hence, each divisional manager will be faced with a probability distribution of transfer prices. Under such conditions it may be appropriate to emphasise the utility of profits in decision-making.

Fourth, existing transfer pricing models do not capture all the relevant organisational and behavioural issues. The pricing mechanism has not as yet completely penetrated all organisational levels, nor has it appropriately taken account of reciprocal or even sequential divisional interactions. Furthermore, the trade-off between corporate optimality and divisional autonomy is an issue of major importance; it is not entirely clear, when in conflict, which of the two should be sacrificed in favour of the other.

The above argument does not imply that the price mechanism should be discarded altogether. All that it implies is that it is necessary for the price mechanism to be buttressed by 'non-market' mechanisms to ensure that resource allocation within the divisionalised organisation more fully reflects the relevant economic, organisational and behavioural characteristics.

References

Bailey, A.D., jun. and W.J. Boe (1976) 'Goal and resource transfers in the multigoal organization', *Accounting Review*, July, pp. 559–73.

Baumol, W.J. and T. Fabian (1964) 'Decomposition pricing for decentralization and external economies', *Management Science*, September, pp. 1–32.

Chalos, P. and S. Haka (1990) 'Transfer pricing under bilateral bargaining', *Accounting Review*, July, pp. 624–41.

Dopuch, N. and D.F. Drake (1964) 'Accounting implications for a mathematical programming approach to the transfer price problem', *Journal of Accounting Research*, Spring, pp. 10–24.

Eccles, R.G. (1983) 'Control with fairness in transfer pricing', *Harvard Business Review*, November–December, pp. 149–61.

Eccles, R.R. (1985), *The Transfer Pricing Problem*, Lexington, Ky: Lexington Books.

Gould, J.R. (1964) 'Internal pricing in firms where there are costs of using an outside market', *Journal of Business*, July, pp. 61–7.

Groves, T. (1973) 'Incentives in teams', *Econometrica*, July, pp. 617–31.

Hirshleifer, J. (1956) 'On the economics of transfer pricing', *Journal of Business*, July, pp. 172–84.

Ravenscroft, S.P., S.F. Haka and P. Chalos (1993) 'Bargaining behavior in a transfer pricing experiment', *Organizational Behavior and Human Decision Processes*, vol. 55, no. 3, August, pp. 414–43.

Spicer, B.H. (1988) 'Towards an organisational theory of the transfer pricing process', *Accounting, Organizations and Society*, vol. 13, no. 3, pp. 303–22.

Swieringa, R.J. and J.H. Waterhouse (1982) 'Organizational views of transfer pricing', *Accounting, Organizations and Society*, vol. 7, no. 2, pp. 149–65.

Vancil, R.F. (1979) *Decentralization: Managerial ambiguity by design*, Homewood, Ill: Dow–Jones Irwin.

Watson, D.J. and J.V. Baumler (1975) 'Transfer pricing: a behavioral context', *Accounting Review*, July, pp. 466–74.

Williamson, O.E. (1975) *Markets and Hierarchies: Analysis and antitrust implications*, New York: Free Press.

CHAPTER EIGHT

Strategic Management Accounting

Richard M.S. Wilson

Introduction

This chapter is structured into three main sections. The first deals with the nature of strategy and strategic decisions, and with some design considerations relevant to developing management accounting systems for strategic purposes; the second with some key concepts relevant to strategic management; and the third with a review of a number of major contributions to the development of strategic management accounting (SMA).

The main aim of the chapter is to give the reader some understanding of why the design of management accounting systems needs to be radically rethought to meet the needs of strategic management. In addition, it seeks to indicate how this might be done.

The emergence of SMA is a recent phenomenon and there is, as yet, no unified view of what it is or how it might develop. As a result, this chapter is intended to convey the flavour of different approaches to SMA rather than offering a definitive statement.

Strategy and Strategic Decisions

We can tackle the issue of strategic management accounting by asking a number of questions. In the first place, what is meant by *strategy*? While strategy has been defined in lots of different ways, there is no standard definition. Early definitions tended to bring in both *means* and *ends* by suggesting that strategy is the determination of the basic long-term goals of an enterprise along with the adoption of courses of action and the allocation of resources necessary for achieving those goals. More recently, there has been a tendency to adopt narrower definitions that focus on means, with ends being taken as given, and in which strategy is seen as being a fundamental pattern of planned resource deployments and environmental interactions that indicate how an enterprise will achieve its objectives.

Some writers have identified different levels of strategy along the following lines:

1. *Corporate strategy* which deals with the allocation of resources amongst various businesses or divisions of an enterprise.
2. *Business strategy* which exists at the level of a particular business or division, dealing primarily with the question of competitive position.
3. *Functional strategy* which is limited to the actions of specific functions (e.g. distribution) within particular businesses.

Our main concern will be with the role of managerial accounting in relation to 2 above – business strategy. In this context we can define strategy as:

> An integrated set of actions aimed at securing a sustainable competitive advantage.

The notion of *competitive advantage* requires that a given business be viewed relative to its competitors, and continuing success requires that a competitive advantage (e.g. superior product quality, lower costs or more efficient distribution) be sought and maintained. It will be apparent from these comments that a period-by-period statement of a business's profits (whether by segment or overall), its cash flow, or any other traditional accounting measure of performance, is blinkered in at least two respects:

1. It is an artificial exercise at best to divide time up into arbitrary periods.
2. Seeking to gauge a business's performance in isolation from changes in its strategic position relative to competing businesses ignores its capacity for generating future cash flows and achieving other aims.

It needs to be emphasised that 'strategy' is not synonymous with 'long-term plan', but rather consists of a business's attempts to reach some preferred future state by adapting its competitive position as circumstances change. Whilst a series of strategic moves may be planned, competitors' actions will mean that the actual moves taken will have to be modified to take account of those actions.

The next question we might pose concerns the *characteristics of strategic decisions*. We can summarise these as follows:

1. They are concerned with the scope of an organisation's activities, and hence with the definition of the organisation's boundaries.
2. They relate to the matching of the organisation's activities with the opportunities of its substantive environment. Since the environment is continually changing, it

is necessary for this to be accommodated via adaptive decision-making that anticipates outcomes – as in playing a game of chess.

3. They require the matching of an organisation's activities with its resources. In order to take advantage of strategic opportunities it will be necessary to have funds, capacity, personnel, etc., available when required.

4. They have major resource implications for organisations – such as acquiring additional capacity, disposing of capacity, or reallocating resources in a fundamental way.

5. They are influenced by the values and expectations of those who determine the organisation's strategy. Any repositioning of organisational boundaries will be influenced by managerial preferences and conceptions as much as by environmental possibilities.

6. They will affect the organisation's long-term direction.

7. They are complex in nature since they tend to be non-routine and involve a large number of variables. As a result, their implications will typically extend throughout the organisation.

In broadening our perspective into a strategic setting we need to recognise that most managers have a functional role (whether as a personnel specialist or as a transport manager), and thus tend to see the world in terms associated with their function. Accountants are no exception to this, and they usually view matters in financial terms that are associated with existing activities. The risk exists, therefore, of managerial accounting systems being designed as a reflection of past experience, with environmental changes being interpreted in the light of what has gone before. This tendency towards retrospective introspection needs to be changed in a fundamental way if strategic control is to be achieved.

For example, traditional managerial accounting methods might propose that attention be given to the following:

♦ controlling working capital
♦ decreasing work-in-progress
♦ reducing wastage rates
♦ negotiating modest wage increases

in order to improve an enterprise's performance. But if the enterprise is in a declining industry, or is suffering from intense competitive pressures, or is lagging behind in the adoption of current technology, no amount of marginal adjustment to insignificant details will improve its fortunes. Of central importance to organisational prosperity is the ability to acquire, allocate and utilise resources in a way that takes advantage of environmental opportunities and avoids environmental threats. The focus for the management accountant is, therefore, outwards and forward.

The contrast between traditional and strategic approaches to cost categorisation is highlighted in Figure 8.1. This suggests that the traditional focus on the top left-hand quadrant is inadequate if a comprehensive view is required. The latter will seek to

Issues in management accounting

	OPERATIONAL	STRATEGIC
TANGIBLE	* Labour * Materials * Energy * Supplies * Contract services	* Debt charges * New plants * Product development * Market development
INTANGIBLE	* Poor quality * Absenteeism * Labour turnover * Low morale * Lost output * Late delivery	* Poor product positioning * Technological obsolescence * Poor location of facilities

Figure 8.1   A total view of cost categories (adapted from Richardson, 1988, p. 30).

encompass strategic as well as operational matters and intangible as well as tangible issues.

As with definitions of strategy, there is no agreed definition of SMA. For present purposes the following definition will be employed:

> Strategic management accounting is an approach to management accounting that explicitly highlights strategic issues and concerns.
>
> It sets management accounting in a broader context in which financial information is used to develop superior strategies as a means of achieving sustainable competitive advantage.

Some key differences between conventional management accounting and SMA are shown in Figure 8.2. Whilst the former tends to have a historical orientation coupled with a focus on single decisions, single periods and single entities, the orientation of SMA is to the future and highlights an enterprise's position relative to its competitors in the context of sequences of decisions over multiple time periods. Despite the fact that the vast majority of commercial enterprises within developed economies are not engaged in manufacturing, it is evident that the training of accountants emphasises a

Conventional characteristics	Strategic characteristics
Historical	Prospective
Single entity	Relative
Single period	Multiple
Single decision	Sequences, patterns
Introspective	Outward-looking
Manufacturing focus	Competitive focus
Existing activities	Possibilities
Reactive	Proactive
Programmed	Unprogrammed
Overlooks linkages	Embraces linkages
Data orientation	Information orientation
Based on existing systems	Unconstrained by existing systems
Built on conventions	Ignores conventions

Figure 8.2 Conventional versus strategic management accounting (source: Wilson and Chua, 1993, p. 530).

manufacturing focus which conditions accountants to look inwards to existing activities rather than outwards towards competitive possibilities. Evidence from both the UK and the USA indicates that current management accounting practice is built on conventions that have more relevance to financial reporting than to SMA.

One variation of SMA is strategic cost management (SCM). This can be defined as follows:

> Strategic cost management aims to reduce unit costs continually in real terms over the long run.
>
> Managers only start to manage costs strategically when they identify the significant costs of the enterprise and then apply effort toward reducing them.

Some of the differences between traditional and strategic cost management are shown in Figure 8.3. Among the limitations of traditional cost management the following can be identified:

1. Responsibility lies solely with operating managers rather than with top management.
2. Costs are only managed during crisis situations rather than on a continuing basis.
3. The focus of cost reduction is limited in scope (e.g. direct labour during the month of May) rather than on an enterprise-wide basis.

ATTRIBUTE	TRADITIONAL	STRATEGIC
Goals	Specific	Competitive advantage
Scope	Narrow	Broad
Time frame	Short-term	Long-term
Frequency	Periodic	Continuous
Trigger	Reaction	Proaction
Target	Labour	Entire value-chain

Figure 8.3 Traditional versus strategic cost management (adapted from Shields and Young, 1992, p. 17).

4. In adopting a partial approach many important costs are ignored.
5. Employees inevitably hold negative perceptions of cost management activities.
6. Personal relationships and emotions typically stand in the way of objective actions.
7. One-time reductions are neither followed up nor maintained.
8. The wrong costs are often cut first if they are the easiest to eliminate.

Subsequent discussion will refer back to cost management in a strategic context.

In a rare attempt at specifying the design parameters for an accounting system intended to help in the process of strategic decision-making, Gordon *et al.* (1978) began by proposing the following (Figure 8.4) as being generally applicable:

---

1. Identification of information preparer(s).
2. Identification of information recipient(s).
3. Identification of the technology employed for information transmission.
4. Specification of the information characteristics:
   A. Which data items are to be communicated.
   B. What the format of the data items is to be.
   C. What the form of the data items is to be.
   D. What the focus of the data items is to be.
   E. What the orientation of the data items is to be.
   F. What the time horizon covered by the data items is to be.
   G. How frequently the data items are to be communicated.

Figure 8.4 Design parameters for an accounting information system (source: Gordon *et al.*, 1978, p. 207).

parameter 1 deals with the question of who should be allowed to enter information into the system, whilst parameter 2 is concerned with who should be allowed access to the output from the system, and parameter 3 refers to the technology to be used. Our main interest, however, is in parameter 4 relating to the specification of information characteristics.

But what might be proposed to meet strategic requirements more specifically? Gordon *et al.* tackle this question by breaking down the process of strategic decision-making into three phases:

1. The problem identification phase.
2. The generation of alternative courses of action phase.
3. The choice among alternatives phase.

Their argument is that each of these different phases requires different specifications for the accounting system's design parameters. These give us some valuable guidelines for designing strategy-oriented management accounting systems. However, the strategic management process logically involves more steps than are captured by problem identification, generation of alternatives, and choice among alternatives. These are shown in Figure 8.5. Each stage in this iterative model warrants separate consideration. For example, in connection with Stage One the following questions might appropriately be asked:

1. How well is the present strategy working?
2. What are the enterprise's strengths, weaknesses, opportunities and threats?
3. Is the enterprise competitive on cost?
4. How strong is the enterprise's competitive position?
5. What strategic issues does the enterprise face?

In connection with Stage Five there seems to be something of a paradox in that recent literature on strategic management advocates the use of strategic control systems to ensure the implementation of strategic plans and to monitor strategic progress, yet, in practice, very few enterprises appear to make use of explicit strategic control measures or build these into their control systems. Johnson and Scholes (1993) have argued that the problems of strategy implementation and control can be dealt with in the following ways:

1. By ensuring that those charged with implementing strategies understand and work within the social, political and cultural systems that regulate organisational behaviour, and which can give rise to a resistance to strategic change.

2. By making use of control and regulatory systems to ensure that the tasks of implementation are clear, that their execution is monitored, that individuals and groups have the capabilities to implement change, and that they are rewarded for so doing.

Prior to reviewing some of the significant contributions to the development of

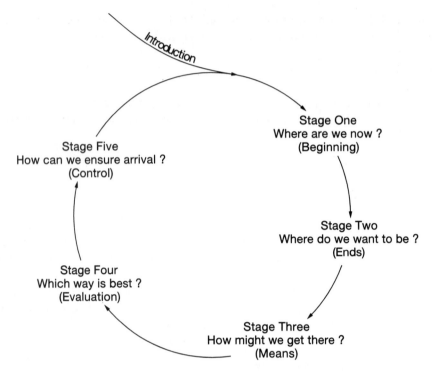

Figure 8.5 Stages in the strategic management process (source: Wilson and Gilligan with Pearson, 1992, p. 4).

SMA, there are some key building-blocks that warrant coverage. These are the product life-cycle, the experience curve and the product portfolio matrix.

Further Underlying Concepts

It is generally accepted that products – and services – typically pass through a series of distinct phases in what is termed the *product life-cycle*. The major characteristics of this concept are as follows:

1. Products have limited lives, and a given product's life can be represented by an S-shaped curve tracing its sales history.
2. The stages of the product's life-cycle are identified by the inflection points in the sales history – introduction, growth, competitive turbulence, maturity, extension, decline.
3. Profit per unit varies as products move through their life-cycles, falling following the growth phase.

4. Each phase of the product life-cycle poses different threats and opportunities that give rise to different strategic actions.

The above points are summarised in Figure 8.6.

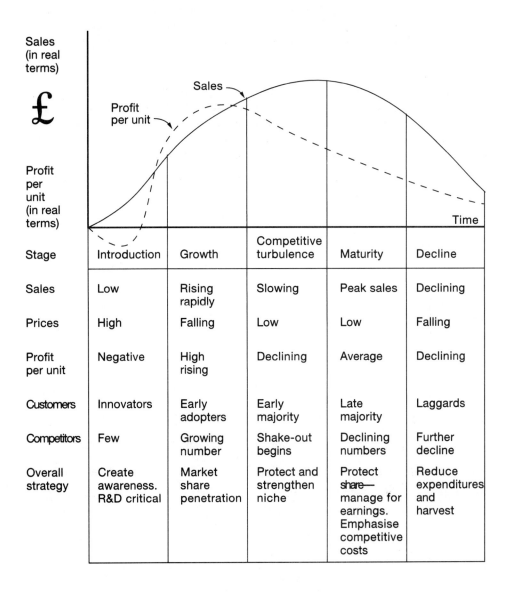

Stage	Introduction	Growth	Competitive turbulence	Maturity	Decline
Sales	Low	Rising rapidly	Slowing	Peak sales	Declining
Prices	High	Falling	Low	Low	Falling
Profit per unit	Negative	High rising	Declining	Average	Declining
Customers	Innovators	Early adopters	Early majority	Late majority	Laggards
Competitors	Few	Growing number	Shake-out begins	Declining numbers	Further decline
Overall strategy	Create awareness. R&D critical	Market share penetration	Protect and strengthen niche	Protect share— manage for earnings. Emphasise competitive costs	Reduce expenditures and harvest

Figure 8.6 The product life-cycle and its strategic implications.

If we simplify Figure 8.6 by removing the competitive turbulence stage we can use the remaining stages to guide SCM activities. Some possibilities are suggested in Figure 8.7.

The strategic *missions* of an enterprise can be linked to the stages of the product life-cycle in the following ways:

1. A *build* mission suggests a goal of increased market share – even at the expense of short-term profit or cash flow. This will be relevant in the introduction and growth stages during which an enterprise adopting this mission would be expected to be a net user of cash.

2. A *hold* mission (which is relevant to the maturity stage) is geared to the protection of an enterprise's market share and competitive position. Such a mission is likely to be one in which cash inflows are roughly balanced by cash outflow.

3. A *harvest* mission (corresponding with the decline stage) implies a goal of short-term maximisation of profits or cash flow – even at the expense of market share. An enterprise pursuing this mission is likely to be a net generator of cash.

These missions will be picked up again later in this section when we look at the product portfolio matrix.

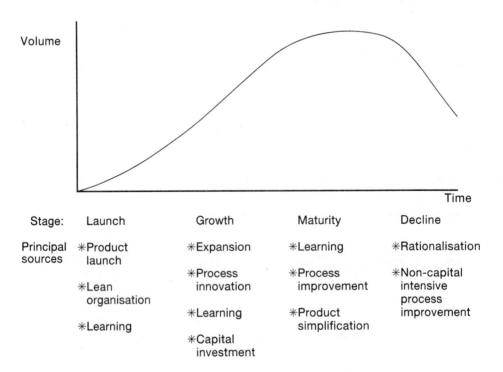

Stage:	Launch	Growth	Maturity	Decline
Principal sources	*Product launch	*Expansion	*Learning	*Rationalisation
		*Process innovation	*Process improvement	*Non-capital intensive process improvement
	*Lean organisation			
		*Learning	*Product simplification	
	*Learning			
		*Capital investment		

Figure 8.7 The product life-cycle: major sources of cost reduction.

It is apparent that the product life-cycle illustrated in Figure 8.7 begins with the introduction of a new market offering. However, in most situations there will be considerable activity prior to the launch. Work carried out by Computer Aided Manufacturing – International (CAM-I) has shown that the cash flow in the stages prior to launch closely follows the matched cost (based on accrual accounting principles) but that the curve reflecting financial commitment is of a fundamentally different shape. This is illustrated in Figure 8.8 which has, as its origin, the 'bright idea' that eventually emerges as a tangible market offering. By the time the design stage has been completed, it is evident that some 85 per cent of costs are already locked-in to the product. The strategic consequence of this is that any subsequent concern to manage costs will be severely constrained by the design characteristics of the product itself. This could clearly inhibit the attainment of a sustainable competitive advantage.

Insofar as life-cycles might be used to facilitate SCM, it is important to distinguish between:

♦ *life-cycle costs* which refer to all the costs that the manufacturer will incur over the product's life-cycle (which include design, manufacturing, marketing, logistics and service costs);
♦ *whole-life costs* which include life-cycle costs as well as costs that will be incurred

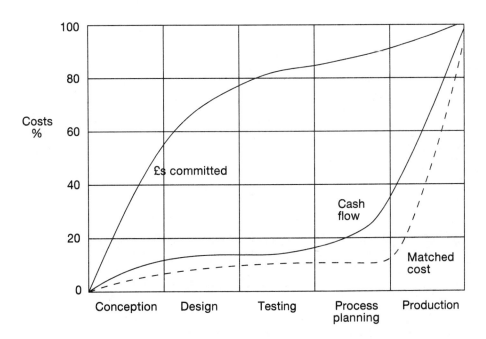

Figure 8.8 The product life-cycle: pre-launch phases (source: Brimson, 1987, p. 5.15).

by consumers (such as costs of installation, operation, maintenance, revitalisation and disposal).

There is a strong argument for making whole-life costs the primary focus of product life-cycle cost management since consumers are becoming much more aware of costs that are incurred *after* the purchase of a product (see Shields and Young, 1991).

The second important concept to understand is the *experience curve*. The essence of experience curve theory is that the real costs of generating products and services decline by 20–30 per cent whenever cumulative experience doubles. Within manufacturing industry, as illustrated in Figure 8.9, with a 20 per cent experience curve effect, if the first 1 million units of output cost £1 each, then the unit cost for a production volume of 2 million units would be 80p (i.e. 80 per cent of £1) and the unit cost of a production volume of 4 million units would be 64p (i.e. 80 per cent of 80p), and so on. The greater the experience curve effect, the greater will be the cost advantage associated with cumulative production volume (which is equivalent to cumulative experience).

An important distinction needs to be drawn between the experience curve and the learning curve. The latter was initially observed during the 1920s and it was a significant feature of the labour hours required for building aircraft during World War II – but it only relates to labour hours (hence labour cost). As a consequence, the reduction in costs due to the learning curve effect is much lower than that due to the

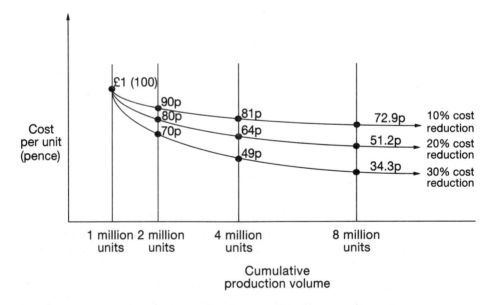

Figure 8.9 Comparison of experience curve effects for 10%, 20% and 30% cost reductions for each doubling of cumulative production volume (adapted from Thompson and Strickland, 1993, p. 60).

broader-based experience curve. *All* costs and cost effects are reflected by the experience curve.

Several causes of cost reduction act together within the experience curve:

♦ the learning experience;
♦ the effect of labour specialisation;
♦ scale effects due to increased volume.

Whilst the experience curve is not equivalent to the long-run cost curve, there are similarities – as shown in Figure 8.10. This indicates some of the sources of cost reduction over time, making it clear that they are not simply a function of volume. The ways in which an enterprise might encourage progress down the long-run cost curve include the following:

♦ investing wisely in plant, equipment and new technology;
♦ building a shared culture between managers and employees in which SCM is seen as being an important, challenging and rewarding activity;
♦ being prepared to innovate in ways that dramatically alter the shape of the cost curve.

The experience curve is derived not from accounting costs but by dividing the cumulative cash inputs by the cumulative output of end products, and the cost decline is shown by the rate of change in this ratio over time. From this rate of change managers can see how – and why – their competitive costs are shifting. If estimates

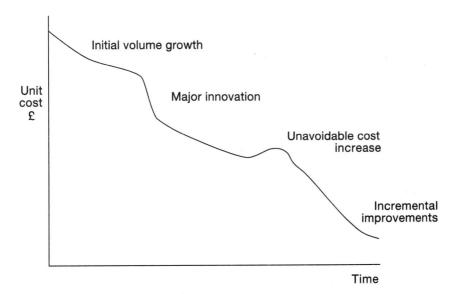

Figure 8.10 Long-run cost curve.

can be made of competitors' experience curve effects, this should reveal which are the low-cost competitors and which are not, hence which are at risk and from whom.

The main strategic message from the experience curve is that, if costs per unit in real terms decrease predictably with cumulative output, then the market leader has the potential to achieve the lowest costs and the highest profits.

Given the empirical existence of the experience curve, it is apparent that the use of cash will be less than directly proportional to a product's rate of growth. Similarly, the generation of cash will be a function of the product's market share. From these relationships the Boston Consulting Group constructed the *growth-share matrix* (which is also known as the *product portfolio matrix*). This is the third important issue and is illustrated in Figure 8.11.

Within the growth-share matrix, market growth serves as a proxy for a firm's need for cash, whilst relative market share is a proxy for profitability and cash-generating ability. Relative market share is given by the ratio of any firm's market share to the market share of the market leader. A high relative market share is deemed to lead to higher profitability on the basis of the experience curve: the market leader should have the lowest costs at the prevailing price level. (This also accords with PIMS findings – see pages 180–3.) A high market growth rate will be associated with a need for investment in both fixed assets and working capital which will usually outstrip the generation of cash from current operations, although securing share now will bring future rewards.

It is possible to superimpose the missions introduced on page 168 into the growth-share matrix. Looking at the four cells of Figure 8.11, starting with the top right-hand cell and moving in an anti-clockwise direction, accords with the Build – Hold –

		Relative market share	
		High	Low
Market growth	High	Star (May be cash generator or cash absorber)	Wildcat (Cash absorber)
	Low	Cash cow (Large cash generator)	Dog (Modest cash generator or absorber)

Figure 8.11 Growth-share matrix.

Harvest sequence, with dogs representing divestment situations. This picture is developed further in the following discussion.

Low market share, high market growth (Build mission)   Any product in this cell will be a cash absorber ('wildcat') because of the need to invest to keep a foothold in a market that is dominated by others. If an aggressive attempt is made to move a wildcat product into a *high* market share position, then it may become – eventually – a cash cow. However, if resources are not available to pursue this strategy, it may be advisable to withdraw.

High market share, high market growth (Hold mission)   This cell contains potential cash cows, at present termed 'stars'. If their competitive position is improved, involving heavy expenditure, they will be cash absorbers until such time as the market growth rate declines and they become cash generators. The important requirement is to obtain and maintain a large market share.

High market share, low market growth (Harvest mission)   This is a position of some strength as the high market share should facilitate economies of scale, low unit costs, etc., and give a position of market dominance. Because market growth is low, the need for new investment will be minimal, with the result that products in this cell will tend to be large generators of cash (i.e. 'cash cows'). A reasonable aim might be to maintain market share to enable the generation of cash to continue, rather than seek to increase market penetration.

Low market share, low market growth (Divest)   Within this cell are the 'dogs' that produce very little cash (if any). It would be prohibitively expensive to seek market dominance from this position, so the best strategy may be to delete dogs from the range. The existence of dogs suggests a failure to obtain a leadership position during the growth phase, so further failures through cash absorption should preferably be avoided.

The choice of a strategy in the light of the growth-share matrix will be influenced by the following:

feasibility (bearing in mind that market share can be influenced more readily than market growth);

desirability (in that a balanced product portfolio will probably be sought in which some products are able to generate cash and acceptable profits in the short run in order to support those that need cash to support their long-run growth).

A strategic success sequence is likely to emerge via the following steps:

1. The cash generated by cash cows (high market share, low market growth) should be invested in building the market share of wildcats. If this is done well, sustainable advantage will be provided by which wildcats will become stars and then cash cows, thereby being able to finance subsequent strategies.
2. To be avoided is the sequence by which wildcats are not supported so that they become dogs when the market matures; low relative share in a low-growth market is not the place to find oneself.

3. Also to be avoided is the sequence by which stars lose position and become wildcats as market growth slows, with the risk of their becoming dogs.

Key Contributions to Strategic Management Accounting

In formulating strategies there is a need to search for alternative directions and means by which those directions might be pursued. We will review five major contributions to these tasks which give a basis for SMA. These contributions come from Porter, the PIMS study, Simmonds, Bromwich, and Simons. Whilst not reviewed here, the outstanding contribution of Shank and Govindarajan cannot pass without appropriate recognition.

Porter's Approach

Porter's influential contributions to strategy formulation and implementation are premised on two basic questions from which some key issues flow:

1. How attractive, from the viewpoint of long-term profitability, are different industries? Differences exist from one industry to another, and changes occur over time: since a given enterprise's profitability will be influenced by the profitability of the industry in which it is operating, this can be seen to be a key question. It is also significant because the choice of an industry determines an enterprise's competitors.

Whatever the industry, there are five competitive forces that need to be taken into account in formulating and implementing strategy:

(a) the threat of new entrants;
(b) the threat of substitute products or services;
(c) the rivalry amongst existing organisations within the industry;
(d) the bargaining power of suppliers;
(e) the bargaining power of consumers.

Taken together, these competitive forces significantly influence the ability of organisations to generate returns in excess of the cost of capital. Thus in the pharmaceutical, soft drinks and database publishing industries, the five forces are favourable and enterprises within these industries are able to earn attractive returns. However, in other industries – including rubber, steel and video games – pressure from one or more of the forces is so intense that few enterprises are able to generate high returns.

Why is it that these forces have such an influence on industry profitability? The answer is to be found in the constituents of profitability – prices, costs and investment. Prices are influenced by the bargaining power of consumers and the threat of substitutes. Costs are influenced by the bargaining power of suppliers and the rivalry amongst competitors. Investment is influenced by the threat of entrants and other factors including rivalry and consumers' requirements.

The relative strength of each of the competitive forces tends to be a function of *industry structure* (i.e. the underlying economic and technological characteristics of an industry). This can change over time, with the result that the relative strength of competitive forces will also change, hence affecting the industry's profitability. At the very least, an enterprise should monitor its environment in an attempt to identify shifts in its industry structure and the competitive forces. But an enterprise can also *induce* change – primarily by its innovative endeavours, such as the development of new products or processes. Any change by one competitor is likely to bring a response from others, and so on, with the result that the final outcome (in terms of impact on an industry's profitability) may be extremely difficult to predict.

2. What is the enterprise's relative position within its industry? This question of position is significant because it influences the extent to which an enterprise's profitability is greater or less than the industry's average. The basic way in which an enterprise might seek to achieve above-average returns into the long term is via *sustainable competitive advantage*. This in turn can be achieved by means of *generic strategies* of which there are three:

(a) *cost leadership*, through which the enterprise aims to be the lowest-cost producer within its industry via the use of the following:

♦ economies of scale
♦ experience curve effects
♦ tight cost control
♦ cost minimisation in such areas as R & D, service, advertising.

Examples:

Texas Instruments – consumer electronics
Hyundai – cars
Black and Decker – machine tools
Commodore – business machines
BIC – pens
Timex – wristwatches.

(b) *differentiation*, through which the enterprise seeks to offer some unique dimension in its products/service that is valued by customers and which can command a premium price via the following:

♦ image (e.g. Coca-Cola)
♦ superior customer service (e.g. IBM)
♦ dealer network (e.g. Caterpillar)
♦ product design (e.g. Hewlett-Packard)
♦ technology (e.g. Coleman).

Other examples:

Mercedes Benz – cars
Cross – pens

Rolex – wristwatches.

(c) *focus*, which has two variants – cost focus and differentiation focus. Whilst cost leadership and differentiation strategies strive for competitive advantage in broad market segments, the focus strategies are directed at narrow segments to the exclusion of others. If the structure of the segments chosen is favourable, then above-average returns should result.

Porter's view is that any enterprise seeking a sustainable competitive advantage must select one or other of these generic strategies rather than attempting to be 'all things to all people' or 'stuck in the middle'.

Insofar as competitive advantage is cost-based we need to recall that conventional management accounting:

♦ concentrates on manufacturing activities;
♦ ignores the impact of other activities;
♦ overlooks linkages between activities by analysing each activity in a discrete way;
♦ fails to assess the cost positions of competitors in relative terms;
♦ relies too heavily on existing accounting systems.

In contrast, SMA focuses on:

♦ the determinants of relative cost position;
♦ the ways in which a firm might secure a sustainable cost advantage;
♦ the costs of differentiation.

Figure 8.12 summarises the SMA implications of cost leadership on the one hand and differentiation on the other.

Following Porter's approach the initial step in undertaking SMA is to define the firm's value-chain. Porter (1985) introduced the *value-chain* as a way of breaking down a firm's strategically relevant activities in order to understand the behaviour of costs. Competitive advantage comes from carrying out these activities in a more cost-effective way than one's competitors.

The value-chain of a firm is composed of nine categories of interrelated activities, as shown in Figure 8.13. These activities are, in part, primary activities and, in part, support activities: the latter exist to facilitate the former, with the particular arrangements reflecting any given enterprise's history, strategy and the underlying economics of its situation.

The value aspect is to be found in the price that customers are willing to pay; hence, the margin depends upon the cost-effectiveness of the primary and support activities on the one hand, and the market's perception of the firm's offering on the other.

Each activity in the value-chain has operating costs associated with it as well as assets (whether fixed or current). The amount of assets assigned to an activity, along with the efficiency of their utilisation, both influence that activity's costs. Assigning assets and operating costs to the activities constituting the value-chain involves

	Cost leadership	Differentiation
Role of standard costs in assessing performance	Very important	Not very important
Importance of such concepts as flexible budgeting for manufacturing cost control	High to very high	Moderate to low
Perceived importance of meeting budgets	High to very high	Moderate to low
Importance of marketing cost analysis	Often not done at all on a formal basis	Critical to success
Importance of product cost as an input to pricing decisions	High	Low
Importance of competitor cost analysis	High	Low

Figure 8.12 Primary strategic emphasis (adapted from Shank and Govindarajan, 1993, p. 18).

problems similar to those found in any allocation exercise – especially in relation to shared assets and costs. Formulae, etc. will need to be established to deal with this problem, bearing in mind the ways in which competitors' cost analyses are to be carried out.

Any enterprise's cost position (relative to its competitors) is derived from the cost behaviour patterns associated with the activities constituting its value-chain. These cost behaviour patterns in turn depend upon a number of causal factors or *cost drivers*. Porter has defined a cost driver as a structural determinant of an activity's cost. Some cost drivers are within the firm's control, but some are not, and a given activity's cost may be due to several cost drivers acting together. It will be evident that a particular firm's cost position on any value activity will depend on whichever cost drivers are at play, but the impact of different cost drivers will vary among firms – even within the same industry.

In order to gain real benefits from this type of analysis, attempts should be made

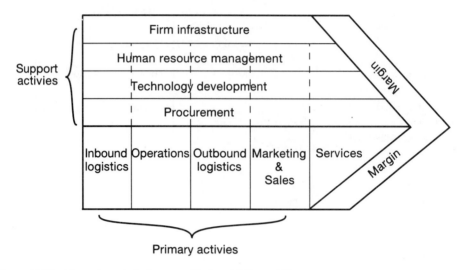

Figure 8.13 The value-chain (source: Porter, 1985, p. 37).

to quantify the impact of each cost driver influencing the cost of a value or activity. However crude the attempt, it should help to indicate the relative significance of each cost driver. Moreover, it will help in showing the extent to which the interactions among cost drivers tend to reinforce or counteract each other.

Having carried out the above analysis for one's own enterprise, the next step is to do it for one's competitors. A given enterprise will have a cost advantage if its cumulative costs of carrying out all the activities within the value-chain are less than those of its competitors. This advantage will only have strategic significance if it can be sustained, which requires that competitors are unable to imitate it readily. The scope for imitation will depend upon the following:

♦ the structure of the enterprise's value-chain relative to those of competitors;
♦ the enterprise's key cost drivers relative to those of competitors.

A cost advantage (which is equivalent to cost leadership) needs to be maintained once it has been achieved, and this requires determined effort on a day-to-day basis in improving cost-effectiveness.

The discussion so far has emphasised the value-chain from a *horizontal* point of view, but there are considerable benefits to be found in looking at it from a *vertical* point of view. Figure 8.14 illustrates this in the context of the paper products industry. Competitor A operates throughout the industry whereas Competitor D is only active at one stage (paper manufacturing), with other competitors spanning two or more links of the value-chain. In this format we can see that the value-chain is that linked set of value-creating activities ranging from basic raw material sources to the ultimate product or service that is delivered to final consumers. Looked at in *vertical* terms the

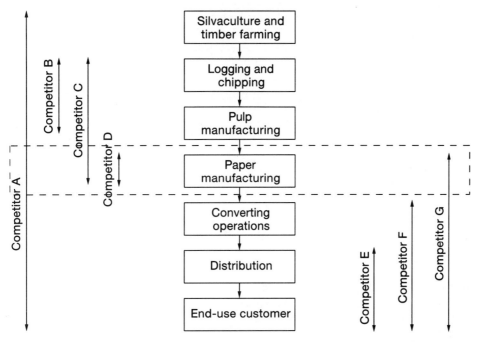

Figure 8.14 The value-chain in the paper products industry (source: Shank and Govindar-ajan, 1992, p. 7).

value-chain typically goes beyond the scope of any individual enterprise and disaggregates an industry into its distinct strategic activities. By analysing the value-chain characterised in this way it is possible to generate insights into the behaviour of costs and the sources of differentiation between one stage (e.g. pulp manufacturing) and another (e.g. logging and chipping in an upstream direction and paper manufacturing in a downstream direction). There may be benefits for a given enterprise to integrate backwards or forwards from its current position, but this may not be apparent if the appropriate analysis is not undertaken. If one is operating at an intermediate stage within a value-chain, it will often be the case that overall performance can be improved by extending the scope of one's activities backwards or forwards, thereby generating for the benefit of the enterprise the value that would otherwise have gone to suppliers on the one hand and customers on the other.

In summary, Porter (1985, p. 118) specifies the steps required in undertaking value-chain analysis as follows:

1. Identify the appropriate value-chain and assign costs and assets to it.
2. Diagnose the cost drivers of each value activity and how they interact.
3. Identify competitor value-chains, and determine the relative cost of competitors and the sources of cost differences.

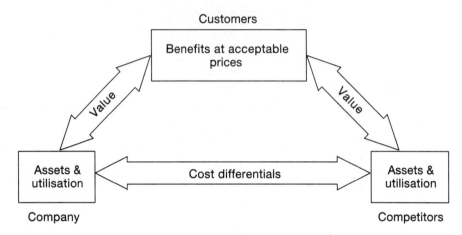

Figure 8.15   The strategic triangle (source: Brock, 1984, p. 226).

4. Develop a strategy to achieve a lower relative cost position through controlling cost drivers or reconfiguring the value-chain.
5. Ensure that cost reduction efforts do not erode differentiation.
6. Test the cost reduction strategy for sustainability.

Brock (1984) has portrayed this diagrammatically as in Figure 8.15.

The PIMS study

Another important and influential approach to guiding strategy formulation is the PIMS (profit impact of market strategy) study. Work has been going on in the USA on this project since 1972, during which time a huge database has been built up. The PIMS database represents over 3,000 businesses, and the aim of the PIMS programme is to identify the features of businesses that account for superior performance (in terms of cash flow and profitability).

Factors that have shown themselves to be persistently influential are as follows:

1. Competitive position (including market share and relative product quality).
2. Production structure (including investment intensity and the productivity of operations).
3. Attractiveness of the served market (as shown by its growth rate and customers' characteristics).

Taken together, these factors explain 65–70 per cent of the variability in profitability among the firms in the PIMS database. By examining the determinants of profitability it is possible to address such strategic questions as:

♦ What rate of profit and cash flow is normal for this type of business?

♦   What profit and cash flow outcomes can be expected if the business continues
    with its present strategy?
♦   How will future performance be affected by a change in strategy?

One of the key notions underlying SMA is that of the relative position of a firm
among its competitors – with regard to unit costs, profitability, market share, etc. This
is reflected in the PIMS approach, as shown in Figure 8.16. The respective
contribution of each of the variables in Figure 8.16 to overall profitability can be
estimated by means of a multiple regression model. This allows the impact of weak
variables to be offset by strong variables -- such as a small market share being offset
by high product quality. Once the model has been applied to one's own company –
requiring as input more than 100 separate variables – it can then be used to assess the
relative strengths and weaknesses of competitors in order to identify the best source
of competitive advantage.

The PIMS approach has been subjected to an increasing amount of critical
comment regarding:

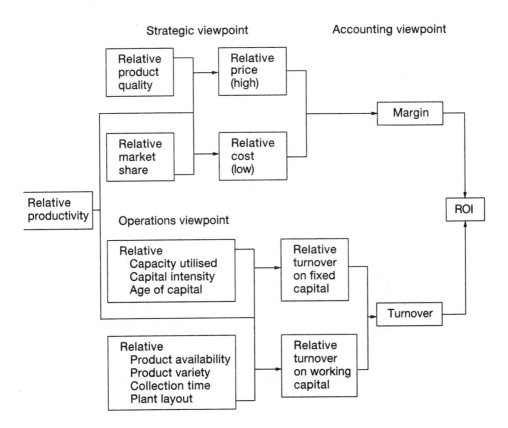

Figure 8.16   The determinants of relative profitability (source: Day, 1986, p. 120).

- ◆ measurement errors
- ◆ deficiencies in the model
- ◆ interpretation of the findings.

Perhaps the main concern is over the practice of deriving prescriptions about strategy from unsupported causal inferences; hence, it is important in using PIMS data to understand the limitations of the approach. When used in this way, the PIMS programme can provide valuable insights.

Some of the broad conclusions from the PIMS programme are as follows:

1. In the long run, the single most important factor affecting performance is the quality of an enterprise's market offerings relative to those of its competitors.
2. Market share and profitability are strongly related:

(a) return on investment (ROI) increases steadily as market share increases;
(b) enterprises having relatively large market shares tend to have above-average rates of investment turnover;
(c) the ratio of marketing expenses to sales revenue tends to be lower for enterprises having high market shares.

The PIMS programme has demonstrated the linkages between superior relative quality, higher relative prices, gains in market share, lower relative costs and higher profitability. These linkages are portrayed in Figure 8.17, which indicates the causal role that relative quality plays in influencing business performance.

3. High investment intensity acts as a powerful drag on profitability:

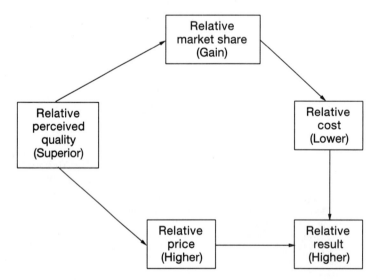

Figure 8.17 Some PIMS linkages (source: Buzzell and Gale, 1987, p. 81).

♦ the higher the ratio of investment to sales, the lower the ROI;
♦ enterprises having high investment intensity tend to be unable to achieve profit margins sufficient to sustain growth.

4. Many dog and wildcat activities generate cash, whilst many cash cows do not.

5. Vertical integration is a profitable strategy for some kinds of enterprise but not for others.

6. Most of the strategic factors that boost ROI also contribute to long-term value.

Simmonds' approach

The third major contribution to consider, that of Simmonds, is – along with the work of Shank and Govindarajan – perhaps the most significant from the viewpoint of showing how SMA might be undertaken. Simmonds (1981) has defined SMA as:

> The provision and analysis of management accounting data about a business and its competitors for use in developing and monitoring the business strategy.

He emphasises the particular importance of relative levels and trends in the following:

♦ real costs and prices
♦ volume
♦ market share
♦ cash flow
♦ the proportion demanded of an enterprise's total resources.

The key notion here is that of an enterprise's position *relative to* competitors' positions. Insofar as strategy is concerned with competitive position it has been largely ignored by management accountants, but in a number of papers Simmonds (e.g. 1981, 1982, 1986) has proposed how this failing might be overcome.

A basic tenet of his argument is the preoccupation that accountants have with the recording, analysing and presentation of cost data relating to existing activities. This 'data orientation' begs some fundamental questions – such as why the data is being collected in the first place. An alternative, and preferable, approach is one of 'information orientation' which starts with the diagnosis of problems, leading to the structuring of decisions, and thence to the specification of information that will help in making appropriate decisions. The focus shifts from the analysis of costs *per se* to the value of information.

The manager wishing to make decisions that will safeguard his/her organisation's strategic position must know by whom, by how much, and why they are gaining or being beaten. In other words, strategic indicators of performance are required. Conventional measures, such as profit, will not suffice.

Let us take comparative costs as a starting-point. It is intuitively the case that organisations having a cost advantage (i.e. lower unit cost for a product of comparable specification) are strong and those having a cost disadvantage are weak. If we relate this to the idea of the experience curve (which was introduced on page 170, it will be appreciated that, if costs can be made to decline predictably with cumulative output, that enterprise which has produced most should have the lowest unit cost and, therefore, the highest profits.

Apart from cost, an enterprise may seek to gain strategic advantage via its pricing policy. In this setting the management accountant can attempt to assess each major competitor's cost structure and relate this to its prices – taking care to eliminate the effects of inflation from the figures being used. Applying cost-volume-profit analysis to one's competitors is likely to be more fruitful than simply applying it internally.

> Clearly, competitor reactions can substantially influence the outcome of a price move. Moreover, likely reactions may not be self-evident when each competitor faces a different cost-volume-profit situation. Competitors may not follow a price lead nor even march in perfect step as they each act to defend or build their own positions. For an adequate assessment of the likelihood of competitor price reactions, then, some calculation is needed of the impact of possible price moves on the performance of individual competitors. Such an assessment in turn requires an accounting approach that can depict both competitor cost-volume-profit situations and their financial resources. (Simmonds, 1982, p. 207)

After dealing with costs and prices, the next important (and related) variable to consider is volume – especially market share. By monitoring movements in market share, an enterprise can see whether it is gaining or losing position, and an examination of relative market shares will indicate the strength of different competitors.

Reporting market share details along with financial details can help in making managerial accounting reports more strategically relevant.

The significance of competitive position has been highlighted by Simmonds (1986) as being the basic determinant of future profits and of the enterprise's value. Moreover, since competitive position can change over time, so can profits and value, but it should not be assumed that an improvement in competitive position will be associated with an improvement in short-run profits. In fact, the opposite is likely to be the case due to the need to incur costs in building up a competitive position, which has the effect of depressing current profits in favour of future profits. This raises the question as to whether competitive position can be measured in accounting terms – not just for a given business, but also for its main competitors; and not just at a point in time, but also over time. Simmonds has attempted to do this by applying SMA. He makes it clear, however, that it is not possible to express competitive position as a single figure. Instead, it is possible to offer an array of indicators relating to the competitive situation. From these indicators managers can gain insights into a business's competitive position which will help them in judging whether or not things are moving in their favour.

Bromwich's approach

In a number of overlapping papers Bromwich has focused on identifying the distinctive characteristics of market offerings in order that these might be costed. Once this has been done for a given enterprise, it should then be done for that enterprise's competitors in order to establish cost positioning relative to rivals, if sustainable competitive advantage is to be secured.

Market offerings are seen as comprising a package of objective attributes or characteristics. It is these attributes that appeal to consumers; hence, the demand for goods is of a derived nature and stems from the underlying characteristics of market offerings. These might include a range of quality elements (such as operating performance variables, reliability and warranty arrangements, physical features – including the degree of finish and trim, and service factors – such as the assurance of supply and of after-sales service). Whether an enterprise is pursuing a generic strategy of cost leadership or differentiation, it is these characteristics of market offerings which need to be the subject of appropriate analysis. Bromwich gives the purpose of this analysis as being the attribution of costs which are normally treated as product costs to the benefits they provide to the consumer for each of those benefits which is believed to be of strategic importance. The recommended approach is, initially, to list separately the benefits to consumers contained in the market offering, and then to relate costs to these. Figure 8.18 indicates how this might be done in the case of a fast-food supplier which supplies prepared and partly processed products to its network of selling outlets. Benefits are listed against the rows and are grouped according to their relationship with either the unit of product (items 1–7) or the sales outlets (items 8–11) or other (item 12). Some allowance is made for product costs that cannot be attributed to consumer benefits. The headings of the columns in Figure 8.18 reflect the source of costs. For example, some are directly volume related whereas others are a function of particular activities or specific decisions.

Whilst there is little by way of evidence to indicate the effective operationalisation of this approach, Bromwich has lucidly argued in its favour and there are good reasons to anticipate that more enterprises will be seeking to adopt it in the near future.

Simons' approach

The focus of Simons' work has been on the interface of strategic management and management control. He has defined a control system as a set of formalised procedures and systems that use information to maintain or alter patterns in organisational activity. He includes planning systems, reporting systems and

Illustrative costs:	Product-volume related costs	Activity-related costs	Capacity-related costs	Decision-related costs	Total costs
Product benefits					
1. Texture					
2. Nutritional value					
3. Appearance					
4. Taste					
5. Consistency of above, over outlets & time					
6. Quality					
7. Low cost relative to competitors					
Outlet benefits					
8. Service					
9. Cleanliness					
10. Outlet facilities					
11. Location & geographical coverage					
Other benefits					
12. Product advertising	....
TOTAL COSTS ATTRIBUTABLE TO CONSUMER BENEFITS	....
PRODUCT COSTS *NOT* ATTRIBUTABLE TO CONSUMER BENEFITS	....
TOTAL PRODUCT COST	....

Product-volume-related costs include material, labour and variable overheads, each of which may be reported separately. Activity-related costs include material handling and transport, quality control, monitoring quality and service, and site and facilities maintenance, each of which may be reported separately. Capacity-related costs include land and building occupancy costs and depreciation and leasing charges, each of which may be separately reported. Decision-related costs include product and site design, product and site engineering, quality improvement, marketing, including product advertising, and personnel and administration – again each of these costs may be reported separately.

Figure 8.18 Benefits and costs of a market offering (source: Bromwich, n.d., p. 11).

monitoring procedures within this definition but, somewhat arbitrarily, excludes such mechanisms as social and cultural control. In his 1987 study Simons examined the way in which enterprises align their control systems to their strategies, using the typology of Miles and Snow (1978). This typology is based on the rate at which enterprises change their markets or market offerings as a means of identifying generic strategies. Three successful generic strategies were identified:

1. *Prospector* – in which market offerings are changed over time and new market opportunities are continually being sought as a means of keeping ahead of competitors.
2. *Defender* – in which market offerings are relatively stable and more limited than those of competing enterprises, with competition being based on cost leadership, quality and service.
3. *Analyser* – which represents an intermediate hybrid having some characteristics of both defender and prospector strategies.

It is argued by Miles and Snow that an enterprise's control system should be congruent with its strategy. Thus, it is likely that defenders will emphasise cost control, trend monitoring and efficiency, whereas prospectors are more likely to rely on scanning the environment for new opportunities, comprehensive planning and the adoption of relatively subjective performance measures. Accounting controls in general tend not to be associated with innovation, hence prospectors will tend to make limited use of them, although they will be important in the case of defenders.

Simons' evidence suggests that high-performing prospector enterprises attach considerable importance to forecast data, set tight budgets, and monitor outputs carefully. Cost control effort is reduced, and frequent reporting is emphasised in larger enterprises. He found that defenders tend to use control systems less intensively but emphasise bonuses based on budget attainment. His conclusion was that there is an important need to gain greater insights into the links between strategy and control. Little is known about the effects of strategy on management control systems or the way in which management control systems might affect strategy. This prompts the question as to the relationship (if any) between the way in which an enterprise competes and the way in which it designs and operates its management control system. The way in which an enterprise competes (i.e. how it achieves competitive advantage) reflects its strategy.

Simons' belief is that management control systems are important for both strategy formulation and strategy implementation. He investigated this line of argument and established that management control system differences among enterprises are due to the ways in which top managers choose to monitor some issues personally whilst delegating others to subordinates. A model was developed to help explain these differences. It was built on four concepts:

1. Limited attention of managers since they lack both the time and the capacity to process all the information available to them.

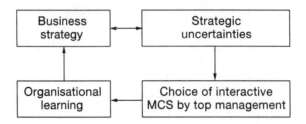

Figure 8.19 Process model of relationship between business strategy and management control system (MCS) (source: Simons, 1990, p. 138).

2. Strategic uncertainties which relate to those issues that top managers feel they must monitor personally if the organisation is to achieve its goals.
3. Interactive management control which reflects a choice between the use of management control systems interactively (i.e. to monitor and intervene in the decision-making activities of subordinates) and the programmed use of management control systems.
4. Organisational learning which describes the ways in which organisations use knowledge to improve the fit between the organisation and its environment.

Figure 8.19 shows the integration of these concepts. They fit together with the following logic: an enterprise's intended strategy creates strategic uncertainties that top management chooses to monitor personally, given the limited attention they possess. The choice of which aspect to control interactively is made once the strategic uncertainties are specified. This leads to organisational learning as further knowledge is built up in relation to the strategic uncertainties and their links to goal attainment.

It is apparent from this model, due to its recursive nature, that management control systems are an important input to strategy formulation in that their operation enables organisations to learn and adapt over time.

Conclusion

In this chapter we have dealt with the nature of strategy and strategic decisions; design criteria for developing SMA; key concepts underlying the analysis and formulation of strategic actions; and some major contributions to the development of SMA.

The primary sources of reference have been Simmonds, Porter, and Shank and Govindarajan. However, additional sources worthy of attention include Gordon *et al.*, Buzzell and Gale, Richardson, Bromwich, Simons, and Shields and Young. All of these can be found listed in the following references.

Bibliography

Brimson, J.A. (1987) 'CAM-I Cost Management Systems Project', in Capettini, R. and D.K. Clancy (eds.) *Cost Accounting, Robotics, and the New Manufacturing Environment*, Sarasota, Fla: American Accounting Association.

Brock, J.J. (1984) 'Competitor analysis: some practical approaches', *Industrial Marketing Management*, vol. 13, pp. 225–31.

Bromwich, M. (1990) 'The case for strategic management accounting: the role of accounting information for strategy in competitive markets', *Accounting, Organizations and Society*, vol. 15, no. 1/2, pp. 27–46.
This approach to SMA reflects Bromwich's background in economics.

Bromwich, M. (n.d.) 'Accounting information for strategic excellence', mimeo, London School of Economics.

Buzzell, R.D. and B.T. Gale (1987) *The PIMS Principles: Linking strategy to performance*, New York: Free Press.
A lucid and intriguing summary of the PIMS project.

Day, G.S. (1986) *Analysis for Strategic Marketing Decisions*, St Paul, Minn.: West.

Gordon, L.A., D.F. Larcker and F.D. Tuggle (1978) 'Strategic decision processes and the design of accounting information systems: conceptual linkages', *Accounting, Organizations and Society*, vol. 3, no. 3/4, pp. 203–13.
This is an early and original contribution focusing on designing SMA systems.

Johnson, G. and K. Scholes (1993) *Exploring Corporate Strategy*, 3rd edn, London: Prentice Hall International.

Miles, R.E. and C.C. Snow (1978) *Organizational Strategy, Structure and Process*, New York: McGraw-Hill.

Porter, M.E. (1985) *Competitive Advantage: Creating and sustaining superior performance*, New York: Free Press.
The cornerstone text on strategic management.

Richardson, P.R. (1988) *Cost Containment: The ultimate advantage*, New York: Free Press.
This book contains valuable guidance on SCM.

Shank, J.K. and V. Govindarajan (1992) 'Strategic cost management and the value chain', *Journal of Cost Management*, vol. 5, no. 4, pp. 5–21.

Shank, J.K. and V. Govindarajan (1993) *Strategic Cost Management: The new tool for competitive advantage*, New York: Free Press.
A compilation of the authors' more recent work on SMA and SCM: a major contribution.

Shields, M.D. and S.M. Young (1991) 'Managing product life cycle costs: an organizational model', *Journal of Cost Management*, vol. 5, no. 3, pp. 39–52.

Shields, M.D. and S.M. Young (1992) 'Effective long-term cost reduction: a strategic perspective', *Journal of Cost Management*, vol. 6, no. 1, pp. 16–30.
This paper focuses on SCM in a stimulating way.

Simmonds, K. (1981) 'Strategic management accounting', *Management Accounting*, vol. 59, no. 4, pp. 26–9. Reprinted in Cowe, R. (ed.) (1988) *Handbook of Management Accounting*, 2nd edn, Aldershot: Gower, pp. 14–36.

This paper introduced the idea of SMA which was developed further in Simmonds' 1982 and 1986 papers.

Simmonds, K. (1982) 'Strategic management accounting for pricing: a case example', *Accounting and Business Research*, vol. 12, no. 47, pp. 206–14.

Simmonds, K. (1986) 'The accounting assessment of competitive position', *European Journal of Marketing*, vol. 20, no. 1, pp. 16–31.

Simons, R. (1987) 'Accounting control systems and business strategy: an empirical analysis', *Accounting, Organizations & Society*, vol. 12, no. 4, pp. 357–74.

This offers a rare attempt to relate control to strategy.

Simons, R. (1990) 'The role of management control systems in creating competitive advantage: new perspectives', *Accounting, Organizations and Society*, vol. 15, no. 1/2, pp. 127–43.

Thompson, A.A. and A.J. Strickland (1993) *Strategic Management: Concepts and cases*, Homewood, Ill.: Irwin.

Wilson, R.M.S and W.F. Chua (1993) *Managerial Accounting: Method and meaning*, 2nd edn, London: Chapman and Hall.

Wilson, R.M.S and C.T. Gilligan with D.J. Pearson (1992) *Strategic Marketing Management: Planning, implementation and control*, Oxford: Butterworth–Heineman.

CHAPTER NINE

Financial Justification of Advanced Manufacturing Technology

David Dugdale and T. Colwyn Jones

In this chapter we review the use of investment appraisal techniques and their relationship to decisions about manufacturing technology. It is structured so that the discussion moves from a close consideration of accounting techniques to progressively wider location of these in manufacturing contexts. First, we consider the nature of the various investment appraisal techniques. Second, we survey the degree of application of these in practice in UK and US companies. Third, we consider the role of investment appraisal in investment decisions. Fourth, we locate these decisions in organisational context. Fifth, we contrast UK practice with that of Japanese manufacturers to begin to identify the influence of the societal environment on the investment process. We conclude with a re-evaluation of current concerns about accounting practices in investment appraisal, recommendations for change, and their prospects for success.

Transformation in manufacturing

The 1980s saw widespread introduction of new production technologies which are usually labelled 'advanced manufacturing technology' (AMT). Of particular importance are technologies utilising computer-based information and control systems including computer numerically controlled machine tools (CNC), computer-aided design (CAD) and computer-aided manufacturing systems (CAM), and flexible manufacturing and assembly cells (FMC and FAC). Together with various management information systems (MIS), these offer the long-term promise of computer-integrated manufacturing (CIM) where these technologies, first used as 'islands of automation', are networked into coherent systems. The claims for the manufacturing benefits of AMT are that it offers opportunities for both *flexibility* and *integration*. Flexibility refers to the reprogramming of AMT so that it can be used for several different products, with the facility to switch rapidly between them, and its usefulness is not limited to the particular purposes for which it was purchased, thus increasing its useful life. Integration refers to the linking of previously separate functions – for example, linking design to production through CAD/CAM systems. Alongside these technological changes, managers were also becoming increasingly interested in 'new' management practices including just-in-time (JIT) production and total quality management (TQM). The success of 'world-class manufacturers', especially in Japan, has been widely attributed to these developments, and to the forms of employment and working practices that sustain them. As US and UK manufacturers became more keenly aware of the challenge posed by international competition, and concerned about an increasing fragmentation and volatility in their traditional mass markets, managers came to see the need for change as growing ever more urgent. Thus, the 1990s have been seen as a period in which all aspects of manufacturing need to be rethought, and where AMT is crucial in facilitating the desired changes. The exploration of this by industrialists, academics and management consultants has produced an 'ideology of crisis and transformation' in manufacturing in which the role of conventional management accounting has come under increasingly critical scrutiny.

The hue and cry over investment appraisal

One of the most widely criticized of accountants' activities concerns the forms of investment appraisal currently practised in industry. In particular, it is argued that accounting handicaps managers and engineers who advocate the adoption of AMT. Accountants have been criticised for refusing, being reluctant, or being too slow to adopt and properly apply the more sophisticated appraisal *techniques* which have been developed over the last thirty years or so. The traditional *measurements* which accountants use as the basis of calculation of costs are seen as inappropriately focusing attention on direct labour costs which are a diminishing proportion of total costs in the new manufacturing environment. The *criteria* adopted for payback periods or discount/hurdle rates are identified as demonstrating a 'short-termism' in which AMT's claims for longer-term flexibility and integration are underemphasised. In this chorus of complaint against current practices of investment appraisal, it is claimed that accounting is a crucial factor which militates against the adoption of new manufacturing technologies, and that companies using these current methods may be restricted in their ability to compete in world markets.

Technicalities of Investment Appraisal

Traditionally, four techniques of investment appraisal have been emphasised: payback; accounting rate of return (ARR); internal rate of return (IRR); and net

Table 9.1   Investment appraisals for two projects.

Year	Project A (£000)	Project B (£000)
0	(100)	(100)
1	10	60
2	30	60
3	60	10
4	60	10
5	20	10
Payback	3 years	1.67 years
Average ARR	32%	20%
IRR	20%	24%
NPV (10% discount rate)	£32,360	£24,670

present value (NPV). The last two are discounted cash flow (DCF) techniques whilst ARR is based on 'return on investment' as calculated from accounting statements. Recently, a new technique, modified internal rate of return (MIRR), has been introduced and this technique seems to address some of the shortcomings of other methods. Some of the theoretical issues are most easily illustrated by an example (see Table 9.1).

The bare cash flows suggest that these projects are not very dissimilar. Both have outlays of £100,000 and both have five-year lives. While cash inflows for Project A are greater than for Project B, they are delayed to the later years of the project. Scrutiny of the various appraisal measures allows a number of points to be made. NPV calculated with a 10 per cent discount rate indicates that Project A is preferable – the theoretical recommendation. Since IRR is based on discounting principles like NPV, we might expect a similar outcome; instead, it indicates that Project B is preferable. This is because of the reinvestment assumption implicit in the IRR calculation. Here the IRR is based on an assumption that the early incoming cash flows in years 1 and 2 can be reinvested during years 3, 4 and 5 to earn a return of 24 per cent. Since the early years produce unusually high cash flows, this produces an optimistic estimate of the value of the project. The deficiencies of payback are graphically illustrated – it ignores the time value of money and cash flows outside the payback period. Project B is thus preferred and, if short payback is demanded, Project A might even be rejected outright. As we shall see, the use of short payback periods is one of the reasons why traditional investment appraisal techniques might militate against investment in AMT. ARR is spectacular for Project A (whilst for Project B it is merely good). This is a consequence of ignoring the time value of money so that Project A cash flows in years 3 and 4 are treated as being as valuable as the Project B cash flows in years 1 and 2. ARR is based on the same conventions as accounting reports and exaggerates return by comparing profits generated with the historic cost of investment. We shall see that the conventional calculation of a company's return on investment (ROI) can also work against investment in new technologies.

Whilst payback, IRR and ARR have theoretical deficiencies, it seems that many managers also have reservations about the use of NPV, preferring a rate of return (such as IRR or ARR) to the single absolute number generated by NPV calculations. However, as we have seen, the IRR reinvestment assumption may be optimistic and ARR calculations ignore the time value of money. These issues can be addressed by the use of modified internal rate of return (MIRR). While not yet used extensively (not appearing in the surveys discussed in the next section), it is theoretically attractive and appears in the most recent edition of Drury's (1992) best-selling text. The theoretical advantage of MIRR is its implicit reinvestment assumption which, like NPV, is the cost of capital (discount rate). This means that MIRR gives the same signals as NPV when, for example, competing investment opportunities have to be ranked, and, because MIRR is not based on a reinvestment assumption which is unduly optimistic, there is less danger of projects appearing overly attractive. The MIRR is calculated by converting all the cash flow after the initial investment outflow into a single cash flow at the end of the project. This is achieved by assuming that each projected cash flow can be invested at the cost of capital until the end of the project. The modified internal rate of return is then calculated as the internal rate of return based on an outflow in year 0 and an inflow at the end of the project's life (see Table 9.2).

Intuitively the MIRR figures for our example seem sensible. There is not a huge difference between the projects but Project A is preferred to Project B – consistent with the ranking derived using NPV – and the MIRR for Project B is significantly less than IRR. This reflects the MIRR reinvestment assumption of 10 per cent compared with the IRR reinvestment assumption of 24 per cent. (Of course, if 24 per cent were

Table 9.2 Modified internal rate of return for two projects.

Year	Project A		Project B	
	Cash flor (£000)	Reinvested @ 10% (£000)	Cash flow (£000)	Reinvested @ 10% (£000)
0	(100)		(100)	
1	10	14.641	60	87.846
2	30	39.641	60	79.86
3	60	72.6	10	12.1
4	60	66	10	11
5	20	20	10	10
Total value of inflows		213.171		200.806
MIRR		16.4%		14.6%

a realistic reinvestment assumption then IRR, not MIRR, would be sending the correct signal as to which project is financially preferable.)

This example serves to highlight some of the technical issues which arise in investment appraisal and the care that must be exercised in interpreting evaluation calculations. Given these interesting technical issues, it is perhaps not surprising that the methods of investment appraisal and their outcomes receive copious textbook attention with, for example, Drury (1992) devoting two whole chapters to the subject.

Applications of Investment Appraisal

In this section we review the manner in which investment appraisal techniques are applied, comparing surveys by Pike and Wolfe (1988) in the UK with those by Klammer, Koch and Wilner (1991) in the USA. We combine the empirical evidence of these surveys with the theoretical insights of Kaplan and Atkinson (1989) in order to demonstrate that uncritical use of appraisal techniques could hinder the adoption of AMT.

Techniques in use

Pike and Wolfe surveyed a sample of the largest UK companies, providing a wealth of data concerning capital budgeting processes, use of appraisal techniques and the take-up of sophisticated ideas such as risk analysis. As their study was based on similar work carried out on the same companies in 1975 and 1981, they provide comparative data so that trends in practice can be observed (see Table 9.3). This indicates an increasing use of DCF methods but, rather than displace the 'inferior' methods of payback and ARR, they are used alongside these methods. In fact, the use of payback has increased so that over 90 per cent of companies surveyed in 1986 used it. (The figures in each year total more than 100 per cent because companies employ several appraisal techniques.) Pike and Wolfe asked respondents to identify which techniques they used most frequently (see Table 9.4). Almost 50 per cent of companies always use the payback technique and, where a discounting technique is standard, IRR is almost twice as popular as NPV.

The study by Klammer *et al.* used similar methods and provides comparative US data for 1980, 1984 and 1988. They do not provide an overall summary because their

Table 9.3 Techniques used in a sample of 100 UK firms (%).

	1986	1981	1975
Payback	92	81	73
Average ARR	56	49	51
IRR	75	57	44
NPV	68	39	32

Source: Pike and Wolfe (1988).

Table 9.4   Frequency of use of techniques in sample of 100 UK firms, 1986 (%)

	Total	Rarely	Often	Mostly	Always
Payback	92	5	16	24	47
Average ARR	56	13	15	10	18
IRR	75	9	11	13	42
NPV	68	16	15	14	23

Source: Pike and Wolfe (1988).

analysis differentiates the usage of techniques by type of project (see Table 9.5). These results indicate some variation in techniques employed by project type. DCF techniques are used fairly consistently except on social investments where 'urgency' becomes the most significant factor. Urgency is also important in replacement and general/administrative investment. Payback is used consistently except for abandonment and social investment decisions. Simple rate of return (SRR – presumably ARR) is used by a minority of companies. If we concentrate on the trend in high-technology investments (see Table 9.6), we find an increasing take-up of discounting techniques,

Table 9.5   Techniques used by project type in a sample of 100 US firms, 1988 (%).

Project	Urgency	Payback	SRR	IRR	NPV
Replacement	41	42	13	58	47
Expansion – existing operations	7	32	15	54	44
Expansion – new operations	17	48	14	74	55
Foreign operations	11	45	16	71	60
Abandonment	18	11	11	40	47
General and adminstrative	42	30	10	30	32
Social expenditure	60	11	4	11	15
High-technology investments	21	42	9	57	46

Source: Klammer *et al.* (1991).

Table 9.6   High-tech investments in a sample of 100 US firms (%).

	1988	1984	1980
Urgency	21	22	22
Payback	42	36	37
Simple rate of return	9	9	10
IRR	57	50	43
NPV	46	35	30

Source: Klammer *et al.* (1991).

but not at the expense of payback which, although not as widely represented as in the UK, is being used in more companies. In general this supports the conclusions of Pike and Wolfe: increasing use of DCF methods but used alongside traditional methods.

Despite its obvious deficiencies, payback continues to be employed extensively, especially in the UK. Pike and Wolfe note managers' justifications: (a) simplicity of calculation and understanding ; (b) help in assessing time-related risk by encouraging quick returns; and (c) complementing other more sophisticated methods. To these we might add its obvious risk aversion and its use when liquidity is a major problem. Pike and Wolfe also discuss managers' preference for IRR over NPV. They cite three reasons. First, IRR is convenient for ranking projects (the absolute NPV is not so convenient and has to be converted into a 'profitability index' if projects have to be ranked). Unfortunately, it is precisely in this area that IRR is suspect because of its implicit reinvestment assumptions. Second, calculation of IRR does not require prior specification of a discount or hurdle rate. Third, and perhaps most important, managers seem to be psychologically more comfortable with a measure expressed in percentage terms, with accountants explaining that 'people are familiar with rates of return', 'percentages are more readily understood by authorising bodies', and 'I can't see the net present value meaning much to a non-accountant – or even an accountant for that matter!'

Having established that particular care is needed in interpreting the results of investment appraisal calculations, and that a variety of appraisal techniques is used in practice, we now consider the implications of these techniques in use for the justification of AMT. Kaplan (1986) stimulated debate with his seminal paper 'Must CIM be justified by faith alone?' He noted that managers seemed to have difficulty in justifying CIM investment using traditional (discounting) methods and this had led some to abandon financial analysis and to see capital investment as an act of faith: 'a commitment to making the future happen'. He could see no fault in the discounting process itself and concluded that problems must be due to the manner in which techniques are applied. These relate to accounting measurements and criteria.

Measurements in use

Not only are practitioners accused of employing inferior techniques, but also it is claimed that their measurements of AMT benefits are often faulty. Accountants continue to emphasise savings on direct labour as a key benefit even though this is now seen as a small and declining proportion of product cost, partly as a result of previous investment in AMT. Items such as better quality, greater flexibility, reduced inventory, reduction of scrap, waste and rework, reduced throughput-time, lead-time and disruption of workflows, and lower warranty and service costs are all more significant in the eyes of advocates of AMT. The solutions offered for this are that accountants should precisely quantify all of these benefits in an accounting which is a true 'appliance of science' (Primrose, 1991) or, where savings from reduction in

Table 9.7 Importance of qualitative factors in a sample
of 100 UK firms (%).

	1986	1981
Very important	13	19
Important	38	44
Average importance or below	49	37

Source: Pike and Wolfe (1988).

inventory/floor space and improvements in quality cannot be precisely calculated, they should be estimated and included in investment justification calculations (Kaplan and Atkinson, 1989). If benefits gained in increased flexibility, reduced throughput/lead-time and organisational learning are too difficult to quantify, they should be identified as intangible benefits. Even if the calculated NPV is negative, these intangibles might still be judged sufficient to outweigh the projected deficit. It appears that UK accountants do regard qualitative factors as having some importance in investments (see Table 9.7), but rather than this perception increasing, these factors are seen as having less importance in the later period.

Again, current practice appears to indicate that, although accountants are often willing to include other items, traditional measures are still emphasised. Although Pike and Wolfe do not supply figures of the type of measurements used in investment appraisal, the perception of direct labour as continuing to be important even with AMT can be gained from the findings of Drury, Braund, Osborne and Tayles (1993) on overhead allocation bases (see Table 9.8). This suggests that although, in AMT environments, the use of other allocation bases is more likely, this does not imply abandoning direct labour measures, which remain the most common.

Criteria in use

Whatever techniques are applied to whatever measurements, further criticisms are levelled at the criteria that are imposed. It is argued that long-lived projects are disadvantaged by the use of short payback periods and high hurdle rates and that this is of particular significance in the case of AMT.

Table 9.8 Overhead allocation bases in a sample of 260 UK firms.

	Automated production activities	Non-automated production activities
Direct labour hours or cost	68	73
Materials consumed	30	29
Machine hours	49	26
Units of capital	42	31
Cost drivers using ABC	9	7

Table 9.9　Hurdle rates used in a sample of 100 UK firms.

Rate for normal-risk projects (after tax in monetary terms)	1986	1981
Below 10%	5	2
10–14%	21	15
15–19%	37	37
20–24%	27	29
25–29%	6	7
Over 29%	4	10
	100	100

Source: Pike and Wolfe (1988).

Kaplan and Atkinson note (1989) that rates in excess of 20 per cent and 25 per cent are used in the USA, and high discount rates also appear to be used in the UK (see Table 9.9). In 1986 37 per cent of respondents used discount rates in excess of 20 per cent (compared with 46 per cent in 1981). A comprehensive survey of management accounting practices in 260 UK manufacturing companies by Drury *et al.* (1993) indicates that matters have not improved in the 1990s. Of companies surveyed, 53 per cent used discount rates in excess of 20 per cent, and 75 per cent required payback of three years or less, for AMT projects.

If discount rates as high as 25 per cent are used, then the value of cash flows in later years declines significantly, and a project which depends on such cash flows for its viability becomes difficult to justify in financial terms. If we apply a 25 per cent discount rate to our original example (see Table 9.1), then the NPV figures for both projects become negative. This is marginally so in the case of Project B (–£1,107) but Project A now looks very unattractive (–£10,950), thus reversing the previous message. If decisions were made on the basis of these numbers then both projects would be rejected, and if Project A represents a typical AMT investment (taking a longer time to become fully operational) then it would be disproportionately handicapped.

A number of sources of error have been identified which can lead to excessive discount rates. First, firms might derive their cost of capital from the profit and loss, and balance sheet accounting statements (Kaplan and Atkinson, 1989). As we saw earlier, ARR could be as high as 32 per cent for a project which has a MIRR of 16.4 per cent. Rates of return based on accounting conventions tend to be excessive because the time value of money is ignored. Profits are compared with investment values which are out of date because accounting statements are based on the 'historic cost' convention. A number of other factors may also cause distortion, including the use of off-balance sheet finance – investment which generates profit but never appears on the balance sheet. Here, it seems, devices of 'creative accounting' employed by financial accountants for communication to outsiders may give managers an overly optimistic view of current performance and influence expectations for the future.

Second, managers might attempt to adjust the discount rate in order to make

Table 9.10   Use of risk analysis in a sample of 100 UK firms (%).

	1986	1981	1975
Sensitivity analysis	71	42	28
Reduced payback periods	61	30	25
Increased hurdle rates	61	41	37
Probability analysis	40	10	9
Beta analysis	16	0	0

Source: Pike and Wolfe (1988).

allowance for perceived risk in the project. Surveys in both the UK and USA indicate an increasing use of measures to deal with risk. Pike and Wolfe, for example, found that 61 per cent of UK firms surveyed reduce payback periods and/or increase hurdle rates in order to allow for risk (see Table 9.10). Klammer *et al.* (1991) found a similar increasing trend toward the use of risk analysis in the USA. The percentage of firms increasing hurdle rates to deal with risk had risen from 31 per cent in 1975 to 35 per cent in 1980 and 40 per cent in 1988.

Kaplan and Atkinson (1989) pinpoint the theoretical shortcomings of increasing discount rates to deal with risk: 'It is a crude mechanism because the geometric compounding of the interest rate over time implies that project risk must also be compounding geometrically, an assumption that is almost always wrong.' They argue that if a project is risky, the risk is likely to manifest itself in the early years. If the project is successful after two or three years, the risk of failure is likely then to decrease, not increase. This may be particularly relevant with AMT since engineers must learn to implement a technology with which they are unfamiliar. Indeed, one of the intangible benefits often cited for such investment is that it enables the company to come up the 'learning curve' so that subsequent adoption of AMT is facilitated and becomes less risky.

Third, an error arises if discount or hurdle rates are based on money market rates (e.g. returns available to equity holders) whilst project cash flows are projected in so-called 'real terms' – without making an allowance for projected inflation. The problem arises because market rates are set at a level which takes account of inflation. When inflation is high, interest rates rise; when inflation falls, interest rates fall. If project cash flows take no account of inflation, then the inflation element in the discount or hurdle rate should also be excluded. Drury *et al.* (1993) provide evidence that this can be a real problem: '85 respondents (44 per cent) incorrectly used a nominal discount rate to discount current price cash flows. This may significantly underestimate the present value of a project's cash flows and lead to profitable projects being rejected.'

Fourth, the 'tax shield' effect of debt finance might be neglected. If a company is financed by both debt and equity, the interest paid on debt finance is tax deductible. This means that the true 'cost' of debt (for a company making profits) is calculated by multiplying the nominal interest rate by $(1-t)$ where t is the marginal tax rate. Kaplan and Atkinson (1989) argue that, with typical equity capital costs of 13 per cent, and after-tax debt costs around 5 per cent, the use of discount or hurdle rates in excess of 20 per cent is indefensible. A similar observation might equally be made about hurdle rates in the UK.

Accounting as a handicap to AMT

Kaplan and Atkinson (1989) concluded that objections raised by critics of DCF techniques 'may reflect nothing more than the frustration of attempting to push innovative projects through a corporate financial process that is systematically biased against investments in long lived assets'. Among the problems are the following:

flaws which occur when managers:-

1) Require payback over arbitrarily short time periods
2) Use excessively high discount rates
3) Adjust inappropriately for risk
4) Compare new investments with unrealistic status quo alternatives
5) Emphasise incremental rather than global opportunities
6) Fail to recognise all the costs of the new investment
7) Ignore important benefits from the new investment

(Kaplan and Atkinson, 1989, p. 475)

All of this appears to be a devastating attack on the manner in which many accountants employ investment appraisal techniques in practice. Even if discounting techniques are employed (and, as we know, many companies use payback and ARR) and even if NPV is the preferred technique (although many managers continue to prefer IRR), it seems that accountants fail to measure the right things, and it is all too easy to employ a discount rate which is inappropriately high. Kaplan and Atkinson find persuasive reasons as to why this can happen and Pike and Wolfe (1988) supply statistics which indicate that it does happen. Does this mean, then, that accounting is hindering or preventing the adoption of AMT? Despite the arguments and evidence so far amassed, we would be cautious of such a conclusion. It is predicated on an assumption that the results of appraisal calculation actually determine which projects are approved. As we shall see, such an assumption is problematic.

Investment Appraisal and Investment Decisions

So far we have focused narrowly on one moment in the investment process – the investment appraisal. We now need to locate this discussion in a broader understanding of the investment decision process.

Investment appraisal

Pike, Sharp and Price (1989) followed up an earlier study (Pike and Wolfe, 1988) in order to investigate the factors which influenced investment in AMT. These authors began by setting out to identify which factors affected investment decision-making in general (not specifically those relating to AMT). Because they expected strategic considerations to be a factor in AMT investment decisions, they included a wider range of factors than had previously been normal in survey-style investigations. They asked respondents to rate a variety of factors on a scale of 1 to 6 and averaged these responses in order to rank them (see Table 9.11).

Initially, the authors 'expected short term, readily quantified considerations to be given far more weight than the longer-term, more speculative ones'. They were therefore surprised to find 'strategy' ranked first, with the highest short-term, quantitative measure – payback – ranked fourth. In fact, the first seven factors are dominated by 'strategic', 'risk' and 'qualitative' factors. This finding underlines the importance of locating accounting practices in their wider context – a point which has repeatedly been made by field researchers but which is still widely ignored by those content to rely on questionnaire-based evidence.

Having established that non-financial factors are important in investment decisions, Pike *et al.* investigated the difficulties their respondents had in justifying AMT. They found that over 50 per cent of manufacturing firms reported problems in assessing the benefits of AMT investment: 'There are difficulties in forecasting the pace of technological change in AMT. Such investments tend to involve many more qualitative or intangible factors.' Perhaps because of this, AMT investment processes did not fit with the researchers, expectations.

> Of particular interest ... because it has not been explicitly considered in previous surveys is the strong emphasis placed by all respondent companies on 'intangible'

Table 9.11 Priority of investment factors in a sample of 100 UK firms, 1986.

Rank	Factor	Average score
1	Degree of fit with business strategy	5.21
2	Sensitivity to changes in key assumptions	5.00
3	Growth rate of markets related to the project	4.35
4	Payback period	4.28
5	Type of project (e.g. cost saving, new technology)	4.11
6	Effect on product quality	4.09
7	Investment track record of project sponsor	4.00
8	Effect on achievement of profit and sales targets	3.83
9	Competitive position of the related business unit	3.81
10	Impact of investment on current year's earnings	3.62
11	Level of agreement (opposition) from interested parties	3.61
12	Effect on productivity	3.49
13	Effect on corporate image	3.34
14	Impact of project failure on corporate financial status	3.32
15	Effect on morale	2.79
16	Effect on trade union relations	2.76

Source: Pike *et al.* (1989).

factors. This was initially surprising to us. It was expected that quantifiable factors, particularly internal rate of return and payback would be rated far higher. However, interviews have confirmed that executives from middle management level upwards pay considerably more attention to an investment's fit with corporate strategy than they do to its financial performance. (Pike *et al.*, 1989, p. 25)

This would indicate that researchers employing survey methods have been, until recently, unaware of the possibility that evaluation techniques might not be foremost in the decision-making process. However, field researchers have been emphasising non-financial factors in investment decision-making for several years, and two of the most recent field investigations, by Nixon and Lonie (1992), and Slagmulder and Bruggeman (1992), relate specifically to investment in AMT. By adopting a field study approach these researchers were not restricted to pre-set survey-style questions and they were sensitive to the possibility that a variety of factors might influence AMT investment decision-making.

Investment decisions

Nixon and Lonie (1992) studied the impact of management accounting on technological innovation through thirteen case studies where they adopted an 'eclectic approach' which examined decisions in the context of strategy, culture and organisational arrangements, including both formal and informal information systems. They concluded that, where decisions relate to entrepreneurial prospects or product differentiation strategies, financial considerations are 'eclipsed' by strategic considerations:

in some cases the financial calculations and information were massaged to accommodate important information . . . commenting on the appraisal techniques used, one Managing Director stated that: *'We did all these (DCF) calculations . . . we did them again and again until they came out right'*. [emphasis added]

Nixon and Lonie noted, 'Only one of our case study companies has developed systems to match the information needed to formulate competitive strategies. . . . Most of the other companies rely heavily on informal information', and they recommended that management accounting control systems should be (further) developed to support strategic decisions.

Slagmulder and Bruggeman (1992) studied the justification of flexible manufacturing technologies (FMT) in six companies, and set out to identify the characteristics of the investment decision-making process including 'financial, strategic, technical and organisational analysis'. They reported that projects could be approved even if IRR did not meet the hurdle rate and, if there was insistence on a 'satisfactory' return, there was a tendency to manipulate savings and benefits. In seven (of nine) projects investigated, strategic considerations/benefits were most important. In only one project was favourable payback cited as most important, and even that project's success was later explained in terms of the fit between FMT and the company's competitive strategy. They concluded that the 'main critical success factor in deciding

on investments in flexible technologies is the quality of the strategic analysis ...
financial justification and the use of capital budgeting techniques in the decision-
making process have become of secondary importance'.

The role of investment appraisal

In the previous section we began with an implicit assumption that investment
appraisal calculations were a key factor in AMT investment decision-making and an
analysis indicating that such calculations could hinder the adoption of AMT. In this
section we have evidence from survey and field research which indicates that
investment appraisal calculations are of secondary importance, with 'strategic fit'
cited as a primary factor in approving investment expenditure. Slagmulder and
Bruggeman (1992) go so far as to suggest that 'the fact that the investment decision
is mainly based on good strategic arguments, appears to be a sufficient condition for
success'. We should be cautious over Slagmulder and Bruggeman's assumption that
capital budgeting techniques have become secondary. As we have noted, survey
questionnaires may simply fail to take such factors into account, and although there
is relatively little field research evidence for earlier periods, what is available is
indicative of a lower degree of importance being attached to appraisal than
commonly assumed by academics. For example, over thirty years ago, Haynes and
Solomon (1962) suggested 'a misplaced emphasis in capital budgeting' and drew
attention to steps in the capital budgeting process which, typically, received little
attention: the search for investment opportunities and the identification of costs and
benefits associated with these opportunities. They noted that the 'literature, however,
stresses an entirely different step in the decision making process: the precise
computation of the relative worth of investment alternatives'. Thus, capital budgeting
techniques may *always* have been of secondary importance, with academics failing to
appreciate this.

We also have reservations about Nixon and Lonie's (1992) recommendations for the
extension of management accounting control systems. Having discovered that formal
systems and calculation might be relatively unimportant in AMT decision-making, it
does not automatically follow that such systems should be modified in an attempt to
make them more relevant. Perhaps the key aspects of investment decision-making
cannot be captured within a formal system grounded in quantification and calculus.
On the other hand, it may be that the influence of accounting on investment decisions
is not limited to its formal application in appraisal, but that it is deeply embedded in
less formal organisational processes. The next section turns to this issue.

Investment in an Organisational Context

This section draws on field research carried out by ourselves in a number of UK
manufacturing companies. Using semi-structured interviews, we explored the

perceptions of investment decision-making held by accountants, engineers and managers.

Investment appraisal in context

In one study (Jones and Dugdale, 1994) we contrasted an academic view of investment appraisal with those of a number of practitioners. Whilst the academic thought that theory 'ought' to be applied in practice and the only sound appraisal technique was NPV, practitioners did not share this view. A plant accountant actually felt that the use of sophisticated techniques could be counter-productive: first, because they would not be understood ('I've always been a bit sceptical of DCF . . . who would I present it to? My local management wouldn't understand that. I'm sure they wouldn't understand that.'); second, because the complexity of NPV calculations would distract from the main task – interrogating the cash flow projections (especially the product volume assumptions) on which the analysis was based. This accountant advocated the use of payback ('Payback? Its strength is it is simple and if you can justify something on simple grounds then why make them more complicated?').

The emphasis on the cash flow projections was reiterated by accountants in a second company. This high-tech organisation had a policy of recruiting highly qualified staff and encouraging them to study for degrees such as the MBA. Here, unlike the first plant, no problems of understanding were anticipated and a senior divisional accountant foresaw no difficulties in calculating and presenting the results of appraisal calculations ('Investment appraisal techniques? Somebody, somewhere is going to ask you for all of them, for each in turn. Invariably you'll end up doing them all.'). But it was emphasised that such calculations were a small part of the decision-making process. The original proposal would usually be driven by perceived market forces (such as capacity, quality and/or reliability), and the importance of projects fitting into company 'strategy' was emphasised rather than their financial justification. If a project 'felt' right but appeared not to meet financial criteria, then the financial justification would be scrutinised for errors rather than the project rejected. Again, the uncertainty inherent in cash flow projections was emphasised and attempts were made to quantify this uncertainty by having managers estimate the probabilities of certain events.

Whilst these practitioners were relatively unconcerned about techniques (payback, NPV, etc.), they were concerned about measurement – estimating projected cash flows. They were prepared to go to considerable lengths to ensure that the financial projections supported company strategy and there is some evidence that such projections may sometimes be a post-hoc rationalisation for a decision made on other (possibly strategic) grounds. However, no particular difficulty was seen in the measurement of AMT since many of the benefits would be 'intuitively obvious – you're buying a machine because you're going to cut down on waste, something like that'. In both companies short payback periods were expected. In one case this was not seen as a problem since even targets of 'a year or so' could be met by many projects. In the other company there had been a reduction in payback periods from 5–8 to 2–3 years. This had resulted from a take-over of the company by a new owning group 'who wanted to milk us dry' and thus represented a strategic decision rather than a criterion based on faulty assumptions or calculations. Whilst practitioners were sensitive to issues of technique, measurement and criteria, they did not regard accounting as a particular handicap to AMT. Indeed, investment in production technology was seen as easier to justify than other proposals such as acquisition of land and buildings.

Investment decisions in context

In another study (Dugdale and Jones, 1994) we explored a number of AMT decisions in a division of a high-tech multinational. We found some scepticism of accounting numbers in AMT investment ('generally those decisions, you can make the numbers support the case for doing it or you can make the numbers support the case not to do it, if you want to'). Much accounting information was kept deliberately low-key ('We did some ROI-type stuff, pretty simple basic stuff.'). There was a fairly relaxed attitude to criteria ('there are no hurdle rates or anything like that') and measurements (engineers had 'complete freedom on the cost model'). Overall, there was no fixed, formal appraisal procedure which people were compelled to follow.

However, this did not mean that accounting was unimportant in investment decisions. Precisely because accounting numbers could be manipulated, a middle manager saw interrogation of the assumptions behind the financial projection as crucial, particularly in building up the credibility of the project sponsor. Proposers should be able to work out unit costs on the new technology and would be asked about this.

> 'If he says it's $[x], it's good that he knows the answer, that gives you confidence that he's thought about it. Then you're going to ask yourself the question, does $[x] sound reasonable? What was it on the previous line, where have your savings come from?'

Whilst the techniques of investment appraisal and the criteria used to judge an investment project are seen as relatively unimportant by practitioners, the process of constructing financial projections is seen as critical. Understanding and gaining consensus regarding these projections is a complex social process and whether the numbers eventually 'come out right' depends on the interaction of several, perhaps conflicting, views. For the middle manager, however, financial justification was secondary to strategic considerations. That was why, when one proposal appeared to meet financial criteria, it was nevertheless rejected. The proposers

> 'went through all kinds of financial analyses. I kept telling them, "look guys [laughter] it's the wrong answer" [laughter] . . . We just don't want to get good at doing that . . . So there was a case when they failed. They failed the strategy test. If they had managed to get the strategy in line . . . then I'd go with the best financial justification.'

This interrogation on strategy and finance

> 'is really aimed at confidence-building, rather than justification. I mean the reality is that if he has answered the questions to a certain level of depth, you form the opinion that the guy knows what he's doing, he's looked at it from a reasoned point of view. Right? Then you say "OK, this guy convinced me that I should back his judgement".'

The engineer who led the team making the proposal did not see it this way, and his manager was concerned that he must learn to get strategy and finance in line because a proposer's task was to 'Convince me that I should trust you'. A year later, the engineer had begun to see investment decisions differently:

> 'Maybe I've learnt a little better how to target ... my mistake was that sometimes I would tailor my justification to the next person in the chain ... not realising that they've got to explain it to the next one up ... everything needs campaigning and following up and seeing other people and getting support and all those things.'

Accounting, credibility and confidence

In this section we located the moment of appraisal as part of an extended process of investment decision-making in broader organisational context. First, proposals may originate outside accounting — coming from engineers and production managers – and already be filtered before formal appraisal begins. The origins of such proposals reflect managerial concerns with increasing capacity to keep up with orders, or the updating of production technology. The economic viability of these proposals may well be assessed – either intuitively, or by simple calculations – before they come to the attention of accountants. Many projects with potentially high financial returns may well be rejected for non-financial reasons and never become formal proposals. Second, once submitted, proposals may not be judged solely on financial criteria. Financial information co-exists with market, production and technology information which all play their part in decision processes. The role of accounting is important in checking out proposals, and giving indication of the consequences of investment, but practitioners do not typically see it as determining decision outcomes. The eventual decision may depend on later strategic judgements.

This does not mean that accounting is irrelevant. Projects require financial scrutiny even if this is not the determining factor. Accounting numbers may be used by decision-makers to interrogate proposers of AMT to ensure that they have business (not narrowly technological) ends in mind and have made a rigorous examination of the means of achieving them. It is not the 'correctness' of accounting numbers which is sought; it is that proposers have considered the investment from a financial perspective. It is this which makes proposals credible, and builds up confidence in proposers.

Thus accounting as a mode of thought, which provides particular views of the ends and means of manufacturing, may have a much broader impact than its narrow role in investment appraisal. Since UK companies are often described as 'finance led' or 'accounting dominated', this may produce particular organisational contexts which discourage investment in AMT. In the next section we explore this issue through comparison of UK and Japanese manufacturing.

Organisational Contexts in Societal Environment

This section draws mostly on Jones, Currie and Dugdale (1993) for discussion of the relationship between accounting and technology in eight large Japanese manufacturers. Although the term AMT is widely applied in the West, Japanese managers seem reluctant to use it, and prefer terms such as 'factory automation' or simply 'production technology'. Nevertheless, many of the specific technologies are similar, and allow us to make some comparisons with UK manufacturing.

Accounting practices

On the surface, many accounting practices in Japan seem similar to those we have identified in the UK. The *techniques* used are 'traditional', with only one of the eight companies using DCF but all using payback. Indeed, it appears that, with decreasing life-expectancy of products and manufacturing systems, DCF is becoming generally less common. Similarly, *measurements* appear to remain focused on direct labour costs, and 2–3-year payback periods are the usual *criteria*. These superficial similarities may, however, have different meanings and consequences in Japanese decision-making. For example, although direct labour is measured this may have different meanings. Japanese employment practices encourage the development of 'polyvalent' or 'multi-skilled' employees, and work organisation centres on teams. Here we may find activities which are identified as 'indirect labour' in the UK (e.g. maintenance) being seen as 'direct labour' in Japan. In addition, long-term management drives to simplify and reduce administrative functions mean that 'white-collar' overhead is probably much lower than in the UK. One consequence of this is likely to be that direct labour costs are identified as a much higher proportion of total product cost. Hence the benefits of AMT may appear higher even if only direct labour costs are measured.

Again, although both UK and Japanese managers typically use 2–3-year payback periods, this may not produce a similar emphasis on short-termism. In Japan, strategic decision-making appears to be more rigorously and formally pursued than in the UK, especially in respect to technology. Thus each technology investment decision may be viewed as merely one step, needing specific justification, on a path to longer-term product, market and production goals. For example, typical practices appear to assume a reduction in production costs of about 10 per cent per annum in the short term, and then a more marked reduction in the longer term (say three-yearly) through product redesign (e.g. by reducing the number of components).

Organisational context

As the above comments indicate, it is again necessary to locate accounting practices in organisational contexts to understand their significance. Whilst both UK and Japanese companies may vary considerably between themselves, we may identify some overall contrasts between the two societies.

In the large Japanese enterprise *management* appears to have broader functional experience at the individual level, to be more strongly organised into teams, and decision-making may be described as 'management by consent'. At the higher levels accountancy seems less widely represented and engineering has 'a strong voice'. This more integrated management structure, and the emphasis on shared responsibility for both decisions and their implementation, may assist in the introduction of integrated AMT systems. In relation to *labour*, patterns of permanent employment which large companies have been able to maintain (for male employees), until recently, have produced a workforce which is often characterised as 'loyal' and 'multi-skilled', and which is represented through single-enterprise (or even single-plant) unions. This may facilitate the introduction of AMT through the existing flexibility and relative security of the workers who are both able and willing to make the work organisation changes which often follow. At the level of *capital*, the largest of the Japanese enterprises (combines or industrial groupings) have close links with banks and other financial institutions (often members of the same groups) and are less vulnerable to the short-termism of shareholders and stock markets. This has been important in securing a supply of cheap, long-term finance for companies and has enabled managers to concentrate their attention on product, production and marketing issues, rather than giving priority to financial concerns. Again, this may support the development of longer-term AMT strategies and their successful implementation, especially since both the supplying and the adopting companies may well be within the same combine or group.

Societal environment

These features of Japanese manufacturers have emerged, and been sustained, in a society which has different characteristics from those of the UK. We will focus on two features here.

The development of AMT in Japan is influenced by *state* direction and intervention. Successive Japanese governments since the start of the 'Meiji period' of 1868 have been involved in creation and restructuring of industries. Economic development has been shaped by the Ministry of International Trade and Industry, and the Japan Development Bank. In education, the Japanese government has focused on the production of graduate-qualified engineers whose numbers surpassed that of the USA by 1970. In respect to technology, the Japanese government has identified key technologies for import and allocated these to selected combines and industrial groups for development. Thus the acquisition, assimilation and diffusion of technology is structured by state planning. In Britain, the picture is much less clear.

Various UK governments have steered an erratic course between 'state intervention' and 'free market' approaches to the economy, business, education and technological innovation – in both ideological pronouncements and actual practices. The situation is further complicated by the uneasy relationship between the UK government and the European Union. The importance of this for the development of AMT, and more generally the fortunes of our manufacturing industry, is difficult to assess. But we would suggest that, at minimum, it may create a climate of uncertainty.

The issue of *culture* is a difficult one since it may be seen as both a cause, and an effect, of business practices. However, a number of Western observers have been impressed by the different values and attitudes which pervade Japanese manufacturing. Hayes and Wheelwright (1984) identified strong values of cleanliness and orderliness, care of equipment, and a 'quality consciousness' that began by 'thinking it in' through design, training and emphasis on every person being responsible for quality screening, feedback and correction. These values may have been encouraged by 'lifetime employment' practices and attempts to secure an 'everlasting customer'; and the drive to reduce stocks and eliminate defects from the plant may have been given impetus by the extremely high cost of industrial land. However, Hayes and Wheelwright also cited underlying cultural factors which are reflected in these Japanese production practices: first, 'group consciousness', where work organisation is group-based, members orient themselves to this group, and actions for the benefit of the group are highly regarded – this becomes embedded in team or participative management and, at a wider level, between core firms and affiliated enterprises; second, a 'do-it-yourself' preference for making extensive modifications to existing machinery, and designing and producing production technology in-house; and third, the pursuit of 'the last grain of rice in the corner of the lunchbox', which suggests an obsessive combination of frugality, orderliness and persistence, and which sustains managers in completing programmes of change (e.g. aiming for 'zero defects' rather than 'acceptable waste') even where the financial justification is not convincing. The central emphasis on quality can be difficult for UK managers to accept since the conventional wisdom is that higher quality implies higher costs, whereas in Japan it is associated with higher productivity. In the 1980s, British managers may have been convinced that Japanese production methods were successful, but they found it difficult to understand why this was. This may indicate that some features are so culturally unique that they are not open to interrogation from other societies nor transferable to them. Having said this, we note that Japanese companies have not seemed particularly constrained in their import of 'Western' manufacturing (and accounting) techniques, their modification to local circumstances and then their re-export to subsidiaries in the UK (and USA).

Accounting and AMT in Britain and Japan

This brief review of Japanese enterprises provides no evidence that their success in developing 'world-class manufacturing' has resulted from use of 'superior' investment appraisal techniques, measurement or criteria. On the contrary, these would be labelled 'traditional' by most Western observers. What it has suggested is that the meanings and consequences of accounting may differ because it reflects, and acts within, different organisational contexts. These contexts are constructed within Japan's particular social formations of capital, management and labour, which are embedded in particular societal patterns at political (e.g. state) and ideological (e.g. culture) levels. This reconfirms our view that the nature of AMT investment, and accounting's role in this, needs to be located in broader organisational contexts and societal environments in order to understand the processes involved.

Does Accounting *Really* Handicap AMT?

We began this chapter by identifying a hue and cry over investment appraisal in which it is seen as a crucial factor in investment decisions, and the failings of traditional accounting (discovered in its techniques, measurements and criteria) are identified as a significant handicap to AMT, thus hindering the development of more competitive manufacturing in the UK and USA.

Our discussion of technicalities showed that the selection of different techniques, and the assumptions under which they are applied, do indeed make a significant difference to the informational output of investment appraisal. We also found the claim that accountants in practice continue to use traditional techniques, emphasise direct labour measurements and often apply short-term/high-return criteria, was backed by survey evidence for both the UK and the USA. All of this would appear to support the case that, both theoretically and in practice, accounting could handicap AMT investment.

We began to diverge from this view by identifying investment appraisal as merely one aspect of investment decisions. Other forms of information (such as production and marketing information) and broader strategic issues were also seen as important. We also identified appraisal as only one moment in decision-making processes which began before the interventions of accounting and continued beyond them. Particular relationships between accounting and non-accounting information, and between moments in the decision process, were related to organisational contexts. Here accounting was seen not only as a formal system of information and control, but also as a mode of thought which could be important in the interrogation of proposers of AMT investment (although perhaps of secondary importance to strategy). Accounting was seen as implicated in managerial processes of gaining credibility for proposals, and building confidence in proposers. In order to explore the influence of organisational contexts, we contrasted UK accounting practices with those of Japanese manufacturers. We found that, although the technicalities of accounting had superficial similarity in the two societies, different organisational contexts implied that their meaning and consequences could differ.

This leads us to the view that, although the argument that traditional accounting handicaps AMT is a logically sound deduction from consideration of technicalities in investment appraisal and survey evidence of current applications, field research suggests it is not an empirically convincing account nor explanation of decisions in manufacturing. AMT investment decisions in the UK do not appear to conform to the assumptions implicit in the academic critique of practice. Neither do Japanese companies, typically cited as exemplars of world-class manufacturing, seem to have adopted the prescriptions advanced as solutions in the West – nor do they show signs of doing so. This is not to imply that detailed consideration of investment appraisal is irrelevant. In our view, it is important that accountants recognise and understand the nature of technicalities – it is part of their expertise. The relevance of considering organisational contexts and their societal environment is not to escape the technicalities of accounting; it is to understand accounting more broadly. If we adopt a myopic view of the financial justification of AMT, we reduce it to merely the technicalities of investment appraisal. If we take a broader view, we understand these technicalities as interrelated with wider decision process, contexts and environments. The narrow view may lead to the conclusion that traditional accounting handicaps AMT, and that new practices will result in significant improvements. The broader view suggests that (at best) this 'handicapping' is unproven, and (more probably) close attention to the technicalities of investment appraisal, abstracted from a wider analysis, is unlikely to impact significantly on the adoption of AMT.

If UK companies have underinvested in AMT, and if this is a cause of uncompetitiveness (see Note below), we do not believe this can be ascribed to deficiencies in investment appraisal (although no doubt they exist) nor that improving this (which is no doubt desirable) will transform either investment or performance in manufacturing. Instead, greater understanding of technological and managerial issues among accountants, increased awareness of financial issues among engineers and manufacturing managers, and closer teamworking between these groups may be a more appropriate focus; and there are some indications that this is the direction a number of companies are taking. In this way financial justification of AMT may be more firmly located in its organisational context.

Note

Here we identify two important assumptions:

1. that UK manufacturers' investment in AMT falls short of some absolute or relative 'standard' which they ought to be achieving; and
2. that this is a significant contributory factor in uncompetitive manufacturing performance.

Neither of these propositions is self-evident. For example, we have noted that Japanese manufacturers put considerable emphasis on modifying existing technology, and on developing in-house innovations, rather than relying on the more advanced products of specialist suppliers. It is not clear that higher rates of adoption of AMT have been a key factor in Japanese productivity. In the UK, one of the companies we researched (Dugdale and Jones, 1994) adopted an advanced (bought-in) assembly system for a new product, but then found that it did not match their expectations or requirements for it. Subsequent expansion in production was achieved by developing a simpler, and more traditional, in-house solution, and may come closer to Japanese practice.

Exploration of the relationship between adoption of AMT and improved manufacturing performance is too large a task to be undertaken here. We do note, however, that the view of accounting as a handicap to AMT rests upon the two assumptions; so when accounting does not demonstrate that the adoption of AMT would be beneficial, then accounting is deemed to be in error.

References

Drury, C. (1992) *Management and Cost Accounting*, Wokingham: Van Nostrad Reinhold.

Drury, C., S. Braund, P. Osborne and M. Tayles (1993) *A Survey of Management Accounting Practices in UK Manufacturing Companies*, London: ACCA.

Dugdale, D. and T.C. Jones (1994) 'Finance, strategy and trust in investment appraisal', *Management Accounting (UK)*, April, pp. 52–6.

Hayes, R.H. and S.C. Wheelwright (1984) *Restoring Our Competitive Edge*, New York: Wiley and Sons.

Haynes, W.W. and M.B. Solomon, jun. (1962) 'A misplaced emphasis in capital budgeting', *Quarterly Review of Economics and Business*, February, pp. 39–46.

Jones, T.C. and D. Dugdale (1994) 'Academic and practitioner rationality: the case of investment appraisal', *British Accounting Review*, vol. 26, no. 1, pp. 3–25.

Jones, T.C., W.L. Currie and D. Dugdale (1993) 'Accounting and technology in Britain and Japan: learning from field research', *Management Accounting Research*, vol. 4, no. 2, pp. 109–37.

Kaplan, R.S. (1986) 'Must CIM be justified by faith alone?', *Harvard Business Review*, March–April, pp. 87–93.

Kaplan, R.S. and A.A. Atkinson (1989) *Advanced Management Accounting* (2nd edn), Englewood Cliffs, NJ: Prentice Hall.

Klammer, T., B. Koch and N. Wilner (1991) 'Capital budgeting practices: a survey of corporate use', *Journal of Management Accounting Research*, Fall, pp. 113–30.

Nixon, W. and A.A. Lonie (1992) *Technological Innovation and Management Accounting Control: Some survey evidence from thirteen case studies* (Paper ACC/9205), Dundee: Department of Accountancy and Finance: University of Dundee.

Pike, R.H. and M.B. Wolfe (1988) *Capital Budgeting for the 1990's*, London: CIMA.

Pike, R.H., J. Sharp and D. Price (1989) 'AMT investment in the larger UK firm', *International Journal of Operations and Production Management*, vol. 9, no. 2, pp. 13–26.

Primrose, P. (1991) 'The appliance of science', *Manufacturing Engineer*, November, pp. 42–3.

Slagmulder, R. and W. Bruggeman (1992) 'Investment justification of flexible manufacturing technologies: inferences from field research', *International Journal of Operations and Production Management*, vol. 12, no. 7, pp. 168–86.

CHAPTER TEN

Management Information Systems, Computer Technology and Management Accounting

John K. Christiansen and Jan Mouritsen

♦

Introduction

Management information systems and computer technology provide organisations with opportunities to make activities such as receiving goods, production processes, distribution, marketing and sales, and services more efficient. While computer technology is important for general administrative and managerial purposes, it also changes and challenges the role of management accounting in organisations. In this chapter we discuss the nature of information technology and the challenges and opportunities it poses for management accountants.

The relationship between information technology (IT), management information systems (MIS) and accounting information systems (AIS) is one where IT supplies the basis on which MIS and AIS are designed. IT includes both hardware and software. MIS and AIS are particular applications used to support organisational procedures through access to information supported by IT. MIS provides information for management in its broadest sense, including accounting information. AIS is thus part of an organisational MIS, which concentrates on financial data. This distinction between AIS and MIS is becoming blurred, and often what organisations refer to as AIS contains non-financial data, just as financial data may be useful in managing inventories, debt-collection and production-processes. Therefore, what is labelled in organisations as MIS and AIS is open to debate. In organisations, however, AIS is mostly seen to be within the regime of the accounting department. It thus designates a division of labour between the functions in the firm. This division of labour is not yet inevitable, but is the result of decisions in that respect and identifies a domain of control.

The first section of this chapter describes the changes in computing technology. The structure of the technology is explained by describing the different layers in the technology. This section then goes on to identify the impact of changes in computer technology on information technology. It is argued that IT has become a critical factor for the survival of the firms, having wide strategic and organisational implications and involving many stakeholders. The next section is devoted to an examination of the implications of these changes for management accountants.

In the section on the design of information systems, parallels are drawn between the development of AIS and MIS. The role to be played by management accountants in the design process is discussed. The design approaches presented deal with the design issue in very different ways. These range from very structured methods, focusing on the life-cycle of systems, to less structured socio-technical methods, stressing parallel development of social and technical systems. End-user computing methods empowering the user with the possibility of and responsibility for designing and testing applications and the idea of business process re-engineering (BPR) are also discussed. The section following presents four typical information systems – decisions support systems, executive information systems, group decisions support systems and strategic information systems – and evaluates the importance of each in turn for the management accountant.

Finally, the natural competition that arises between management accountants and information systems specialists in the design and control of information systems is discussed. It is argued that in many respects management accountants are in a favourable situation, since their intellectual technology focuses on how organisational decisions and processes can be integrated. In contrast, information systems specialists' competence concerns the relationships between technologies rather than those between technologies and organisational processes.

The Changes in Computing and Information Technology

The changes in computing technology and IT during the last decade have been dramatic in terms of the development of both software and hardware. Such developments are intermingled, with advances in one area affecting the other. Parts of tasks performed earlier by software are today integrated into hardware, and the more sophisticated software demands better and faster hardware.

Table 10.1 summarises some of the most important changes in computing technology that have occurred during the last ten years.

Until late in 1979 nearly all computers were large machines used for number-crunching and routine bookkeeping. Outside the universities and government establishment, they were acquired mainly by large companies, which could afford to pay the prices and to employ professional programmers and technicians to maintain the machines. The machines were available in two broad categories: mainframes and minicomputers. Both types could have several users working at terminals simultaneously, entering and printing data. Mainframes played a key role in data

Table 10.1 Trends in computing technology during the last decade.

	1960s to 1980s	Late 1980s to present
Hardware		
Size	Large mainframes and some minicomputers	Some mainframes and lots of PCs and servers
Users	Large companies and government organisations	Large and small firms in the public as well as in the private sector
Price for computing power	Expensive in most areas. Only few organisations could afford IT	Medium to low – according to the types of IT required. In general, though, IT becomes less expensive
Performance	Mainframes' performance amounted to the performance of one PC of today	A PC's capacity is typically not fully exploited by one single user
Standards and compatibility	The individual vendor and supplier created their own IT standards, thus disabling different IT solutions from communicating	Industry-wide standards improve compatibility between products from different vendors
Use of computers	Automated routine calculations controlled by central computing departments	Widely dispersed use at all organisational levels, both by groups and by individuals
Storage and retrieval of data	Centralised database systems which were often difficult and time-consuming to operate	Central and distributed local databases and personal ones – with improved access and retrieval capabilities
Software		
Types of applications	Designed specifically for tasks and functions in companies	Many types of applications including functional and cross-organisational ones, with extensive networking facilities and sharing of data
Performance	Designed for the task and difficult to alter. Access to data not easy or possible by end-users themselves	Designed for integration and distribution of data between different applications
Designers of applications	Engineers and specialists in computer science	Some specialists with users, or users themselves
Price	High	Still high for mainframe applications, but very low for 'off-the-shelf' products
Standards and compatibility	Software designed for specific platform (machine from single vendor)	Industry-wide standards – for applications and operating systems
User interface	Command oriented – abstract coding languages – required much training	Graphic user interfaces – dialogue and object-oriented languages, closer to natural language – less training

processing operations in most large companies. Smaller and less expensive mini-computers were often used by divisions of the same companies, or by medium-sized firms which could not justify spending the amount necessary to buy a mainframe.

Due to the complexity of mainframe machines, customers had only a few large established suppliers from which to choose. It was difficult for newcomers to enter the market. The introduction of microprocessors or 'chips' made the personal computer (PC) a cost- and performance-competitive alternative for small and medium-sized companies as well as for single users. The introduction of more 'open standards' that enable machines across different platforms to talk and work together has made it easier to connect, replace and exchange information between different machines and software. Customers now require their data to be used across multiple platforms and even across different applications, for example between different word-processing systems (see Note), or for example the incorporation of data from the company database into a spreadsheet and finally into a word-processing document. The open standards in computing grant smaller companies access to the market, where they compete in all areas and at every stage of the value-chain, from chips to distribution. The establishment of open standards made it possible to break the market dominance of the biggest supplier, IBM.

The integration of platforms through the introduction of networks and distributed computing has increased the usefulness of PCs, although the larger mainframes have not completely disappeared. The mainframes have proved to be useful in large organisations with specialist applications and a need for processing large amounts of data, or where storage and security issues make it important to concentrate computer processing at a few central locations, for example airlines and the financial sector.

The fastest-growing segment of the computer business is now the 'networking' area, where computers and other output and input devices are connected together. One type of connection between PCs is known as 'peer-to-peer' computing, which allows users to send information between PCs. In a 'client-server' network, a large number of PCs (clients) are connected to a central computer (the server). The server performs many of the same tasks as did the old mainframes, but at a fraction of the cost. However, much computing is done locally on the client-computers by running the applications on the individual PCs in the network. This type of network also supports sharing information and documents among several users simultaneously. This allows several users to have access to and work on 'shared' information, such as customers' orders or the integration of accounting information directly into letters to the customers. Local area networks (LANs) connect several client PCs with their server. Wide area networks (WANs) connect a number of LANs, e.g. connecting several geographically dispersed business unit LANs with a company WAN.

The structure of computer technology today is on the one hand simpler, and at the same time more complex, than just three to five years ago. It is simpler because the introduction and demand for standards and compatibility between products have produced a set of standards. It is more complex because today there exists a large number of suppliers of many different types of products, and with no single player dominating the whole computing scene. Where the 'old' computer scene could be described as a series of manufacturers, each having their own 'tower' of products where one or a few manufacturers controlled all the levels (products) of the tower, computing equipment today consists of an assembly of products from different manufacturers.

The computer products of today might be described as consisting of five levels or layers. The *first layer* is the microprocessor that performs the basic manipulations in the computer. The *second layer* is the computer-platforms, including every form of assembled PC, such as desktops, workstations, laptops and notebooks. The *third layer* is the operating system software, which is divided into operating software for running central network servers and software for running client machines (PCs). A few million machines function as servers, while more than 90 million machines work as clients. Microsoft and Apple dominate the client section, while a number of products are represented on the network server side, such as Novell netware and IBM, among others.

The *fourth layer* is the applications software that performs one or several tasks for the user. This layer can be divided into different categories for each task such as spreadsheet, bookkeeping, word-processing, graphics and so on. Bookkeeping packages such as Sage, Pegasus and Maconomy are examples of brand names. The *fifth layer* is the distribution layer, where assembled and installed computers and different accessories, such as printers and modems, are shipped off and services are offered.

The distribution level contains a growing number of services offered to business, such as consultation on the purchase of computers, installation of networks and the implementation of technology in order to make the best use of the computers, and integrating technology with organisational restructuring (re-engineering). System integration enables the different platforms and applications to talk with one another.

These substantive changes in computing technology, with their implications for information technology, are altering the way that firms work. Thus Earl (1989) notes that the organisational arguments for, and the role of, IT have changed throughout the 1980s.

First, IT is increasingly being regarded as an investment rather than as a cost. New IT is justified not only on how it will improve the speed of the administrative and bookkeeping process, but also on the grounds of how it can improve overall competitiveness.

Second, the role of IT has shifted from being mostly a support tool to being a critical factor for the survival of the firm by giving it a competitive advantage in controlling distribution of goods and information between a manufacturer and the customers using electronic data interchange technology (EDI). Electronic communications with suppliers and customers connect the firm more closely with its environment, thereby expanding the 'effective boundaries' of the firm. IT also makes it possible to implement just-in-time manufacturing processes, reducing costs of keeping inventories and speeding response time to market changes (see, for example the discussion in Chapter 5).

Third, whilst previously IT was mostly operational/tactical, it now increasingly becomes strategic. Until recently, IT has mostly been applied to production planning, and to bookkeeping activities. IT has subsequently permeated to all levels throughout the organisation. Thus IT now provides information to chief executives with the use of executive information systems (EIS), by which executive management is able to oversee most of the activities of the firm. Hence, IT has become an indispensable part of firms' strategic planning processes. Many corporate strategies emphasise the need to collaborate across space and time. IT is one way in which firms can compete globally.

Fourth, IT changes the conditions for organisations and individuals, influencing nearly all aspects of organisational life. Individual users recognise that their daily work often consists of spending most of their working hours in front of a screen. This changes power structures within organisations between those who are providing data and those who are able (or allowed) to access and decipher the information.

Fifth, IT has moved from being useful for computerisation of existing administrative tasks, such as computing of large quantities of data in bookkeeping, to being utilised to solve tasks in new ways, e.g. by linking departments and business processes. The restructuring and rationalisation of business processes and companies through IT is given more attention through business process re-engineering (BPR), which is discussed in more detail later in this chapter.

Sixth, the number of stakeholders in IT, MIS and AIS has increased. Those affected directly or indirectly by the technology have multiplied from just a few stakeholders to many. The use of IT to link a business unit with its headquarters, customers and suppliers illustrates how company-wide databases can be accessed and analysed by different groups for different purposes. When IT is used as a means of BPR, it naturally becomes an important issue to many different groups of employees.

Finally, the nature of the technology involved in IT has changed, with the emphasis moving away from merely concentrating on raw computing power to focusing on the interface with the user. This has considerably increased the access and usefulness of IT throughout the organisation.

These changes have all served to increase the importance of IT, and Earl argues that IT is now a key element in the strategy of any firm, in that it underwrites most of the activities performed in modern organisations. The pervasiveness of IT is therefore also a challenge to management accountants, accustomed, as they are, to having a monopoly on information in many organisations. IT is a new field of expertise which management accountants need to master if they are to continue to operate effectively in any organisation.

Computer Technology and the Management Accountant

Computer technology is regarded by many management accountants as the most important issue facing management accounting. This is evidenced by a recent survey among the largest firms in Denmark, which found the following ranking of the most important issues facing management accountants: introduction of information technology (58%), increased co-operation with the sales function (45%), increased co-operation with top management (45%), improvement of product calculations (44%), introduction of new production technology (37%), improvement of budgeting procedures (35%), improvement of variance analysis (39%), increased co-operation with the production function (32%) and improvement of communication with owners (19%).

It is also interesting to note that about two-thirds of accounting departments in these firms were responsible for information systems development and introduction of computer technology.

Computer technology presents the management accountant with several challenges. First, computer technology is involved in mechanising parts of the accounting department's tasks, such as reporting, invoicing and data collection. IT in many different forms is integrated into production equipment, with chips controlling operations and production facilities, and data may be produced and stored automatically in the production process. This increases the productivity of the accounting department by speeding up the production of reports. Thus the 'score-card' role of management reports is supported and enhanced.

Second, computer technology makes available more complex financial databases than before. The extension of the number of 'dimensions' to an accounting record is possible. It is, for example, possible to pay much more attention to dimensions related to customers, products, production processes, etc.' and thus empower management accountants in their *ad hoc* analyses of business processes. Today, many standard accounting systems contain ten or more dimensions on which a particular transaction may be recorded. This extension of dimensions in AIS enhances the possibilities for firms to increase their information matrix, providing a richer 'picture' for the monitoring and analysis of their operations.

Third, computer technology also changes management accounting's involvement with the wider organisational issues because its flexibility makes possible analyses previously only dreamt about. Suddenly, the management accounting department is not merely providing information, it is also producing new and perhaps even competing representations of the organisation.

Fourth, computer technology facilitates the production of contingency plans. Simulations and 'what if' scenarios enable a more thorough analysis of the possible consequences of decisions. The flexibility of modern computer technology to support the development of models in spreadsheet applications underscores this. Management accountants are able, through this technology, to make their own models quickly – and modify them – without having to consult computer specialists.

The previous points refer to the tasks presently faced by management accountants, and thus identify areas for productivity improvements. IT also creates new roles for management accountants since the technology creates new relationships between firms and customers and suppliers. Through EDI, these relationships between firms, suppliers and customers become more visible. This presents management accountants with information about the demand for the firm's products and the production processes involved. Thus, management accountants can gain new insights into the operations of the firm. IT potentially changes the role of the management accountant and provides a basis for intervening more thoroughly in the general management of the organisation.

While IT may support the role played by the management accountant, an enhancement of the management accountant's power-base is not automatic. Other groups in firms may want to exploit the increased flexibility of IT as well. The general access to IT challenges the previous monopoly position of the management accountant in the collection, storing and production of information. Information is collected throughout the organisation, and the storing, calculation and presentation of data can be performed on individual PCs distributed widely throughout the firm. This places management accountants in competition with other groups in defining, producing and using information.

The Design of Information Systems

Management accountants may strongly increase their power through their active participation in the design and implementation of information technology and the models used therein. The design of information systems involves important decisions on how to structure the organisation and workflows and how, and where, to collect and process information. This makes it important for management accountants to appreciate different design methods and perspectives.

The design of information systems can be organised in a variety of ways, each of which uses its own definition of the problem area of systems development, of the principal agent in the design process, of the methods applied to reach a solution, and of its result. Table 10.2 illustrates four methods, which differ on these dimensions, and indicates that systems design can be organised in four corresponding ways. The four methodologies will be discussed in more detail below, and their relationship with management accounting will be analysed.

Structured methods

Structured methods see the development of a system as a technical problem laying out the formal structure of a business process. 'Tasks' are pivotal inasmuch as systems are to be developed to match the inherent logic of particular tasks. Structured approaches are useful when there is clear understanding of the problem to be addressed and when the procedure for solving the problem can be laid out in a sequential procedure, as in 'Yourdon's structured method' (Yourdon, 1989), 'Jackson System Development', 'SSADM' and 'Euromethod' (Robson, 1994). SSADM – Structured Systems Analysis and Design Method – is the preferred method to be used in projects for the UK government. Euromethod is an initiative of the European Union (EU).

The development of new systems – often large mainframe systems – involves a

Table 10.2 Four methodologies for systems development.

	Structured methods	Socio-technical approach and soft systems methodology	End-user computing	Business process re-engineering
Problem area	To analyse the task to be supported by information technology	To identify and integrate organisational and user needs for IT solutions	To make end-users develop their own systems according to their wants	To develop and leverage lateral processes through IT
Principal agent in design process	The analyst/designer/programmer designs systems with only limited input from users	The analyst interacts with users to make the technical solution acceptable to users	End-users define their own problems, they program the IT solution, and they modify it continuously	Top management heads a process of organisational redesign in which IT is a major mechanism of integration
Method	Analysis of information needs, design and programming of the solution based primarily on formal logic, deduction and rational inference	Map and socially understand users' wants and queries and match them with technological solutions to reduce resistance to IT and support IT solutions to be used	End-users define their needs and solve them alone or with the help of other users	Experts define relevant value-chain activities and support lateral processes through IT. IT leverages new ways of organising and supports ongoing organisational redesign
Result	The information system is a logical mapping of the task at hand	The information system integrates organisational needs and individuals' interests	The information system reflects the individual user's idiosyncratic wants	Information systems substitute formal organisational arrangements and facilitate networking
Parallels with management accounting	Management accounting develops logical and consistent financial models of a firms' cost-revenue relationships	Management accounting involves users in the design of accounting systems to reduce resistance to change and to help users understand and accept the system	Local information systems often conflict with global information systems. They are more process oriented and capture budgetary variances before they materialise	Activity-based costing encourages management accountants to be concerned with the firm's lateral flows *vis-à-vis* its products and customers

great number of computer specialists, user representatives and others, and makes a well-defined set of procedures important. The set of structured phases through which an individual information system will pass is called a *systems life-cycle*. Through this, the development and operation of a new system evolve by application of a consistent and logical process. It progresses from phase to phase, such that one phase has to be completed before the next phase can begin. The output of one phase is input to the next phase. Each of the systems life-cycle's phases can be subdivided into several activities. A generic illustration of the life-cycle of a computerised information system with phases and activities, condensed from the literature on structured methods, is shown in Table 10.3.

The socio-technical approach and soft systems methodology

The socio-technical approach suggests that systems design is concerned with matching the human and technical issues in an integrated socio-technical solution. Organisations need to satisfy users to make them accept and take advantage of the systems, otherwise, systems may be resisted. Socio-technical methods introduce the notion of taking into account both the social and the technical aspects when analysing and designing technology (Mumford and Weir, 1979). In situations with some opposition to technology, socio-technical methods offer the prospect of aligning the human and technical dimensions of the problem. The involvement of users in systems design ensures a greater chance of user acceptance of the technology.

Participation is seen as the remedy to the need of communication with users, and resistance to change is expected to be reduced if people are actively engaged in suggesting changes which will benefit the individual. For example, the ETHICS method (Effective Technical and Human Implementation of Computer-based Systems), presented by Mumford, shows how a socio-technical design can be undertaken by simultaneously identifying the social and the technical objectives and alternatives and matching these, as shown in Figure 10.1 (Mumford and Weir, 1979).

Thus, the socio-technical design approach requires the technical parts of a work system to be carefully evaluated in terms of their human consequences, and the technical choices to be made both in terms of the contribution of the technology to efficiency and in terms of its ability to contribute to job satisfaction. Its aim is to achieve both technical and human objectives, and it does so by identifying human and technical alternatives that fit together. The final choice is made after taking account of cost and other constraints.

The socio-technical approach and management accounting share a common ground in the importance attached to the fit between system, user, task and organisation. The observations from behavioural accounting research stress the importance of user acceptance of accounting systems (Markus and Pfeffer, 1983). If systems are not accepted by the users, they might ignore the system, enter data randomly or carelessly or even manipulate the system. Thus, designing an account-

Table 10.3 A generic description of phases and activities in the systems life-cycle in structured approaches.

I	**DEFINITION PHASE**	
	0. Perception of need (initiation)	A need or a problem is defined and an IT project is set up
	1. Analysis of current physical system	Understanding existing system employing data from users and user review of result
	2. Analysis of current logical system	Deduction of logic: what does the system do? – with users providing information and approving the description. Focus on business requirements
	3. Specification of required logical system	Understanding requirements and designing future system as a logical system: what is the system supposed to do (not in technical terms)? – future logic system must be approved by users. Focus on business requirements
	4. Specification of required physical system	Physical design considerations for choice of specific hardware and software platform. Less user involvement – but their approval needed
II	**DEVELOPMENT PHASE**	
	5. Programming	Program specification. Coding. Program testing and documentation of individual modules of program. System testing.
	6. Development of procedures	Instructions for users, input/output personnel and operating staff. Conversion procedures
III	**INSTALLATION PHASE**	
	7. Conversion	Training. Creation of new files. Parallel running. Acceptance testing
IV	**OPERATION PHASE**	
	8. Operation and maintenance	Operation of system and modifications of system
	9. Post audit	Review of objectives and cost/benefit. Operational evaluation
	10. Termination	Should current system be abandoned or replaced by a new system ?

ing system must involve simultaneously identification of the possible technical solutions, its fit with the organisation, the tasks to be performed, the individual employee and her/his motivation and attitude towards the system.

In situations of unclear objectives or many stakeholders a more open approach like soft systems methodology (SSM) (Checkland and Scholes, 1990) may be appropriate. Through an iterative process of debating problems, taking action and then reflecting again on the consequences of this action, the soft systems methodology places more emphasis on users' definition of issues and problems than on technical design. Users' definitions of the problems at hand are considered to be real. Users are privileged in this method. Only users' definitions of problems count, and analysts function merely as translation mechanisms between the problem as perceived by the user and the technical formulation of an IT solution. The designer here must be sensitive to the users' statements rather than to his or her ideas about the problem area at hand. SSM thus emphasises 'who' defines the situation (Avison and Wood-Harper, 1990).

End-user computing

End-user computing sees systems development as a trial-and-error process by which information systems are iteratively developed, tested and redefined by users

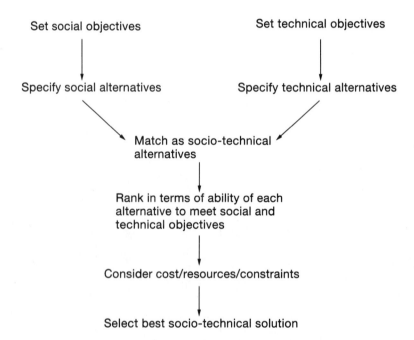

Figure 10.1 A socio-technical approach with parallel design of technical and social aspects (source: Mumford and Weir, 1979).

themselves. End-user computing is oriented towards the design of tailor-made systems to suit the emerging needs of individual users.

Users have become able to develop computer programs without having to consult computer specialists. End-user computing is the direct, hands-on use of computers by end-users – not indirect use through systems professionals or the data processing staff (McNurlin and Sprague, 1989).

One area where end-user computing has become common is office automation, with users setting up their own standards and exchanging information through the use of office systems and networks. Users manage and retrieve data from databases, or they design databases for their specific need and integrate these data into other 'products' like a customer database. Users develop and use decision-support applications designed by themselves, e.g. spreadsheet applications that can make 'what if' calculations.

Although end-user computing frees the user from the discipline of formal development methodologies and thus may foster creativity, there are potential problems (Robson, 1994, pp. 284 ff.). Users may solve the wrong problem, there may be a waste of computing time and machinery, little or no organisational co-ordination and integration of the use of local computer power and equipment, lack of error-checking and testing, incompatibility between the local PC solution and other PCs and between the PCs and the company server or mainframe. Likewise, end-user computing challenges central computing staff over control of computing resources, and it poses a threat to security issues like making back-ups, error-checking of applications and testing them.

End-user computing focuses on single users solving their own problems, but management might often want to use a broader organisational perspective in their attempts to rationalise the firm. The concepts and perspective presented in business process re-engineering are thought to apply in this situation.

Business process re-engineering

Business process re-engineering (BPR) concerns linking development of accounting information systems with organisational restructuring. IT is seen as a medium used to change organisational structures and patterns of communication. Through IT, organisations are 'de-constructed' to facilitate organisational arrangements that allow the lateral processes to take the lead in an attempt to align more carefully the customer with the combined efforts of the organisation. BPR pays attention to business processes along the dimensions of the value-chain. The dialectic between organisational structure and information systems makes the organisation one that is changing.

BPR does not provide a strict methodology, although Hammer and Champy (1993) provide the following eight principles:

1. Organise around outcomes, not tasks.
2. Those who use the output of a process should perform the process themselves.

3. Subsume information-processing work into real work that produces the information.
4. Treat geographically dispersed resources as though they were centralised.
5. Link parallel activities instead of integrating their results.
6. Put the decision point where the work is done, and build control into the process.
7. Capture information once and at the source.
8. Think big!

BPR is described as 'the fundamental rethinking and radical redesign of business processes to achieve dramatic improvements in critical, contemporary measures of performance, such as cost, quality, service, and speed' (Hammer and Champy, 1993).

BPR focuses on extended cross-functional business processes covering the whole organisation, including processes between the organisation and its customers and suppliers. IT is used as an enabler in the re-engineering processes. This is done by focusing on the use of company databases as replacement for paperwork, making it possible to collect data for management control when information is created, storing data centrally and making them accessible to those who need the information. IT solutions, created using BPR, 'empower' employees by providing an IT package that allows the employees to perform all necessary operations related to a particular market-related case, e.g. an insurance claim.

BPR thus radically redesigns business process flows, job definitions, management and control processes and organisational structures. The guiding principles are to facilitate dramatic improvements in cost, quality, service and speed.

Management accounting and systems development

The four methods of systems development resemble and parallel methods used by management accountants to design their accounting systems. The development of accounting systems can be grouped into categories that parallel the ones described above.

In accounting, the parallel to structured methods is the design of logical models of a firm's financial structure, its revenue–cost relationships and its relationships between profitability and liquidity. The deductive logic of accounting modelling parallels the nature of the structured approach since both rely on the rationality of a formal procedure. In accounting, the analysis of the decision situation resembles the orientation in structured methods towards analysing tasks to be executed in business processes. The formal analytical properties of a decision situation resemble, in accounting modelling, the attempt to generate better and more relevant decision-oriented accounting systems. Likewise, in structured methods, the interconnections between the task's components 'guarantee' the usefulness of the solution. Logic, rather than feelings and personal opinions, determines the proper systems in accounting modelling, as in structured methods.

The socio-technical model and the soft systems methodology are also important ideas for management accounting due to the emphasis of the social aspects when implementing accounting systems. In large parts of behavioural accounting, usefulness of accounting depends on people's acceptance of it. The design, implementation and use of accounting systems are seen as one interconnected process where failure to incorporate the psychological needs of people will alienate them from the system. If people are not taken properly into consideration, systems will continue to fail. Resistance and lack of understanding are important factors in this. To generate commitment and to reduce hostility, employees need to feel assured that systems are not being used to make them redundant or to give them less interesting jobs. Their understanding of the need for changes in the accounting system is a prerequisite for its successful implementation. Studies have shown that successful implementation of accounting systems requires a fit between the system and three factors (Markus and Pfeffer, 1983). A fit must be achieved with the dominant view in the organisation or perception of the situation. Second, the accounting system must fit the way problems are normally solved, i.e. the technology of the organisation. Finally, the accounting system must fit with the culture, i.e. the norms and value system that characterise the organisation. These findings on accounting systems implementation are important, since these are some of the issues that the soft systems methodology and the socio-technical methods address.

The end-user computing perspective also has a parallel in management accounting. Local, unofficial accounting systems are developed by budget-responsible people to facilitate decision-making in a situation where global, formal systems are either too crude or too slow to respond to the needs of decision-makers. Jönsson and Grønlund (1988) suggest that experimentation with locally designed information systems may enhance creativity and improve the profitability of the firm. Local systems may actually improve the firm's functioning, when used to cope with budgetary variances before they materialise in formal systems, or when they are used to monitor processes rather than output, or when they transform and set standards rather than comply with established standards. Often in these cases formal systems are too crude and too late to be of any direct help in decision-making as typically they are oriented towards score-card purposes. The support of decision-making requires specially designed systems that consider the particular aspects of the particular situation.

Last, the BPR perspective also has parallels in management accounting. The discussion of cost drivers sets a similar agenda. It proposes to look at the firm not only in terms of vertical budget variances but also in terms of the supply of activities to the customer (Cooper and Kaplan, 1991). The cost driver helps identify the resources needed to integrate the firm *vis-à-vis* an external market. It suggests that the lateral flows can be described and investigated in the name of the customer. Although the cost driver cannot define the measures that need to be taken, it encourages attention to the firm's commitment of resources to customers. It draws attention to the role of the customer in the firm's value-chain, just as it supports a more or less systematic consideration of the division of labour between company and customers. Although the cost driver *per se* does not define how relationships with customers should be, it does direct attention to the problems of configuring the firm's resources in the light of its services to the customer. Like BPR, activity-based costing looks at ways to transform the firm in terms of technology, organisation, procedures and services in the name of the customer. Neither has a strong logical method for supplying this solution. Both, however, promise that it is possible through new representations and configurations of the firm's activities to redirect its focus from hierarchical relations to lateral relations.

The parallels between systems development and management accounting identified here suggest that management accounting methods and intellectual technologies are in line with the procedures used in the development of IT. Consequently, management accountants are likely to have good opportunities to engage in systems development. Their interest in systems development is supported by a domain-specific knowledge which makes it possible for them to contribute to the development of the models and reporting practices that are important for the success of systems.

Different Types of Information System

IT supports different kinds of systems. Apart from conventional data-processing systems (financial accounting systems, etc.), management accountants need to be concerned particularly with information systems that support management decision-making (such as DSS, GDSS and EIS) as well as strategic information systems.

DSS, GDSS and EIS

Decision support systems (DSS), group decision support systems (GDSS) and executive information systems (EIS) integrate flexible technology with management concerns by providing information for on-line 'what if' analyses. All three types of system allow the user to explore the structure of the information provided on the computer screen. If, for example, a particular result is not deemed appropriate, the system facilitates either a thorough variance analysis (e.g. EIS) or simulations of the critical assumptions (DSS, GDSS). Some systems also address the idea-generation and collection of suggestions for possible solutions from a dispersed group of people linked through IT. Whiteboard software makes it possible to transmit, share and work on a whiteboard using IT, while interactive video can provide interactive television between distant locations and persons.

Both DSS and GDSS support decision-making in different ways. A DSS may be defined as a computer system, which helps decision-makers confront ill-structured problems through direct on-line interaction with computer-based models and data. DSSs do not provide 'results' as the so-called expert systems would do. Rather, they provide the opportunity to explore the consequences of potential decisions through 'what if' analyses. For management accountants, this is typically a financial model of the firm or a set of operations or a project within the firm. They also depend on database technology since the value of DSSs increases with the number of different sources of data on which they can draw. A special version of this is the geographical information system (GIS) that contains physical data as well as economic and demographic data.

Whilst a DSS is oriented towards individuals, in contrast a GDSS assumes that groups make decisions rather than individuals. A GDSS may be defined as a computer-based system that allows people to work together on problem-solving in a way which supports development of positive group behaviour. Its technology can be distinguished in four different situations. The 'Decision Room' is one in which a screen makes a DSS visible to a group of people who meet in the same room. Based on collective enquiries into the assumptions of a result and a continual development and testing of appropriate alternatives, the group is supposed collectively to reach a better solution than the individuals would have reached by themselves. The 'Local Decision Network' is one where there is ongoing decision-making activity amongst geographically dispersed people. Through LANs there is less friction of time/space than in a 'Decision Room', but people still communicate on decision-making. 'Teleconferencing' brings together groups of people located in one room with other groups of people in other locations. Through video-cameras all members can see each other across space and thus simulate a meeting – a virtual meeting. Last, 'Remote Decision-making' facilitates decision-making where there is a need for continual contact between decision-makers over large geographical spaces. Long-distance communication, for example through e-mail systems, supports decision-making with people in partnership with whom one must regularly make decisions.

Whereas both DSS and GDSS are oriented towards decision-making, EIS is oriented towards organising the firm's databases in a way which makes it possible for top management to 'drill-down' on any variance in (say) production or sales to elicit additional explanations. In contrast to DSS and GDSS, EIS is more oriented towards providing information than the direct analysis of that information. EIS is not only based on internal data. Couplings to external databases make it possible for managers to combine internal and external pieces of information, making such EIS particularly powerful. EIS both gives executives immediate insight into the 'score-card' data and provides them with real-time information on issues.

These systems are crucial to the work of the management accountant. The organisation of flexible models for planning and decision-making purposes is of paramount importance for the managerial competence of the firm. Management accountants need to use these tools to enhance their capacity to engage in company-wide decision-making activities.

Strategic information systems

A different class of system from DSS, GDSS and EIS is the so-called strategic information system, which in contrast to the former group is mostly oriented towards connecting the firm with its suppliers and customers, for example through electronic data interchange (EDI). This, and other communication solutions, allows an exchange of information between the firm and its environment. Such systems can be used to transmit and exchange orders, transportation documents, banking transactions, airline reservations, etc.

IT is able to link the company's product with the customer to enhance the service provided. For example, Otis Elevators provided their elevators with a small computer that collected information about the use and status of the elevator and reported this information directly to the company. This enabled Otis to provide the customer with a service that matched the use of the specific elevator and enabled Otis to plan the service visits and utilisation of the service staff more efficiently.

In this way, computer technology made it possible for Otis to design an information system with updated information on the use of the products, to provide information for planning the services of the products, to market the company as having an outstanding service and to provide the customer with a service that was competitive. The information from the product has ultimately made it possible for Otis to supervise the use of its products, the quality of the maintenance, the quality of any repairs made, and to make calculations of the profit from different installations and service contracts.

Such use of IT is strategic inasmuch as it connects customers (and products) more closely with the firm. IT not only facilitates a better execution of the products and services that a firm offers, but it also holds the customer in a closer relationship with the firm by reducing attention given to other possible providers of services. IT may contribute to making monopoly in this respect.

Management accountants may benefit from such a technology in two respects. Such systems provide more information regarding the customers, suppliers and products due to the wide automatic registration of different forms of data (cf. the Otis case above). The possibility of modeling relationships between suppliers, customers, product use and services more carefully by financial models enhances their role in aligning financial resources with production and sales planning. Second, strategic information systems also provide an important source of information on efficiency and quality of production and services, but this requires the management accountant to design appropriate data capture systems and provide the templates for the analysis of the data.

Management Accountants and Information Systems

The above discussion suggests that management accounting parallels information systems in many respects and can benefit from using new computer technology. The growth of IT together with the analysis, design and planning methods also present an independent area of organisational activity, which also challenges and competes with management accounting.

While IT analysis and design theory might provide guidelines for solving issues in information processing, the methods do not comprise any actual guidelines for what the technology should actually do. For example, IT specialists might be involved in the setting up of a credit system, but would not know how a reminder procedure should be arranged. Such specialists might perhaps identify the need for an improved financial system, but they cannot define the criteria for segmentation of turnover, principles for cost accounting or depreciation. Such issues cannot be resolved through a systems design process. These examples illustrate that IT, at least to some extent, focuses on form rather than content (Christiansen and Mouritsen, 1994). The users need to deliver the models. This identifies a key role for management accounting in resolving these design issues.

Earl (1989) presents his view on the wider perspectives for the role of the IT community in modern organisations and companies as follows:

> One characteristic of the IT era is that IT and information systems are regarded as a management function alongside finance, production, marketing, and the like. There may be two sorts of directors required in organisations where IT is important. Besides a corporate IT director, local IS directors may be required to direct the use of IT, ensure that IS strategies are formulated and perhaps manage some IS development. The overall IT director is likely to require considerable social and political skill [and] the local IS directors who are expected to connect IT with business needs must possess credible business knowledge. (pp. 2–21)

Here, Earl argues that in general IT planning and design opens up, and perhaps requires, a change in corporate management structure and organisational build-up. It is emphasised that IT requires new forms of knowledge, which are often difficult to handle for those who organise data retrieval in conventional companies. It means that members from the IT community participate in the general competition about who will be allowed to define information requirements, data registration and information processing. For example, it is no longer only the marketing and financial staff that can access and analyse sales data. The 'IT community' could provide such a service. Which group performs the service in a particular firm will depend on the strength of their organisational function as well as their ability to mobilise their interests in the most effective way.

This argument has arisen in several situations (Armstrong, 1985). In such circumstances different specialist groups mobilise their interests by referring to their professional competence. The problem is that, to some extent, all groups comprising professional specialist competence in a certain sense have a 'right' to provide this service. All 'professional' management disciplines focus more or less on analysing the problems and future prospects of a company. However, the various disciplines differ in the approach they take. As a result, the competition will be between different theoretical frameworks of reference and will focus on which framework enjoys the most attention.

Conclusion

The management accountant faces competition from other groups, who through the widespread access to data can provide, and acquire, information without the use of management accountants. Yet the diffusion of computer technology supporting decision-making in different forms, such as GDSS, DSS, EIS and strategic information systems, makes it even more crucial for that information to be used properly. Here the accountant has a considerable competitive advantage in the analysis of financial data and the building and interpretation of financial models. Hence, it is essential that the management accountant actually gets involved in the design and implementation of the new technology. A passive attitude on these issues will create opportunities for other groups who will know how to exploit the potential. Participation in, and understanding of, the use, design and implementation of computer technology must be a highly prioritised area if the management accountant wishes to maintain his/her position in the future.

Note

This chapter was created and edited using several different word-processing systems on different computer systems. It has been transmitted electronically between computers in the UK, Denmark and California using the Internet datanet – no hard copies were sent by 'snail-mail'. The authors and the editor responsible for the chapter have never met and have communicated only by e-mail and the occasional fax. We hope that this does not show in the final product!

Bibliography

Structured systems analysis and design

These titles provide an overview of systems design issues and methods, and Robson has a good introduction to end-user computing as well.

McNurlin, B.C. and R.H. Sprague (1989) *Information Systems Management in Practice*, 2nd edn, Englewood Cliffs, N.J.: Prentice Hall.
Robson, W. (1994) *Strategic Management and Information Systems. An integrated approach*, London: Pitman.
Yourdon, E. (1989) *Modern Structured Analysis*, Eglewood Cliffs, N.J.: Prentice Hall.

Socio-technical approach and soft systems methodology

Alternative approaches to systems analysis and design, focusing less on the structured aspects and presenting the socio-technical and soft systems methodology, are presented in:

Avison, D.E. and A.T. Wood–Harper (1990) *Multiview. An exploration in information systems development*, Oxford: Blackwell Scientific Publications.
Checkland, P. (1981) *Systems Thinking, Systems Practice*, Chichester: John Wiley.
Checkland P. and J. Scholes (1990) *Soft Systems Methodology in Action*, Chichester: John Wiley.
Mumford, E. and M. Weir (1979) *Computer Systems in Work Design – the ETHICS Method: Effective technical and human implementation of computer systems: a work design exercise book for individuals and groups*, New York: Wiley.

The role of the management accountant

The role of the management accountant in organisations, both in competition with other groups and in collaboration with others, is described in:

Armstrong, P. (1985) 'Changing management control systems: the role of competition between accountancy and other organisational professions', *Accounting, Organizations and Society*, vol. 10, no. 2, pp. 129–48.
Jönsson, S. and A. Grønlund (1988) 'Life with a subcontractor: new technology and management accounting', *Accounting, Organizations and Society*, vol. 13, no. 5, pp. 512–32.
Mouritsen, J. (1993) *Økonomifunktionens rolle* (The role of the management accounting function), Copenhagen: Børsens Forlag.

Business process re-engineering

The original texts in this area are the two below:

Hammer, M. (1990) 'Reengineering work: don't automate, obliterate', *Harvard Business Review*, July–August, pp. 104–12.
Hammer, M. and J. Champy (1993) *Re-engineering the Corporation: A manifesto for business revolution*, New York: Harper Business.

Strategic information systems

Introduction to strategic information systems and a critical comment on the issue can be found in:

Earl, M. J. (1989) *Management Strategies for Information Technology*, Hemel Hempstead: Prentice Hall.
Christiansen, J.K. and J. Mouritsen (1994) 'Information resource management. A critical analysis of a new intellectual technology', *Proceedings from The Second European Conference on Information Systems*, 30–31 May, Breukelen, The Netherlands: Nijenrode University Press.

Designing management accounting systems

A comprehensive presentation of the issues can be found in:

Cooper, R. and R.S. Kaplan (eds.) (1991) *The Design of Cost Management Systems*, Englewood Cliffs, NJ: Prentice Hall.

Political issues around implementation

An overview of political issues when dealing with implementations of information and accounting systems is described in:

Markus, M.L. and J. Pfeffer (1983) 'Power, and the design and implementation of accounting and controlling systems', *Accounting, Organizations and Society*, vol. 8, no. 2/3, pp. 205–18.

CHAPTER ELEVEN

Accounting Measures, Motivation and Performance Appraisal

Stephen Lyne

All large companies employ a range of formal control systems to ensure that they operate efficiently and effectively; many medium and small companies do likewise. Many formal control systems make use of accounting measures to appraise the performance of individuals and business units, and most seek to motivate individuals to perform at their best or to behave as required. Control systems usually operate at every level within the organisation, from managing director to the most junior trainee. Different control systems will be appropriate at different levels; it would be unusual to control the managing director by means of a clock card system, just as it would not usually be effective to control a cleaner by means of a return on investment target.

In this chapter the role of accounting measures in motivation and performance evaluation will be discussed. First, there will be a brief discussion of the concept of control, followed by a review of various motivation theories. A number of key issues that have dominated research in this area will then be discussed, including the use of accounting measures as targets, the creation of slack and the role of participation. The chapter will end with a consideration of non-accounting aspects of motivation and control.

The Concept of Control

The term 'control' has many meanings and even more connotations, many of which are not appropriate to accounting and management. The basic meaning of control in this context is the idea of regulation and monitoring of activities. Regulation has been defined as 'fulfilling what has been laid down' and 'adapting to requirements'. So, control is concerned with ensuring that what was intended actually occurs or that appropriate adjustments are made in the light of changed circumstances. Control does not presuppose that one group dominates another; rather, control is synonymous with the efficient and effective running of a business. Whether a business is run on highly authoritarian lines or is a loose arrangement of equal partners, it will still need to be controlled, albeit by very different means. Part of the concept of control is therefore motivation, another part is the measurement of performance.

'Organisational control' is a term which encompasses all forms of control used within the firm. It is helpful to distinguish between 'control' which is an objective, and 'controls' which are the means by which control is achieved. Controls are a set of procedures and practices unique to each organisation. Hopwood (1974) categorises controls and shows their relationship with control in the diagram shown in Figure 11.1.

Each of these categories of controls is important to overall control of the organisation. Each has an impact on motivation but only some of the administrative controls make use of accounting measures. It is important to note at the outset of this chapter that motivation and control are very broad concepts which extend far beyond accounting controls. At the end of the chapter the importance of non-accounting controls and their relationship with accounting controls are discussed further.

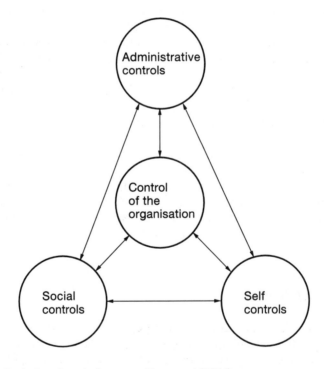

Figure 11.1 Control and controls as per Hopwood (1974).

However, for the majority of this chapter accounting control is the focus of attention.

There are many definitions of accounting control in the literature and most are broadly similar to that discussed by Otley and Berry (1980) and summarised below. For an accounting control system to operate effectively there must be:

♦ clear objectives set in such a way that they can be quantified;
♦ measured output in a form which is directly comparable with the objectives;
♦ a predictive model which enables an appropriate revised objective to be determined and which is fully comparable with the conditions that produced the measured output; and
♦ the ability to take action if objectives and outputs are not the same.

An accounting control system of this type is an example of a feedback control system. In accounting terms the objectives may be a budget, a target return on investment or given level of profit. The objective must be set *ex ante* in a specific and measurable form such that comparison can be made *ex post* and any remedial action taken. The predictive model may take many forms. For example, where the objective is a budgeted level of profit or costs, a flexible budget could be a predictive model. This form of feedback control system can be represented diagrammatically as shown in Figure 11.2.

A further development to the feedback model in the figure would be to include a second loop around the top of the diagram. This would indicate that one possible action would be to alter the objective, for example revise the budget. It appears from empirical research that companies are loath to alter objectives during the period of time for which they have been set; they seem particularly reluctant to change a budget or other financial target which has been set for a period up to one year.

The feedback model of control as described above is both static and backward-looking. Clearly a business would much prefer to take action to prevent matters becoming out of control rather than find out after the event. At first sight many

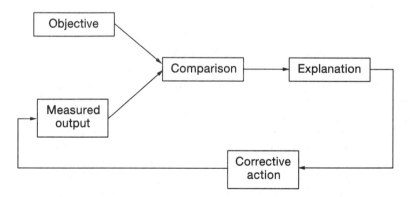

Figure 11.2 Feedback control loop.

accounting control models appear to be backward-looking feedback systems but they are operated in such a way that this disadvantage is overcome. In practice they become 'feedforward' systems. The fact that an appraisal will take place and that differences between objectives and outputs will be highlighted will cause good managers to predict the measured output. If the prediction does not compare favourably with the objective, managers will take action to remedy the situation. The real control is the forward-looking operation of the system even though it may appear that the formal control is a feedback system.

To enable this feedforward approach to work and to enable the appropriate revision of the initial objective to incorporate exogenous changes, the predictive model is vitally important. Without the ability to predict what will happen under changed circumstances, these basic accounting control models will not operate. How a business might deal with that situation is considered later. At this stage uncertainty will be assumed to be low enough to allow the possibility of a predictive model.

A predictive model is not a purely technical procedure. To set the original objective and to make revisions requires an understanding of the behaviour of the individuals involved. The most important feature for this purpose is knowledge of what motivates individuals to perform at their best and what conditions will encourage high levels of performance. The next section describes various theories of motivation that management accounting writers have used in constructing a predictive model as part of an accounting control system. It is unlikely that practising management accountants consciously think in terms of these theories, yet the decisions they make are based on a view of what will motivate individuals within their firm. The purpose of the next section is to make explicit some of the theories that are available and to see the implications that follow for the design and operation of accounting control systems.

Theories of Motivation and Their Application

One of the interesting features of accounting as an academic discipline is its interrelationship with other disciplines. Accounting, more than most disciplines, draws on the understanding and expertise of other disciplines. Theorisation of accounting control systems requires an understanding of how individuals can be motivated, and accounting theorists have turned to psychology for help in this matter. Unfortunately there is no single, simple theory of motivation; rather, the accounting theorist is faced with a huge range of theories developed over many decades. Most of these theories have empirical justification which leads one to conclude that motivation is a complex issue which cannot be encapsulated in a single theory. In this section four commonly used groups of theories will be presented in outline, and then the theory which has been most widely used in accounting will be discussed in more detail. Each of these theories adds to the total picture of what motivates individuals to perform at their best. The four groups of theories each have within them many writers and theories but there is a common basis which unites them into a group. The four groups discussed in outline are: need-satisfying theories, achievement theories, motivation/hygiene theories, and equity theories; expectancy theory is dealt with in more detail.

Need-satisfying theories

Maslow developed one of the earliest forms of this class of theory. His theory states that within each individual there are various 'needs' which will influence behaviour. Where one of the needs is absent, the individual will be motivated to behaviour that will lead to the need being satisfied. Furthermore, Maslow states that these needs do not have equal effect. In fact, there is a hierarchy of needs in which certain needs will dominate other needs until they are met, and once they are met they will no longer have any motivating effect. This hierarchy of needs is shown in. Figure 11.3. In practice, therefore, the theory states that physiological needs will dominate all other needs if they are not met. Physiological needs include basic requirements for physical life such as food, drink, shelter and warmth. If a worker perceives these as needs, then money is likely to be a highly effective motivator as all these needs can be met by purchasing the appropriate goods. However, most workers live well above the poverty line and will not be motivated by physiological needs; this may mean that simply paying more may not be a sufficient motivator. In times of high unemployment security needs may be a powerful motivator. For people in well-paid employment affiliation needs (feeling a sense of group belonging) and esteem needs (being recognised for doing high-quality work) may be more powerful motivators than simply higher salaries. Maslow stresses that not all individuals perceive these

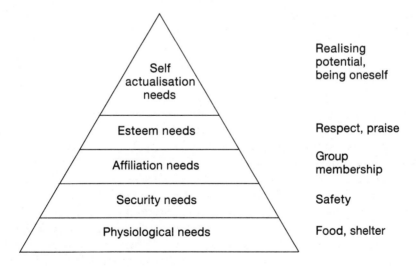

Figure 11.3   Maslow's hierarchy of needs.

needs in the same order of importance, that is, an individual's hierarchy may not match the general theory. Thus, motivation is not so straightforward and possibly different individuals will need to be motivated in different ways. This issue will arise again later.

Need-satisfying theory has many implications for accounting control. First, it raises questions concerning the concepts of motivation commonly used in textbooks. Often, elementary texts consider motivation in terms of payment, bonuses or possibly promotion. Maslow and others suggest that there may be much more powerful motivators in many circumstances. For example, reorganising the way in which work is carried out in such a fashion as to enhance teamwork and feelings of belongingness is likely to be a very powerful motivator for certain individuals.

Need-satisfying theory has been subject to much criticism. Some have criticised its logic, and the nature and measurement of its variables. Others have attempted to test these theories empirically with only limited success, although it is not clear whether this is a reflection on the theory or the tests. Nevertheless these theories are still commonly referred to and are frequently used in management teaching.

Achievement theories

These theories arose in response to the problems with need-satisfying theories and were initially developed by McClelland in the early 1960s. McClelland's theory also has a hierarchy of factors which motivate behaviour; in his case there are three: achievement, power and affiliation. In achievement theories the hierarchy is much less rigid. Different people, and the same people at different times, may have a different order for the hierarchy. Achievement motivation is particularly strong in individuals whose personality is such that they have a strong need to achieve. Where this is so, the achievement needs can become strong motivators if the work circumstances have the appropriate characteristics. In particular, there must be opportunities to take responsibility and to receive credit for so doing. Similarly, power motivation and affiliation motivation are particularly effective for certain individuals. Different individuals will respond in varying degrees and the circumstances must be right to bring out the maximum motivating effect.

Many writers developed and refined the initial theories, and a large number of empirical studies were undertaken. The conclusions of these studies broadly substantiated achievement theory, although it is recognised by most theorists that this is only a partial theory. There are practical applications for achievement theory in a business context. Perhaps the most important is that different individuals will need to be motivated in different ways. It is argued that achievement theories can help to determine the appropriate forms of motivation for managers at different levels within an organisation.

Motivation/hygiene theories

In the mid-1960s Herzberg proposed a theory of motivation which divided the factors which affect behaviour into two broad categories. These were motivating factors and hygiene factors. The important feature of Herzberg's theory was his contention that the factors which have a positive effect on motivation were quite different from those which have a negative effect. Herzberg also proposed that there was a significant relationship between job satisfaction and motivation (this relationship will be considered further later in the chapter). Where job satisfaction is high, motivation will be high and vice versa. Hygiene factors reduce job satisfaction and thus reduce motivation. These factors include: company policies, work conditions, interpersonal relations, job security and salary. Motivating factors include: achievement, recognition, a challenging job, promotion and responsibility. All these lead to increased job satisfaction and thus increased motivation. This theory states that removing negative hygiene factors will have only a limited effect on motivation as the strong motivating effects arise from the motivating factors themselves. However, the existence of the hygiene factors acts as a constraint on the effective working of the motivating factors. So a two-pronged attack is necessary to obtain high levels of motivation. Hygiene factors must be removed and motivating factors must be established or encouraged.

Empirical support for these theories came from a number of studies. However, there were methodological problems with some of the studies which cast doubt on the substantiation of the theory. The link between job satisfaction and motivation is also more complex than that posited by Herzberg. Nevertheless, these theories have been used extensively in the management and accounting literature, where there are some clear implications. It will not be possible to motivate individuals beyond a certain point by means of purely financial rewards. Budget-based reward systems where the reward is in financial terms alone will therefore have limited applicability. On the other hand, use of the Herzberg-style motivating factors such as the establishment of work teams and a general empowerment of staff will have little effect if there are hygiene factors acting as a constraint. For example, it may be necessary to improve the level of pay and conditions before the motivating factors can be fully effective.

Equity theories

Herzberg's theory raised the issue that job satisfaction is an important aspect of motivation. In equity theory, however, a key feature is job dissatisfaction which arises where one individual compares circumstances with another and feels that the position is unfair. Equity theory is a generalised form of this feature based on the concept of social exchange relations. In an exchange an individual gives something (an input) in exchange for something else (an output). Where the individual considers the inputs and outputs are not of comparable value, an inequity occurs.

The individual usually perceives this inequity by comparison with another. The inequity can be of two forms and both lead to adverse motivational consequences. If the individual perceives an unfavourable inequality, dissatisfaction leading to anger and frustration occurs. Whereas if there is a perceived favourable inequality, this will lead to feelings of guilt.

The perceived inequities lead to motivational effects. An individual will be motivated to remove or reduce the tension that is caused by the perceived inequities; the greater the dissatisfaction, the greater will be the motivational effect. Various conclusions have been drawn by equity theorists that have relevance in a management context. For example, the theory predicts that where there is unfavourable inequality individuals will work less hard if they cannot change the inequality and that they will eventually leave employment if unfavourable inequality persists. This theory highlights the fact that it is relative payments, not the absolute amounts, which are likely to have the strongest motivational effect.

Expectancy Theory

Expectancy theory has probably been most used by accounting researchers. It can be used as an analytical tool or as a means to quantify motivation in empirical studies. The basic theory has a long history but it was popularised in accounting by Ronen and Livingstone (1975). The essence of this theory is that an individual's behaviour is influenced by various internal and external factors. This results in a theory which includes a wider range of variables and as such is slightly more complex. Ronen and Livingstone present the theory in the following mathematical expression. The expression can be appreciated intuitively and no mathematical manipulation is required to understand the considerable insight that this theory contains.

$$M = IV_b + P_1 \left(IV_a + \sum_{i=1}^{n} P_{2i} EV_i \right)$$

where

M = motivation to work

IV_a = intrinsic valence associated with successful performance of the task

IV_b = intrinsic valence associated with goal-directed behaviour

EV_i = extrinsic valences associated with the ith extrinsic reward contingent on work-goal accomplishment, $i = 1,2, \ldots, n$

P_1 = the expectancy that goal-directed behaviour will accomplish the work-goal (a given level of specified performance); the measure's range is $(-1, +1)$

P_2 = the expectancy that work-goal accomplishment will lead to the ith extrinsic reward; the measure's range is $(-1, +1)$

Some of the terms used in this theory are well known in psychology but possibly need explanation for those less familiar with the literature. The motivation to work is a combination of a number of internal and external features perceived by the individual. The importance of this theory is its attempt to incorporate a wide range of features which can be customised for different situations. A valence is a feeling of satisfaction that may be caused by internal or external features and may be positive or negative. Economists use the term 'utility' in much the same way. Expectancies are subjective probabilities determined by each individual.

From the expression it can be seen that there are two basic parts to the motivation to work which are substantially independent. IV_b represents the satisfaction felt by individuals from working towards the objectives of their work. Thus if work is enjoyable for its own sake, IV_b will be positive and approaching the value 1. This motivation is independent of actually achieving any objective that may have been set; it is intrinsic to the nature of the work itself. Where the work is hated, this feature of motivation will be negative.

The second part of the motivation to work is related to achieving objectives that have been set and any rewards that might be associated with them. There are two features within the parenthesis of the expression. First, an intrinsic valence from successfully meeting an objective or target that has been set (IV_a). This is independent of any reward and primarily a feature of an individual's personality. There is also an extrinsic valence gained by receiving a reward for attaining the objective. This extrinsic valence must be multiplied by the probability that meeting the objective will lead to receiving the reward. If the reward was a financial bonus payable for a certain level of performance that was detailed in a formal agreement, then the probability (P_{2i}) would be virtually 1 or certainty. However, if the reward was promotion there is likely to be an indirect relationship between meeting the objective and receiving promotion. The individual will have a subjective probability which reflects the likelihood of obtaining promotion if the objective is met. The expression allows for i possible rewards, each with their own probability. The sum of all these extrinsic valences is added to the intrinsic valence from achieving the objective and the result is multiplied by the actual probability of achieving the objective (P_1).

This expression formally represents many features which are understood intuitively. For example, if there is almost no chance of achieving an objective (that is, P_1 is virtually zero) there will be almost no motivating effect even if there were very large rewards available and there was a high degree of certainty that achievement of the objective would lead to the reward being given. In accounting terms for example, a budget target which is set so high that no one believes it is attainable will have no motivating effect irrespective of the rewards which would result from achieving the target.

Expectancy theory can incorporate a wide range of features and show their interrelationships. It demonstrates clearly that setting targets at attainable levels is vitally important if the objective is to motivate. It also shows that there are major aspects of motivation which cannot be directly affected by the company as they are intrinsic to the individual. For some individuals these intrinsic features dominate all others and rewards will play only a small part. The management of a company need to have reasonable knowledge of its staff to motivate them effectively. Another important implication of the theory is that different aspects of the total motivation to work are likely to be important at different levels within the company and in different parts of the company. For example, research staff are likely to be motivated by features different to those that are important to sales executives.

Concluding comments on motivation theories

This section has discussed a small number of the wide range of theories of motivation. If nothing else, this should serve to demonstrate that any simple understanding of motivation is in fact simplistic. Unless a realistic concept of motivation is used, any attempt to improve performance using evaluation based on accounting measures is likely to prove unsuccessful.

Accounting Measures and Motivation

For an accounting measure to have motivational properties it must be accepted as a relevant target; this statement conforms to common sense and expectancy theory. In practice this is usually operationalised by setting a target level for the accounting measure. There have been various laboratory-based experiments and field studies to investigate which type and level of target will produce the best performance. Stedry attempted both these forms of empirical research in the 1960s and reported similar results. Where targets, in the form of accounting measures, were set at high levels the results were either very good or very poor. Stedry explains this in terms of aspiration levels but it is equally well understood from expectancy theory. As long as there exists a reasonable probability of achieving the demanding target it will motivate, but when that probability drops the motivation will fall dramatically. Hofstede (1968) wrote, after examining this issue in a small group of Dutch companies, that accounting-based targets 'will have a more positive effect on motivation when they are tighter and less easily attained. This works up to a certain limit; beyond this limit tightening of standards reduces motivation.' At the same time E.A. Locke conducted a series of experiments into targets, motivation and performance and came to the conclusion that 'the results are unequivocal. The harder the goal the higher the performance.' (See Locke (1968) for a summary). Most of Locke's experiments were laboratory based and may not have included targets that reached the cut-off level that Hofstede found in company-based experiments.

Locke and others investigated the form that the target should take for it to have the maximum motivational impact. They summarised much of this work in three statements:

1. Specific hard goals produce a higher performance than a more general goal of 'do your best'.
2. Hard goals produce less overall task-liking than easy goals.

3. Specific hard goals produce more interest in the task than a general goal of 'do your best'.

Many issues follow from these findings. There is clear evidence that individuals will respond better to clearly stated specific goals. Accounting measures are an obvious form in which this can be achieved. In terms of expectancy theory it is easier to see if a target has been achieved if it is clearly stated and quantifiable. Thus it is likely that targets presented in this way will lead to higher values for P_1 and P_2 than more generally framed targets. In simple terms, there is evidence that people like to know where they stand; both in advance when targets are set and later when they are evaluated against a target. The second and third statements lead to the issue of motivation and job satisfaction which will be covered later.

There is a general issue of relevance of the target or objective and the effect of this on motivation. One aspect of equity theory was the de-motivating consequences of perceived unfairness. This can arise when a target is first set and it is perceived as too hard or unfair in some other way. A target may also be perceived as unfair if the initial target were considered realistic but a revised target, caused by a change in circumstances, is perceived as unfair. This may occur when a flexible budgeting system produces a revised budget target for the actual output level but this is not considered fair or realistic under the changed conditions. Often the method of flexing the budget level (a predictive model in the feedback control system described earlier) is primitive and produces a revised budget which the manager does not consider relevant. One of the attractions of recent developments in activity-based budgeting is the claim that they produce relevant flexible budgets. This is possible because activity-based budgets incorporate a range of different factors which will vary in different ways under different sets of circumstances. In one company the flexible transport budget was produced using a simple linear adjustment with the traditional division between fixed and variable costs. The transport manager claimed that this was a nonsense and that there were many factors which changed as output levels varied. The adverse variances that the system produced as output levels rose had a serious dysfunctional effect on the company. In fact, it was in danger of undermining confidence in the whole accounting system. The situation was resolved by implementing an activity-based budget for transport costs in which the transport manager had confidence. Under the traditional budgeting system all motivational and control aspects had been lost because the accounting measures were not considered a relevant representation of the true costs.

Accounting Measures and Performance Evaluation

The basic model that we are using is that accounting measures can be set *ex ante* and these have motivational features. These same measures can be calculated *ex post* and a comparison of the two will serve as a valid means of evaluating the performance of the unit and its managers. Various aspects of this basic model are challenged and developed in this chapter. The complexity of motivation and the nature of the target have already been discussed. Linked to these two issues is a matter which has been widely commented upon in the accounting literature (and beyond). This matter is usually termed the creation of 'budget slack' but it relates to all accounting measures, not solely the budget. In essence the issue is whether it is likely that managers will attempt to manipulate the *ex ante* accounting measures that will be used in performance evaluation and so create a target which is easy to attain. Such a practice would of course drastically reduce the motivational effect of the target and, if the theory discussed above has validity, will result in lower performance levels. Budget slack is not simply forecasting error; it is a predetermined attempt to manipulate the objective or target. Usually the objective of creating budget slack is to gain higher rewards (broadly defined) for less effort. However, other reasons advanced for this practice are the desire to smooth accounting results or to reduce pressure on the manager, neither of which is necessarily bad for the firm. Some attempts have been made to measure the amount of slack that is built into the system and figures of 20–25 per cent have been reported.

To enable budget slack to be created two conditions must exist. First, it is necessary that personal and organisational goals are not fully congruent. This is the usual position in normative organisations where there is a trade-off between personal goals and organisational goals. This assumes that individuals do not have an intrinsic desire to work with maximum efficiency for an employer. The organisation offers a package of 'rewards' to the employee to motivate maximum effort. Thus, most individuals will be happy to take the maximum reward without offering maximum effort. Second, the employee must have some relevant knowledge that is not available to the employer so that the employer cannot always know when budget slack has been created. As these conditions are usual, it is argued that the creation of budget slack will be common. Employers will operate on the assumption that this is the behaviour of employees. However, because of the personality differences between individuals some are much more likely to create the maximum amount of budget slack than others. Agency theory has developed these ideas and good reviews of the implications of agency theory for management accounting can be found in Chapter 12 and Walker and Choudhury (1987).

In the setting of targets the likelihood of budget slack must be recognised. Certain forms of reward structure will increase the probability of budget slack creation, particularly those which are based on accounting measures over which the employee has more control than the employer. General rules for minimising budget slack cannot be issued. However, it is possible to note where it is most likely to arise and senior managers must then act appropriately to minimise its consequences. There is good evidence to suggest that non-accounting-based measures are the most likely to succeed in minimising slack, especially measures which reduce the difference between personal goals and organisational goals. In recent years there has been a great deal written about creating organisational cultures, enhancing team-building, creating positive attitudes, etc., all of which are designed to improve the congruence of personal and organisational goals.

Many firms use accounting measures as a major part of performance evaluation in the manner that has been described above. It appears that many firms are either unaware, or choose to ignore, that there are often serious dysfunctional consequences which follow from using accounting measures in this manner. Argyris (1952) documented the consequences of pressure to meet targets which had been set in terms of accounting measures. He noted consequences in managerial behaviour such as: undue concentration on the manager's unit, not the firm as a whole; much time and effort spent in shifting blame to someone else; the creation of small-group loyalties; and the building of budget slack. These consequences were not so much the result of the use of accounting measures; rather, they were caused by pressure to meet these targets. However, where targets exist there will frequently be pressure applied to meet them. The important question that has interested researchers for many years concerns ways to exert pressure to achieve targets in such a manner that dys-functional consequences are minimised.

Hopwood in a study in 1972 investigated this issue in one large US manufacturing company. Four styles of evaluation were identified:

1. Budget Constrained style (BC) where meeting the budget was more important than general cost control.
2. Budget Profit style (BP) where meeting the budget and cost control were both important.
3. Profit-Conscious style (PC) where concern for costs rather than meeting the budget was important.
4. Non-Accounting style (NA) where neither meeting the budget nor general cost control were important.

The managers who were evaluated under the BC and BP styles reported a range of dysfunctional feelings and behaviour, including: higher levels of job-related tension; deteriorating relations with superiors; less favourable relations with peers; and a greater likelihood of engaging in manipulative behaviour. There was also no evidence that the BC style of evaluation led to a higher incidence of meeting the budget. Hopwood concluded that dysfunctional consequences were likely to occur when pressure to meet the budget was such that meeting the budget became an end in itself.

Otley (1978) replicated and commented on this study using fifty-seven managers from a UK company. The results were not wholly in agreement with Hopwood's. Otley found that the BC style resulted in the following: a decrease in job ambiguity and better performance; no significant increase in job-related tension; budgets being met more frequently; more manipulation and creation of budget slack; and better general performance. The differences between the two studies gave rise to further research which attempted to test various factors which might explain the differences. Hirst introduced a variable 'reliance on accounting performance measures' (RAPM). He suggested that when task uncertainty was low, RAPM did not lead to dysfunctional consequences and the opposite applied when task uncertainty was high. There followed a series of papers which examined different intervening variables that might explain the relationship between the style of performance evaluation and the consequences which resulted.

A great variety of research has been carried out in this area, using various methodologies such as laboratory experiments and company questionnaires. However, the varied results do not allow firm conclusions to be drawn. Nevertheless, it is clear that the way in which accounting measures are used for performance evaluation will have an effect on outcomes. It is clear that dysfunctional consequences often result when accounting measures are relied upon to a large extent and that these consequences will worsen as pressure to meet the accounting-based target increases. Other features such as task uncertainty and personality types further complicate the picture. Many of these same variables are also important in the next section and performance evaluation, pressure to meet targets and participation have often been studied together. A comprehensive review of the literature in this area and that referred to in the next section can be found in Briers and Hirst (1990).

Participation, Accounting Measures and Motivation

Various ways in which the objective can be made relevant to the individual and ways in which an accounting control system can become a powerful motivating force have been mentioned above. In this section another important feature will be discussed. Many writers have examined the role of participation in the setting of accounting-based objectives, usually participation in the budget-setting process. Participation requires that subordinate managers and employees have some influence in the setting of the budget. Genuine participation is more than mere consultation and requires that lower levels of management can have a real effect on the final budget. As such, there are degrees of participation but this aspect will not be considered directly in this chapter. Most of the comment and research has been in terms of the firm's budget but the findings and comments are directly applicable to other accounting measures which are used in performance evaluation or for motivation.

The simple textbook approach is that increased participation will lead to a greater acceptance or internalisation of the budget which will lead to greater motivation to meet the budget and thus to a higher level of performance. Hofstede (1968) summarised this in the diagram shown in Figure 11.4. Many of the early research studies into participation found evidence for this simplified view of a positive relationship between participation and higher performance. Performance is a slightly problematic variable as different studies have various definitions and methods of measurement. Initially, higher performance meant better job performance, but some

Figure 11.4 Simplified view of budget participation as per Hofstede (1968).

of the studies use budget performance as the dependent variable. There are important differences between these two variables (note the Budget Constrained and Profit-Conscious styles in the Hopwood and Otley studies). In an important study Kennis (1979) tested the effects of participation on both of these variables and found a positive relationship between participation and budget performance but no significant overall relationship with job performance. As further research was conducted the picture became less clear. Some studies continued to support this simplified view, others gave no support and one or two suggested that participation would lead to lower performance. Such a divergence in the research findings required a development of the theory.

Before discussing the more complex and problematic relationship between participation and other variables, it will be helpful to present three research findings where there has been general agreement – although the most recent research is beginning to complicate these issues! An increase in genuine participation is likely to lead to improvement in three dependent variables set out below.

1. *Job satisfaction*. Various studies have concluded in similar vein to Vroom in 1964 who stated, 'There is considerable evidence that the satisfaction of subordinates is positively associated with the degree to which they are permitted an opportunity to participate in making decisions.' It is important to note that this relationship between participation and job satisfaction says nothing about the level of performance in the job, only whether the job is enjoyed. It could be that participation allows easier targets and so the subordinate enjoys the job more as less effort is required.

2. *Job tension*. There is a large body of evidence which suggests that increased participation leads to reduced job tension. There is also evidence that reduced job tension is preferred by the individual and will usually lead to better performance, but the research findings are not unanimous regarding the effects on performance. The basis for this result is that many of the factors that cause job tension will be removed or moderated if the subordinate participates in decision-making and target-setting.

3. *Job attitudes*. A number of studies have reported that increased participation leads to improved attitudes towards the job, the firm, the budget system and superiors. Again, there is no direct evidence that this improves performance.

There seems to be good evidence that participation will improve the perceived quality of working life as all of the three features discussed above have this effect.

The relationship that researchers were originally seeking to demonstrate, and which has proved so problematic, was that participation increased motivation which resulted in improved performance. The simple relationship could not be proved and so more complex interrelationships of the variables involved were examined. The very mixed results from early research on the effects of participation led researchers to conclude that there were other variables involved. It was hypothesised that where these intervening or contingent variables existed in the appropriate form, the positive relationship between participation and performance would be found. Thus the focus of research turned to the intervening variables.

One of the earliest attempts to do this was 'an improved model of the effects of

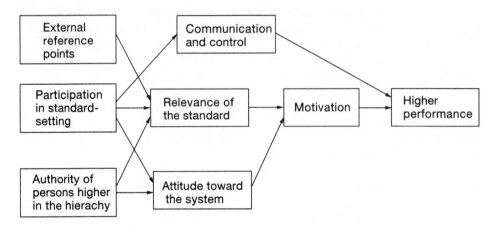

Figure 11.5   An improved model of participation as per Hofsteded (1968).

participation on standard setting' in Hofstede (1968), which is shown in Figure 11.5. This figure shows a range of different variables which affect higher performance, motivation and participation among them. Other variables also affect performance and some affect motivation, which results in a complex situation. There are five intervening variables which have been extensively investigated. The conclusions of these studies will be discussed in this section and further details are given in Briers and Hirst (1990) and Lyne (1988). There has been a large amount of research into these issues, which is ongoing, and much of it has been carried out by a group of researchers including Merchant, Brownell, Hirst and Dunk.

For each of these variables the important feature is the way in which it affects the relationship between participation in setting *ex ante* accounting measures and the resulting performance. A secondary issue is whether increased motivation is part of the process which results in higher performance. The five intervening variables will each be discussed.

Personality types

Most of the discussion to this point has assumed that all people behave in similar ways. Clearly they do not. Some individuals are workaholics and others are lazy; some are easily satisfied and others always find cause for complaint; some thrive when 'left to get on with it' whereas others are much happier when told what to do. So early on, attempts were made to bring personality types into the theory of participation. One study showed that increased participation produced improved performance for 'low authoritarian persons with high independence needs', but there was no improvement for other types.

Two studies examined the personality variable 'locus of control' which classifies individuals into internals and externals. Internals feel that the rewards and punishments they receive are determined by their own actions; externals feel that the force that yields reward and punishment is beyond their control. The predictions of previous theory were supported by the results of the study by Brownell. Internals in a participative system produced high performance, as did externals in a non-participative or authoritarian system. Where the personality type matched the style of the accounting or budgeting system, high performance resulted. The studies also showed the reverse, in that where the personality type and system style were incongruent, performance was low. The conclusion drawn from these studies is that participation will produce high performance in certain personality types but other personality types will perform poorly under participative conditions.

An interesting study reversed the usual causality and attempted to predict the type of budget system from the personality types of the people involved. The study found that authoritarian, inflexible persons with high independence needs were found in non-participative systems, and that the reverse was also true. This led to the conclusion that if individuals were attracted to companies where the evaluation style matched their personality, it could be dangerous for the company to change its style. Overall, these studies were in agreement with the intuitive predictions that certain types of people would perform better in participative systems and that participation is not a panacea.

Organisational attitudes

The hypothesis examined here is that unless there are positive attitudes towards the firm, superiors and the performance measurement system, participation will not be beneficial. In fact, it is predicted that if participation is introduced where these attitudes are not favourable, there would be a high probability that performance would deteriorate. There is increased scope for manipulative behaviour in participative systems which will be exploited unless the individuals involved have positive attitudes towards the firm (there is empirical support for this in a recent study by Dunk). Theoretical evidence strongly supports this contention and there is a small amount of empirical evidence to support it also. This is a very clear example of an intervening variable: participation will have a beneficial effect only when the conditions are appropriate.

Motivation

Two studies by Brownell in the 1980s attempted to show that the primary cause of the link between participation and improved performance was through increased motivation. This had been the main theoretical view for some time but it had not been directly tested. An expectancy theory approach was adopted in both studies but neither produced support for this link. However, the studies did find a strong positive link between participation and performance but 'only a small proportion of this was accounted for by the path through motivation'.

Another approach to this issue was to test whether motivation was a moderating variable between participation and improved performance. In this context a moderating variable is one which is not directly related to either of the other two variables but to the relationship between the variables. This approach was tested and produced very positive results indicating that there is an important relationship between participation and performance but it is complex. Action to increase participation and motivation would lead to improved performance.

Uncertainty

Galbraith had hypothesised that participative forms of organisation would increase as uncertainty increased. The logic was that greater and more relevant knowledge could be gained by participation and this would help to overcome the problems of increasing task uncertainty. Direct attempts to test this have not proved successful. However, a study which used a formal contingency model where environmental uncertainty was one of two contingent variables produced positive results. In this study seventy-seven managers from a large business organisation gave 'clear and strong support' for the hypothesis that 'the greater the environmental uncertainty, the greater the positive impact of participation in the budgetary process on managerial performance'. The relationship here is not fully proven but there is evidence that greater uncertainty leads to participation having a beneficial effect on performance.

Role ambiguity

This final intervening variable reflects the situation where the expectations for managers are such that they cannot be clearly translated into behaviour or performance. In simple terms high role ambiguity is where a manager does not know exactly what is required. In the test of this variable it was hypothesised that increased participation would produce better results in situations of high role ambiguity. The evidence strongly supported this hypothesis, and gave another situation where participation is likely to produce better performance.

There have been two decades of active research developing earlier research into the relationship between participation and improved performance. It is now possible to draw some conclusions with reasonable confidence. Clearly the general proposition that increased participation will increase motivation and improve performance does not hold. However, the fact that increased participation can lead to higher levels of performance has also been clearly demonstrated. The preceding section has set out various personality types and different circumstances where this result will occur. There is now enough evidence to allow management accounting system design to incorporate these features. As a result, accounting measures can be more effectively used to motivate individuals to achieve improved performance.

Systematic Approaches to Accounting Measures, Motivation and Performance Evaluation

Over the years there have been many attempts to systematically deal with accounting measures, motivation and performance evaluation. One of the most well known, management by objectives (MBO), will be considered briefly. MBO dates back to the 1920s but it was made popular under this title by Drucker from 1954 onwards, and it is still in use in the 1990s. The essence of MBO is a formal system of setting objectives, motivating managers and appraising performance. Its proponents claim that it is an integrated approach to total management, that it is a powerful control mechanism, that it incorporates motivation and reward structures, and that it is universally applicable. Such a set of claims would be hard to live up to and most of the appraisals of MBO find that it falls short of the mark (a good summary and comment can be found in Dirsmith and Jablonsky, 1979).

The proponents of MBO usually describe a participative style for setting objectives for almost all aspects of organisational life. A high proportion of these objectives use accounting measures. There are usually formal reward structures based on accounting measures and regular performance evaluation in terms of the objectives set. Rewards are typically monetary and the whole approach seems based on an economic view of people. It is also a very rationalist approach and there appears to be little scope for dealing with uncertainty. Many large companies have adopted MBO in some form but a significant proportion have reported that it was not successful.

The basic feedback model described earlier in this chapter is the underlying model for MBO, on to which an elaborate structure is built. It appears that the full MBO system does not incorporate behavioural and organisational aspects sufficiently. Thus, for all its elaboration, it is not sufficiently realistic to be practical in most of the complex environments in which large firms operate.

Conclusion

At the outset of this chapter it was stressed that motivation and performance appraisal were both very broad subjects and that accounting measures played only a small part. Figure 11.1 shows that control of the organisation comprises three sets of controls, in which accounting measures form part of the administrative controls. The other forms of control, which each have motivational aspects, can be very powerful and in some circumstances will override accounting-based controls. There are examples of firms with very strong organisational cultures where accounting controls are much less important than the social controls. In such companies far less accounting data will be collected and analysed as the key element of control is the personal commitment of employees to the company. The strong commitment necessary for this form of control cannot be engendered by monetary payments alone. It requires an all-embracing culture where individual goals and organisational goals have been closely aligned.

In other companies self controls may be used as the primary feature of organisational control. Where this is the case, considerable effort will be spent on recruiting and training individuals to obtain staff with the appropriate self controls. Where this is successfully implemented, there will be a much reduced need for all forms of administrative controls. It is likely that summary accounting data will be used to assess overall performance of the business and senior managers.

The problems that face a firm within an environment containing a high degree of uncertainty were also overlooked earlier. In such circumstances it is difficult or impossible to set meaningful *ex ante* accounting measures. If the environment is rapidly changing or contains a high degree of unpredictability, budgets may have little relevance for control purposes. They may have to be set a year or more in advance and may be totally inappropriate by the time they are used to evaluate performance. The standard feedback control system becomes meaningless and a different approach to motivation and performance appraisal must be found. It may still be possible to set high-level accounting targets, but it will not be possible to specify in detail how these targets should be met. Senior management are forced to delegate increased powers to their subordinates and the non-accounting controls discussed above become even more important. Motivation must involve attitudes, culture and commitment to the organisation, rather than a monetary payment for attaining an accounting-based target. Performance appraisal will have to be over the medium term and not based on short-term accounting measures.

In conclusion it should be noted that there is a clear role for accounting measures in motivation and performance appraisal. However, it is equally important to be aware of the wider context. Motivation is often based on non-accounting and non-monetary features. Performance needs to be evaluated against objectives that cannot be measured in accounting terms. The successful firm is one where motivation is seen in its widest context and where performance appraisal and motivational techniques are carefully suited to the circumstances in which the firm operates.

Bibliography

Argyris, C. (1952) *The Impact of Budgets on People*, New York: The Controllership Foundation.

Briers, M. and M. Hirst (1990) 'The role of budgetary information in performance evaluation', *Accounting, Organisations and Society*, vol. 15, pp. 373–98.

Dirsmith, M.W. and S.F. Jablonsky (1979) 'MBO, political rationality and information inductance', *Accounting, Organisations and Society*, vol. 14, pp. 39–52.

Ezzamel, M. and H. Hart (1987) *Advanced Management Accounting: An organisational emphasis*, London: Cassell Educational Ltd.

Hofstede, G.H. (1968) *The Game of Budgetary Control*, London: Tavistock.

Hopwood, A. (1974) *Accounting and Human Behaviour*, London: Haymarket Publishing Limited.

Kennis, I. (1979) 'Effects of budgetary goal characteristics on managerial attitudes and performance', *Accounting Review*, LIV no. 4, pp. 707–21.

Locke, E.A. (1968) 'Towards a theory of task motivation and incentives', *Organisational Behaviour and Human Performance*, pp. 157–189.

Lyne, S.R. (1988) 'The role of the budget in medium and large UK companies and the relationship with budget pressure and participation', *Accounting and Business Research*, pp. 195–212.

Otley, D.T. (1978) 'Budget use and managerial performance', *Journal of Accounting Research*, vol. 16, pp. 122–49.

Otley, D.T. and A.J. Berry (1980) 'Control, organisation and accounting', *Accounting, Organisations and Society*, vol. 5, pp. 231–44.

Ronen, J. and J.L. Livingstone (1975) 'An expectancy theory approach to the motivational impact of budgets', *Accounting Review*, October, no. 4, pp. 671–85.

Vroom, V.H. (1964) 'Work and motivation', New York: John Willey.

Walker, M. and N. Choudhury (1987) 'Agency theory and management accounting', in Arnold, J.A., R. Scapens and D. Cooper, *Management Accounting: Expanding the horizons*, London: Chartered Institute of Management Accountants, pp. 61–112.

CHAPTER 12

Introduction to Agency Theory in Management Accounting

Miles Gietzmann

One of the potential costs of decentralisation or delegation of decision-making is that if a manager delegates decisions to a worker, then the worker may take decisions that are not in the interest of the manager. If these decisions were observable by, or entirely transparent to, the manager, then the manager would be able to govern the worker's actions and controls could be applied when decisions did not conform to requirements. However, with such transparency one may question whether there is actually any delegation. Agency theory addresses this issue of the 'costs' of delegation by assuming that certain decisions are not transparent, or are what is more commonly referred to as *unobservable*. The simplest form of unobservable decision is the action by a worker or *agent* concerning what level of effort to supply in a job. At issue, then, is how best the manager or *principal* can incorporate incentives into a contract of employment, to ensure that the agent acts in the best interest of the principal by providing the required level of effort. As we shall see, this question is of concern to management accountants because the incentives will frequently be based upon variables measured and communicated by the management accounting system. The ideas explored in agency theory can be illustrated by the example of a travelling salesperson (agent) who is constantly away from the office. The sales manager, or principal, will have little idea as to the effort put in by the agent. Typically therefore the salesperson's contract of employment will specify a performance-related element based on sales. However, the number of sales an agent makes cannot be determined perfectly by the level of effort provided because of uncertainties such as the preferences of customers. Given this uncontrollable event, performance-related payment schemes subject the agent to risk. A hard-working agent may sometimes receive low commission payments, while an agent who puts in little effort may still be rewarded with a major contract.

There are a number of thorough reviews on the application of agency theory to management accounting, which are detailed in the References at the end of this chapter. For the most part these reviews assume students have some acquaintance with agency theory concepts such as moral hazard and incentive compatibility as well as a substantial degree of mathematical sophistication. It is the intention of this chapter to present an elementary coverage of agency theory so as to make the material referenced at the end of the chapter more accessible to the reader. In the next section we discuss the relationship between the classically posed management accounting control problem and the agency theory characterisation of the problem. A numerical example of an agency control problem is then discussed, along with the interpretation of the solution. The example illustrates why information such as product unit costs, generated from the management accounting system, have relative 'productive' and 'information' values which are not co-extensive. In the appendix to this chapter we discuss generalisations of the results as an introduction to the academic literature on agency theory. This section is more abstract and may be omitted. Throughout the main body of this chapter we will try to keep the use of mathematics to a minimum. The only prerequisite is a knowledge of elementary linear programming and calculus.

The Inferential Control Problem

Given our concern with incentives, motivation and control, there are a number of natural questions that we need to consider. What are the appropriate performance measures (statistics) available from the management information system (MIS) and how effective are these at controlling agents? How exactly should statistics extracted from the management accounting information system be used to control perform-ance? What are the theoretical limitations to the control of agents by the information produced by accounting systems?

In the agency theory model presented in this chapter, we will assume that the decision to be controlled/influenced is the agent's choice of effort level. Since we will assume the agents operate in an uncertain environment, it is not possible to infer perfectly what input (effort) was provided purely by observing output statistics such as revenue or cost. Consider now a formal modelling of these ideas in which the output in the form of revenue or profit increases with the agent's effort in some stochastic way. Thus on average the greater the agent's effort (e) the greater the output q, where output is related to effort by the (stochastic) equation

$$q = e + \varepsilon \tag{12.1}$$

Here ε is a random variable with a zero expected mean. The problem for the manager or principal is that effort is not directly observable and the only information that the principal has is the output from the *combined result* of effort (e) and chance (ε) in the form of q. Hence the principal cannot disentangle the separate effects of e and ε on any observed q. A 'good' realisation could have resulted from a high level of effort e, combined with a poor ε realisation arising from poor market conditions. Altern-atively, the same output could have resulted from little effort and a good ε realisation arising from favourable market circumstances.

Equally, the agent is aware that his/her effort does not uniquely determine q because there are uncontrollable random events leading to a particular realisation of ε. For example, an agent who works extremely hard (e high) to sell a good for which demand is low (ε poor) because of (say) a sudden unpredicted change in consumer tastes might generate less sales revenue than an agent working not very hard (e low) to sell a good for which demand is high (ε good). This simple model is intended to capture the fact that the complex interrelated environments in which we operate are often subject to shocks and uncertainties.

Given the principal's inability to observe or even deduce with certainty the agent's effort, it is important to ask how we could best control the agent's actions or choice of effort. This requires us to model the agent's choice of action. We shall do this using the standard agent's preference function employing the utility preference model of microeconomics. (For more details see any standard text in microeconomics.)

The agent is assumed to be wealth maximising and risk averse. The agent is also averse to work. Such a purely self-interested agent will trade-off effort against the likely return or money wage W. For mathematical convenience we will assume that the agent's net utility can be represented as a utility over money less a (separate) utility over effort.

$$\tilde{U}_A(W,e) = \text{agent's separable utility function} = U_A(W) - V(e)$$

$$U'_A(W) > 0 \qquad V'(e) > 0$$
$$U''_A(W) < 0 \qquad V''(e) > 0$$

Thus, effort aversity implies $V'(e) > 0$ while $V''(e) > 0$ implies that the harder the agent works the more the agent must be paid to increase effort. This last condition is a mathematical condition which will ensure that the problem will have a solution. The conditions imposed on the first and second derivatives of U_A ensure respectively that the agent is wealth maximising and risk averse.

The principal would like to reward the agent for the effort provided and hence condition the wage directly on effort, which we could denote as $W(\bar{e})$, where the bar denotes 'observed' effort. Given that effort cannot be observed directly, this is not possible. However, since effort and output are related, albeit only stochastically, we can condition the wages on the observed output q. This we can denote as $W(q(e))$. Thus, the wage is a function of the output q which in turn depends on the effort e in some random way.

Clearly then, the way the principal can affect this trade-off is through the choice of the wage rate function $W(q)$, which could be viewed as a productivity-related wage. It may at first seem intuitive to expect to see the wage rate increasing for higher realised values of the output statistic. For example, if the output measure were revenue, the more revenue the agent's operations generated, the higher the agent's wage. As we shall see shortly, this is not always the case!

Given the agent's effort is not observed by the principal, let us consider how a 'self-interested' agent would select a level of effort to provide. We assume the choice of productivity-based wage $W(q(e))$ by the principal will lead to the agent selecting effort level e^* to maximise the value of his/her utility of wage income less the disutility of effort, as represented by expression (12.2)

$$U_A(W(q(e)) - V(e)) \qquad\qquad (12.2)$$

We say the agent 'self-selects' his/her effort choice.

The principal may influence this effort choice by changing the wage schedule or bonus system to $\tilde{W}(q(e))$ so that the agent then chooses $\tilde{e}$ such that $\tilde{e}$ now maximises $U_A(\tilde{W}(q(e)) + V(\tilde{e}))$. The effort level $\tilde{e}$ is the corresponding effort level that the agent (self-) selects given the change in the productivity wage 'schedule' from W to $\tilde{W}$. If we assume that this change is an increase with $\tilde{W}(q(e)) > W(q(e))$, then since a 'unit of effort' now earns more commission, the agent will provide more effort and will choose $\tilde{e} > e^*$. However, note that although we are confident that at the margin, higher rewards result in higher effort, we cannot be sure whether such a change is desirable. Without also considering what is the value of extra output, induced by the extra effort, relative to the extra cost of rewards, we cannot recommend such a change a priori. Rather than attempting to fully resolve this issue here, we merely emphasise the point that the agent trades off reward and effort and thus 'freely' chooses the effort level that best suits him/her. The principal therefore must choose an appropriate schedule of rewards W such that this schedule leads to 'incentive-compatible' behaviour by the agent, ensuring that the agent freely selects to provide the level of effort compatible with the principal's desires. Although the principal can manipulate the agent's incentives so that the desired level of effort is achieved, it is costly to generate such incentives. This arises because any increase in wage to generate appropriate incentives reduces the residual income available to the principal. In fact, we will show in the next section that sometimes it is 'too costly' to the principal to induce the highest agent effort and it becomes desirable to induce some lower level.

This problem of the agent having freedom to self-select effort is commonly called 'moral hazard' or alternatively described as a 'hidden action mode'. The terminology arises out of the following type of insurance industry problem. If you insure your car against theft, your effort to take anti-theft measures such as closing windows, locking doors and removing valuables may reduce. That is, the provision of insurance may result in your taking less preventive acts, and the insurance company has to take this *hazard* into account when costing the service. Of course the insurance company is aware of these problems and uses no-claim bonuses to encourage the owner to be careful. It also frequently makes the owner bear the first £100 (say) of any loss. Thus the insurance company attempts to write an 'incentive-compatible' contract which encourages the insured to act in a way that reduces its own exposure to moral hazard.

Let us now consider how similar ideas can be used to conduct an optimal contract of employment. First, consider how the principal would act if they could observe the agent's effort. When analysing the incentive properties of agent compensation, conditioned on management accounting statistics, it is conventional to assume the principal is risk neutral and hence has a utility function U_p of the form $U_p(\Pi) = \Pi$, where Π is expected residual profit after the agent's wage has been paid. This assumption of risk neutrality by the principal serves to simplify the mathematical analysis. Thus, the principal attempts to maximise expected output or profits, where expected profits are calculated after paying the agent's wages.

If the principal could perfectly observe the agent's effort e, then the principal would ensure the agent's reward was such that a fixed wage would be paid only if a required level of effort was observed or, more formally, a wage dependent on observed effort e_o such that:

$$U_A(W(e_o)) - V(e_o) = \overline{U}_A \tag{12.3}$$

where $\overline{U}_A$ is the 'wage' or utility the agent could obtain in alternative employment.

Constraint (12.3) is sometimes called the participation or individual rationality constraint. It assumes agents will not participate and will seek alternative employment if they could expect to improve their wages elsewhere. It should be noted that the wage can be conditioned on observed effort and the principal can in effect choose the appropriate effort level. Issues of control are largely irrelevant. This is the traditional economic model of decision-making in which the question concerns only which level of effort to induce. However, if we assume that effort is not directly observable, the principal can only reward an agent on the observed level of profit on output. The principal cannot condition the wage on the effort level. It can now only be conditioned on observable output level q. Different realisations of q will help the principal to make (imperfect) inferences concerning which level of effort the agent (self-) selected. The following section develops a simple example which demonstrates these principles.

A Worked Example

Suppose there are four possible states of the world, S_1, S_2, S_3 and S_4, where in general S_1 can be considered more favourable than state S_2, with S_4 being the least favourable. Each state is assumed equally likely and thus has a probability of 25 per cent of occurring. In our example the agent can only choose one of three effort levels: high (e_H), medium (e_M) or low (e_L). In general, of course, there are many more states of the world and the output or profit is likely to depend in some continuous way on the effort. We assume effort choice and state realisation lead to the following revenue pay-off matrix.

Effort state revenue matrix

	S_1	S_2	S_3	S_4
e_H	6500	6500	3200	1500
e_M	6500	3200	3200	1500
e_L	6500	3200	1500	1500

Assume the agent's preferences are such that:

$$\tilde{U}_A(W),e_i) = W^{\frac{1}{2}} - V(e_i) \text{ where } e_i \text{ takes one of the values } e_H, e_M, e_L.$$

The agent's utility derived from wealth is given by the square-root function, while the agent's disutility associated with the three discrete effort levels is assumed to be

$$V(e_H) = 10, \ V(e_M) = 7, \ V(e_L) = 4$$

We will also assume the agent's outside wage is such that the participation constraint has $\overline{U}_A = 20$. Thus, unless the agent's expected net utility is 20, he/she will seek employment elsewhere.

Suppose the principal wanted the agent to provide high effort. Since effort is assumed unobservable, how can such effort be induced? This question can be addressed by considering what management accounting information is available. In this simple model, three values for revenue can occur and the principal should make the agent's wage conditional on the observed revenue. Why? If the realised revenue was 6,500 then the principal knows there is a 50 per chance chance the agent used high effort, and a 25 per cent chance respectively that s/he used either medium or low effort. On the other hand if a revenue of 1,500 were observed, there is only a 25 per cent chance that high effort was used. Thus the revenue statistics are valuable in the 'effort inferential process' and it seems intuitive to reward the agent more for those revenue realisations that signal the agent did in fact use high effort. The principal's problem is to choose a wage or reward function which depends on the observed revenue and which will motivate the agent to act in the principal's best interest. Thus, the principal must choose the values of W_{65}, W_{32} or W_{15}, where W_{65} is the wage if a revenue of 6,500 is observed, W_{32} is the wage if a revenue of 3,200 is observed and W_{15} is the wage if a revenue of 1,500 is observed. The principal will also need to satisfy the agent's individual rationality condition (see equation (12.3)). To see how to formulate this problem, let us consider the case where the principal would like the agent to provide a high level of effort. The expected utility of the agent *if* s/he chose to provide high effort would be:

$$\tfrac{1}{2}W_{65}^{\frac{1}{2}} + \tfrac{1}{4}W_{32}^{\frac{1}{2}} + \tfrac{1}{4}W_{15}^{\frac{1}{2}} - 10$$

This expression is the expected utility of the wage received, less the disutility (10 units) of putting in the highest level of effort.

For the agent to prefer providing high effort to medium effort we require that the net utility from putting in the highest level of effort is greater than that from putting in only medium effort. Hence we require that:

$$\tfrac{1}{2}W_{65}^{1/2} + \tfrac{1}{4}W_{32}^{1/2} + \tfrac{1}{4}W_{15}^{1/2} - 10 \geq \tfrac{1}{4}W_{65}^{1/2} + \tfrac{1}{2}W_{32}^{1/2} + \tfrac{1}{4}W_{15}^{1/2} - 7$$

which simplifies to the condition $W_{65}^{1/2} \geq W_{32}^{1/2} + 12$

This illustrates the nature of the constraints of the mathematical program that the principal needs to 'solve'. Thus, formally, the principal needs to find $W_{65}^*, W_{32}^*, W_{15}^*$ such that these values minimise the expected wage costs, i.e.

$$\text{minimise } \tfrac{1}{2}W_{65}^{1/2} + \tfrac{1}{4}W_{32}^{1/2} + \tfrac{1}{4}W_{15}^{1/2}$$

subject to constraints (1) to (4):

1. Incentive compatible for the agent to prefer to provide high effort rather than medium effort:

$$\tfrac{1}{2}W_{65}^{1/2} + \tfrac{1}{4}W_{32}^{1/2} + \tfrac{1}{4}W_{15}^{1/2} - 10 \geq \tfrac{1}{4}W_{65}^{1/2} + \tfrac{1}{2}W_{32}^{1/2} + \tfrac{1}{4}W_{15}^{1/2} - 7$$

2. Incentive compatible for the agent to prefer to provide high effort rather than low effort:

$$\tfrac{1}{2}W_{65}^{1/2} + \tfrac{1}{4}W_{32}^{1/2} + \tfrac{1}{4}W_{15}^{1/2} - 10 \geq \tfrac{1}{4}W_{65}^{1/2} + \tfrac{1}{4}W_{32}^{1/2} + \tfrac{1}{2}W_{15}^{1/2} - 4$$

3. Individually rational for the agent to work for the principal, whereby the agent must receive a minimum net utility of 20 units:

$$\tfrac{1}{2}W_{65}^{1/2} + \tfrac{1}{4}W_{32}^{1/2} + \tfrac{1}{4}W_{15}^{1/2} - 10 \geq 20$$

We will also assume that the wage paid is always a positive amount, hence

4. $W_{65} \geq 0, W_{32} \geq 0, W_{15} \geq 0$

The optimal solution to the mathematical program is:

$$W_{65}^* = 1521, \; W_{32}^* = 729, \; W_{15}^* = 225$$

Thus the principal should pay a wage of 1,521 when a revenue of 6,500 is observed, a wage of 729 when the revenue is 3,200 and a wage of 225 when the observed revenue is only 1,500. This gives an expected wage bill of 999 ($= \tfrac{1}{2}$ 1521 + $\tfrac{1}{4}$ 729 + $\tfrac{1}{4}$ 225). The expected revenues are 4,425 ($= \tfrac{1}{2} \times 6500 + \tfrac{1}{4} \times 3200 + \tfrac{1}{4} \times 1500$), giving a net revenue of 3,426. If the principal could have observed the amount of effort directly, then s/he would have had to pay the minimum wage needed to ensure that the agent performed at the highest effort level. This is given by W_o, where the subscript denotes that the principal can observe the effort and does not need to infer the effort from the revenue

$$W_o^{1/2} - V(e_H) = W_o^{1/2} - 10 = 20$$

Hence $W_0 = 900$. The difference in wages represents a loss to the principal from an imperfect information system. Not being able to observe the agent's effort directly, is costly. In this case the cost is 99 ($= 999{-}900$) to the principal because the wage schedule must be structured on revenue realisations which are only a partial signal of the effort used by the agent.

It is worth summarising at this point just what we have calculated. We have identified the optimal wage schedule for the principal that will ensure that the agent puts in the highest level of effort and thus maximises the revenue. Of course, the principal is really interested in maximising the expected profit (i.e. expected revenue less expected wage cost). We need to repeat the above programming exercise conditioned on inducing medium and low effort in turn and evaluate the effect on profits of other revenue and wage costs. A summary of the solution of the three programming problems is as follows:

Effort induced in agent

	e_H	e_M	e_L
Expected revenue	4425	3600	3175
Expected wage cost	999	892	675
Expected profit	3426	2708	2500

Thus for this problem it is in fact optimal to induce high effort. It can be shown, however, that this will not always be the case. This can be illustrated if we replace the revenue of 6,500 by 3,600 in the original effort choice state realisation matrix. In terms of the mathematical programs all that we need to do is replace W_{65} by W_{36} and the same solutions would result, since from an 'inferential statistics' point of view, the revenue of 3,600 is identical to the previous revenue of 6,500. Thus the expected (incentive) wage costs will be identical, but clearly the expected revenue will be lower.

The summary solution to the revised problem is as follows:

Effort induced in agent

	e_H	e_M	e_L
Expected revenue	2975	2875	2450
Expected wage cost	999	892	675
Expected profit	1976	1983	1775

It is now optimal for the principal to induce the agent to self-select medium effort since it is, relatively, too costly to induce high effort.

In our original problem wages were increasing in conditional revenue, i.e. $W^*_{65} > W^*_{32} > W^*_{15}$. Now we need to ask whether we always expect to see wages increasing monotonically in the conditional statistic, i.e. the agent's wage being required to be larger for larger realised revenues. An extreme variant of our original problem provides us with an easily understood answer. Suppose now the effort choice state realisation matrix becomes:

	S_1	S_2	S_3	S_4
e_H	6500	5000	3200	1500
e_M	6500	3200	3200	1500
e_L	6500	3200	1500	1500

this is identical to the original problem expect for $R(S_2, e_H) = 5000$.

If we solved the associated incentive programming problems, we would find that the optimal solution was such that $W^*_{50} > W^*_{65}$.

Clearly the 'monotonicity condition' has been violated. For this incentive problem it is easy to see by inspecting the revenues in states S_1 and S_2 that a revenue realisation of 5,000 tells us a lot about the agent's effort choice, more so than a revenue realisation of 6,500. That is, from an inferential point of view a revenue realisation of 5,000 has more information content than a realisation of 6,500. Thus the productive and information values of managerial accounting statistics may not be co-extensive. From a production value point of view the best revenue realisation is 6,500. From an information content (control) point of view the best revenue realisation is 5,000. In the appendix we explore this issue in more detail and discuss the conditions that ensure that the agent's compensation will increase with increasing output. This section also serves the purpose of introducing the reader to the mathematical structuring of the problem that is used extensively in the literature. An alternative treatment of the mathematical structure of continuous effort and reward models in agency theory can also be found in Ashton (1991).

Linear Contracts

In the appendix we discuss the likelihood ratio property which ensures that the agent's compensation will increase the more revenue s/he earns. In practice, we frequently see linear compensation schedules. Holmstrom and Milgrom (1987) have used an agency theoretic approach to establish that a linear wage schedule of the form:

$$W = a + b (R + cy)$$

(where a, b and c are constants, R denotes revenue and **y** refers to other management accounting statistics besides revenue which have value when trying to make inferences about the agent's actions) can be optimal for certain environments. The amount a has the obvious interpretation of being the fixed wage, with the remaining component being the bonus/incentive element. Thus b is chosen to determine how strong the bonus element should be. Thus, if b = 0.9, the agent when generating revenue from a sale would keep 90 per cent as commission (assuming for the moment that c = 0). Thus the coefficient c determines the weight of these other statistics in the bonus formula. We will not present the details of the assumptions that must be made for such linear schedules to be optimal. Instead, we give a brief intuitive discussion regarding why linear schemes may be optimal.

Suppose you were an agent required to produce some fixed output at a budgeted cost of $\overline{Z}$ and were only rewarded for achieving $\overline{Z}$. Hence, incentives are dichotomous: if costs were greater than $\overline{Z}$, you may get no reward, and if they were less than or equal to $\overline{Z}$ you receive a fixed bonus. You may work hard to control costs so that this budget is achieved. However, if you could envisage other opportunities that would lower cost even further, but which required additional effort, the existing budget would give you no incentive to implement such opportunities because of the discontinuous nature of incentives. Thus, we may desire a budgetary system to apply uniform incentive pressure such that the manager will desire to search for, and to implement, cost reduction possibilities no matter what the existing predicted achievable cost conditions are. Thus, when we require such uniformity of incentives, linear wage schedules can be optimal. For the interested reader, the text by Milgrom and Roberts (1992) provides an excellent discussion of these issues.

Conclusion

We have given a very elementary introduction to agency theory as it applies to management accounting. We have concentrated on showing how management accounting statistics can be used optimally to control agents behaviour. We have then discussed the extent to which agency theory predicts the use and form of the managerial accounting performance measures that we observe in practice. Our coverage of this now large research area has been extremely selective. It is hoped that the approach adopted here has made the somewhat technical agency theory research area more easily accessible to an undergraduate audience and motivated such an audience to embark on study in the area. Classic review papers in the area include Baiman (1982), Namazi (1985) and Baiman (1990).

References

Ashton, D.J. (1991) 'Agency theory and contracts of employment', in Ashton, D.J., T. Hopper and R.W. Scapens (eds.) *Issues in Management Accounting*, 1st edn, Hemel Hempstead: Prentice Hall.

Baiman, S. (1982) 'Agency research in managerial accounting: a survey', *Journal of Accounting Literature*, Spring, pp. 154–213.

Baiman, S. (1990) 'Agency theory research in management accounting: a second look', *Accounting, Organisations and Society*, July, pp. 341–72.

Holmstrom, B. and P. Milgrom (1987) 'Aggregation and linearity in the provision of intertemporal incentives', *Econometrica*, March, pp. 303–28.

Milgrom, P. and J. Roberts (1992) *Economics, Organisations and Management*, Hemel Hempstead: Prentice Hall.

Namazi, M. (1985) 'Theoretical developments of principal–agent employment contract in accounting: the state of the art', *Journal of Accounting Literature*, Spring, pp. 113–33.

Appendix: General Conditions for Monotonicity of Conditional Incentive Wage Schedules

$$\blacklozenge$$

The following analysis uses calculus and provides a bridge between the simple discrete problems and the more advanced reviews of the agency theory literature in management accounting. In particular we will explore the conditions under which wages are an increasing function of revenue.

We assume that the agent chooses an effort level from the continuous interval between $\underline{e}$ and $\bar{e}$ and that revenue is denoted by R. We assume that revenue has a continuous probability density function on the interval $[\underline{R}, \bar{R}]$ induced by effort choice e. Thus the principal's problem is to determine a conditional wage schedule W which depends on R such that W(R) maximises the expected value of net revenue R − W(R). The expectation is taken with respect to the conditional probability of a revenue R conditioned on the agent's effort e. Mathematically, this takes the form

$$\int_{\underline{R}}^{\bar{R}} (R - W(R)) p(R|e) dR$$

The principal's choice of wage schedule is constrained by the fact that the agent chooses a level of effort to maximise the expected utility based on the wage schedule less the disutility of effort. Thus the agent chooses e to maximise

$$\int_{\underline{R}}^{\bar{R}} U_A(W(R)) p(R|e) dR - V(e)$$

By differentiating with respect to e in order to determine this optimal effort level, this constraint can be rewritten as

$$\int_{\underline{R}}^{\overline{R}} U_A(W(R)) \frac{dp(R|e)}{de} - V'(e)) = 0 \qquad (12.1)$$

The next constraint (12.2) says the agent expects to achieve at least the reservation level of utility. This constraint can be written as

$$\int_{\underline{R}}^{\overline{R}} \{U_A(W(R)p(R|e)) - V(e)) - \overline{U}_A\} p(R|e) dR \geq 0 \qquad (12.2)$$

using the fact that

$$\int_{\underline{R}}^{\overline{R}} p(R|e) dR = 1$$

to bring the p(R|e) term outside the bracket.

We now reformulate the constrained optimisation problem utilising the Lagrangian $\mathcal{L}$, in which we have a Lagrange multiplier λ for the first constraint and Lagrange multiplier μ for the second constraint. This gives us:

$$\mathcal{L} = \int_{\underline{R}}^{\overline{R}} \{(R - W(R))p(R|e) + \lambda (U_A(W(R)) \frac{dp(R|e)}{de} - V'(e))$$

$$+ \mu (U_A(W(R))p(R|e) - V(e) - \overline{U}_A)p(R|e)\} dR$$

On differentiating the Lagrangian with respect to W(R) to determine the necessary condition for the optimum wage schedule, we find that W(R) must satisfy

$$-p(R|e) + \lambda \frac{dp(R|e))}{de} U'_A(W(R)) + \mu \, p(R|e) U'_A(W(R)) = 0 \qquad (12.3)$$

which can be rearranged to give

$$\frac{1}{U'_A(W(R))} = \mu + \lambda \frac{\dfrac{dp(R|e)}{de}}{p(R|e)} \qquad (12.4)$$

Assuming sufficient regularity such that the second order condition for a maximum is satisfied, we are then left with how to interpret (12.4). In the simple case when effort is dichotomous, either high or low, the equivalent equation to equation (12.4) becomes:

$$\frac{1}{U'_A(W(R))} = \mu + \lambda \left(1 - \frac{f_{eL}(R)}{f_{eH}(R)}\right)$$

Since $U'_A > 0$ and $U_A'' \leq 0$, $U'_A(W(R))$ is a decreasing function and so

$$\frac{1}{U'_A(W(R))}$$

must be increasing. Hence

$$\left| 1 - \frac{f_{eL}(R)}{f_{eH}(R)} \right|$$

must be increasing or

$$\frac{f_{eL}(R)}{f_{eH}(R)}$$

decreasing. The term

$$\frac{f_{eL}(R)}{f_{eH}(R)}$$

is called the likelihood ratio and thus the optimal incentive wage schedule is increasing in realised conditional revenue if the likelihood ratio is decreasing. Thus, for our model we do have the monotonicity condition, provided this likelihood ratio property holds. It may be reasonable to assume this property holds, if higher revenue is in fact a correct signal of higher effort. Under such conditions agent incentive wages increase with conditional revenue.

CHAPTER THIRTEEN

Budgeting, Creativity and Culture

Alistair Preston

The purpose of this chapter is to explore the way in which budgeting may contribute to, or impede, the creative process within organisations. The first section examines the model of the creative process implicit in the conventional textbook treatment of budgeting. This model is referred to as the rationalist model of creativity. The chapter then explores the characteristics of organisations and budgeting prescribed under this model for dealing with high environmental uncertainty. It is suggested that the rationalist model is an inadequate representation of how creative or innovative behaviour manifests itself in organisations, which casts doubt upon the efficacy of using traditional budgeting techniques in conditions of high environmental uncertainty. The second section proposes an alternative model of creativity, referred to as the social constructionist model. Drawing on contemporary research on budgeting, the social constructionist perspective is seen to shed a different light upon the process of budgeting in organisations. Budgets are seen to be part of, and give shape to, the shared meanings, beliefs, values and distribution of power within the organisation. It is argued that these elements must be considered in making prescriptions about the appropriate nature of budgeting under conditions of high environmental uncertainty. The final section tentatively considers what form budgeting systems intended to foster creative behaviour in organisations might take.

The Rationalist Model

The rationalist model is part of a general theory which professes to explain the natural order. The natural order is seen to be an interlocking system of objective elements, arranged in a logical and rule-governed manner. This natural order is ultimately knowable and may be fully explained, provided that all the relevant variables in the system are identified and the rules governing their relationship understood. Events within the natural order, including physical, social, economic and organisational, events are the inevitable outcome of a determinate principle and therefore, with the correct knowledge, may be predicted. The reason why creativity is still regarded as being mysterious is simply that all the relevant factors have not been identified, and the interplay between the elements is still ill understood. Research into creativity, as with research in general within the rationalist perspective, involves uncovering those variables and rules of which we are still ignorant.

The following explores how rationalist assumptions are used in the management and accounting literature to explain the workings of organisations environments, uncertainty and various organisational processes, including budgeting. The ways in which organisational characteristics may impede or enhance creativity will also be explored.

Organizations, environments and uncertainty

Environmental uncertainty

In the management accounting literature, environment is defined as a complex system of interrelated economic, market, technological and, to a lesser extent, social and political variables. These variables may be placed on a continuum ranging from low to high uncertainty. Low environmental uncertainty is characterised by situations in which future events may be extrapolated from the past with some degree of accuracy. In this case, the variables and rules which make up the environment are well understood. Therefore the outcome of a course of action – say, a proposed investment in plant and equipment – may be predicted with a high degree of confidence. In contrast, high environmental uncertainty is characterised by dynamic, variety-rich environments which manifest themselves in highly unpredictable changes. In this case, the relevant variables and rules of the environment are misunderstood or only partially understood. The outcome of a proposed investment may therefore be highly uncertain.

In accounting, considerable effort has been directed towards improving quantitative techniques for dealing with uncertainty. These techniques, which include probability theory, conform to the rationalist perspective in that they are directed towards determining all the relevant environmental variables and the rules governing their relationship, based upon the belief that environments operate according to a predetermined order. The reduction of uncertainty may be achieved by gathering information, and therefore knowledge, about the environment. Perfect information would permit a reliable predictive model to be constructed, and the outcomes of particular courses of action would then be determinable.

However, even within the rationalist perspective it is generally accepted that perfect information, and therefore adequate predictive models of highly uncertain environments, is unobtainable. It is recognised that an organisation's strategy for dealing with high uncertainty may not be restricted to the application of quantitative or statistical techniques. Rather, an organisation's survival is dependent upon its ability to respond creatively to the threats and opportunities posed by a highly uncertain environment. Creativity – or, as it is usually expressed in the management literature, adaptability and flexibility – is seen to occur when the correct combination of variables or organisational characteristics is brought into play. These characteristics include the organisational structure, leadership style, the information system and the planning and control process. Each of these elements may be seen to be part of, or interact with, the budgeting process. Implicit within this perspective is the assumption that particular combinations of these elements are appropriate to different environmental conditions. Some combinations foster bureaucratic and highly rigid behaviour, while other combinations result in creative, adaptable and flexible behaviour.

In essence, organisational structures and processes may be designed to promote creativity. The following examines three organisational characteristics typically associated with budgeting under conditions of high environmental uncertainty. These are the organisation structure, the information system and the management control system. Although the three elements are highly interrelated, each will be explored separately.

Organisations as a combination of elements

Organisations are traditionally portrayed as a series of interlocking subsystems, representing patterns of authority and control, communication and information flow. Organisations are seen to differ in the ways their subsystems are arranged, the ways in which information is communicated and the ways in which control is exercised. Under conditions of high environmental uncertainty, where creativity is at a premium, the ideal combination of structure, information and control systems conforms to the *organic* type of organisation rather than to the *mechanistic* type.

Organic structures are typically decentralised, with relatively low degrees of hierarchical authority and with few formal rules and regulations. Ideally, subsystems within the organisation will have a high degree of autonomy in decision-making, planning and control. Within an organic structure, contact with the environment, and therefore information-gathering, is dispersed throughout the organisation. In conditions of high environmental uncertainty, organisations are required to produce greater volumes and varieties of information in order to plan for, and respond to, changes in the environment. For example, organisations will need information about the future as well as about the past, about events within the organisation and about external events in the environment. Much of this information will be generated through informal sources and may be qualitative and non-financial in nature. The planning and control of the organisation's activities are likewise dispersed throughout the organisation to facilitate adjustments in current operations and future plans, in response to environmental conditions. Ideally, there will be few formal rules and regulations, to allow for flexible and adaptable behaviour. Organic structures are loosely coupled, flexible and adaptable, and permit creative and innovative behaviour.

Without going into details, mechanistic organisations are essentially the opposite of the organic type and are characterised by rigid hierarchical structures, formalised information and control systems, and numerous formal rules and regulations.

Two questions are posed by the depiction of organic organisations. First, does budgeting, as typically presented in management accounting textbooks, conform with the organic type of organisation? Second, does the rationalist depiction of organisations represent the way in which organisations actually operate? These questions are explored below.

Budgeting, organisations, information and control

The extreme case

There is a close relationship between budgeting and organisational structure. Budgeting is based upon the concept of responsibility accounting, which emphasizes formalised, hierarchical structures. Organisational subsystems are defined as responsibility centres with individual managers held responsible and accountable for the performance of their divisions or departments. Typically, performance is measured against some clearly defined target or standard, often determined by senior managers in the organisational hierarchy and communicated downwards through the budgeting process. Budgeting is involved in co-ordinating the activities of the individual subsystems so that the goals of the organisation as a whole are achieved. As such, budgeting, through its formalised system of responsibility and accountability, may have the twin effects of establishing and reinforcing structures which emphasise hierarchical and rigid patterns of relationships within the organisation. The typical organisational charts found in management accounting textbooks appear to be more in keeping with mechanistic than with organic organisations. Such monolithic structures may promote inflexible responses with little room for creativity, thus impairing an organisation's ability to respond adequately to rapidly changing and dynamic environments.

As noted above, organic organisations need a considerable variety of information, often informal. Yet the information which budgeting systems typically provide is highly quantitative and economic in nature and forms part of the formal and often computer-based information system. Indeed, budgets are typically defined as a quantitative or financial expression of a company's plans. However, formal information systems have been criticised for their failure to provide the correct type of information in conditions of high environmental uncertainty (Mintzberg, 1975). The criticisms are as follows, and are applicable to budgeting systems as well:

♦ Budgeting concentrates on easy-to-measure events.
♦ When events are rapidly changing and unpredictable, information from budgets is often outdated, is historical rather than future oriented, and arrives too late for managers to base their decisions on.

♦ Formal information is not rich enough to describe complex and unfamiliar environmental events adequately.
♦ Finally, formal systems tend to concentrate upon events internal to the organisation rather than upon events in the external environment.

These criticisms have led to the suggestion that formal information systems produce an overload of irrelevant information about routine events and very little relevant information about important unfamiliar events.

To illustrate these inadequacies: a group of managers at a large plastic container factory were found to systematically ignore formal production information which reported labour and material variances as part of the budgetary control system. One production manager claimed that the information was too late. He said, 'Information is bound to be so far behind and managers must react much quicker. They've got to react on an hour-by-hour basis.' The production planner claimed that 'The overall picture might be good enough, it's just that the detail is not good enough in some cases.' Another production manager commented on the type of information provided: 'I don't know what I can do about it, they are just showing me some bloody figures, aren't they? What can I do about figures? They just mean 60, 70, 80 or whatever the bloody figure is. It doesn't tell me how to get better figures.' Finally, even the factory accountant admitted that 'there are too many inaccuracies. If you get it wrong at one stage then it's invariably wrong throughout.'

Mintzberg argued that these insufficiencies are not the result of a poorly designed system but are inherent to all management information systems, including budgeting systems. Given the type of information provided by the typical budgeting system, it is questionable whether it contributes to creativity, flexibility and adaptability in organisations.

The model of control which has dominated management accounting and budgeting thought is that of 'control over'. Managers set and communicate targets or standards, measure and evaluate performance, and prescribe corrective action if actual performance deviates from planned. Within the conventional textbook wisdom, control is typically portrayed as being located at the top of the organisation and the allocation of tasks, setting standards, evaluation of performance and budgetary process are top-down. Control is exercised through managerial dictate and the establishment of numerous rules and regulations to guide behaviour. Motivation is based upon a system of incentives designed to provide economic reward for good performance. The underlying assumption of this style of control has been characterised by 'Theory X', which suggests that individuals are rational economic beings, are inherently lazy, and require constant supervision and motivation through economic gain. However, such autocratic control is typically associated with mechanistic organisations. The concentration of authority and control at the top of the hierarchy creates a monolithic organisation which will have difficulty responding to changing environmental conditions. Such methods of control within a budgeting system are said to impede organisational learning by positively reinforcing existing practices rather than developing new, innovative and creative strategies.

Softening the case

The above portrayal of budgeting may seem extreme and to some extent dated; nevertheless, it is still common in textbooks. Others, while still operating within the rationalist perspective, suggest that budgets need not reinforce mechanistic structures, nor incorporate all of the problems associated with formal information systems, and need not rely on autocratic control. In particular, contingency theorists (see Otley, 1980) suggest that budgetary control systems may be designed to respond to, rather than ignore, changes in the environment. Decentralised structures may be complemented by decentralised systems of budgeting. Greater autonomy in formulating plans, setting standards, evaluating performance and determining corrective action may be devolved throughout the organisation rather than being concentrated at the top. The type of budgeting system operating within an organisation will be contingent upon the environmental conditions which confront it. Flexible budgeting and control systems are ideal for uncertain environments, and more bureaucratic methods are applicable for organisations operating in stable conditions. In addition, informal, non-quantitative and non-financial information may complement the more formal and quantitative calculations found in the typical budget.

In terms of control, these authors would suggest that autocratic control need not be the only form practised in rational organisations. Consensual control, which emphasises participation in budgeting, when setting standards and in the evaluation of performance, may be practised. This style of control is based upon 'Theory Y', which emphasises the 'human' side of management. Individuals are defined as responding to a wide range of incentives such as greater autonomy and control over their own tasks, job enrichment and group participation. By encouraging participation in the budgetary process, a greater variety of information and perspectives will be introduced which will promote more innovative strategies. By dispersing information throughout the organisation and allowing all members to participate in the budgeting and control process, organisations will be better able to identify, learn about and respond to changing environmental conditions. Under consensual control, the budgeting process will be bottom-up, with top management's role confined to approving standards proposed lower down in the hierarchy. It is assumed that if individuals are involved in the setting of standards and in the evaluation of their own performance, they will internalise and strive to achieve the standards set.

Another alternative to Theory X which proposes even fewer formal controls is 'Theory Z' (Ouchi, 1979). A Theory Z organisation is likened to a clan, where each individual becomes a member of the organisation in a much more intimate sense. The clan functions by socialising the individual completely, so that the goals of the individual merge with the goals of the organisation. The clan is culturally homogeneous and members share a common set of values and beliefs. Unlike hierarchical organisations, in which each member is dependent on the structure to provide guidance for action and levels of performance to which to aspire, clan organisations are said to have relatively few rules, regulations and control systems.

This enables the members to adjust individually and adapt their behaviour to suit changing conditions. Chaos is avoided because a system of mutual interdependence is established between the individual and the organisation. This relationship is characterised by the motto 'what is good for the organisation is good for the individual'. Thus, formalised control systems for ensuring consistency between individual and organisational goals are unnecessary, because the goals of the organisation are already the goals of the individual. In clan organisations, control takes the form of socially integrating the individual into the organisation. Theory Z was apparently developed by observing the practices of Japanese firms and has been prescribed as an appropriate model of control in rapidly changing environments.

In summary, certain authors advocate organic structures, a budgeting system which provides relevant and timely information and a style of control that minimises the number of rules and regulations, either through participation or through a process of social integration. It is argued that suitably designed budgeting systems are possible and may facilitate the flexibility and adaptability necessary to promote creative and innovative responses to environmental uncertainty. However, these prescriptions are based upon the same rationalist perspective which underpins mechanistic structures, formal systems and autocratic control. Implicit in all of the above models is the assumption that creative and adaptable behaviour will automatically result from the correct combination of organisation structure and information and control systems.

Dismissing the case

What is missing from this perspective is that organisations *create* as well as *respond* to their environment. Take, for example, the deregulation of financial services in the United Kingdom. The environment, namely the financial services market within which brokerage firms and investment banks operated, underwent a radical transformation. The environment became highly uncertain; Japanese and American investment firms moved into London. London companies began to restructure through a rash of take-overs and mergers, and by introducing new operating procedures to position themselves better for the new conditions they anticipated. So far, this is consistent with contingency theory. However, after deregulation, the nature of the financial services market was created by the actions of the people and companies in that market. The mergers themselves, reducing commissions, offering different services and the introduction of American and Japanese styles of management, all helped shape the environment within which the firms operated. In this respect the organisations created their own environment.

There is a degree of reciprocity between organisations and environments. Environments may be contingent upon the actions of the organisations, and in turn an organisation's structure and process may be contingent upon events in the environment. Where an environment begins and an organisation ends is a lot less clear, and the relationship between organisations and their environment is more complex and mutually interrelated than contingency theory would lead us to believe. Even budgeting, and the plans of action it contains, may impact upon and change the environment. In short, environments do not operate according to immutable laws but rather are created and reproduced by the actions of individuals and organisations. The idea of mapping out environmental variables and matching them with organisational variables and appropriate budgeting systems is a fallacy, simply because environmental and organisational variables do not exist as discrete entities which can be identified, measured, modelled and predicted. Rather, environments are constructed by the actions and interactions of competing organisations, governments and customers. As we shall see in the next section, these entities are themselves constructed by the actions and interactions of individuals and need not operate according to a single determinate principle of order.

Another criticism of the traditional perspective of budgeting rests upon the fact that consensual and clan control have an important characteristic in common with autocratic control. All three are premised upon the principle of 'control over' or of coercing individuals into behaving in accordance with the goals of the organisation, normally reflected in the top management's ideology. The purpose of consensual control which allows, and indeed encourages, individuals to participate in the budgeting process is as much to do with enduring commitment to the budget by the participant, as it is to do with promoting creativity. In a similar way, clan control appears to subordinate the expression of individuality to the organisation. Clan control may be likened to a dictatorship of the majority. It is based upon a docile and mute membership, including management, which will comply with unspoken norms and values as if they were its own. There is also the suggestion that the unspoken norms and values are those of the senior management which are internalised by the clan. Conformity rather than creativity may be the likely result.

What is also notable from the rationalist perspective, whether it relates to creativity budgeting, organisational structure or the natural order in general, is the absence in the analysis of human beings as self-directing individuals. Within the rationalist perspective, the behaviour of individuals is seen to be determined by the situation – that is, by the combination of structure and process, including the budgeting process, of the organisation. There is no provision within the rationalist perspective for the conscious, self-determining actions of individuals. For this reason, the rationalist model is referred to as being determinist in nature. Behaviour is explained by the stimulus–response model. An individual's response will be determined by the stimulus or situation which is brought into play, and is therefore predictable. The image of the human individual is that of a passive object being tossed around by the force of circumstance.

The absence of the creative human individual in traditional perspectives on budgeting is their most severe limitation. In response, a number of studies have sought to introduce the human being into their analyses of the budgeting process. We shall refer to these as the social constructionist perspectives. There are a number of overlapping schools of thought within the social constructionist perspective, each emphasising different aspects of social reality or individual behaviour. In the following, we will examine two of these.

Before progressing, it should be noted that contingency-based research, which has relied heavily on analysing questionnaire data, has been recognised by some of its principal practitioners to contain a number of limitations. For example, Merchant and Simons (1986) note that the possibility of respondent bias and the potential of superficiality of questionnaires are very real problems, as is the fact that 'organiz- ational context is often a construct of the researcher rather than a description of perceived reality in the terms used by the organization under study'. In an attempt to overcome these limitations, *case study* research in which the researcher interacts with the organisational participants is advocated. Unfortunately, the results of the case study research are surprisingly similar to the results generated under questionnaire surveys. Organisations are still defined in terms of interlocking subsystems and formal processes, change is still seen as a result of changing environmental conditions, and finally there is rarely any mention of human beings.

The Social Constructionist Model

In the social constructionist perspective, behaviour, including creativity, is not the result of the correct combination of elements or a predeterminate order, but is a product of the creative individual. One school of thought, called symbolic inter- actionism (see Blumer, 1962), suggests that human behaviour may be understood in the following manner. First, individuals act towards 'things' – that is, towards objects, situations, events and possibly each other – on the basis of the *meaning* that things have for them. There is a critical process between encountering an object, situation or event and an individual's response to it. This is referred to as the process of interpretation, in which the individual constructs a meaning or definition of the situation, event or object and acts in accordance with that meaning. Meaning is therefore not inherent in the object or situation, but is brought to it by the individual. Second, meanings do not simply pop out of the air; rather, they are said to be derived through social interaction – that is, through the ways in which people meet, talk, work and play together and in turn construct and share meanings. Meanings are therefore socially constructed, internalised and shared between individuals. Third, meanings may be expressed symbolically through language (hence the title 'symbolic interactionism'). In this respect, words, formulas, information, financial accounts and budgets are all symbolic representations of reality and carry meaning which may be communicated to others. Finally, meanings are not immutable but rather may be changed by individuals themselves and/or through further social interaction.

For example, during a lorry drivers' strike, when pickets refused to permit products to leave the plastic container factory mentioned earlier, the managers met to discuss the problem. Throughout the interaction various managers suggested that the factory should be closed, that stock should be built up until the strike was over, or that part of the factory should be closed and certain select items of stock should be built up. The managing director finally asked the following question: 'If we cut back or close down, how do our customers stand?' One of the production managers commented, 'It doesn't matter. If we are picketed they're going to be picketed as well! If they can't get anything out they won't need any containers.' The production planner, however, interjected: 'Ah, is that right? They're not picketing food manufacturers ... Birds Eye, Express Dairies, Rowntree, Van den Berghs won't be picketed' (these companies were the factory's largest customers). The managing director then said, 'If you look at it that way, we're part of the food industry ourselves.' After discussions with the regional offices of the union, plastic containers used in the food-processing industry were allowed to leave the factory. The factory was able to continue operations at a slightly reduced capacity throughout the strike.

This example demonstrates how meanings and definitions may be altered through social interaction. In effect, the managers had redefined the very nature of their business. From being in the plastic container industry, the company was now defined to be part of the food-processing industry. The interaction is also an example of the creative process at work. The redefinition of the business brought a significantly different meaning to the situation, and it resulted in a creative solution to the problem. The source of creative and adaptable behaviour lies in the ability to construct and redefine meanings.

Recently, the work of Bruno Latour (1987) and others in a school of thought called the social construction of technology has provided useful insights into the way in which new technologies and scientific discoveries are introduced and accepted by others in the scientific community or organisation. The work of the social constructionists of technology has begun to influence our thinking about creative processes in general and about how budget and control systems are introduced into, or resisted in, an organisation (see Preston, Cooper and Coombs, 1992). Latour focuses not so much on the creation of new ideas but rather on how ideas are taken up and developed into full-blown new facts, new products or new systems, or else rejected or resisted by members of a community or organisation. For Latour, the process of interaction between individuals is critical to this process. However, his depiction of interaction is more political and intriguing than the somewhat harmonious notions implied in the work of the symbolic interactionists. For Latour, the process of innovation has a lot to do with persuading others that one's idea is the best. Within this perspective, successfully introducing new management ideas, new products or new systems is a process of taking weak, hesitant possibilities and *translating* them into convincing arguments – arguments that others will buy into. In our own study of the attempted introduction (the initiative eventually failed) of a management budgeting system into the British National Health Service (NHS), we observed a range of different strategies adopted by the advocates of the system to enrol allies in an attempt to ensure success. These strategies ranged from official dictates handed down from the Region and NHS Management Board, requiring Districts to develop budgeting systems, to strategic attempts to maintain control over how the initiative was defined and presented. Here, rhetoric was very important. For example, one Health Notice from the NHS Management Board defined the initiative thus: Management budgeting should not be seen as an accounting exercise, or as a device for containing costs. The key purpose is to improve services through more effective management at all levels.' It was thought by the proponents of the initiative that if it were associated with previously unpopular cost-cutting exercises in the NHS, medical professionals in particular would refuse to participate in the initiative. However, such attempts to control the way in which the initiative was perceived were not always successful. One participant in the study commented that:

> The Region has tried to down play the role of accountants, and has said it is a management information system and all that kind of baloney. But no matter how you look at it, it is an accounting system. So we're trying to go along with that, but we've got our reservations.

It is interesting that after the management budgeting initiative failed, it was resurrected as the 'Resource Management' initiative. Therefore, even in failure the initiative was re-created, but with the lessons of the previous initiative well learned. Creativity in this perspective is a very Machiavellian affair, and yet these processes of translating weak, hesitant possibilities into convincing arguments to enrol others are clearly evident in the dynamics of interactions in organisations.

The creative process is often defined as being intuitive or inspirational. However, these are only metaphors for an individual and social process that eludes rational enquiry, because the creative process does not conform to the rationalist model. First, creativity ultimately rests upon the potential in individuals to look at the world anew and to interpret what they see differently. Here, symbolic interactionism can help explain this process. However, no one lives in a vacuum. The successful adoption of a new idea, product or system requires the creative individual to convince and enrol others and carefully navigate his or her idea through the political and sometimes adversarial environment of the organisation. The social constructionists of technology have much to teach us here.

The question the social constructionist perspective poses concerns which organisational context and budgeting process will promote and which will impede creative ideas and their adoption by the organisation and its members. To answer this question, it is first necessary to redefine the nature of organisations under the social constructionist perspective.

Organisations as culture

Within the non-rationalist perspective, organisations are seen as gatherings of people. However, football crowds may also be described as gatherings of people, yet in many obvious respects they differ from the typical organisation. What makes an organisation different from a football crowd or indeed one organisation different from another, is the manner in which people gather – that is, the manner in which individuals interact with one another and thereby for the most part align their individual courses of action. As noted above, human behaviour is not determined by a rational order, but neither is it completely irrational or anarchic. Rather, an individual's behaviour is guided by the meanings, values and beliefs that are constructed by, and shared between, the members of an organisation. An organisation may therefore be defined as socially constructed order. It must, however, be noted that the actions of organisations may ultimately be traced to the actions of individuals.

These shared values, beliefs and meanings have come to be collectively defined as organisational culture. Within the organisation and accounting literature two conceptions of culture have emerged, and it is important to distinguish between them. On the one hand, culture is defined as merely another variable to be combined with the organisation structure and processes in order to bring about desired results. Organisations are portrayed as *having* a culture which may be crafted and manipulated by management intervention to instil particular company values and attitudes and to create particular forms of behaviour. The work on clan organisations belongs to this tradition, as it interprets culture as a 'thing' which may be manipulated. On the other hand, organisations may be thought of as culture (Dent, 1991). From this perspective, culture is not a separate element, but rather it constitutes or *is* the organisation. Organisations *are* the shared meanings, values and beliefs – that is, the culture, over time, has been formed by the organisational members.

This social constructionist perspective does not preclude the existence of organisational structures and processes, but rather it suggests that they are symbolic representations of a particular view of organisational reality. They are subject to interpretation by individuals who will act towards them on the basis of the meaning they have for them. In this respect the structure, and in particular processes including budgeting, may form part of the culture of the organisation, and indeed may be active in shaping the pattern of shared meanings, values and beliefs.

A particular organisational culture may impede or enhance creativity. Culture may be seen to define the limits of currently acceptable behaviour or of current practices and beliefs. In other words, it prescribes a line between that which is 'done' and that which is 'not done'. Such prescriptions may be seen as rules, but these differ from the predetermined rules of the rationalist model. They are 'rules in process' and are often unstated. They are continually produced and reproduced, or else modified and changed, through the actions and interactions of the participating individuals. Creativity, by definition, lies beyond acceptable or current practice: it operates on or beyond the border of 'that which is done'. For creativity to thrive, individual behaviour which transcends the current order must be accepted by other members and, if judged worthy, be incorporated into, or change, current practices. In short, a culture of acceptance of new and innovative behaviour will have to evolve. The above perspectives on individual behaviour, organisational culture and creativity provide some interesting ways of reinterpreting budgeting in general and also budgeting under conditions of high environmental uncertainty.

The meaning *of* budgets

Budgeting, like any other object or activity, is subject to the interpretation of individuals. While many of the meanings of budgeting may be shared by the organisational participants, there need not be complete consensus. Budgets may mean radically different things to different people.

For example, during a study of the introduction of management budgets into a district in the NHS a number of conflicting meanings of the budgeting process were evident. The Department of Health and Social Security (DHSS) defined management budgeting in the following manner: 'The overriding objective of introducing management budgeting in the NHS is to give better services to its patients, by helping clinicians and other managers make better informed judgements about how the resources they control can be used to maximum effect' (DHSS Health Notice, January 1985). The above definition conforms fairly closely to traditional definitions of budgeting, which emphasise efficiency and improved services. However, an administrator in the district revealed his scepticism of this definition and offered his own:

> The general view is that this is yet another tool for cuts within the District. So no matter how cleverly one might attempt to disguise this in a language that talks about improvements in services, what we are actually talking about in this District is achieving less for less money ... In this district we want to be doing less by 1993 at less unit cost than we are doing now.

For this administrator, budgeting meant cost-cutting or the constraining of financial resources. For the doctors within the NHS budgets meant a device which would impinge upon their clinical freedom. Doctors defined budgets as an 'Orwellian nightmare' and argued that if they participated in the process, it would be a 'Trojan horse' to their autonomy.

All of these and other definitions were laden with deep-felt meaning and guided the various individuals' responses to the management budgeting initiative. Ultimately, the entire national initiative to introduce management budgets was suspended because of the conflict it caused between national and district managers and the entire medical profession. The outcome of the budgeting process is in part determined by the meaning that it holds for people and the culture within which it is placed. In the case of the NHS, the proposed new budgeting system was placed in a complex culture in which there were multiple shared meanings, values and beliefs. Indeed, the NHS at the time of the study could be defined as a culture of conflict. The new budgeting system not only reflected this conflict but helped to fan the flames. In this sense, the new system increased and even created conflict within the organisation.

Another example of the meaning of budgets found in the literature is that the presence of budgets within an organisation gives the impression of a rational, efficiently run operation. In this sense, budgets are synonymous with good management and confer legitimacy upon the organisation. They create the appearance of a rational approach to the uncertainties of the future. This may be very important to organisations trying to raise funds from financial institutions or government departments. Financial institutions usually require operations and capital budgets before considering a loan. For example, one author noted that the power of the administrators in the Polaris missile programme came from their ability to convince others both inside and outside the US Defense Department that they were effective and rational managers. They did this through the use of sophisticated management techniques, including forms of budgeting, even though these techniques were not employed in making the critical decisions (Sapolsky, 1972).

In this sense, budgets are a form of advertisement for rational economic behaviour. Budgets may also be used as advertisements in another sense. Managers may inflate their expected level of performance in the budget, against which they will subsequently be evaluated. This advertises determination and motivation, which may be valued and rewarded qualities within the organisation. While this strategy may seem risky, the same budgets may be used as a means of defence if the budgeted performance is not achieved. Budgets contain numerous assumptions about anticipated future events. Managers who fail to achieve their budgeted performance can appeal to these assumptions, claiming that events outside of their control did not work out as expected. In essence, they may claim retrospectively that the budget was rendered meaningless by unpredictable and uncontrollable events.

Given that budgets may be interpreted differently in different situations by different people, the budget as an artefact, and budgeting as a process in itself, can neither impede nor promote creative behaviour. However, the meaning that budgets and budgeting have for people certainly may do so. If budgets are seen as a divisive means of cutting cost and constraining growth, or as a pernicious form of control (as in the case of the administrator in the NHS), this may influence values and beliefs in an organisation and create a culture in which creativity is stifled.

To avoid the possibility that budgeting might impede creativity, the directors of an independent record company simply refused to budget in the early days of the company. One director commented as follows: 'I think budgets are totally irrelevant, you are never going to know [whether a record is going to be profitable] in this kind of business. It's either going to be a good idea or a bad idea.' When asked what constituted good or bad the director replied, 'It's good if you like it.' He then asked rhetorically, 'Do you make a record because you think the man on the street is going to like it? Na, you're going to make it because *you* like it.' The principal philosophy of the company was to subordinate economic analysis to aesthetic appreciation in order to allow creative music and ideas to surface and develop. Their principal concern was that a good idea should not be rejected on its perceived unprofitability, when revenue and costs were highly uncertain. Budgets were therefore seen as meaningless or might mean giving up a good idea.

Budgets are not only meaningful to people, they may be involved in the shaping of meaning. The following section explores this point.

The meaning *in* budgets

Budgeting is typically presented as a neutral process, or as a passive technique which mirrors but does not create a purely objective reality. However, this claim to neutrality and objectivity has been criticised because it neglects to consider that budgets are symbolic representations of the reality they express. Budgeting brings a selective visibility to particular events or particular characteristics of events and thus sets the agenda for the future. In this respect, budgets or budgeting may define what is important and in need of consideration. Budgets emphasise the economic aspects, the revenues, expenses and cash flows, of future anticipated events or current operations. Budgets, by what they measure and how they measure it, may shape the interpretative process of individuals and the meaning that things have for them. Because of budgeting's focus upon the measurable, quantitative elements of a situation, the hard-to-measure non-quantitative elements may be ignored. What is measured gets attention, what is not measured gets ignored. Budgets may have the effect of narrowing the focus of managers' interpretations to consider only the economic and in turn stifle the possibility of new and innovative interpretations. It must be noted that the capacity of budgets and budgeting to shape meaning is not inherent in the budget or the process of budgeting. It is because budgets have come to *mean* something that they in turn shape meaning. Budgets may be seen as part of the overall management trend towards quantitative and economic analysis – that is, towards an increasingly rational organisational culture. It is because quantification and economic measure have come to mean so much in commercial organisations that budgeting and other quantitative techniques may in turn shape people's interpretative process and create meaning.

An example of how meanings may be affected by accounting concerns the independent record company mentioned above. One of the bands which recorded with the company was investigated by the Inland Revenue. The record company was required to provide information on earnings for each album and single, tape and CD that the band had recorded with them. This required calculating the sales revenue and costs of each item, something the company had not done until this point. This constituted an enormous elaboration of the accounting system of the company. What is relevant is that after the investigation, the new accounting system continued in operation. It began to be used to evaluate the success of particular projects. For example, one director commented to the manager of a band, 'You know your last single made a loss.' The band manager replied, 'I dispute that.' The director interjected, saying, 'You can't dispute the figures [referring to the new accounts]. Costs: recording and mixing 60, video 40, printer's bill 110 . . . that's where we really got caught. Pressing was 65; with royalties, the total costs are 315 grand. Total money in was about 260. . . . We made a loss of about 55 grand.' The new accounts finally evolved into a crude form of budgeting which would not have been acceptable a few years previously.

This example suggests that budgets and accounting in general may not only shape the meaning given to events but might impact upon the culture of an organisation more generally. With the increased use of accounting, the directors of the record company admitted that they had moved into an era of financial realism. In turn, other practices within the organisation changed. More aggressive 'hyping' (meaning advertising and promotion) of the music and a greater concern for profits began to emerge. In consequence, the culture of the organisation slowly evolved from one which emphasised aesthetics to a more economic orientation.

Another example of how budgets may shape culture is found in a study of a company referred to as European Rail. Dent (1991) noted that when financial considerations were given a greater profile in the organisation, economic interpretations began to eclipse the engineering interpretations which up until this reorientation had had a significant impact upon the culture of the organisation. This example of European Rail and the new financial realism at the record company suggest that accounting in general and budgets in particular may be mechanisms of change and power within organisations.

The power of budgets

Within an organisation, groups of individuals or indeed a single individual may have the ability to influence the budgeting process and therefore the allocation of resources. Resource allocation is subject to a considerable amount of power play in organisations, in that it may set the level of resources assigned to departments and determine which capital projects will be funded. Budgets have been defined as a political bargaining process which reflects systems of power and influence in organisations. The manner in which resources are allocated and the capital investment projects chosen are not necessarily the outcome of a rational decision-making process but, rather, reflect the ability of certain groups or individuals to influence the allocation process.

For example, a media director of a leading advertising company in London commented that he wished to have the largest media budget in the advertising industry. He admitted that it was important for him to have a large budget because this would reflect the relative importance and status of the media department within the company and the industry as a whole. Higher status would enable him to have a greater say in the running of the company. Given this interpretation, the media director was deliberate in his attempts to influence the budgeting process in his favour. Thus the size of the media budget, relative to other departments in the organisation and the industry, reflected the director's power and his ability to affect subsequent resource allocation.

Thus, budgets may mirror the extant patterns of power and influence in the organisation and may reflect changes in these patterns. Apart from the political bargaining of powerful individuals, the allocation of resources and the acceptance of projects under capital budgeting may be influenced by those individuals involved in the budgeting process. Certain individuals may have the influence to determine the selection of information to be included in the budget; this may help shape the outcome of the budgeting process and affect the future direction of the company, and possibly the distribution of power and influence. In this respect, budgets are an instrument of power as well as being a reflection of power. Determining the input of data may have other consequences. Certain managers may underestimate performance and build slack into their budgets. Subsequently, when their performance is evaluated they appear efficient and effective. This in turn may improve their positions in the organisation.

Lastly, budgeting, especially capital budgeting, through the manipulation of data may be used to justify decisions already made rather than playing a role in the decision-making process *per se*. In this respect a capital budget may be a *post hoc* rationalisation of a decision that has already been taken. For example, a company which ran a chain of catalogue showrooms in the United Kingdom determined that any new showrooms must show a positive net present value using the company's regular cost of capital figure. The estate manager, who was responsible for searching out and evaluating new showroom sites, was set the objective of opening twenty new stores per year. As the prime sites were slowly used up, it became increasingly difficult for prospective showrooms to satisfy the company's investment criteria. In order to fulfil his quota, the estate manager used more and more generous estimations of those factors which would affect his anticipated revenue calculations, such as the spending power in the area and flow of pedestrian traffic past the store. In effect, the capital budget was manipulated to justify the opening of new stores and satisfy the quota requirements set by the company. Budgets and the process of budgeting are complex, and tightly interwoven with organisational life. In particular, budgets form part of, and help shape, the shared meanings, values, beliefs and distributions of power which make up the culture of the organisation. The question remains as to how this conceptualisation of organisations and budgeting impacts upon the creative process.

Budgeting and creativity

Budgets and budgeting in themselves neither impede nor enhance creativity. Rather, it is what budgets mean to organisational members, what meaning budgets bring to situations, and how budgets are used to reinforce or shape the patterns of power in an organisation that will impact upon the creative process. This impact may enhance or impede creativity. For example, in the case of the media director mentioned above, his striving to increase his budget had a more pragmatic intention than simply to increase his status and power. By increasing the size of the media budget the director could buy in talent, meaning the best media planners and buyers in the industry. This would enable the director to operate the media department more effectively. In fact, the department won a number of national awards for best media campaign. This success in turn enhanced the media department's standing in the company and in the advertising industry.

Here, influencing resource allocation increased creativity in the media department by permitting the buying in of talent. The buying in of talent is a common way for organisations to attempt to increase creativity. However, if the power to influence resource allocation lay in the hands of those committed to preserving the status quo, new and innovative projects might not receive funding, or departments which might increase the company's ability to operate in conditions of high uncertainty might be starved of funds. For example, organisations which experience a downturn in earnings after a period of high profitability tend to develop rigid budgetary control systems and cut research and development, even though it was product innovation which created their success in the first place. Such organisations become inward-looking rather than exploring possible new products and markets, and fail to meet the challenges of the environment.

Even if powerful individuals in an organisation are committed to creativity, change and development, the dominant culture or cultures of the organisation might suffocate the best intended attempts to change. Rigidity may be integral to the socially constructed order. Particular approaches to problems or situations may become ossified into culturally accepted 'ways of doing things'. Innovation and novelty may be socially unacceptable and mechanisms may exist to resist change and restrict creative endeavour. The notion of rigid cultures suggests that there are particular characteristics of organisational culture which might impede creativity. March (1976) identifies a number of agents of rigidity commonly found in organisations. He notes that in organisations decision-making and subsequent action are typically viewed as being purposive – that is, directed towards achieving a predetermined goal or objective. March notes, however, that in highly ambiguous situations, managers often have to act in order to find out what they are doing. Even if managers operate on a trial-and-error basis, they are obliged to rationalise their actions to appear as if they were purposive and goal-directed. Managers are required to give the impression that they know what they are doing, and most organisations place a premium on rationality. Indeed, rational behaviour is rewarded and non-rational behaviour is frowned upon. Decisions clouded by emotions are actively discouraged in most organisations and justifying a choice because it 'feels right' is rarely acceptable.

In addition, in most organisations, courses of action are evaluated in terms of whether they are consistent with the actions of other managers and sub-units and with the goals of the organisation. Actions are also evaluated in terms of whether they are consistent with past actions, which coerces managers into familiar and routine patterns of behaviour. Purposiveness, rationality and consistency have a strong appeal in organisations and are often highly valued and rewarded. However, organisations confronted with rapidly changing and highly uncertain environments require a very different type of culture. Purposiveness, rationality and consistency may promote a cautious and risk-averse approach to unfamiliar situations. Procedures may become standardised and formalised and create a culture of preserving established customs and practice. Such a culture may promote repetitive and imitative rather than original behaviour.

If we examine the principles and practice of budgeting, we can see how they may be involved in reinforcing a culture of rationality, consistency and purposiveness. Budgets, by reducing events to financial measures according to basic accounting formulas, represent a paragon of rationality. Moreover, because managerial perform-ance is often evaluated against these measures, budgets may not only reflect rationality but may also actively promote and reinforce rational behaviour. The role of budgeting in co-ordinating the activities of the various sub-units in an organisation is valued because it promotes consistency and goal congruence. But insistence upon goal congruence and consistency may limit creative ideas and experimentation and instead may promote imitative behaviour which displays very little originality. Finally, budgets, conceived as a means of compelling planning in organisations, promote the ideal of purposive behaviour and the need to justify decisions and actions in terms of intent and purpose. When one's intention has been expressed through the budget, one's performance may be evaluated against achieving the goals set. Failure will be defined in terms of the inability to meet the budget. This may promote rigid, undirectional behaviour as well as slavish adherence to budgets even if they are made obsolete by changes in the environment. Budgets represent a highly formalised approach to planning in organisations and, as we have seen, represent a narrow picture of reality. These characteristics may have the effect of guiding behaviour down one path in accordance with one strategy. Therefore, budgeting may constrain and limit an individual's ability to explore creatively and experiment with alternative approaches to decision-making and planning and thus with different ways of representing or interpreting environmental conditions.

Below, we explore how organisations might design or develop organisational processes which either complement or replace traditional budgeting procedures and which may in turn stimulate creative and adaptable behaviour. This final section is necessarily tentative, in that there are few examples of creative forms of budgeting in the management accounting literature.

Budgeting for Creativity and Creativity in Budgeting

What is notable in research which advocates alternative conceptualisations of budgeting in conditions of high environmental uncertainty (see Cooper, Hayes and Wolf, 1981) is the absence of concrete prescriptions for appropriate budgets or budgeting systems. This is understandable, given the perspective these papers normally adopt. When one considers that within a single organisation budgets mean different things to different people and different organisations evolve different cultures, and given that cultures are dynamic and changing, or at least have the potential to change, then a simple formula for budgeting is inappropriate. A budgeting system which in one organisation might compel planning and encourage innovative ideas might be the source of conflict and retrenchment in another organisation. It might, therefore, be undesirable to prescribe or construct a general model of budgeting for all people in all organisations.

A normative, model-based conception of budgeting belongs to the rationalist perspective which believes that an organisation's structure and processes, including the budgeting process, may be modelled to match environmental conditions. Therefore, a particular model of budgeting will have a general application for all organisations existing in similar environments. Within the social constructionist perspective this is simply not the case. The interpretations and interactions of people, within a shared culture of meanings, values and beliefs, shape how organisations operate, rather than predetermined, immutable laws. Thus, budgets and the budgeting process must reflect the role of the human individual in interpreting and constructing reality and the meanings, values and beliefs of the organisation. Boland (1979) suggests that the design of information and control systems should be 'action based' rather than 'model based'. He notes that an action-based approach is not a question of the way in which a system fits a particular model of the environment, but rather how it fits into the culture of the organisation and how it is used in the symbolic process of constructing meanings and definitions. This fit may be achieved only by active participation of the organisational members in the design process. An appropriate metaphor of this principle of design is that of the jazz 'arranger'. Mike Westbrook (1981) describes the role of an arranger of jazz music as follows: 'My job is to provide a structure and then work on it within the band. The music is a collective concern with ample room for improvisation and individual ideas. Working together we create a chain reaction and that's what provides the thrills.' Compare this to an orchestra playing a classical arrangement where the music is precisely defined and minutely specified, with little or no room for individual interpretation. The design process of a budgeting system should likewise provide ample room for improvisation and individual ideas, rather than being based on the imposition of a precisely defined model. In this respect, the outcome of the design process – that is, the way in which a budget may look and operate – is unpredictable. The outcome is a product of the process rather than a product of a predefined model.

The outcome of such a design process could be that the members of an organisation might choose to ignore budgeting, as did the independent record company in its early days. However, in our increasingly rationalist and measurement-prone society there is considerable pressure for managers to seek the reassurance that budgets give in guiding and justifying action. In addition, financial institutions, government agencies and investors provide additional pressure for rational accounts and business plans. There are strong imperatives towards rational, purposive and consistent behaviour. It is therefore difficult for organisations to give up budgeting and rely instead on creative and intuitive behaviour for which there is no clear means of evaluation and no rational or quantitative way of accounting.

The action design approach might relax mechanisms within an organisation which foster purposive, rational and consistent behaviour. Certain authors, notably Cohen, March and Olsen (1972), advocate quite different modes of management for organisations operating under conditions of high environmental uncertainty. These may be referred to as organised anarchies. Cohen and his colleagues describe the 'garbage-can model' where, amongst other things, there is a partial decoupling of problems and solutions. Decisions and the choice of a course of action are the fortuitous confluence of streams of problems, solutions, participants and choice opportunities. These come together like streams of garbage in a garbage-can (or rubbish in a dustbin). The outcome is an unpredictable but creative matching of solutions and problems. The garbage-can provides an interesting, if a little unfortunate, metaphor of organisations which represent less rigid imperatives, less formalised systems and less standardised procedures. March (1976) provides further suggestions, in the form of aphorisms, about how organisations might generate less rigid, formal and standardised responses. He refers to these, again in a somewhat unfortunate metaphor, as the 'technology of foolishness', which is designed to encourage playful, experimental and creative behaviour. The aphorisms are as follows.

1. *Treating goals as hypotheses.* This prescription implies that minimum faith should be placed in goals under conditions of high environmental uncertainty. Rather, they should be treated as ideas or possibilities with the recognition that these are possibilities that may never actualise. The plans which budgets represent must be taken for what they are – a series of assumptions or hypotheses about the future. In this sense, they should not be slavishly followed as if they were objective facts. Goals, plans and budgets should be continually reconsidered and challenged by other and possibly more appropriate interpretations of the future.

2. *Treating intuition as real.* Although the origins of creative ideas are not clearly understood, the potential for new and surprising ideas should be recognised. Such ideas may not be easily rationalised within a conventional framework, but should nevertheless be accepted as legitimate. Accepting ideas and behaviour for which no 'good' reason exists opens up new arenas for analysis and comparison. Budgets, which require a rationalised and quantitative justification for proposed courses of action, cannot accept intuition as real in their present form. It may be necessary to have budgets that 'don't add up' or budgets that are part quantification and part narrative. Storytelling, analogies, anecdotes and parables may be included in budgets to allow the expression of intuitive ideas.

3. *Treating hypocrisy as transitory.* Hypocrisy may be defined as a discrepancy between actions and stated goals or plans. Inconsistencies between action and goals are typically referred to as deviant or goal-incongruent behaviour and not normally sanctioned in organisations. Budgeting is a process where actual outcomes are compared with plans, and performance is judged on discrepancies between the two. Yet behaviour which contradicts goals may be providing new opportunities to enrich the organisation's stock of experience and provide new and innovative strategies. It has been suggested that semi-confusing information and control systems which recognise and report contradictory data should be used to promote the inconsistencies necessary for generating new forms of behaviour. Another strategy may be to decouple planning and control. If people are not held responsible and accountable for plans, perhaps more interesting ones will develop.

4. *Treating memory as an enemy.* This prescription is intended to break the link between the past and the future. Treating past and current practices as something to

be avoided places a greater reliance upon the generation of novelty. It has been suggested that organisations should disbelieve the familiar, taken-for-granted ways of doing things and encourage minimal commitment to the status quo. Instead, they should be encouraged to have faith in the new, the unfamiliar and doubtful. Although textbooks on budgeting caution against the use of the past as a model of the future, they nevertheless proclaim the need for consistency with the past and claim that historical information may be the best gauge of the future. As an alternative, budgets which deviate most from previous plans and those that might seem most outlandish or have no supportable, rational explanation might be valued and rewarded. Such budgets might not be fully implemented, but they might provide a wider variety of alternatives.

5. *Treating experience as a theory.* This aphorism suggests that experience may be seen as a process of learning rather than as a given, indisputable fact. Experience may be re-examined, possibly by different groups, in order to reveal what lessons it may teach. The past may be reinterpreted and expressed in new and unique ways, thereby promoting new ways of thinking and allowing the organisation to learn about itself. Within budgeting, the evaluation process should not be based simply upon analysis of variance, but rather should be seen as a learning experience. The underlying assumptions built into the budget about anticipated future events, and the theoretical underpinning of budgeting itself, should be open to question, analysis and reinterpretation within deliberately set-up group processes.

As a final point, most of management theory, including budgeting theory, is normative. This means that it prescribes how organisations ought to be and how budgeting ought to be done, according to the rational economic model. Few management theories are based upon how organisations actually operate. The dearth of descriptive studies on alternative ways of budgeting is due in part to the reluctance of researchers to study budgeting in action or within its organisational context. There are, however, companies which respond creatively to environmental conditions. In this sense, the creative potential is there and needs to be explored before any more prescriptions are made.

For example, in the plastic container factory mentioned above, the managers who systematically ignored the formal production information system, constructed their own processes of informing whereby they gathered and shared information within the organisation. These processes of informing included interaction by which managers met and swapped information. As one departmental manager commented, 'One of the most effective ways of keeping things ticking over, is obviously fairly regular word-of-mouth contact.' The sales manager likewise commented, 'It is back to word-of-mouth. We'd like to think that people can come over, which happens a lot, and say they've got a problem.' Another source was direct observation, where, when it was possible, managers directly observed the problematic event taking shape. The material control manager commented, 'I've got to get on my feet and walk down there to see what's going on. I come in . . . in the morning and see a machine still running [when the order quantity should already have been produced] and have to go to the machine setter and ask what is going on.'

Another mode of informing was keeping personal records, in which important and often hard-to-measure events were recorded, for future reference. The sales manager kept customer record cards on which he recorded the number of containers produced and the quantity dispatched in order to calculate the level of stock on hand. This enabled him to answer customer enquiries promptly and compensate for inaccuracies in the official stock reports. The managers actually created arrangements to inform, by which individuals could be relied upon to provide richly descriptive, accurate and timely information. Moreover, these arrangements to inform were forums in which unfamiliar or intractable problems were analysed, interpreted and made meaningful. Based upon the meanings that the managers constructed, new and innovative courses of action were decided upon. As the sales manager commented,

> You hear something and then you go and check on it. You probe and you try and find out what is happening and you then find out what you feel to be the true picture. There are a lot of cases still, where you think you ended up with the true picture. Then you talk to somebody else about it or you put forward your theory, just to find you've got the whole thing wrong anyway, or there have been developments.

Although this example relates to production managers and information systems, there is evidence to suggest that informal planning and control systems, in addition to information systems, exist at all levels in organisations. Within the rationalist perspective, informal processes are referred to as 'grapevines', or as 'butcher or black books', or as 'gossip' and 'hearsay'. They are criticised for their inconsistency, for duplicating effort and for not being factual. Conventional textbook wisdom suggests that they should be eradicated and replaced with more formal, efficient and rational planning, information and control systems. Yet these informal processes are an integral part of creativity in organisations. They provide a rich source of alternative interpretation and are a means by which novel and innovative behaviour may emerge. They are also an integral part of the process of modifying the organisational culture and with it current custom and practices. In this sense, the potential for creativity may already exist in organisations. The informal processes, which are systematically ignored or criticised in conventional textbooks on management accounting, may already generate the kinds of creative and innovative behaviour necessary in a rapidly changing environment. The irony is that, by imposing formalised systems, the very behaviour necessary for an organisation's survival may be systematically eradicated or at best severely constrained.

Bibliography

Blumer, H. (1962) 'Society as symbolic interaction', in Rose, A. (ed.) *Human Behaviour and Social Process*, Boston: Houghton Mifflin.
A good article outlining the basic tenets of symbolic interactionist thought.

Boland, R.J., jun. (1979) 'Control, causality and information system requirements', *Accounting, Organizations and Society*, vol. 4, pp. 259–72.
The earliest application of interactionist thought to information and control systems.

Cohen, M.D., J.G. March and J.P. Olsen (1972) 'A garbage can model of organizational choice', *Administrative Science Quarterly*, vol. 17, no. 1, pp. 1–25.
A great challenge to the orthodox view that solutions follow problems. The authors argue that the reverse is often the case in organisational life.

Cooper, J.D., D. Hayes and F. Wolf (1981) 'Accounting in organised anarchies: understanding and designing accounting systems in ambiguous situations', *Accounting, Organizations and Society*, vol. 6, no. 3, pp. 175–91.
An early attempt to incorporate unorthodox organisational theory into the accounting literature.

Dent, J.F. (1991) 'Accounting and organizational cultures: a field study of the emergence of a new organizational reality', *Accounting, Organizations and Society*, vol. 16, no. 8, pp. 705–32.
A thorough field study of accounting and organisational change with an explicit focus on organisational culture.

Latour, B. (1987) *Science in Action*, Cambridge, Mass.: Harvard University Press.
A striking challenge to the conventional depiction of the practice of science. Latour argues that scientific facts and technological artefacts are constructed in a complex socio-technical milieu.

March, J.G. (1976) 'The technology of foolishness', in March, J.G. and J.P. Olsen (eds.) *Ambiguity and Choice in Organizations*, Bergen: Universitetsforlaget.
An extension of his work on garbage-cans. Here he argues for more playfulness in order to promote creative problem-solving in organisations.

Merchant, K.A. and R. Simons (1986) 'Research and control in complex organizations: an overview', *Journal of Accounting Literature*, vol. 5, pp. 184–203.
A good overview of the conventional approaches to control in organisations. This paper marks Merchant's move into case study research.

Mintzberg, H. (1975) *Impediments to the Use of Management Information*, New York: National Association of Accountants.
There are a great many insights in this paper into the problems that managers encounter with formal information systems.

Otley, D.T. (1980) 'The contingency theory of management accounting: achievement and prognosis', *Accounting, Organizations and Society*, vol. 5, no. 4, pp. 413–28.
A clear articulation of the conventional contingency theory approach to control systems.

Ouchi, W. (1979) 'A conceptual framework for the design of organizational control mechanisms', *Management Science*, vol. 25, no. 9, pp. 833–48.
Apparently an insightful paper on first reading but really quite insidious. The paper advocates a kind of docile acceptance of authority through creating an unquestioning devotion and loyalty.

Preston, A., D. Cooper and R. Coombs (1992) 'Fabricating budgets: a study of the production of

management budgeting in the National Health Service', *Accounting, Organizations and Society*, vol. 17, no. 6, pp. 561–93.
Here we attempt to employ Latour's framework to the creation of management budgeting in the NHS.

Sapolsky, H.M. (1972) *The Polaris System Development*, Cambridge, Mass.: Harvard University Press.
A paper which exposed capital budgeting as a decision justification rather than a decision-making tool.

Westbrook, M. (1981) 'Jazz and the art of living dangerously', *The Sunday Times*, 10 May, p. 35.
A nice article on the seemingly contradictory positions of improvisation and arrangement in jazz.

CHAPTER FOURTEEN

Management Accounting in Global Firms

Jan Mouritsen

Marco Polo's journey to China in the thirteenth century and Columbus's voyage to America in 1494 are early examples of internationalisation. They combine an interest in adventure, trade and commerce and their travels were accompanied by physical and psychological hardships, since they were exposed to the unknown and to laborious travel where paths did not exist.

Today internationalisation is not so adventurous, as it is helped by a considerable knowledge about the contours of the world geographically, socially and politically (Dicken, 1992). Knowledge about the world makes it accessible: roads, railways, flights, etc. connect the various places of the world, and the symbolic representation of the world in information systems and the use of communication systems such as the telephone make people readily available to each other. Now, travelling and communication are ordinary rather than adventurous activities.

The improvement of transportation and communication reduces the barriers of geographical distance. Whereas a journey for Columbus to America took a couple of months, today from Europe a flight lasts about seven hours and a telephone call is instantaneous. The reductions in time to travel and communicate across space in modern societies allow people located in different places to be easily available to one another.

International firms use management accounting to co-ordinate and integrate their activities in different countries. Through symbolic representations, it helps managers create an understanding of the world which is necessary for executing international activities. Financial knowledge makes visible what is happening in different subsidiaries across the world, enabling central control at a distance and the integration of activities of spatially separated organisational segments (Belkauoi, 1991).

Management accounting is thus a medium to create knowledge which makes travelling across countries less adventurous as it helps stabilise international transfers of money, goods and knowledge in global organisational systems. It has been argued that 'accounting and structure were most instrumental in internationalising coordination, monitoring and allocation within the giant enterprise' (Chandler and Daems, 1979, p. 18). The contribution of accounting to the globalisation of economic activities and the rise of international conglomerates has been crucial, although it has often been neglected.

Management accounting in international firms

Co-ordination, monitoring and resource allocation are partly contained within systems of budgeting, performance measurement and currency management in international firms. While these issues are relevant to ordinary national firms, their importance is augmented in international firms due to problems of size, the uncertainties of currency fluctuations and possible political upheavals in host countries.

International firms are typically depicted as large with respect to revenues, assets and having many subsidiaries spread across many countries. This does not necessarily mean, however, that the bulk of their activities are primarily international – for example, many US international firms generate only about 50 per cent of total revenues in the international sphere, whereas many European small firms' foreign sales amount to more than 95 per cent of their total revenues. It is its geographical spread and power in the world that gives the international firm its distinctiveness, rather than its proportion of international to national revenues. Such firms can use their power, capital and expertise to exploit the specific conditions and comparative advantages offered by a particular geographical location, and integrate these different locations into a multinational network of research and development (R&D), production and sales/marketing.

Management accounting is a mechanism that weaves together these locations within a broader design of organisational control mechanisms. Organisational structure and corporate strategy are other components of control that influence the major role for management accounting within specific firms. For example, whereas in integrated global firms management accounting primarily co-ordinates the activities of the different subsidiaries, in the multidomestic, conglomerate international firm it is primarily a means of evaluating the performance of each subsidiary (see later for a detailed discussion).

Management accounting's involvement with currency management is also important for international firms because the volatility of financial markets can blur the results of their productive efforts (Eiteman, Stonehill and Moffet, 1992). Many international firms therefore attempt to manage the risk of currency fluctuations through financial instruments such as options and futures. Sometimes this is reinforced by performance evaluation and standard cost systems that single out the impact of currency fluctuations.

Management accounting is also involved in the political relationships between international firms and host governments. Some international firms show in their internal accounting reports the tax savings from decisions to locate production and sales abroad by measuring after-tax profits rather than pre-tax profits (Murray, 1981). Thus the managers of foreign divisions or subsidiaries must not only consider the efficiency of their unit but they must also interact politically with local host governments over items such as conditions of work, subsidies, tax breaks and cheap land (Neimark and Tinker, 1986). Transfer prices are part of this political process as they enable firms to allocate their profits to low-tax regions, giving rise to host government attempts to curtail this practice when they believe their interests conflict with those of the firms.

Thus internationalisation sets a complex agenda for management accounting which is resolved in different ways in different firms. Holzer and Schonfelt (1986) illustrate that accounting systems of major international European and US firms differ greatly and, although internationalisation affects their management accounting systems, it does not do so in a linear fashion.

To pursue these points in more detail this chapter is organised into five major sections. The first section outlines three types of international firm: the global firm, the multidomestic firm and the exporting firm. Each differs on questions of co-ordination and integration and how they use management accounting. In the second section, the different methods of co-ordination, integration and the roles of management accounting are illustrated through a comparison of two international firms, IBM and Superfos. The third section discusses performance evaluation in international firms, pointing out how global firms differ from multidomestic firms in this respect. Then, in the fourth section, problems of currency fluctuations are presented and a layered model for currency management with varying time horizons is discussed. Lastly, in the fifth section, the role of management accounting in international firms is related to the political processes between firms and host governments.

Global, Multidomestic and Exporting Firms

International firms differ in their organisation of international activities. Porter suggests a threefold classification of international firms: the global firm, the multidomestic firm and the exporting firm (Porter, 1986; Sheth and Eshghi, 1990).

The *global firm* is characterised by its large geographical reach, its considerable organisational interdependence and its ability to integrate coherently activities carried out in different countries. Each organisational segment is highly dependent on other segments as an output from one division or subsidiary is often an input to another, so it must manage its network of operations in an integrated way. For example, for a manufacturer, some components may be produced in one country, other components in a second country, final assembly located in a third country, and the products may then be sold in a fourth country. The dependence between the various manufacturing plants and the sales company is considerable. In this situation, co-ordination between the subsidiaries from corporate HQ is extensive.

In contrast, a *multidomestic firm* manages itself through a decentralised structure making each subsidiary as independent of the others as possible. This may range from independence in geographically detached market-places, such as selling a single product in different independent regions of the world, to a conglomerate structure by which each subsidiary manufactures and sells its own products. In both situations, management accounting primarily supports top management by providing performance information to control each division or subsidiary. Since the subsidiaries are not dependent on each other, management accounting concentrates on financial resource allocation between subsidiaries rather than on their integration and co-ordination.

Exporting firms tend to be simpler as they primarily export through other firms, for example independent agents who sell their products in a particular region. Exporting firms rely on others for their international sales and marketing, preferring to concentrate on production issues. In this situation, management accounting plays little part in the management of international affairs.

The above distinction between international firms is important for management accounting because each has a distinct type of organisational interdependence. The global firm requires extensive integration and co-ordination through corporate planning. Its management accounting is involved in the detailed co-ordination of international activities across geographically scattered divisions and subsidiaries. In contrast, a multidomestic firm co-ordinates its relatively independent divisions and subsidiaries at arm's length through delegation of responsibility, so that central management's co-ordination efforts are less pervasive. Its management accounting is a monitoring and resource allocation mechanism which reports composite financial ratios such as return on investment (ROI). Exporting firms only infrequently use management accounting to co-ordinate and integrate international activities since they are typically organised by local agents.

The value-chain, co-ordination and integration

Porter's (1986) analysis of internationalisation claims that the firm's efficiency and effectiveness depend on the design of its value-chain which separates the strategic components of a firm into primary and support activities. The primary activities comprise the firm's logistical structure (inbound logistics → production → outbound logistics → sales and marketing→service), and the support activities are the overheads needed to manage logistics appropriately (infrastructure, human resource management, technology development, procurement).

Porter argues that two factors, configuration and co-ordination, are the major management issues facing international firms. Configuration is the world-wide dispersion of the firm's activities within the value-chain. Configuration ranges from concentration, where an activity is set up in one location only, to dispersion, where the activity is set up in many locations. Dispersed configuration, for example, occurs when R&D is located in one place, manufacturing in another, and sales in a third place. Alternatively, concentrated configuration is where all these activities are in one place.

Co-ordination refers to how activities within the value-chain but performed at different locations are aligned with each other. No co-ordination occurs when organisational segments have total autonomy over specifications, use of technology and choice of markets. There is no co-ordination if subsidiaries in different locations can operate independently of each other over their choice of products, production technology and marketing. Extensive co-ordination occurs when there is a high degree of corporate involvement in aligning the activities of its segments. This comes about when production activities in one location, R&D activities in a different location, and sales activities in a third location must integrate their work with each other.

Questions about configuration and co-ordination can be raised for each of the value-chain's activities. For example, for *operations* configuration involves decisions concerning where the production of components and end-products are to be located. Co-ordination involves the extent to which different plants transfer technology. For *marketing* activities, configuration decisions are about the level of uniformity of product lines and prices across locations. Co-ordination of marketing activities involves questions about world-wide brand-names, sales to mutinational accounts, similarity of sales channels and product positioning world-wide, and how prices are set in different countries. For *service* activities, configuration is about whether they are concentrated in one or a few locations or are dispersed to the regions where sales take place. Co-ordination questions concern the similarity of standards and procedures world-wide.

In general, configuration concerns choices about organisational structure and the location of tasks across space. Co-ordination is about which mechanisms ensure appropriate interaction between organisational segments in day-to-day activities. When configuration is concentrated, co-ordination between locations is less stressful because each is 'self-contained'. However, when configuration is dispersed the requirements to co-ordinate are more demanding, for it requires a continual effort to integrate the different activities beyond the individual subsidiary.

The significance of management accounting resides in its ability to support an appropriate form of co-ordination, while being responsive to the strategies behind configuration decisions. It is a useful tool for corporate management to control value-chains either within or across subsidiaries but management accounting's role is different in each situation.

Management Accounting, Configuration and Co-ordination

Configuration and co-ordination set an agenda for management accounting in global and multidomestic firms framed through the following questions: (1) what is corporate strategy, and how does it affect configuration and co-ordination?; (2) what

Table 14.1 Some differences between management accounting in a global integrated firm and in a multidomestic conglomerate firm.

Issue	Global firm	Multidomestic firm
Strategy	To internationalise the value-chain	To balance risk through portfolio management
Role of HQ	To develop and co-ordinate subsidiaries in an integrated effort. Co-ordination of subsidiaries is strong	To enhance the management of financial resources. Corporate co-ordination of subsidiaries is weak
Role of subsidiary	To carry out and suport a detailed strategy developed at HQ	To develop its own strategy towards market and production
Role of budgeting	To integrate activities across subsidiaries with an emphasis on products and markets	To establish targets for each individual subsidiary with an emphasis on accountability
Performance evaluation	Many and diverse financial and non-financial performance measurements oriented towards products and markets	Relatively few, but aggregated financial performance measures oriented towards individual organisational entities

is the role of corporate headquarters?; (3) what is the role of the subsidiary?; (4) what is the role of budgetary controls?; (5) what are the roles and methods of performance evaluation? Table 14.1 answers these questions for the global firm and the multidomestic firm respectively. The different sets of answers portray two distinct approaches to management accounting in international firms.[1]

The global firm's strategy is to manage its subsidiaries spread around the world in an integrated effort. Each subsidiary has a clearly defined role in the integrated effort to align production, sales and R&D in different locations towards one or more global product lines. Central management produces plans and procedures that specify the relationships between subsidiaries, for example product line budgets that reflect their interdependence in production and sales.

In contrast, in multidomestic firms subsidiaries have more influence on defining their strategy and acting upon it. HQ concentrates on general financial management, managing its subsidiaries through arm's-length controls such as financial ratios. Each subsidiary produces and realises its business plans with limited co-ordination with others. Relations of dependence amongst subsidiaries are often managed through market-based internal transfer prices. These reinforce the sovereignty of each subsidiary to decide whether to buy from other subsidiaries or from the open market.

A comparison of strategy and management accounting in two major international firms, IBM and Superfos, illustrates the different roles management accounting plays in global and multidomestic firms. IBM is the world's largest firm (revenues amount to about £40 billion) in the computer industry. It has manufacturing facilities in the

USA, Europe, and several Third World countries and has sales subsidiaries in most countries in the world: IBM is virtually omnipresent throughout the world.

Superfos is a major Danish conglomerate (revenues come to about £700 million) which operates in four business areas (seeds, plastics, road construction, and chemicals).[2] Each business area is managed through a subsidiary that develops its marketing and production strategies largely by itself. There are few, if any, synergies between the different business areas. For example, the plastics division has no operations (e.g. production or marketing) in common with the road construction division. Superfos is located mainly in European countries and, particularly within road construction, in the USA.

The two firms are good examples of how integrated global firms and conglomerate multidomestic firms constitute their corporate strategy, organisational structure and management accounting differently.[3] IBM is an integrated global firm where central management intervenes in the affairs of the individual subsidiaries in a controlling and managing capacity. In Superfos, a conglomerate multidomestic firm, the subsidiaries are more autonomous and their responsibilities are broader and extend to strategy.

These differences, described in detail below, demonstrate that management accounting is integrally tied to strategy. Configuration and co-ordination are mechanisms for combining organisational structures with markets and international divisions of labour. Management accounting is a means of co-ordinating established configurations and its form depends on the strategies a firm adopts for configuration and co-ordination (Tomkins, 1991).

Strategy

IBM develops, manufactures and sells computer hardware and software. Its international division of labour integrates R&D, manufacturing and sales on a global basis. Most of its research activities take place in the USA, whereas production takes place all over the world with sub-assemblies often in third world countries and final assemblies and testing in the USA or Europe. All manufacturing facilities are part of a world-wide division of labour. Sales take place globally since all products are marketed world-wide as world-products; all sales subsidiaries sell the whole product range to their individual geographical markets. Each of IBM's locations has its distinct position in the corporate value-chain, being specialised to support an integrated strategy of supplying a world market. This configuration requires extensive co-ordination, as is detailed below.

Superfos, in contrast, locates the responsibility for most of its value-chain activities directly with the subsidiaries. Corporate HQ focuses on diversifying its financial risk through portfolio management of the subsidiaries. Corporate strategy is formulated through financial criteria such as a required rate of return on investment. In Superfos the responsibility for R&D, manufacturing and sales is located with the subsidiaries. HQ has no R&D function, nor does it attempt to align the subsidiaries' activities with each other to integrate sales and production. Superfos's HQ is concerned with profitability per subsidiary and it seeks to pool financial risk from currency and interest rate fluctuations. This configuration requires less co-ordination from HQ as each subsidiary executes all of its value-chain alone and activities with different time horizons for costs and revenues are confined to the individual organisational segment.

The role of headquarters and subsidiaries

In IBM the role of HQ is to produce an integrated system of R&D, production, sourcing and global sales throughout its subsidiaries. Consequently, configuration activities emphasise uniformity: product lines, service contracts, the organisational structure of subsidiaries and accounting systems are standardised across the world. As a result, the subsidiaries' responsibilities are concentrated upon carrying out the strategies and plans developed centrally. Each subsidiary carries out only a limited portion of the firm's total value-chain and it is located in a corporate organisational matrix that emphasises the profitability of global product lines rather than that of the individual subsidiaries.

In contrast, Superfos lacks highly standardised processes, procedures and objectives since products, markets and production processes differ for each sub-sidiary. Each develops its own organisation, procedures and accounting systems. For example, the plastics division has a standard cost accounting system, whereas the road construction division has a project management system that feeds financial data into the accounting system. Superfos's HQ is interested in the strategies and plans of subsidiaries but it is the responsibility of the subsidiaries to develop and materialise them. HQ is not interested in a continual involvement with the subsidiaries in a controlling capacity. Instead, it has developed an organisational control system that offsets risk in different business sectors, and a financial control system that offsets the effects of volatile currency and interest rates.

The role of budgeting

The role of budgeting in IBM is to ensure that what is produced in one part of the world can be sold in another part. Detailed product-line budgets encourage each subsidiary to focus on individual product lines rather than on a composite measure of performance for the subsidiary. In this way, subsidiaries are encouraged to follow the strategic design of the firm world-wide. The budget superimposes corporate product lines over subsidiary performance and it emphasises the need to integrate sales and production across subsidiaries. Although the subsidiary is a company in the legal sense, the focus of its budgeting and planning activities is not primarily on this entity, but rather on its relationships with other subsidiaries through product-line budgets.

In Superfos, budgeting defines the financial targets to which each subsidiary is held accountable. This embraces a composite residual income profit target that forces subsidiaries to invest effectively and to be economical in their operations. The budget superimposes the corporate organisational hierarchy and reproduces the ethos of each subsidiary being independent of the others. Product lines are thus not essential to corporate budgeting as each subsidiary's managers can choose their products and technology in the knowledge that they are responsible for the results of their decisions.

The role of performance evaluation

In Superfos, performance evaluation is conducted through monthly accounting reports typically containing only two figures – revenues and profits (on a residual income basis). Only a small amount of financial information comparing actual with budgeted performance is supplied to HQ. A narrative accompanies the accounts, but little emphasis is put on supplying financial data beyond the required minimum. In Superfos, the subsidiaries' accounting systems are not integrated and data transfer is not automated between HQ and subsidiaries.

In IBM a total of about 470 non-financial and financial measures, and a set of measurements on resources and strategy, are produced monthly. These measures are largely defined by HQ and are intended to provide feedback upon product-line profitability across all the individual subsidiaries. IBM's accounting system is an on-line, world-wide system that can provide daily, world-wide consolidated information, for example concerning order statistics. The accounting system is consolidated monthly within the first week of the following month, thereby making information very timely.

The International Dimension to Performance Measurement

The above comparison between IBM and Superfos illustrates how performance measurement and performance management are designed differently due to the different approaches each takes to configuration and co-ordination. The analysis of performance evaluation was broad and brief and related merely to overall strategic issues. Questions about the specific content of performance evaluation systems and their role in accountability are explored in more detail below.

The multidomestic conglomerate firm

In Superfos, the conglomerate multidomestic firm, performance measurement is primarily designed to enhance corporate control in decentralised organisational systems. Individual divisions or subsidiaries have a relatively large degree of influence not only over their operational decisions but also on strategic issues and interrelated investment decisions, and the different divisions and subsidiaries only marginally draw on each other's resources. They are thus able to organise their activities independently of activities carried out in other divisions or subsidiaries. This is a situation in which financial control of organisational entities is particularly apt. Composite financial ratios such as ROA (return on assets), ROI (return on investment), ROCE (return on capital employed), ROE (return on equity) and RI (residual income) can be deemed to reflect the efficiency and effectiveness of the division or subsidiary in question.

ROI (and ROA and ROCE) portray the division's or subsidiary's ability to use its assets to generate profits through the Du Pont formula (ROI = profits/assets). ROE (= profits after interest/equity) considers the capital structure of the firm and thus the efficiency of its financing decisions. Residual income (RI = profits less imputed interest on capital employed) steers divisions with an ROI higher than their cost of capital to invest in projects with yields below the ROI but above the cost of capital.

These formulas are important for the control of decentralised organisational segments as they both aggregate and simplify. They aggregate the financial position because they simultaneously incorporate the profit and loss account (the cost-management aspects of the business) and the balance-sheet (the investment aspects). They simplify because they provide a formally and analytically consistent basis for evaluating divisions or subsidiaries on one, or a few, financial ratios. All line-items of the profit and loss account and the balance-sheet add up to the financial ratio in question (ROI, etc.).

Empirical studies give strong support to the managerial importance of such composite financial ratios, at least in Western firms. Bailes and Assada (1991) compare divisional performance measurements in US and Japanese firms as illustrated in Table 14.2.

Table 14.2 illustrates that US firms frequently use financial ratios for performance measurement. ROI is by far the most important, followed by controllable profit. It also shows that, to a degree, the choice of performance measurement system varies according to the nationality of the firm Japanese firms pay less attention to ROI than US firms and they seem to pay more attention to individual line-items in the budget

Table 14.2 Percentage of firms in which the different budget goals are important for divisional managers in Japan and in the USA (Bailes and Assada, 1991).

	Japan (%)	USA (%)
Sales volume	86.3	27.9
Net profit after corporate overhead	44.7	35.0
Controllable profit	28.2	51.8
Profit margin on sales	30.7	30.5
Sales growth	19.4	22.4
Return on investment	3.1	68.4
Production cost	40.7	12.4

such as sales volume and production costs. Table 14.2 shows that Japanese firms are more likely to use operational indices and line-items for their performance evaluation procedures than US firms. The latter emphasise composite financial ratios, above all ROI. Such controllability principles seem not to play a large role in Japan. As the table shows, in Japanese firms corporate overheads are more readily allocated to divisions and subsidiaries than in the USA and ROI plays a minor role in divisional performance evaluation in Japan.

In a European context, Horovitz (1978) compared management controls between UK, German and French firms as illustrated in Table 14.3. Horovitz's findings show a differentiation of control systems in the European region. Table 14.3 suggests that UK companies emphasise general financial targets and focus on exceptions from budgets or targets with control delegated to product/market business units within a conglomerate structure with limited central staff. In contrast, German control systems are very detailed and emphasise production levels and operational efficiency. Central staff is large, highly specialised and highly involved in the divisions' operations through tight and frequent involvement with production issues, amongst other things. In France, control is more a personal matter left to the top executive, although central staff is as extensive as in Germany. Unlike in Germany, French management control systems are individualised and committee management is scarce. French firms are typically organised by functions (sales, production) rather than by divisions, and the chief executive often heads the sales function rather than the production function.

Returning to Superfos, composite accounting measures are very important in this firm: whilst it does report ROI at least quarterly, the major performance indicator is residual income. Despite its Danish ownership, Superfos looks more like a US or UK firm than a Japanese, German or French firm in the context of characteristics of the control in Table 14.3. Whilst there is evidence that the location of ownership of

Table 14.3 Key characteristics of top management control in different European countries (Horovitz, 1978).

	Great Britain	Germany	France
Use of control			
– stick to plan	Medium	High	Low
– police operations	Low	High	High
– reward and/or sanction	Low	Low	Low
Primary functional emphasis	Finance	Production	Production
Control decentralised	Yes	No	No
Degree of detail	Overall	Very detailed	Detailed
Time orientation	Future	Past	Past
Degree of quantification	Some	High	High
Frequency	Monthly	Weekly	Weekly
Involvement of central staff	Low	High	High
Standardisation	High	High	Low

multinational firms affects the philosophy and design of management control systems, there is considerable scope for managerial choice and variation.

The integrated global firm

Although performance measurement systems in conglomerate multidomestic firms differ from firm to firm and from country to country, composite accounting measures tend to form the basis of these systems. However, for an integrated global firm such systems may be inappropriate. As described above, IBM uses about 470 different ratios in its performance measurement system, and it has about 320 financial line-items, about 110 volume-related line-items and about 40 line-items related to resources. Its financial measures comprise a battery of different measures of cost structure and revenues for individual products and product lines. Its volume-related indicators emphasise the order performance for each product or product line and its resource-related measures are about employment etc. In all, the 470 performance measurements report on a large variety of issues – for example, cost as a percentage of revenue per product or product line, the number of days to handle customer complaints, accounts receivables, the number of errors in bills, days of inventory, precision of forecasts, number of deliveries, number of replacements, timely payment of creditors, response time in the computer centre and market share are all reported systematically locally as well as at HQ.

These examples suggest that performance in an integrated global firm tends to be evaluated on a broad combination of financial and non-financial measures. This is very different from Superfos. IBM in this sense resembles more the German and French approach than that of the USA and UK described in Table 14.3 since it incorporates non-financial measures about sales and production.

In contrast to ROI, these performance measurements are not analytically consistent. They are not neatly related to each other in a mathematical form that adds up to a composite performance measurement. Instead, they are partial performance measurements which have to be incorporated into a set of decision points and detailed management issues. In a global firm, the dependence of one subsidiary on another is substantial. Consequently, it is often important for one subsidiary – or for the controlling HQ – to know in detail what goes on in another subsidiary. For example, information on product-line performance is useful for the global planning of production and sales/marketing efforts around the world, since a shortfall of orders in one region feeds back to production planning in a different region of the world. Similarly, information on customer complaints from any part of the world may be fed back to corporate R&D if systematic quality defects have been found in a particular product. The rectification of this quality problem has consequences for production planning in factories and for the services yielded in sales subsidiaries world-wide.

The role of financial performance measures is different in IBM as the local subsidiaries' profit is not the only or the most important concern for corporate management. Instead, corporate management wants an organisational system that attends to the interdependencies of subsidiaries within the global organisation. This influences performance management in at least two ways. First, global product-line profitability is more important than the individual subsidiary's own profitability. In an integrated global firm, investments in production plants in one country have implications for what should be sold in another country. Because production investments are spread world-wide, organisational segments throughout the world are obliged to follow the corporate strategy and must sell what is produced regardless of the country of origin. Each subsidiary cannot determine itself what is to be sold in the individual market-place. Therefore, product-line profitability is important.

Second, because of the broad geographical domain of the integrated global firm, pricing decisions are centralised to a considerable degree. Often, pricing in each individual subsidiary has to be aligned with pricing strategies in other countries to prevent product arbitrage. When subsidiaries are situated close to each other, mechanisms must be installed to prevent them from competing with each other. The pricing strategy often pursued by integrated global firms is to transfer the products at full-cost-plus, thereby locating much of the responsibility for total profitability centrally whilst allowing each subsidiary a limited influence on pricing.

An integrated global firm's performance measurement system does not primarily seek to evaluate the business of the individual subsidiary *in toto*. It is part of an organisational configuration that binds the individual organisational entities into centralized, highly co-ordinated relationships with each other. The effectiveness of such systems depends on having available information which accurately mirrors the affairs of the subsidiary. However, in international firms problems due to currency fluctuations can seriously mitigate against this.

Currency and Exposure Management

International firms must trade in multiple currencies. Although currencies are often pegged to each other through international agreements, they can fluctuate unpredictably. This creates uncertain cash flows in corporate currency, i.e. the currency in which corporate accounts are consolidated. Currency fluctuations can also influence the operational performance of organisational segments, for example sales and raw materials costs, and if performance is measured in the currency of corporate accounts, then the financial expressions of overseas operations are sensitive to relative changes in exchange rates.

Currency and exposure management are corporate attempts to manage cash flows susceptible to changes in currency, inflation and interest rates. At least three kinds of exposure management can be identified: short-term transaction exposure to debtors and creditors; medium-term budgeting of international cash flows; long-term strategic currency and exposure concerns over the firm's strategic planning period. The following discussion does not cover the full complexities of international cash

Table 14.4   Short-term economic exposure.

Currency	Accounts receivables (local currency)	Accounts payable (local currency)	Net exposure (local currency)	Net exposure (corporate currency)[1]
US$	14.2[2]	17.2	− 3.0	− 20.3
UK£	0.8	1.1	− 0.3	− 5.4
DM	6.9	2.9	4.0	12.5
Yen	1017.4	0	1017.4	32.5
				19.3

Notes: 1. Corporate currency is Danish Kroner. 2. All numbers are in millions.

management (Eiteman *et al.*, 1992), but it frames a set of issues relevant to management accounting in international firms.

Short-term transaction exposure

A firm's short-term economic exposure depends on the sensitivity of cash flows, expressed in corporate currency, to currency rate changes affecting debtors, creditors and unexecuted forward contracts. For the company to estimate the immediate currency risk for each currency (pounds, dollars, Deutschmarks, etc.) the net exposure must be translated into corporate currency in order to calculate total corporate short-term economic exposure. This is illustrated in Table 14.4. Changes in currency exchange rates will influence the cash flows expressed in Danish Kroner (DKr). For example, if DKr depreciated by 10 per cent against the Deutschmark, short-term cash inflows in DKr would be 1.25 millions higher than expected, giving a positive exposure of 12.5 millions as shown in Table 14.4. On the other hand, if DKr depreciated by 10 per cent against the US dollar, short-term cash inflows would decrease by 2.03 millions. Companies can insure themselves against such currency risk through financial instruments such as options and forwards (hedging).

Medium-term economic exposure

Currency fluctuations influence cash flows in corporate currency and they impact on the competitive position of the firm's different subsidiaries since they influence effective prices and thus the patterns of demand. Assumptions on currency fluctuations are thus important for decisions about pricing and tactical measures in the market-places. When budgeting and planning, the firm may consider how its competitive position is influenced by expected currency fluctuations. For example, if a country's currency depreciates, the firm may reconsider its pricing and its composition of sales to different locations. Depreciation reduces the effective price to the firm which might respond by increasing its price, which reduces demand, and shifting some production to other regions. Expected currency fluctuations may thus influence tactical decisions made by the firm in areas of pricing and production. The management of middle-term economic exposure is thus not merely about cash. It bears upon sales, marketing, production and financing decisions. Sales and marketing are affected by the effective change in demand caused by changes in local prices, production is impacted by the resulting shifts in demand, and financing decisions are impacted by expected inflation and interest rates which follow currency rate depreciations.

The management of middle-term economic exposure makes *ex ante* budgeting and planning activities more complex. Under conditions of currency fluctuations, *ex post* performance measurement is also more complex although the principles of variance analysis apply (Lessard and Lorange, 1977). Conventional variance analysis considers the utilisation of materials, labour and possible overheads. Currency adds complexity to this since in addition to conventional variances the effects of changes in exchange rates are abstracted into separate currency fluctuation variances. However, variances are interdependent and they must be interpreted carefully. For example, currency changes can affect the demand for the firm's products, which shows up in sales and profit variances.

Long-term economic exposure

It is impossible to predict long-term rates of currency, interest and inflation in countries or regions across the world. Long-term economic exposure manages the financial aspects of the strategy of firms either by balancing cash flows through relocating production, sales and financing, or by balancing the structure of financial assets and liabilities to match those of major competitors. Both strategies attempt to reduce the relative risk of currency fluctuations upon the firm's competitiveness. A firm may compose a financial position similar to that of its major competitors to reduce the threats to relative competitiveness that accrue from financing decisions. In this way, if they are risk-averse, firms may adopt a strategy which makes them no more vulnerable to changes in exchange rates than their competitors.

The management of long-term economic exposure cannot be reduced to the mere calculation of cash flows as it involves broader decisions about the strategic development of sales, production and capital structure. It has to be understood in the context of the firm's attitude to risk associated with financing decisions and their possible effect on its competitiveness. All international firms are involved in cash management to varying degrees; for example, IBM and Superfos both pay specific attention to this. Currency fluctuations make international firms very aware of their dependence on international capital markets, and their reactions are complex and extend beyond technical measures to mitigate financial uncertainties.

International firms face forms of risk and uncertainty other than those of a financial nature. Their relationships with host governments around the world give rise to political risk.

Accounting and the Politics of the International Firm

Global firms are powerful not only because of their comparative advantages world-wide but because they can exert considerable influence, individually or collectively, over host governments who do not necessarily share their interests. Part of the international firms' power accrues from their ability to influence the policies of host governments and to persuade them to set up measures favourable to the firms. This is apparent in the ways in which international firms use transfer prices (Murray, 1981) and manage their political risk (Herring, 1983; Raddock, 1986).

The role of transfer prices

Transfer prices are used when one organisational segment sells products or services to another. In global firms the internal but international transfers between sub-sidiaries often amount to 30–50 per cent of their total revenues. The prices of such transfers tend to be based on either the cost or the estimated market prices for the product or service in question, but neither unambiguously determines the economic value of the transfer because it is an administrated price.

Transfer prices help firms maximize their after-tax global profits since they provide, to a certain degree, an opportunity for them to allocate profits around the world irrespective of the productive results of the individual subsidiary (Radebaugh and Gray, 1993). Thus, particularly in global firms, transfer prices may not be set for purposes of productive efficiency or internal management control and decision-making. As described above, the corporate strategies of global firms are often leveraged through detailed plans and budgets rather than through composite profit measures significantly determined by transfer prices.

Governments are interested in transfer prices because they can allocate income between subsidiaries in high tax regions to ones in low tax regions. The incorporation of tax issues into the repertoire of corporate concerns means that international firms often operate at a political level and are not merely concerned with productive efficiency.

Although governments attempt to control transfer pricing through tax laws, transfer prices create a set of financial flows that may be only loosely coupled with the flows of products and services, as transfer prices are essentially administered. Even when the prime cost of an intermediate product can be defined accurately, it is possible to invent new additional overhead services that can be treated as costs through the accounting system. All kinds of organisational relationships such as advisory services, insurance, general management, R&D expenses, telephone calls and loans can be entered as costs by choice.

The power of global firms emanating from their ability to relocate their profits quickly by changing a few codes in their computerized accounting systems can challenge the policies of host governments and force them to create favourable tax havens or lenient tax administration systems (Murray, 1981). The threat of withdrawal and the ensuing loss of jobs, or the prospect of attracting new investments, may persuade host governments to institute benign procedures for the control of transfer prices. Global firms may have the choice over where to locate profits, but for the local governments this is often a zero-sum game from which only the firms can benefit. This process influences the distribution of income rather than its absolute amount. Income is not tied to any particular space for the international firm, whilst local nation-states, in contrast, occupy a fixed space. The opportunities for relocating income presented by transfer prices make the control of production a political issue for individual nation-states. Financial flows and thus the distribution of income can only be controlled to a limited degree by host governments. Thus, sometimes they may intervene directly in production matters – say, by offering cheap sites for production plants, or by funding the continuance of production to support employment.

The construction of financial statements thus amounts to a more fundamental political struggle over the distribution of wealth and the control of production, and is not merely a question of how to design tax laws (Neimark and Tinker, 1986). This means that international firms try to manage political risk.

International firms' management of political risk

Political risk is concerned with a firm's evaluation of the political stability of a particular country, typically a Third World one. The firm fears radical political changes such as the nationalisation or expropriation of its assets. Political risk hinges on firms' uncertainty about governmental motivation to support free markets and their property rights. Thus, many firms are actively committed to monitoring not only their business environment but also their political environment to offset and manage political risk.

Political risk cannot be calculated directly and technically: it has to be understood socially. Raddock (1986) claims it involves international firms confronting the following strategic imperatives:

1. *Have options!* The threat of withdrawal if adverse situations should arise can be supported by several measures. One is to make capacity scarce and thus limit possible losses. Another is to locate similar organisational segments in several countries.

2. *Be indispensable!* If the firm provides relatively high revenues and output, local governments will view the operation favourably.

3. *Accept more value-added activities 'than necessary'!* A certain involvement in the industrial development of the country in question persuades local governments to accept the firm's presence. This is possible even if the firm's commitment is more a symbolic token than a thorough transfer of technology and knowledge.

4. *Sequence investments!* Firms can stage investments in a series that would provide local governments with something new when they put pressure on the firm.

5. *Use project finance!* In some situations firms can set up local sites without any

cash flow implications. This happens when they can finance investments through cash flows from operations or if they can attract equity from the capital markets. It includes backing from international capital markets (including the World Bank), which also puts pressure on the local governments to conform with the firm's wishes.

6. *Select local partners!* If a firm engages with a private local partner, this can provide protection under the widest range of political contingencies.

These strategies and imperatives may be phrased cynically but they show what it means to control political risk: make as few concessions as possible. International firms' strategies tend to be conservative and involve as little commitment as possible. While these strategies may be difficult to execute, they provide a possible framework to evaluate any location on its productivity and its locational advantages. Such processes and the relationships between host governments and international firms influence labour markets and people's lives across the world.

There are two theories of the effects of this. The optimistic free market theory argues that it is in the interest of everybody since it encourages an optimal international division of labour according to the law of comparative advantage. The emergence of the international firm, according to this view, is one of continual economising on transaction costs. International firms emerge because they represent transaction cost-minimising entities that outperform the market since they are more efficient in transferring knowledge and skills (Williamson, 1986). An alternative, more radical, explanation is that the international division of labour enables global firms to exploit the world. The global firm aligns its resources according to the needs of enterprises rather than the needs of people. As Neimark and Tinker (1986) explain, international firms are agents of social change: they can withdraw (economically and technologically) from any country where the social and working conditions are not to their liking and they can influence nation-states' social and welfare programmes. The subsequent weakening of the nation-state in potential or actual production sites challenges the autonomy of governments and their programmes for employment, demand and tax payment. The debate continues, but since the issue of democratic accountability and autonomy within nation-states in the face of globalising markets and firms is a central one world-wide, management accounting's influence, however modest, should be explored.

Conclusion

This chapter discussed the role of management accounting in international firms. The global firm is a particular type of international firm characterized by its large geographical reach, its considerable organisational interdependence, and its ability to integrate activities in different countries in a coherent way. The global firm differs from the international multidomestic firm as the former is an integrated unit whereas the latter is a conglomerate that achieves control by making its subsidiaries as independent of each other as possible.

The role of management accounting in international firms is related to their strategies of co-ordination and integration. In the global firm, management accounting supports a dispersed configuration of the value-chain located across the world. The dispersed location of its activities calls for extensive co-ordination and central management intervention in the affairs of its subsidiaries. Through attention to global product-line profitability, central management can use management accounting to establish an integrated organisation. Production, sales, R&D, etc. are positioned globally according to specific locational advantages and they are integrated through planning and budgeting activities. Management accounting in the global firm is a finely tuned information mechanism. It relies not only on composite financial measures but also on non-financial measures that help integrate different subsidiaries in the furtherance of global rather than local objectives.

In contrast, in the multidomestic conglomerate firm, subsidiaries are not responsible for executing a detailed, centrally imposed plan but are relatively free to devise their own strategies and plans and to monitor their progress towards them. In the multidomestic firm, central management monitors subsidiaries from a portfolio management perspective which evaluates subsidiaries largely on financial rates of profitability. There is little integration of activities across subsidiaries as they are typically in different businesses. Management accounting in multidomestic firms concentrates on setting financial targets and controlling their implementation through composite financial ratios such as ROI. There is little emphasis on information which integrates activities across subsidiaries.

International firms are exposed to volatile international financial markets and currency exposure may blur the effects of the firms' operational activities. The management of currency risk is particularly important in international firms. Consequently, a substantial part of their accounting monitors their short-term transaction exposure by monitoring outstanding debtors and creditors; their medium-term economic exposure by integrating currency management into budgeting; and their long-term economic exposure by examining currency aspects of their competitiveness.

The role of management accounting is, however, not restricted to monitoring uncertainties and organisational interdependencies. It can impinge directly onto political debates. Through transfer prices firms may divert profits to regions where taxes are low and, by changing a set of parameters in their computerized accounting systems, global firms can transfer profits from one location to another. The threat of this puts pressure on governments to make and administer tax laws that benefit the firms. However, the firms seek to be as independent of the individual location as is possible, to minimize political risk such as nationalisation.

The important question is whether management accounting contributes to the welfare of the people being influenced by the international firms, or whether it contributes to their exploitation. Theories disagree on this: one set argues that internationalisation helps create more efficient and effective international business systems which support value creation for the benefit of all; whereas others claim that internationalisation produces domination and exploitation of people and nation-states in a manner advantageous primarily to international firms.

Notes

1. The differences between the two kinds of international firms are idealized and to an extent caricatured. In practical situations a firm may have both characteristics at different levels of analysis. For example, a firm may be organized as a conglomerate in its general set-up and still have the chracteristics of an integrated firm in each of the subsidiaries or divisions. Thus, from corporate management's perspective the firm may be a conglomerate, but for divisional management it may be an integrated firm.
2. As a conglomerate, the business areas of Superfos are variable since it buys and sells companies all the time.
3. This information is supplied by managers from the two companies when they described their management accounting strategy to the author. The following discussion is not an evaluation of the effectiveness and efficiency of the accounting strategies of the two firms but merely an illustration of how management accounting varies according to two types of corporate strategy.

Bibliography

Bailes, J.C. and T. Assada (1991) 'Empirical differences between Japanese and American budget and performance evaluation systems', *The International Journal of Accounting*, pp. 131–42.

Belkauoi, A. (1991) *Multinational Management Accounting*, New York: Quorum Books.
This book is rare because it discusses international accounting from a pure management accounting perspective. In most international accounting texts, management accounting is relegated to a few inferior chapters. Belkauoi's book focuses on currency management, on the relation between strategy and accounting, and budgeting and performance measurement.

Chandler, A.D. jr. and H. Daems (1979) 'Administrative coordination, allocation and monitoring: a comparative analysis of the emergence of accounting and organization in the U.S.A and Europe', *Accounting, Organizations and Soceity*, vol. 4, no. 1, pp. 3–20.

Dicken, P. (1992) *Global Shift. The internationalisation of economic activity*, 2nd edn. London: Chapman & Hall.
This book is a wide-ranging, yet very readable book which seeks to integrate economic, social and political theories of internationalisation.

Eiteman, D.K., A.I. Stonehill and M.H. Moffet (1992) *Multinational Business Finance* 6th edn, Reading, Mass.: Addison-Wesley.
This finance book gives a good introduction to exchange risk management in language which is not too technical.

Herring, R.J. (ed.) (1983) *Managing International Risk*, Cambridge: Cambridge University Press.
This is a collection of papers which attempts to support international firms in their efforts to free themselves from their possible dependencies on host governments.

Holzer, H.P. and H.M. Schonfelt (1986) *Managerial Accounting and Analysis in Multinational Enterprises*, Berlin: de Gruiter.
This book describes the accounting systems and reporting systems of leading US and European international firms.

Horovitz, J.H. (1978) 'Management control in France, Great Britain and Germany', *Columbia Journal of World Business*, vol. xiii, no. 2; pp. 16–22.
This seminal paper discusses the implications of national cultures for management control systems.

Lessard, D.R. and P. Lorange (1977) 'Currency changes and management control: resolving centralisation/decentralisation dilemma', *The Accounting Review*, vol. II, no. 3, pp. 628–37.
This is a seminal paper on the management of currency risk. It contains a good example of variance analysis of currency issues.

Murray, P. (1981) *Multinational Beyond the Market*, Hemel Hempstead: Harvester Wheatsheaf.
This book critically analyses international firms' transfer pricing practices. It demonstrates the problems of achieving neutral transfer prices. Doing this, it shows how transfer prices can be mechanisms for firms to influence policy-making in host countries.

Neimark, M. and T. Tinker (1986) 'The social construction of management control systems', *Accounting, Organizations and Society*, vol. LII, no. 4/5, pp. 369–96.
This is a critical study of the strategies pursued by General Motors. The paper identifies the ways accounting contributes to mystifying the social conditions of corporate activities.

Porter, M. (ed.) (1986) *Competition in Global Industries*, Boston, Mass.: Harvard Business School Press.
This book contains a selection of papers about a variety of aspects of the global firm such as strategy, manufacturing, accounting, finance, marketing, relationships to host governments, competition and collaboration, and a few case studies. Most of the papers are analytical, and the book draws implicitly on transaction-cost theory to justify global arrangements.

Raddock, D.M. (ed.) (1986) *Assessing Corporate Political Risk*, Totowa: Rowman & Littelfield.
This book has the subtitle 'Guide for international businessmen' and lays out the ways in which firms can benefit from interaction with host governments.

Radebaugh, L.H. and S.J. Gray (1993) *International Accounting and Multi-national Enterprises*, 3rd edn, New Yor: John Wiley.
This is a good book that covers a broad set of issues including the global environment, financial accounting, and management accounting related to international issues. Its management accounting chapters are better than in most books on international accounting.

Sheth, J. and G. Eshghi (1990) *Global Organizational Theory Perspectives*, Cincinnati, Ohio: South Western Publishing.
This book provides an introduction to a variety of issues in relation to the management of global operations, including management accounting.

Tomkins, C. (1991) *Corporate Resource Allocation*, Oxford: Basil Blackwell.
This book integrates literatures on strategy, accounting, finance and organisational theory. Although it does not specifically relate to international firms, it does illuminate accounting's relationship with strategy.

Williamson, O.E. (1986) *Economic Organization. Firms, Markets, and Policy Control*, New York: Harvester Wheatsheaf.

CHAPTER FIFTEEN

A Comparative Analysis of Management Accounting in Japan, USA/UK and West Germany

Wendy Currie

◆

Introduction

The background of this chapter is the debate on management's choice and application of costing and investment appraisal methods and techniques for the evaluation of advanced manufacturing technology (AMT) in the manufacturing sector. In particular, it considers some of the management control issues surrounding the use of accounting techniques for the performance measurement of new advanced technologies. It forms part of the wider debate on the competitive decline of Anglo/ American manufacturing companies and the emerging technological gap between the West and Japan.

Searching for a solution to the problems facing Western manufacturers, Anglo/ American governments, academics and industrialists have focused on the competitive advantage which underpins the Japanese 'miracle'. The impetus behind some of this work is to identify appropriate Japanese practices for adoption in the West. Yet questions arise about the suitability of Japanese [solutions] for Western business cultures. This is because the management areas deemed problematic by Western academics (investment appraisal and evaluation) are not given equal priority and attention by Japanese managers. This is particularly the case with regard to selection and appraisal criteria for AMT (Jones et al., 1993). The chapter draws from empirical work on cross-national comparisons of AMT and management accounting in twenty-four companies operating in four countries.

Management Accounting and AMT in Japan

The last decade has witnessed a plethora of academic and practitioner literature on Japanese management. A large proportion of this literature addresses two inter-related debates. The first is the decline of Anglo/American manufacturing and the consequent threat to those markets from Japan and the Pacific rim countries. The second focuses attention on the success of the Japanese enterprise system and questions the extent to which Japanese management methods can be transported to the West.

Having attributed Japanese economic success to their effective exploitation of the 'new manufacturing methods and techniques', such as just-in-time (JIT), materials requirements planning (MRP), manufacturing resource planning (MRP II) and TQM (total quality management), among others, many have overlooked the fact that a number of these solutions originated in the post-war period in the USA. Researchers have further considered Japanese management development and training. Here, managers are seen as creating a 'multi-skilled' or 'polyvalent' labour force with the accent on 'teamworking', loyalty to one's company and high motivation. Forceful arguments have therefore encouraged Western managers to adopt 'Japanese manage-ment practices' to enhance the international and domestic competitive position of their firms – a process which has been labelled the 'Japanisation' of Anglo/American industry.

In parallel with the focus upon 'new' manufacturing methods and human resource practices, research has considered how the Japanese exploit process and product technologies. This technology refers to decision support systems (DSS), management information systems (MIS), local area networks (LANs), client server technology, open systems, computer-aided design and manufacture (CAD/CAM), flexible manufacturing systems (FMS), numerical control (NC), computer-integrated manu-facture (CIM) and robotics, among others. The Japanese, however, are reluctant to refer to any form of technology as 'new' since they perceive technology development and diffusion as an evolutionary and ongoing organisational activity. In the case of AMT, Japanese manufacturing managers prefer the terms 'production technology' or 'factory automation'. As a result, the exploitation of CAD/CAM and robots, etc., in Japanese manufacturing firms is not perceived as a 'quick-fix' panacea to cure problems of low productivity and profitability. Instead, technology diffusion is simply one aspect of an all-embracing corporate/manufacturing strategy planned over a three- to five-year period. Yet the very fact that 'technology decisions' are taken at board level is indicative of the importance senior managers attach to technology as a tool to enhance performance and competitive position. A further line of enquiry into reasons which underpin Japanese economic success concerns their use of accounting methods and techniques. Whilst research into this area is sparse, it is important given the growing Anglo/American preoccupation with identifying new management accounting techniques (e.g. activity-based costing (ABC) and through-put accounting). Here, management accounting is elevated to centre stage.

Much of the current academic critique of Anglo/American management accounting stems from the US accounting literature. Focusing upon 'traditional' or 'conventional' accounting practice, two key problems are identified. The first is in the area of costing systems and the second is investment appraisal.

Cost systems

The underlying assumption of this critique into Anglo/American companies is that accounting information is the 'dominant, indeed the sole, determinant of decisions to adopt AMT. It further assumes that AMT is crucial for successful manufacturing performance. Thus problems in existing UK accounting practice, discovered in its measurements and techniques, are held to generate inadequate or incorrect account- ing information which has central significance for UK manufacturing' (Jones *et al.*, 1993). Critics of conventional accounting practice cite examples where managers rely on distorted accounting information on the cost of particular production processes and profitability of products. Kaplan (1990) cites five key areas of cost system distortions. First, costs may be allocated to products that have little relation to the products being produced. For example, research and development costs, excess capacity costs and corporate overhead costs such as pensions. Second, costs may not be attributed to certain products being produced or to customers serviced. They include marketing, sales, general, admin and warranty costs. Third, 'distortion can be introduced by costing only a subset of the outputs of the firm as products'. Here, Kaplan differentiates between 'tangible' (manufactured) and 'intangible' (service) products, in that costs may only be assigned to the former. Fourth, distortion occurs where costs are 'inaccurately' assigned to products. Kaplan highlights two forms by which this may occur. The first is price distortion. This may occur 'when the cost system is too aggregated and average prices are used instead of specific prices. For example, some cost systems use an average price per direct labour hour despite wide differences in actual wage rates for both skilled and unskilled individuals.' Quantity distortions, on the other hand, occur when costs are 'indirectly assigned to products using a basis that is not perfectly proportional to the actual consumption of resources by products'. Kaplan points out that labour-intensive products are often 'overcosted when direct labour hours are used to assign all overhead costs to products' (1990, p. 4).

Interviews with Japanese engineers and accountants confirmed the use of 'conventional' management accounting techniques in eight Japanese manufacturing firms (Currie and Seddon, 1992). This is also confirmed by other research on Japanese management accounting (Williams *et al.*, 1991; Yoshikawa *et al.*, 1989). In turn, many of the inadequacies of traditional management accounting outlined above were reinforced by Japanese managers. The reduction of direct labour and enhanced productivity through AMT were seen as two key performance goals. Japanese managers were also keen to reduce costs as a consequence of capital rationing and facilitating management philosophies such as JIT and TQM. As Williams *et al.*, (1991, p. 14) point out, 'As far as one can judge, there is no general retreat from labour centred measures.' Many Japanese firms remain preoccupied with the reduction of (direct and indirect) labour hours. However, Japanese firms, unlike their Western counterparts, were uninterested in the 'new' management accounting techniques such as ABC. One or two managers had heard of ABC but showed little interest in exploring it further. They felt that knowledge that some products were more expensive to produce than others was not in itself important to determine product strategy decisions (Currie and Seddon, 1992). On the contrary, expensive products were likely to have real strategic importance to the company and their elimination on the basis of simple product costing information could prove disastrous.

Japanese companies differed from their Western counterparts in the areas of cost management, investment appraisal, market orientation and strategic awareness of AMT. In the area of cost management, Japanese managers perceived *target costing* as important. They felt it was important to calculate the right price for a product at the pre-manufacturing stage. Financial planning for the entire product life-cycle was therefore carried out prior to manufacturing. Product pricing had to relate to 'what the market could bear'. This is reinforced in the work of Yoshikawa *et al.*, (1989) who state that 'Japanese companies show more attention to product costing at the pre-manufacturing stages with earlier and more sustained attempts at target costing and reduction. They also make positive use of quality control feedback' (p. 22). Similarly, Kharbanda and Stallworthy (1991) claim that, as opposed to cost control being the sole responsibility of the accounting function, in Japan it is 'everyone's job'. Relating this to cost control in product development, the authors claim that Japanese manufacturers 'develop the cost of a design and then establish the market price'. Prices are fixed according to market tolerance. Thus the Japanese 'work backwards to the basic cost of the product' and design it to an 'acceptable quality' at the right cost.

Investment appraisal

Investment appraisal was also practised differently by Japanese and Western managers. In recent years, the problems of traditional investment appraisal techniques have been well documented. The fixation on labour costs by perceiving the range of new technologies as *labour saving* has arguably distorted the real strategic advantages of this form of capital investment. The continuing decline in direct labour costs as a proportion of total manufacturing costs suggests this performance indicator is less relevant (Kaplan, 1990). It has also eliminated one of the key justifications for introducing AMT.

Whilst Western managers appear over-concerned with the quantitative advantages of AMT, Japanese managers instead include a wider array of performance indicators when assessing the benefits from production technologies. Some claimed to quantify the *qualitative* benefits of AMT, with particular attention on quality control costs, scrap, rework, warranty, service costs, wastage, space saving and machine performance.

Interviews with Japanese managers confirm the difficulty of quantifying the so-called intangibles, but it was stressed on a number of occasions that payback from AMT was geared to the long term (two to five years). This differs from the Anglo/American tendency to adopt short-term performance targets which invariably over-estimate the cost of capital leading to discounted cash flow (DCF) hurdles that are too high.

One notable difference between Japanese and Western management accounting was managerial level of responsibility for investment appraisal. Here it was difficult to discuss preferences for management accounting techniques in isolation from other important considerations. For example, the notion that individuals could be responsible for departmental capital budgets (as is the case in the West) seemed surprising to many Japanese managers, who instead emphasised the value of teamworking and co-operation. Out of eight large Japanese manufacturing firms, only two middle managers were given budgetary responsibility at levels of only £4,000 and £20,000 per annum respectively. The 'technical champion' – a term that refers to individual effort of technical personnel (commonly used in the West) – was not recognised by Japanese managers. On the contrary, Japanese managers were keen to explain that individual performance was assessed along with group performance. In six of the eight case studies, expenditure on AMT was decided at management meetings comprising the president, board-level directors and associated expert teams from the organisation. Technology strategy was not devolved to even senior-level management where board-level directors simply served to rubber-stamp capital budgets. One reason for the centralisation of the capital budgeting process was indeed the vast cost of introducing AMT. All Japanese companies confirmed an increase in the annual level of expenditure on AMT in the five years to 1990. Further, expenditure on AMT was commonly planned over five years where investment was likely to exceed several million pounds.

Japanese manufacturing firms' use of management accounting techniques for investment appraisal of AMT was interesting. Table 15.1 shows that in spite of

Table 15.1 Management accounting and AMT in Japan.

Case no.	Capital budget per annum – company (£m)	AMT – investment site (£m)	Discounted cash flow (DCF)	Payback
1	–	2	No	Yes
2	500	40	No	Yes
3	–	4	No	Yes
4	268	–	Yes	Yes
5	1296	29	No	Yes
6	14.8	3.2	No	Yes
7	217.1	40	No	Yes
8	135.1	4	No	Yes

large-scale annual expenditure on AMT, only one company used the more sophist-icated technique of DCF. All companies, however, used some form of simple payback.

Management control and accounting measurements and techniques

Payback periods of two to three years were typical but Japanese managers said that the ever-decreasing life-expectancy of products and process technology meant that traditional accounting techniques including DCF were inappropriate. It was stressed that accounting measures for hardware and labour costs tended to exclude other important costs such as software development, training and vendor support services. Some Japanese managers expressed the difficulty in identifying the real costs of software and associated research and development activities. Commenting on software development, one Japanese manager said that the new PC-based languages and packages required new programming skills. This is similar to comments made by managers in the West, given that capital expenditure that was difficult to cost-justify would be described as 'strategic'. But whereas Western managers would seek to impose more financial pressures to support capital projects, Japanese managers actually imposed less! Both sets of managers, however, conceded that some projects were simply too difficult to quantify, although there was an intuitive recognition at senior levels of their strategic importance.

Labour-centred measures were important in Japanese firms largely for perform-ance measurement as opposed to headcount reduction. Several managers reported a severe skills shortage in systems engineering and other IT professional positions. One Japanese manager at an automobile plant said, 'You have to be careful when you talk about eliminating jobs through technology. Here, we do not get rid of people. We move them to another area if their job has become redundant.' In this context, jobs became redundant rather than people! As part of a major JIT programme, this company had 're-engineered' the plant and reduced forty control rooms to only one and organisational functions from seventy-eight to forty. This manager agreed that some jobs were 'in the past', but he balanced this view by saying that many new jobs had been created. He saw technology as both an exciting challenge and a threat to the working environment. On the one hand, it threatened the status quo and people would have to learn new skills and, on the other, it posed a challenge to managers and staff as new *broader* skills were constantly demanded. He said that 'good systems engineers' were at a premium in Japan (e.g. the writers of programs which drive industrial robots, CAD to point-of-sale stock control, etc.).

This comment is reinforced by a *Financial Times* survey on Japanese industry which stresses 'The shortage of systems engineers has been a subject of popular complaint by [Japanese] employers'. Part of the shortage is related to employer perceptions of the software engineer. As the FT survey demonstrates, employers wish to groom software engineers with wider business skills than simply being proficient at programming. 'Engineers must understand the business of clients and be able to give them consultation' (*Financial Times*, 16 December 1991, p. 5).

Whilst Japanese companies were committed to training and skills development, they agreed that it was 'difficult to quantify' the advantages which accrue from high-calibre staff. However, the realisation that technology demanded retraining and re-skilling of the workforce did not discourage high-level capital investment. To realise strategic goals from AMT, managers in the majority of Japanese companies stressed the importance of having 'an all-embracing strategic plan'.

AMT strategy and implementation

The commitment to the development and implementation of AMT strategy was company-wide and not simply a middle-level management responsibility, as is largely the case in the UK. Important technology decisions such as level of expenditure on AMT, cost savings, market share objectives, procurement, vendor contracts, maintenance and training formed part of the corporate strategic plan for AMT. Moreover, AMT strategy was not simply a 'mission statement' to guide middle-management decision-making. Rather, it was an 'all-encompassing' strategic plan incorporating guidance on implementation and performance milestones.

A plant manager at a company which manufactured automatic control device equipment said that in recent years upper management had 'formalised' the strategic and operational decision-making process for AMT. Starting with a long-range strategic plan (LRSP), board-level managers discussed the perceived advantages and disadvantages of AMT with a 'multi-disciplinary', 'expert' team from the organisation (Figure 15.1). The LRSP covered a five-year period. Performance criteria for AMT included financial and non-financial objectives. For example, detailed financial information was presented to the board in the form of perceived payback from AMT in addition to non-financial benefits such as increased flexibility, improved quality of process and product technology, better customer service, reduced waste and space savings. The plant manager said that sometimes qualitative benefits would be quantified, but this was not always possible in a five-year plan.

The Japanese approach differed significantly from Anglo/American approaches to

Level			Term
Top management	T O P	Long-range strategic plan	5 years
Director	D O W N	Long-range operational plan	3 years
Manager		Annual operational plan	1 year

Figure 15.1 Business planning architecture.

strategy formulation in the former's emphasis upon implementation. Once the LRSP was agreed, a long-range operational plan (LROP) was developed to cover all aspects of implementation. This was an implementation plan under the direction of upper management and covering a three-year period. Although the strategic planning process was described as 'top down', it was actually a company-wide commitment and junior and middle-level managers were expected to plan their activities to meet the overall corporate strategy.

Writing on the US strategy formulation process, Mintzberg and McHugh (1985) claim that

> Strategy making still tends to be equated with planning – with the systematic 'formulation' and articulation of deliberate, premeditated strategies, which are then 'implemented'.... This view of strategy, however, is unnecessarily restrictive; it is inconsistent with more contemporary forms of structure and sometimes with the conventional forms as well.... If strategy is defined only with intention, the researcher is reduced to studying perceptions, devoid of behaviour. Defining strategy with respect to realisation, however, enables the researcher to track the rise and fall of strategies in empirical terms (p. 160).

The authors therefore argue that empirical investigation should differentiate between deliberate strategies (intentions realised) and emergent strategies (patterns realised despite or in the absence of intentions).

Empirical research into Japanese companies by the author confirmed a strict adherence to a corporate strategic plan, although Japanese managers said that *ad hoc* sub-strategies emerged as a result of shifting markets for products and the rapid pace of technological change. For example, the annual operational plan (AOP) was designed to track the progress of the LRSP and LROP. Whilst the AOP was largely introduced to monitor expenditure on capital equipment, labour and overhead, it also served to inform senior managers of necessary changes to the original performance milestones of the LRSP and LROP.

What was clear about the Japanese approach to strategy formulation and implementation was their commitment to working as part of a team. Individual ego was eclipsed by a desire to work towards a shared goal rather than for personal financial gain or promotion. Two important cultural explanations reinforced team-working and co-operation. First, the tradition of lifetime employment (at least in the large Japanese corporations comprising about 10 per cent of the labour market) encouraged a long-term view of one's career goals and conduct. One interviewee said that 'a person loses something if he/she leaves to join another [rival] company'. Indeed, the loss could be significant as the individual may lose all their accrued benefits and may be treated like a junior at their new company and retrained accordingly. Second, the route to promotion was length of service, seniority and loyalty to one's company. Individualism and eagerness to 'shine' in addition to 'fast-track' promotions were unusual. However, in the light of recent Japanese economic difficulties and the growing tendency to question 'lifetime employment', it is argued that many indigenous Japanese firms will gradually adopt Western-style job-reduction programmes. Such a strategy would undoubtedly undermine the stability and cohesion of the traditional work ethic and commitment to one's company.

Strategy formulation for AMT was further achieved by the effective restructuring of organisations. One Japanese electronics giant which was split into nineteen business groups had restructured to facilitate innovation, growth and market leadership (Figure 15.2). This company believed that technical innovation was too important to be managed in isolation from other activities. The company therefore 'pooled' technical expertise to assist in the formation, implementation and management of AMT strategy. As Figure 15.2 shows, the matrix structure was designed to provide the nineteen business groups with technical expertise from the Computer-Aided Engineering (CAE) Division comprising 100 technical specialists, the Factory Automation (FA) Division comprising 1,400 people and operating as a profit centre in its own right, and an Investment Committee where 20 directors and senior management considered a range of investment proposals from the various business groups. One manager said, 'The business groups are encouraged to buy production technology from FA. If they want to go to West Germany for equipment, they are discouraged by the Investment Committee. This sometimes makes our lives difficult, but we are one of the most successful companies in Japan!'

The CAE and FA Divisions were described as 'internal consultancy'. However, individuals appointed to these Divisions were expected to act for the corporation by ensuring that the appropriate technology was installed in the business groups. On the subject of external management consultants, some Japanese managers were surprised that Anglo/American companies even considered using 'outsiders' for advice and guidance, particularly in crucial matters such as AMT strategy and implementation.

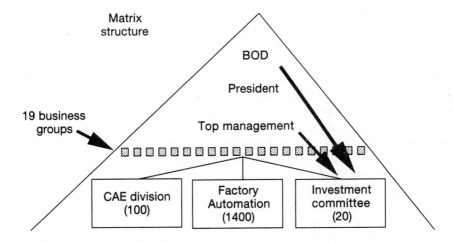

Figure 15.2 Investment appraisal of AMT in a Japanese company.

Many Japanese companies 'outsourced' small IT projects, but their concern to retain control ensured that strategic decision-making was kept strictly in-house.

Japanese management accounting

The significant reason for the scant attention paid to Japanese management accounting, particularly in the USA and UK, is because the methods and techniques used are 'traditional' and do not, in isolation, explain the Japanese 'miracle' or Japan's position as a 'world-class manufacturer'. Indeed, Japanese management accounting has arguably played little part in Japan's post-war pursuit of economic success. In fact, some Japanese managers described management accounting activities simply as 'good housekeeping'. Even the focus on cost reduction through the redeployment of direct labour suggests that while traditional accounting may *influence* rather than simply *inform* decision-makers (Hiromoto, 1988), manufacturing goals were nevertheless achieved by an all-embracing corporate strategy and not by cost-cutting and performance measurement alone. Japanese companies focused upon a wide array of multi-disciplinary financial and non-financial performance indicators and a strong 'engineering voice' was present at board level. Explanations for these differences cannot be attributed to one or two simple factors alone but to a wider socio-economic and cultural explanation which looks at government support for manufacturing, the banking and education systems, human resource practices and Japan's post-war 'backwardness' and keen desire to catch up with the West, particularly the United States, Britain and West Germany.

Japanese managers' definition of JIT also differs from that of UK managers since it incorporates production management methods, total quality management (TQM) and total preventive maintenance (TPM). JIT was described as a 'simple all-embracing manufacturing philosophy' designed to continually improve manu-facturing and reduce costs. Inventory control was just as important as preventive maintenance strategies. Many Japanese managers stressed that post-production-run maintenance shifts ensured the smooth running of the JIT system. Machine breakdown was addressed immediately and communicated to operators through the load ringing of alarm bells. Indeed, operators were expected to carry out routine machine repairs and only alert maintenance staff if necessary (Currie and Seddon, 1992). Performance targets and achievements were also displayed on the shopfloor in many Japanese firms, suggesting that JIT was more than a set of diverse techniques or system for inventory control.

Field research in Japan confirmed the view of Williams *et al.* (1991) that deficiencies in management accounting addressed by Anglo/American academics and consultants are not considered important to Japanese practitioners. The following section considers this issue in relation to field work into five US manufacturing companies visited by the author in 1991.

Management Accounting and AMT in the USA

Interviews with managers in five north-eastern US companies ranging from only 40 employees to 3,500 found that a three-year strategic plan for AMT was followed in only two companies. This signalled an immediate difference between US and Japanese manufacturing firms regarding strategic time-scales for AMT implementation. Even where US companies were spending over $1 million per annum on AMT, payback and/or return on investment (ROI) was expected within a year in two cases.

Interviewing the treasurer (a management accountant) at a paper-making company, recently taken over by a Finnish firm, it was stressed that capital rationing had made it difficult to raise money for *new* equipment as opposed to *replacement* equipment. Advanced manufacturing technologies such as CAD and FMS, for example, were perceived by upper management as new technologies, whereas an investment in a paper-making machine was described as replacement technology. According to the treasurer, 'The stringent demand for cost justification of AMT is a disincentive to innovation.' He gave the example below of the investment appraisal process for CAD.

Identifying productivity savings from CAD

The investment appraisal process at this company was administratively simple since a positive net present value (NPV) was seen as adequate financial justification. Capital expenditure exceeding $50K required a signature from the president and all investments in AMT had to demonstrate their worth post-implementation. Five years ago the company invested in a CAD system to reduce manufacturing costs. This particular experience of CAD had proved unsatisfactory as 'the vendor subsequently went out of business'. As novices in CAD technology, lack of trained personnel and no supplier resulted in a 'support nightmare'. On reflection, the treasurer said that ongoing vendor support was crucial and should have been considered in the investment appraisal process.

To avoid a recurrence of this situation the company had moved away from the act of faith approach to AMT investment in favour of a methodical and more stringent financial approach. Investment appraisal of CAD was therefore assessed by comparing the cost of manual drawing to that of automated design. However, the selection of performance indicators could be described as 'spurious'.

According to the treasurer,

> Specific estimates of savings are based upon a combination of practical experience, and on experience gained during the pilot project. This company generates approximately 2,000 drawings per year. Estimated time to generate a new drawing varies from two hours to a maximum approaching 80 hours, with an average of approximately six hours. Without the use of CAD software, it is estimated that design modification of an existing drawing (when practical) results in a 50 per cent saving (three hours based on the

average drawing but higher for more complex shapes). CAD software has features which facilitate geometry modifications (i.e. stretching, re-positioning and associated re-dimensioning). With the use of CAD software the estimated savings resulting from design modification increases to 85 per cent (approximately five hours on average). It is estimated that successful retrievals will occur in approximately 15 per cent without the use of CAD software, and in approximately 50 per cent with the use of CAD software.

The treasurer said that CAD was introduced to enhance performance in the following areas:

- ◆ enhance design retrieval
- ◆ improve design standardisation
- ◆ standardise process planning
- ◆ enhance production process (work cell formulation)
- ◆ enhance production scheduling.

Engineers at the company were sceptical of this approach and described it as 'mechanical' and 'narrow in orientation'. They also pointed out that it was 'too quantitative' and 'failed to consider the quality of design work'. The fact that it was possible to 'retrieve' drawings was not important in isolation from design quality and customer requirements. This approach also 'failed to consider the skill and flair of individual engineers' and assumed equal status and ability of the design team.

Quantifying manual and automated design work

The treasurer stressed that investment in CAD was only possible if a 'cast-iron' financial case could be put to upper management. Using a Group Technology (GT) database, automated design work (CAD) had several cost advantages. He reflected on the philosophy behind the GT database:

> The basic philosophy of group technology is to analyze a collection of manufactured items and classify them into subsets (families) based on common attributes. A single manufactured item is readily identified as a member of a given subset by a GT code. There is a wide base of knowledge regarding how to formulate a GT classification. Perhaps the foremost criterion for determining the structure of a GT cost is its intended purpose.

Table 15.2 gives the figures based upon the estimated time savings (man-hours) using manual and automated (CAD) design work on the GT database. The time-saving cost is deducted from the cost of using the GT database – the latter remaining fixed in both cases. The estimated cost savings using CAD against manual methods are much higher. The treasurer conceded that, 'Because CAD typically permits more complex modifications to be performed in a simpler manner, a higher percentage of drawings are modifiable. This leads to a greater retrieval rate.'

The GT database cost $6,900. This figure was calculated using a 'ten-minute search' for a drawing on the database. This is equal to 330 man-hours at a cost of $21 per

Table 15.2 Estimated savings from Group Technology and CAD.

Activity	Manual drawings using group technology database ($)	CAD drawings and group technology database ($)
Cost of GT database	(6,900)	(6,900)
Drawing savings	12,100	98,100
Bill of materials/routeing savings	8,500	28,500
Total	13,700 PA	119,700 PA

hour ($6,930) or 2,000 (drawings) multiplied by ten minutes (one-sixth of an hour). Similar calculations were made for the time-saving advantages of the GT database whilst undertaking manual and CAD design work, in addition to the time-savings in modifications of existing drawings stored on the GT database (i.e. stretching, repositioning and associated re-dimensioning).

The treasurer produced a document which concluded that:

> In either case, a CAD or non-CAD environment, some additional benefits will also occur in the manufacturing area. Manufacturing engineering and pre-production planning review engineering drawings and prepare Bill of Materials and Routings. At this company six people are involved with this process approximately thirty per cent of their time. The other seventy per cent involves similar work on non company x designs and on miscellaneous support activities. When BOM and associated routings can be retrieved and modified, a conservative estimate is that between sixty and seventy per cent savings can be achieved. With a fifteen per cent retrieval rate (non-CAD environment) the estimated savings are 390 man hours (approximately $8,500). With a fifty per cent retrieval rate (CAD environment) the estimated savings are 1,300 man hours (approximately $28,000).

Figure 15.3 gives a comparison between estimated manual drawing times and proposed options (using CAD).

In spite of attempts to quantify some of the qualitative advantages from CAD, engineering managers felt that the real justification for CAD was fivefold: process innovation, product innovation, better quality, ability to undertake complex design work and ease of modification/retrieval. One engineer said, 'Without CAD, we simply couldn't produce complex mechanical and electrical design drawings – which means we wouldn't be able to compete in the domestic, let alone international, market-place.' A further criticism by engineers was the 'short-term payback' from CAD expected by upper management. It was stressed that 'Any new purchase of software requires a learning period. In the case of CAD, it takes nine months to become proficient in using it. This means you have a further three months to meet the payback period.' The present investment appraisal process for CAD also assumed a fixity in skills profile and productivity rates of engineers, customer orders, competition, annual number and quality of drawings, delivery times and obsolescence of hardware/software. Given these factors, engineers argued it was difficult to produce

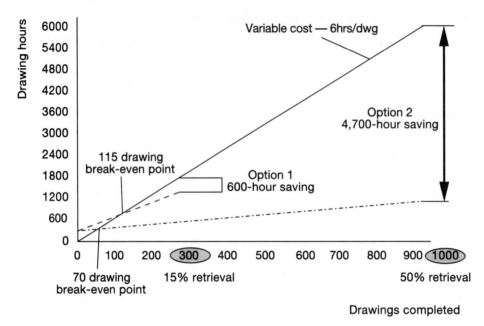

Figure 15.3 Comparison between manual drawing times and proposed options.

hard statistics about likely productivity gains from CAD in an ever-changing organisational and external climate.

The desire to prove the success or failure of CAD through financial performance indicators reinforced an earlier study on CAD procurement and implementation. If anything, the US experience confirmed the high value placed upon traditional management accounting methods and techniques in spite of reports (both academic and practitioner) of their inadequacy. Insufficient financial information on the benefits of CAD led to demands by senior managers for tighter financial control, even though the solution resulted in greater complexity and not necessarily better information.

Management Accounting and AMT in the UK

Research into five UK manufacturing companies on accounting and AMT strategy highlighted many dissimilarities with the Japanese experience. Capital rationing programmes in three companies affecting all functional areas had forced accountants and production engineers to identify cost savings through AMT. In parallel with the US company described above, the capital budgetary framework in UK companies signalled strategic intentions. Yet the relationship between strategic aspiration and practical implementation was somewhat tenuous. This was also the case in an earlier study into the evaluation and implementation of CAD in twenty UK companies between 1985 and 1988.

Peculiar to the British experience was the perception by engineering managers that capital budgeting for AMT was an art-form characterised by game-playing and numerical manipulation. Two reasons were paramount. First, the strong 'accounting voice' at senior management level reflected a lack of understanding about the strategic capabilities of AMT for manufacturing. Engineers were keen to stress that whilst the techniques of investment appraisal for CAD equipment were 'easy to understand and apply', upper management's preference for a narrow range of financial performance indicators excluded important non-financial considerations. In parallel with Japanese manufacturers, UK companies emphasised labour-centred measures but, unlike the former, imposed short-term payback periods for CAD investment.

Second, strategic evaluation of AMT omitted associated costs such as training, skills development (including project management skills), vendor services (maintenance/support contracts) and software updates. To circumvent what was described as a 'narrow financial focus' by senior managers, engineers said that necessary AMT-related expenditure would be allocated to other budgets. For example, a two-day software update course would be met by a centralised training budget, although this form of expenditure was strictly AMT related. More serious problems arose when engineers wished to purchase the latest software update and found that money was unavailable until the next financial period. The study therefore concluded that capital budgeting for AMT was a fragmented and *ad hoc* managerial activity with little cross-fertilisation between functional or hierarchical levels. Payback periods for AMT were particularly short and failed to address issues of skills shortages (i.e. programming languages), training needs and vendor/client relationships relating to support.

Investment appraisal at a UK automobile plant

An interesting empirical observation on the UK experience was the tendency to employ simple payback methods rather than the more complicated DCF techniques in evaluating AMT (Jones *et al.*, 1993). At a UK automobile plant, a senior production engineer said that greater financial controls were now imposed on all capital expenditure. In the case of AMT, a sound financial case was the single most important factor in investment appraisal. Whilst he was not opposed to providing detailed financial evaluation for proposed expenditure on AMT, he was highly critical of the 'fragmented approach' adopted by the organisation. Figure 15.4 outlines the key stages in the investment appraisal process for AMT. First, the project engineer devises a cost proposal which forecasts the benefits of investing in, say, a new CAD system. This is discussed with the engineering manager who assesses the proposed investment according to its strategic importance to the department/plant. The cost proposal is then sent to a project analyser (who may be a trainee management

ENGINEERING ACCOUNTANCY

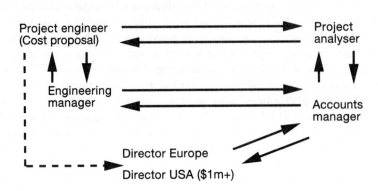

Figure 15.4   Investment appraisal of AMT at a UK car manufacturer.

accountant) for scrutiny. Cost proposals exceeding $1 million are sent to the USA for approval (rubber-stamping). The accounting function checks the figures and records the expected cost savings before proceeding with the order.

According to the senior production engineer, the whole process may last nine months and sometimes a year. He pointed out that often the project analyser failed to grasp the meaning behind engineering terminology used to justify the proposed expenditure. Information was thus 'diluted' to facilitate understanding, and so occasionally lost its meaning. Apparently, poor communication characterised the investment appraisal process since accountants and engineers occupied 'separate buildings' and used 'different canteens'. As Jones *et al.* argue,

> Divisions between accountants and engineers tend to fragment AMT decision-making and, although organisational patterns differ, even the most integrated forms of middle management decision-making do not correspond to Japanese 'team management'. Accountants are either remote from production, or are restricted in their participation in planning teams by their narrowly specialised knowledge and skills. (p. 125)

AMT strategy and implementation

The fragmentation of AMT decision-making was nowhere more apparent than in the pursuit of new manufacturing philosophies such as JIT. Unlike the Japanese approach which perceived JIT as an holistic (company-wide) approach to world-class manufacturing status, many UK companies saw JIT as an inventory control system (Currie and Seddon, 1992). Indeed, one or two UK companies had confined JIT implementation to the responsibility of an individual engineering manager. At the UK automobile manufacturer described above, JIT appeared to be perceived separately from technology decisions. For example, preventive maintenance (PM) was carried out in isolation from a wider manufacturing plan and was the sole responsibility of the maintenance department. In recent months maintenance had been streamlined in line with the corporate labour-elimination policy. Such measures had significantly affected the service offered to production (see Figure 15.5). According to one maintenance manager, 'They [upper management] seem to like it when a machine breaks down because they see us working. They don't like the idea of us reading newspapers in the maintenance crib.'

Such shortsightedness on the part of senior management had resulted in a firefighting approach taken by maintenance, where preventive work had given way to simply fixing machines at the point of breakdown (usually several hours after). Maintenance costs were treated as 'overhead' and, whilst production engineers received monthly reports on machine breakdown, this information was not costed and highlighted in accounting reports. Nor was it required by senior executives.

Whilst many academic studies urge the need for effective maintenance policies, the UK experience suggests an absence of Japanese-style TPM. Even Anglo/American and Japanese comparative studies show that the two-shift production system adopted by Toyota, Kamigo is more productive (with regard to inventory, products, operators, wages, line rate/day, labour engineering hours) than the three-shift system of the UK car manufacturer. Part of the reason is the emphasis upon TPM and the importance attached to short maintenance shifts following production runs.

The failure to support maintenance activities at the UK car plant became apparent over time as PM actions decreased (e.g. to maintain equipment) in conjunction with

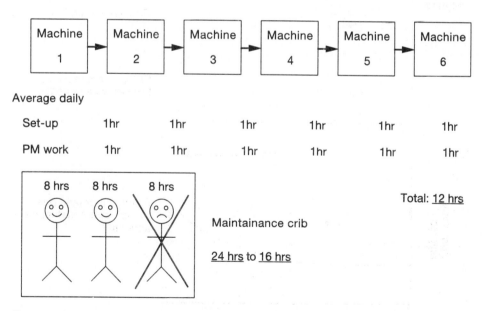

Figure 15.5 Labour elimination in the maintenance function.

Issues in management accounting

an increase in machine failure (see Figure 15.6). The shortfall of maintenance personnel meant that only 90 per cent of PM work could be carried out according to an agreed schedule. Over time the decrease in PM work was reflected by an increase in machine failure, so that downtime increased to 61 per cent. Even at the end of the year, downtime was running at 58 per cent (uptime = 42 per cent) although the forecast year-end uptime was 60 per cent. (Figure 15.7) This example reflected the difference between strategic intentions and actual practice and suggested that key performance indicators were not communicated to management accountants and senior executives. In addition, the pursuit of labour elimination went but a little way to increase production efficiency. On the contrary, the tendency of senior executives to view production problems of labour shortages, poor machine performance and lack of capital investment as issues for production managers highlighted an absence of a manufacturing strategy.

This company seemed to stereotype all the common problems associated with the decline of British manufacturing industry. Severe demarcation lines were drawn between those with 'technical' skills (engineers) and those with business acumen (usually accountants and marketing people). Lack of capital investment in the latest advanced manufacturing technologies contributed to poor performance, as did the failure on the part of senior non-technical managers to act on important production information such as downtime records. In this context, it could be argued that

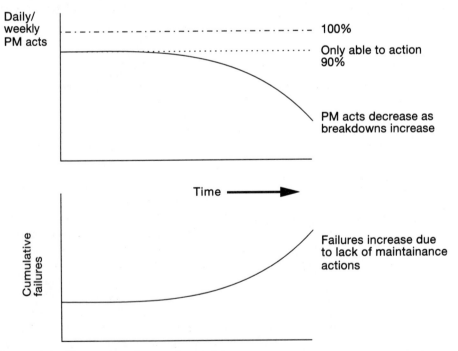

Figure 15.6 The erosion of preventive maintenance.

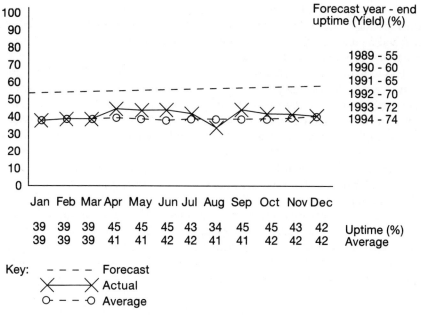

STATUS — DECEMBER 1990

Forecast year - end
uptime (Yield) (%)

1989 - 55
1990 - 60
1991 - 65
1992 - 70
1993 - 72
1994 - 74

	Jan	Feb	Mar	Apr	May	Jun	Jul	Aug	Sep	Oct	Nov	Dec	
	39	39	39	45	45	45	43	34	45	45	43	42	Uptime (%)
	39	39	39	41	41	42	42	41	41	42	42	42	Average

Key: – – – – Forecast
      ✕———✕ Actual
      O- – -O Average

Figure 15.7 Production line uptime at an automotive manufacturer.

management accounting could serve a vital function if accounting information on technical performance was given priority. Unfortunately, accounting information was only concerned with investment appraisal (pre-implementation of technology) and, to a much lesser extent, a simple post-audit to determine if the investment was a success. What seems to be lacking is an ongoing 'Japanese-style' monitoring of technical performance in both the quantitative and qualitative environments.

Management Accounting and AMT in West Germany

Management accounting in West German companies has gained little attention in academic and business circles, although several studies focus upon production methods and techniques. Much of this research emphasises the strong *engineering* voice at the apex of West German manufacturing firms and their underlying long-term commitment to capital investment and R & D. Comparative research highlights the competitive edge of West German companies over their British counterparts. Parallel to the Japanese experience, West German companies have traditionally been less subject to short-term pressures from the stock market, less vulnerable to take-over bids and have enjoyed long-term relationships with their banks and major shareholders. West Germany has fewer publicly quoted companies than Britain, and within this small group only a minority have widely dispersed shareholdings on the

Anglo/American model. Most have a dominant shareholder with at least 25 per cent of the equity. This is usually a non-financial enterprise rather than a bank. In this context, it is important to consider the following factors. First, there is a larger industrial output from West German owner-managed firms than is the case in Britain. Small and medium unquoted West German industrial enterprises are dominant in the industrial sector, unlike Britain where corporate governance issues concentrate on the gap between manager's interests and those of their shareholders (e.g. long-term growth versus short-term profits). Second, the notion that bank representation on supervisory boards is key to the success of West German companies is doubtful, given that companies with this reporting structure comprise only 30 per cent of total turnover in the German economy. Edwards and Filcher (1994) argue that there is no evidence that long-term strategies for growth are pursued due to the presence of banks on supervisory boards in West German companies. Nor is there evidence to suggest that banks confer the advantages of long-term finance. The authors argue that, unlike Japanese banks, West German banks 'do not in general get directly involved in the reorganisation of a firm in financial distress and do not possess any personnel who are specialists at turning unprofitable firms around'. Whilst the authors concede that large quoted West German firms with bank representation on supervisory boards may have 'some limited positive effect' (e.g. knowledge of impending financial constraints leading to intervention), this is not enough to explain industrial success. Third, corporate governance is important in West German firms where a single shareholder may own as much as 25 per cent of stock. Arguably, a major shareholder will carefully monitor corporate performance, unlike those in Anglo/American institutions whose shareholdings rarely exceed 1 or 2 per cent. In addition, a large investor has greater powers to stave off hostile take-over bids. Edwards and Filcher argue that the absence of the take-over threat has allowed many West German companies to pursue expansionist policies such as investment in new plant and buildings. The holders of large stakes are usually clients of or even suppliers to the company. An in-depth knowledge of the company is possessed by the shareholder and 'implicit contracts' are developed which encourage a high degree of trust and co-operation. This stability and commitment is arguably absent in Anglo/American enterprises.

At the other end of the spectrum, West German companies have been criticised for being 'too long term' in orientation. Whereas Anglo/American companies rapidly dispose of loss-making businesses and constantly pursue a policy of radical restructuring, West German firms may be reluctant to dispose of poorly performing companies. Similarly, Japanese companies who have offered numerous examples of top-class performance (particularly in gaining competitive advantage from AMT) are now questioning the principle of life-time employment (Hori, 1994).

Learning from West German manufacturing companies

The recent preoccupation by Western academics with the 'Japanese miracle' is similar to past interest in the success of West German manufacturing industry. The impetus behind these studies is to explain the relative decline of UK manufacturing compared with other industrialised nations. But instead of management accounting theory and practice occupying centre stage, researchers have attributed economic success to industrial policy, corporate governance, manufacturing techniques, human resource practice, the education system and even the background of senior managers.

A recent comparative study on West German and UK management accounting concluded that:

> A comparison with German theory and practice in engineering suggests that British management accounting overemphasises the single-minded pursuit of profit. This may have contributed to Britain's relative industrial decline. German management accounting was found to be more modest in its goals, more restricted in its use and more accurate in content. (Strange, 1991).

But as we saw above, management accounting practices employed in West German manufacturing companies are determined by the corporate governance structure – whether they are owner-managed or large quoted companies.

In a recent comparative study on management accounting and AMT in six West German manufacturing companies with similar Anglo/American and Japanese firms it was found that the role of management accounting neither helped nor inhibited AMT strategy. In fact, the practice of management accounting in West Germany was similar to the Japanese experience. For example, DCF was used in only two of the five West German companies (and in only one out of eight Japanese firms). One West German engineering manager said:

> Ten years ago we installed CAD. At the time it was a bit of an experiment as nobody knew much about CAD, or what it could achieve. After about a year, two of our senior designers became very knowledgeable about it. They designed a database (i.e. a collection of all our production drawings). Initially we thought CAD was an expensive toy and we could not demonstrate that it had any cost advantages whatsoever. However, after about eighteen months, we saw the real benefits. We could retrieve and modify drawings from our newly acquired database. This helped to reduce design lead times as our drawings reached production much more quickly. In short, CAD has been vital in design and production. But it is impossible to quantify the many hours of intellectual effort and the painstaking attention to detail of our engineers. This is why a DCF is not appropriate to capital projects of this type. Implementing new technology costs more than the price of the hardware and software packages. Perhaps if the true costs of AMT were known, there would not be any future investment!

West German companies devised AMT strategies at senior executive level where engineers often outnumbered finance directors (Table 15.3). Long-term (five-year) strategies were also implemented as part of an all-embracing manufacturing strategy (incorporating JIT, TQM, Statistical Process Control (SPC), etc.). Interestingly, cost justification for AMT was often undertaken by engineers in West German firms because 'it is important to understand the technical capabilities of technology which lead to competitive advantage'. Unlike the Japanese, however, West German

managers were keen to differentiate between *new* and *dedicated* (traditional) technology. They argued that whilst conventional management accounting was more easily
applied to the latter, it was unsuitable for cost justification of AMT.

AMT and performance measures

Another similarity between West German and Japanese manufacturing firms was the
choice of performance indicators for AMT. Only one West German manager at a
textiles firm said that labour elimination strategies were expected from AMT
investment (Table 15.4). This same company also hoped to increase productivity
through AMT, unlike the remaining five who claimed that productivity was not a key
performance indicator. Instead, there was a great emphasis on the reduction of
product lead times through CAD, FMS and robots in the two countries. JIT was also
part of a wide-ranging manufacturing strategy and not to be confused as a technique

Table 15.3   Management of AMT in West Germany.

	Machine tools for sheet metal	Consumer goods (plastics, detergents and food)	Components for textile industry	Textiles	Components for automobile industry	Control units for machine tools
How are decisions taken by management to acquire AMT, e.g. committees / working groups / project teams / functional heads / individuals, etc.?	Project teams reporting to the Board	Inter-disciplinary work groups	Direct level (enginering)	Director level (engineering)	Steering group (engineers, accounting, sales and planning)	Director level (engin-eering)
How many levels of management hierarchy are involved in capital budgeting for AMT?	5	3	2	2–3	1	2
Is DCF used for AMT? (time period in years)	Not used	2 years	3 years	Not used	Not used	Not used

for inventory control. Like Japanese companies, West German manufacturers prided themselves on possessing a thorough understanding of production and information technology. Skills development and training at all levels were a key priority. One West German manager commented:

> If I believed everything I read in vendor literature, I would have invested in every CAD system or CNC machine I had come across. The truth is, you need a lot of skill and judgement when you do a feasibility study on AMT. Many of our engineers know more about CNC machines than the vendors – and more importantly, the shortcomings of the machines.

Recognising the pitfalls of conventional management accounting theory and practice, West German companies had no plans to introduce ABC or any other new cost management system. Alternatively, most said that accounting information had to be used in conjunction with non-financial (qualitative) considerations. An interesting observation from the West German study (and one which is reinforced in the work of Strange, 1991) was that management accountants were trained in production engineering cost accounting techniques and seemed to agree with engineers about the full range of strategic (financial and non-financial) benefits from AMT. In short, management accounting in West German companies was seemingly used for performance monitoring and did not significantly influence long-term AMT strategy.

Table 15.4 Performance measures for AMT.

	Machine tools for sheet metal	Consumer goods (plastics, detergents and food)	Components for textile industry	Textiles	Components for automobile industry	Control units for machine tools
What are the criteria for assessing the benefits of AMT?						
Increase productivity	No	No	No	Yes	No	No
Minimise capital in work-in-progress	Yes	No	No	No	No	No
Shorten lead times	Yes	Yes	Yes	Yes	Yes	No
Increase flexibility	Yes	Yes	Yes	Yes	Yes	Yes
Improve quality of manufactured components	Yes	No	No	No	Yes	No
Delivery to customers	Yes	Yes	Yes	Yes	Yes	Yes
Reduce headcount	No	No	No	Yes	No	No
Develop process technology	Yes	Yes	Yes	No	Yes	Yes
Reduce R&D costs	Yes	Yes	Yes	No	Yes	Yes

Accounting and AMT were best understood in the wider context of corporate governance in West German manufacturing firms. As we saw above, owner-managed firms and large quoted companies tended to pursue longer-term strategies for growth rather than short-term profits for shareholders. Like Japanese firms, many West German manufacturing firms forged close relationships with banks, although this was not in itself an explanation for West German industrial strength. An important reason underpinning corporate industrial success in West Germany was their strong science and engineering culture. This manifested itself in the management of technology. Management accounting, on the other hand, occupied a service role by supplying financial information to decision-makers. It was not a service which required radical change in its theoretical content or practical application, according to West German managers.

Conclusion

This article has concentrated on the management of advanced technology in Anglo/ American, Japanese and West German companies. Important themes emerge which relate to industrial policy, corporate governance, management methods and tech- nology strategy in the four countries. Whilst it is unwise to offer general explanations in isolation from the wider institutional and societal context, some tentative conclusions will nevertheless be put forward. The Anglo/American preoccupation with identifying problems with management accounting was not shared in West Germany or Japan. In Anglo/American firms, strategies for AMT translated into mission statements and visions for progress. Here, AMT was seen as a 'strategic device' by many managers, although a closer examination found that few managers actually understood how AMT would achieve strategic or competitive advantage. Anglo/American senior managers preferred a 'hands-off' approach to technology, leaving its implementation and management to engineers and technologists. Manage- ment accounting techniques used in Anglo/American companies tended to concen- trate on investment appraisal and performance measurement. However, the content of investment appraisal documents was seen by non-accountants as 'spurious', particularly by engineers. The key difficulty with investment appraisal was twofold. First, the time-scale for a return on investment was seen as restrictive and unnecessarily short. In the case of CAD, engineers argued that the learning curve must be taken into consideration. Second, investment appraisal tended only to measure financial criteria. Traditional labour-centred and productivity measures were seen as outdated for today's 'knowledge worker' environment. Intellectual work such as software development was seen as an important part of working with new technology. But there were no such measures for assessing quality in software engineering and programming skills.

The recognition in Anglo/American companies of the inappropriateness of traditional management accounting measures, however, had produced the opposite of what one might expect. Rather than abandoning management accounting measures as inadequate, many Anglo/American managers were seeking a solution by applying even greater financial control over technology investments. As we saw in the US case study above, CAD equipment was subject to considerably detailed analysis of estimated drawing and retrieval periods. Whilst this solution undoubtedly provided vast quantitative data on the use of CAD, it failed to incorporate any information regarding the outcome of CAD. In other words, had CAD contributed to new and improved products down the production line? Or would the company be able to design certain products without the use of CAD in today's manufacturing environment?

Placing management accounting at centre stage of our analysis in West German and Japanese companies was difficult simply because it was not seen as central to technology decisions. Japanese firms had survived and prospered in spite of their management accounting. This was also the case in West German firms which, like the Japanese, shared a long-term view of AMT strategy and company expansion. In Japanese companies, we saw that traditional management accounting measures were used, such as payback and, to a lesser extent, DCF. Japanese managers were aware that these measures were not wholly adequate but they saw strategic returns from AMT in a wider organisational context. For example, internal training and skills development were seen as key to achieving positive results from AMT. Measures such as market share and improved product quality were also important. This sometimes meant that shareholder wishes were given a low priority.

Similarly, in West German companies, long-term corporate development was secured by major shareholder interests where short-term profit was not favoured above long-term capital investment. In turn, management accounting was described as a 'service function' in West German firms. As with Japanese firms, investment in AMT could not easily be justified purely on cost terms. High-risk forms of capital investment were often described as 'strategic'. This also occurred in Anglo/American companies. However, strategy for AMT in Japan and West Germany was largely about implementation, not intention. One of the problems in British companies was that strategic intentions rarely included detailed plans about managing technology. Here, management accounting could arguably play a vital role in the ongoing monitoring of technology performance. The present tendency, which is to evaluate technology pre-implementation (investment appraisal) and at the end of its estimated life (usually after three years), leaves a wide gap in our knowledge of how it was managed during its life-cycle. In this context, two firms buying the same technology may not achieve the same benefits even though their investment criteria may be similar. Information is therefore needed throughout the technology life-cycle. This is particularly the case in software development where skill levels between programmers and project managers vary considerably between departments and companies.

In conclusion, it is contended that in spite of similar management perceptions about the benefits of AMT in the four countries, wide differences occurred in the corporate governance structures of manufacturing firms. Anglo/American firms tended to pursue short-term gains from technology and this was determined by the annual financial reporting structure. Long-term capital investment was rarely pursued. Japanese firms, on the other hand, adopted Western-style accounting techniques and, like their global rivals, actively pursued rationalisation policies. Where they differed from their rivals was in their perception of strategic planning for AMT. A more appropriate term is perhaps 'strategic implementation'. West German firms also shared common goals through AMT such as headcount reduction, productivity enhancement and improved quality. But these firms differed from their Anglo/American rivals in two important areas, one concerning their shareholding arrangements and the other, their emphasis upon the practical exploitation of engineering and technical knowledge. Like Japanese firms, technical expertise in West German companies was not viewed as a low-grade function but, instead, a major contributory factor in gaining competitive advantage. In this context, it is argued that lessons to be learned by Anglo/American companies on sustaining competitive advantage would be better served by concentrating on the wider institutional and societal features of West German and Japanese industry. This is because the narrow focus on management accounting theory and practice simply distorts our understanding of the key competitive strengths and weaknesses of industrial enterprises.

References

Currie, W.L. and J. Seddon (1992) 'Managing AMT in a JIT environment in the UK and Japan', *British Journal of Management*, September, pp. 123–36.

Dugdale, D. and T.C. Jones (1991) 'Discordant voices: accounting views of investment appraisal', *Management Accounting*, November, pp. 54–9.

Edwards, J. and K. Filcher (1994) *Banks, Finance and Investment in Germany*, Cambridge: Cambridge University Press.

Financial Times (1991) 'Survey on computerised manufacturing', 14 May.

Hiromoto, T. (1988) 'Another hidden edge: Japanese management accounting', *Harvard Business Review*, July/August.

Hori, S. (1994) 'Fixing Japan's white collar economy: a personal view', *Harvard Business Review*, November/December, pp. 157–72.

Jones, T.C., W.L. Currie and D. Dugdale (1993) 'Accounting and technology in Britain and Japan: learning from field research', *Management Accounting Research*, no. 4, pp. 109–37.

Kaplan, R. (ed.) (1990) *Measures for Manufacturing Excellence*, Boston, Mass.: Harvard Business School.

Kharbanda, O. and E. Stallworthy (1991) 'Let's learn from Japan', *Management Accounting*, vol. 69, no. 3, pp. 26–33.

Mintzberg, H. and A. McHugh (1985) 'Strategy formation in an adhocracy', *Administrative Science Quarterly*, 30, pp. 160–97.

Strange, N. (1991) 'Management accounting and competitive advantage: a comparison of British and German management accounting', *Management Accounting Research Conference*, University of Aston, September.

Williams, K., C. Haslam and J. Williams (1991) 'The Western problematic against the Japanese application', *3rd Interdisciplinary Perspectives on Accounting Conference*, Manchester University.

Yoshikawa, T., J. Innes and F. Mitchell (1989) 'Japanese management accounting: a comparative survey', *Management Accounting*, vol. 68, no. 11, pp. 20–3.

CHAPTER SIXTEEN

'Caught in the Act': Public Services Disappearing in the World of 'Accountable' Management?'

Christopher Humphrey and Olov Olson

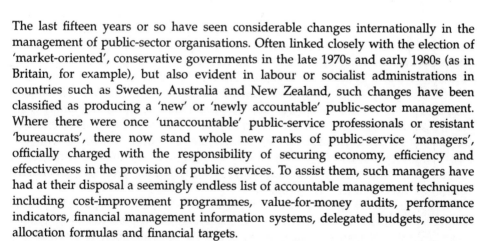

The last fifteen years or so have seen considerable changes internationally in the management of public-sector organisations. Often linked closely with the election of 'market-oriented', conservative governments in the late 1970s and early 1980s (as in Britain, for example), but also evident in labour or socialist administrations in countries such as Sweden, Australia and New Zealand, such changes have been classified as producing a 'new' or 'newly accountable' public-sector management. Where there were once 'unaccountable' public-service professionals or resistant 'bureaucrats', there now stand whole new ranks of public-service 'managers', officially charged with the responsibility of securing economy, efficiency and effectiveness in the provision of public services. To assist them, such managers have had at their disposal a seemingly endless list of accountable management techniques including cost-improvement programmes, value-for-money audits, performance indicators, financial management information systems, delegated budgets, resource allocation formulas and financial targets.

Implicit in the promotion of accountable management techniques in public-sector organisations is a sense of incredulity that such organisations could have survived for so long without formal systems of managerial and financial control. As Plowden (1985) noted, it must be right

> to identify the tasks to be done and the resources used in carrying out each of the multifarious activities of government to ensure that someone is clearly responsible at each level for managing these resources, and to devise information systems that provide
> people at each level – including ministers – with accurate information about activities

and resources down the line of command. The development of the techniques of management, in this sense, in the civil service (and elsewhere in the public sector) is long overdue. (p. 394)

Twenty-five years ago, talk of the management of financial resources and the need for accounts would most likely have conjured up the boring images so often associated with accountancy – perhaps most classically illustrated in Monty Python's lion-tamer sketch.[1] Such images, though, are long gone. Nowadays, one does not have to look too far to find mention of the enabling, decentralising capacities of delegated budgets or financial management information systems. Further, major accounting firms, far from being held up to ridicule á la Monty Python, have been some of the most significant recruiters of university graduates in the 1980s. In public-sector financial management, they have been classified on varying occasions as the 'expert explorers', as catalysts for change – not just by fellow accountants, but even by senior public-service officials:

> what the likes of Price Waterhouse and Coopers and Lybrand have, is a conceptual model which can be applied in a practical way. What they can do is approach our issues from a broader background than just social services, and that's helpful; they can act as a catalyst for the development of thinking within our organization. (*Social Services Insight*, 10 October 1990)

That said, it would be wrong to suggest that recent developments have gone uncontested. Indeed, there exists a considerable body of opinion that has called into question the role and functioning of accounting practices and the accounting profession in general (for an introduction, see Puxty, 1993). In the public sector, such perspectives have been used to question the restrictive, old-fashioned assumptions of accountable management reforms concerning organisational behaviour and to raise concern about the way in which the narrow pursuit of efficiency has undermined long-held public-service values (see Broadbent and Guthrie, 1992; Humphrey *et al.*, 1993). Such concerns, however, do not yet appear to have had any marked effect on the promotion of accountable management systems. Indeed, problems with one initiative seem persistently to be met only by the next 'new' accountable management reform, with some authors concluding that such reforming processes, essentially, have only just begun (see Thomson, 1992).

The aim of this chapter is to contribute to such a debate by providing some descriptions of, and critical reflections on, international experiences with public-sector accountable management systems. Particular consideration is given to the international status of such systems and to the range of explanations for their existence. It is apparent from such a review that there are no simple relationships across nations with respect to the pursuit of accountable management. Indeed, there remain a number of contrasting, and at times quite paradoxical, aspects to the reforming processes. The chapter seeks to highlight some of these by paying specific attention to the experiences of public-sector organisations in Britain and Sweden, two countries which in the 1980s had governments of quite distinct political perspectives and yet saw considerable resort to notions of accountable management. The chapter concludes by considering the implications for both the practice and research of 'accountably managed' public-sector organisations.

An International Perspective on Accountable Management

In conducting a national, let alone international, study of the changing nature of public-sector management systems, problems of definition arise. A variety of phrases such as 'accountable management', '"new" public management' and 'managerialism' have been used as a means of labelling reforms pursued to varying degrees of interest over the last fifteen years or so. For purposes of clarity and consistency, we have chosen to utilise the term 'accountable management' throughout this chapter. This phrase closely reflects our principal concern with management accounting issues (such as the setting of plans and objectives, specification of performance targets, calculations of costs, the determination of budgets and the provision of information on resource usage for the purposes of management decision-making). It also usefully captures the sense of duality present in many accounting-based public-sector reforms, i.e. the way they are concerned both with management at the local level and with giving an account of organisational performance to senior management or government authorities.

In one of the few genuinely comparative studies of cross-national experiences with accountable management reforms, Hood (1994) identified two general aims:

1. The desire to lessen or eliminate differences between modes of private and public-sector organisation.
2. The intention of exerting more control over the actions of public-service professionals.

Within these two aims he categorised international accountable management reforms as having had up to seven key dimensions. Relating to the first aim, such systems had sought a greater disaggregation of public-sector organisations (establishing smaller, more distinct, financially responsible corporate units), a stronger competitive ethos, a greater use of private-sector management techniques and a heavier emphasis on the efficiency of resource usage. With respect to the second aim, accountable management reforms had sought more active control and 'hands-on' management by senior staff, a clearer specification of input–output relationships and a greater use of explicit and measurable performance standards/targets.

In considering the cross-national application of such approaches to public management in countries belonging to the Organisation for Co-operation and Economic Development (OECD), Hood identified marked differences. Sweden, Canada, New Zealand, Australia and Britain were nations highly active in the pursuit of accountable management, while Germany, Japan, Switzerland (three of the OECD's 'showcase' economies), Greece and Spain had done comparatively little in respect of adopting accountable management, or what Hood referred to as 'new' management principles. Countries such as Denmark, Finland, Italy, Portugal and the

United States of America were classified as falling in a middle range of activity with respect to accountable management.

Hood explored a number of conventional explanations of public-sector reform including the views that accountable management was principally an Anglo-American (deriving from the Thatcher–Reagan era of the 1980s) or a broader 'English-speaking' national phenomenon, or was essentially related to matters of party politics, government size or economic performance. However, all of these were found to be difficult to sustain given the observed form of cross-national variations. For instance, the extensive promotion of accountable management reforms by Sweden's Social Democratic governments contradicted claims that the reforms were an essentially 'English-speaking' phenomenon or were closely associated with right-wing governing parties.

Such observations left Hood to hypothesise that more sophisticated explanations were needed for the promotion (or lack of promotion) of accountable management systems. He introduced the notion of initial endowment, suggesting that the promotion of such reforms was dependent on both motive and opportunity. From this perspective, accountable management systems could be expected to have been promoted most actively in those nations facing fiscal stress or 'outsize' governments (where there was potentially much to be gained from the reforms in terms of resource savings) and where there existed an integrated public sector offering politicians a direct opportunity to influence/secure the desired organisational change. Reflecting on such ideas, Hood also suggested that accountable management reforms had been pursued in 'different political circumstances for diametrically different reasons and with quite different effects'. Thus, in some countries there was the feeling that such reforms had been implemented to fend off the 'new right' agenda whereas in others they had been seen as the first step in realising such an agenda.

Hood's study was motivated essentially by what he saw as an inappropriate labelling of accountable management as a global phenomenon (for other international reviews, see Gray *et al.*, 1992; Broadbent and Guthrie, 1992). While his analysis makes clear the degree of cross-national discrepancy in its application, some of his reflections above are, nevertheless, suggestive of a potential narrowing in acceptable modes of administration and activity in public-sector organisations – an impression reinforced recently by the way in which some countries not traditionally noted for their promotion of accountable management techniques, such as Germany (see *The Financial Times*, 2 July 1993, p. 17), have resorted to such reforms. When coupled with the lack of simple, all-encompassing explanations for international responses to accountable management and the continuing imbalance between the scale of expenditure being incurred by some national governments in the pursuit of such management[2] and understandings of the operation of such systems in practice, it serves to emphasise the need for more detailed comparative analyses of national experiences. The remainder of this chapter seeks to provide such an analysis through its consideration of the promotion of accountable management reforms in Britain and Sweden.

The Comparative Development of Accountable Management in Britain and Sweden

Accountable management reforms in the 1960s and 1970s

While terms such as 'accountable management' have come to describe a variety of public-sector management reforms undertaken since the late 1970s, it is important to realise that internationally a concern with the performance of the public sector has not been the sole preserve of governments of the last fifteen years. Indeed, the practice of utilising inverted commas when referring to 'new' public management processes has been one of the methods by which some authors have sought to reflect the way in which such reforms have in many respects repackaged ideas about the administration of public services which were expressed long before the 1980s (see Hood, 1994).

In both Britain and Sweden, the 1960s and 1970s saw a growing interest in managerial technologies such as 'management by objectives', 'cost-benefit analysis' and 'planning, programming and budgetary systems'. Such reforms drew heavily off initiatives in the USA and were seen as offering the possibility of a more (and much-needed) rational and scientific means of planning and organising the provision of public services; of modernising the 'amateurish' way in which resources were currently being administered.

However, the impact of such reforms was highly questionable. In Britain, for instance, many of the recommendations for reform of the civil service proposed by the Fulton committee in the late 1960s either were never implemented or failed to change traditional Whitehall culture. The Policy Analysis and Review (PAR) initiative of the Heath administration of the early 1970s similarly lost momentum when the problems of the 1973 oil crisis assumed political prominence. In Sweden, initial programme budgeting experiments in the 1960s and subsequent reformulations in the 1970s struggled to live up to ambitions. Reviews by the National Audit Bureau (*riksrevisionsverket*) found that they had floundered on the measurement of outputs and the coupling of such outputs with their respective costs of provision (see Premfors, 1991; Czarniawska–Joerges and Jacobsson, 1989). Criticisms were also made of the commitment and interest of national ministries and politicians (see Sandahl, 1992).

Deepening public-sector 'problems' and more accountable management 'solutions': the British experience post-1979

The late 1970s and early 1980s witnessed a considerable extension in efforts devoted to the 'accountable management' of public services. In Britain, relative economic decline and the public-service strikes in the 'winter of discontent' of 1978/79 stimulated a desire not just to control, but also to reduce, public expenditure. The public sector was quite clearly classified as a 'problem'. Statements such as 'public expenditure is at the heart of Britain's economic difficulties' peppered the early years of the first Thatcher administration of 1979/83, being backed up by demands for value for money in the provision of public services. The welfare state was held to have had a morally damaging effect on individual initiative, enterprise and responsibility. Promises were made to reduce the share of public expenditure in national income, to curtail the range of functions being performed by government, while at the same time seeking to impose, nurture and stimulate the business values, attitudes and practices necessary to relaunch Britain as a successful capitalist economy.

In the early years of the first Thatcher administration, direct attempts were made to reduce public-sector expenditure, with the government specifying required levels of savings to be made by local government, health authorities and central government departments, or more directly transferring public-service organisations to the private sector through privatisation processes. A variety of initiatives such as cost-improvement programmes, efficiency scrutinies and value-for-money audits were also promoted with the claimed desire to improve the efficiency and effectiveness of public-service delivery. In practice, however, the overriding concern with levels of financial expenditure ensured that such exercises seldom got beyond narrow-based notions of inputs and cost control. In 1982, in response to criticisms that its public-sector management policies were neglecting issues of service quality, the British government launched what was represented at the time as something akin to a 'grand strategy' in the form of the Financial Management Initiative (FMI). This had the official aim of promoting in each central government department:

> an organisation and system in which managers at all levels have:
> a. a clear view of their objectives and means to assess and, wherever possible, measure outputs or performance in relation to those objectives,
> b. well defined responsibility for making the best use of their resources, including a critical scrutiny of output and value for money and
> c. the information (particularly about costs), training and access to expert advice which they need to exercise their responsibilities effectively.

That success was now to be judged in terms of outputs rather than reduced costs and inputs was suggestive of a more comprehensive approach to resource management. However, the FMI still bore considerable similarities with management-by-objectives initiatives of the 1960s/1970s and showed little indication of the way in which the practical implementation problems of such reforms were to be overcome. Some researchers classified the FMI's view of management as being essentially 'impoverished', relying on conventional management accounting techniques at a time when their use was increasingly being questioned in the private sector (see Hopper, 1986). Such arguments suggested that the FMI confused management with control. Management really starts where control is problematic, where situations are encountered which defy the corpus of available knowledge. It is an interactive process requiring an ability to manage people and not just information systems. As

Earl and Hopwood (1980) noted, 'it is the managers . . . who put the management into Management Information Systems'.

Suggestions that the government remained principally concerned with matters of financial control were provoked by its reforms in local government. Rhodes (1987), for instance, argued that since 1979 central government policy had been dominated by cost-cutting objectives – which resulted in capital and cash limits, the introduction of the block-grant system, the abolition of supplementary rates, the introduction of rate capping (and later the 'poll tax') and the privatisation of local government services. Between 1979 and 1983, for example, there were seven major changes to the system of local authority grant allocations. More recently, central government has come to speak of the 'enabling local authority' and a desire to devolve responsibility to local service providers, but in many respects the reforms implemented have resulted in a considerable tightening of central control, not least through the ever-expanding role of (centrally determined) 'delegated' budgets. Local government expenditure has been significantly restricted, now forming just 13 per cent of gross domestic product (GDP) (and 25 per cent of public spending – or £58bn (in 1991/92) of revenue expenditure in absolute terms). Much of this reduction has been achieved by transferring the responsibility for such expenditure to 'quangos' (quasi-autonomous non-governmental organisations), which now are responsible for nearly a third of all public spending (the *Independent on Sunday*, 22 May 1994, p. 1). It has been estimated that over £24bn of former local authority-controlled services has passed into the hands of such democratically unelected bodies, staffed by central government appointees.

In relation to the British public sector more generally, it is the latter aspects of local authority reform, namely the devolution of financial management responsibilities and the promotion of 'delegated budgets', which have come to characterise reforms in major areas such as the civil service, health, education and the police. In the civil service, the 'Next Steps' initiative was implemented with the official intention of rectifying deficiencies in the FMI and of enhancing central policy-making and securing a greater alignment in the operational and financial responsibilities of civil servants. In the National Health Service, relevant reforms have included the FMI, its successor – the 'Resource Management Initiative', and, in the late 1980s, legislation to establish an 'internal market' for the supply and consumption of health services and to introduce the concept of 'fund-holding' general practitioners. In education, the devolution of financial management has been introduced through the Local Management of Schools (LMS) initiative, while in the Police Service, the Audit Commission, amongst others, has been active in promoting the delegation of resource management responsibilities and a greater usage of budgets and performance indicators at the operational level.

Such reforms reflect the recoding that is taking place in the role and position of the state in Britain, from a 'provider' to a 'regulator' of public (and other) services. Accounting techniques have proved particularly attractive in this respect, because they have offered the possibility of extending spheres of individual discretion and choice, while also helping to ensure that actions are taken in accordance with broader economic and social objectives of government. As Miller and Rose (1991) illustrated with respect to the role of budgets:

> [T]o be in charge of a budget is to have the freedom to spend as one sees fit, whilst remaining the point at which responsibility resides in cases of deficits or surpluses. Not only do budgets individualise, they also tie individuals into networks of calculation. The individual endowed with a budget ... is not an isolated individual, but is linked to centres of calculation. Firmly located within the networks of figures and accounts that flow back and forth from the centres to the budget holder, the individual is made calculable and made to calculate. Professional discretion is shackled not by attempts to claim jurisdiction over the content of expert judgement, but by encircling expert judgement within the discourse of budgetary calculation. (p. 133)

Twenty years ago, consideration of the work of a surgeon would have routinely spoken of their professional skill in saving lives (often with such ability generally being taken on faith). Now, with trust in public-service professionals long undermined (at least from the standpoint of successive Conservative governments), their actions have been seen to require a greater harnessing. No longer are standards of performance presumed – their cost-effectiveness or value for money must be shown to have been maintained, and hopefully improved. In principle, devices such as delegated budgets and performance indicators offer central authorities the opportunity of securing such goals without having actively to intervene. As Miller and Rose put it, budget-holders are 'not being set free, but are "made to be free", and in a very particular way and in relation to quite specific criteria' (p. 34). General practitioners are free to provide the best services for their patients but have to do it within the constraints of their budgets and the availability and price of medical services on the internal market. Teachers consider the needs of their students (or 'customers') with an awareness of their school's cost-per-pupil ratio or its position in league tables of examination results, while the police can pursue innovative policing strategies knowing that lengthy criminal investigation and surveillance exercises are not costless. Even the 'Bill', it might be said, has a price to pay.[3]

For some, the possibility of greater control over strategic operations and their funding arrangements through accountable management reforms has proved attractive, as evidenced most notably by the growing number of schools, hospitals and general practitioners choosing to 'opt-out' of the previously unavoidable local authority control. Where resistance has been encountered, this has often been due to perceptions of the reforms as being an extension of central control and likely to lead to challenges to the existing culture and its – valued – modes of practice. In considering the different responses to accountable management reforms, recognition should also be given to the growth in management that has taken place over the last twenty to thirty years in many public-sector organisations. For instance, in relation to the Probation Service, it was not unusual for the chief probation officer of an area service to carry a substantial client case-load. Such practices are unheard of today. Accountable management reforms have clearly contributed to such changes, both offering 'new' management technologies to existing managers and generating whole new intermediary ranks of managers, auditors and inspectors whose very jobs depend on the utilisation of such techniques.[4] Some writers have even gone so far as to refer to managerialistic tendencies in the public sector as the 'acid' being used 'to dissolve the chains of welfarism', stressing that the most valued, and trusted, skills in the public sector are now those of managing budgets and understanding management information systems (e.g. see Cochrane, 1992, pp. 12–13).

Replacing public-service 'solutions' with the 'promises' of accountable management: The Swedish experience in the 1980s and 1990s

In Sweden, the early 1980s also saw a marked increase in impetus with respect to reforming public-sector management systems. Premfors (1991) emphasised the scale of the shift from the earlier reforms of the 1960s and 1970s, concluding that in 1982 Sweden went from pursuing public-sector reform 'as an ad hoc activity' to viewing such reform as 'public policy' (p. 87). To appreciate the similarities and differences in the approach taken in Sweden, it is first necessary to examine more general views with respect to the welfare state and the role of public services.

Attitudes towards the welfare state in Sweden have for a long time stood in some contrast to the position in Britain, and indeed in a host of other Western nations. As Rothstein (1993) noted, the Swedish Social Democratic Party regarded the creation of the welfare state as their greatest achievement and political asset, pointing out that a commitment to it still helped them to win two elections in the 1980s. In Sweden public-sector expenditure amounts to around 70 per cent of GDP, the highest proportion of any country in the world (*The Financial Times*, 21 December 1993, p. III; 25 January 1994, p. 21). The average for OECD countries is about 51 per cent (with the share in Britain being 45 per cent). Governmental consumption expenditure is about twice as much per capita than in Britain (although Britain spends about three times more in terms of total government consumption expenditure). The Swedish approach to the welfare state has generally been classified as following an institutional model as distinct from a residual model (see Rothstein, 1993). The emphasis in an institutional welfare state is on high rates of taxation, universal (and high) welfare benefits (such as child allowances, day care and part-time pensions) and no means testing to determine eligibility to receive state benefits. Britain has tended, with its growing reliance on privatisation and the application of market-based principles in the public sector, towards the other extreme of a residual welfare state (providing a limited range of benefits, with means testing and service charges), although it has not proved a country which has been easy to place in such a typology.

Despite such contrasting positions, the last two decades have seen a growing expression of concern in Sweden with the welfare state. In part, such concern came from those on the political left who argued for more redistributive policies and more flexibility and direct democracy in the functioning of public services. One of the criticisms of the Social Democratic Party when it lost power in the mid-1970s had been that it was too closely associated with a rigid, bureaucratic system of public-service provision. Later, challenges to the Swedish welfare model came from the political right, as concern began to be expressed as to the escalating nature of the country's budget deficits and as public expenditure began to assume a more problematic status (see Premfors, 1991).

When returned to power in 1982, the Social Democrats made explicit attempts to respond to such challenges, establishing a new Ministry for Public Administration to secure change. With the scope for tax increases limited, improvements and advancements in the provision of public services were seen to reside not in expenditure increases but in the restructuring of public-service organisations and in the better management of existing resources.

The government's programme for public-sector renewal announced in 1985 spoke of four key objectives: wider democracy and a restoration of commitment to local affairs; greater freedom of choice for individual citizens; increased efficiency and improved quality; and reduced bureaucracy and improved services. Initiatives were launched to secure greater decentralisation in, and broader community participation in decisions concerning the provision of central government services. Budgeting systems in central government agencies were reformed. A new three-year budgeting cycle was piloted from 1986 and then fully implemented in all agencies in 1989. This required agencies to provide evaluation reports of their performance in relation to stated plans and objectives but allowed them to carry over surplus funds from one year to the next. It also sought to secure a closer link between operational and financial responsibilities (see Sandahl, 1992; Fudge and Gustafsson, 1989).

Comparisons of the British and Swedish reforms have traditionally spoken of the differing spirit underlying them, with the view being that appeals to decentralisation and flexibility in Sweden were genuine and not merely rhetorical as they have often been claimed to be in Britain. For instance, Fudge and Gustafsson classified the Swedish approach as being a 'social responsibility' model of public-service management compared to the British government's promotion of 'market-led models':

> It is different from 'market-led' private sector models in its concern for economic efficiency; for responsiveness to need as well as demand; for both outputs and outcomes; for humanistic values in organisations; and prefiguring an improved social reality in terms of how organisations manage their affairs. (pp. 33–4).

In contrast to Britain, the reforming desire has generally not been labelled by researchers as seeking to dismantle (or 'roll back') the welfare state or to have been as dogmatic in its preference for private-sector service provision/modes of organisation and as strong in its pursuit of central control of public resources. As Rothstein (1993, p. 495) aptly illustrated, the Social Democratic governments of the 1980s managed to eliminate a huge inherited budget deficit at the same time as expanding some of their most popular welfare reforms.[5] Further, Rothstein suggested that an over-reliance on 'fashionable management ideology' and 'quick-fix management recipes' on the part of Bo Holmberg, the first head of the Ministry for Public Administration, were key reasons behind his removal from office in 1988.

The image of a less centrally driven approach to reform in Sweden than in Britain is well illustrated through the case of Swedish local government (or municipalities).

At 70 per cent of total government expenditure, local government expenditure represents a far greater proportion of public expenditure than in Britain.[6] Swedish municipalities also retain considerable revenue-raising powers, with their proportional local income tax raising about 40 per cent of their overall resources. Although a number of local government-provided services in the areas of health and education are directly mandated by central government, the long tradition of self-regulated municipal government in Sweden seems to have made it less vulnerable to central government intervention than in Britain. Indeed, in terms of accountable management reforms, these have tended to be promoted either by individual local governments or through their representative body, the Federation of Municipalities. Historically, the Swedish central government has only sought to influence such processes of reform through what can best be described as indirect pressure, with the clear initiative remaining at the local level as individual municipalities experimented (with the help of auditors or academic accountants) with ideas extracted from the Swedish private sector or from international public- or private-sector developments. In this respect, it has even been suggested that discussions and experiments with budgetary systems in the municipalities did much to place issues of accounting and accountable management more prominently in the minds of central government officials (see Bergevärn and Olson, 1989).

In attempting to explore what precisely has been done differently in Sweden and the varying strategies utilised to secure change, one is confronted with a significant difficulty in that there are relatively few studies of the practical application and achievements of Swedish accountable management reforms. Further, the studies that exist and which go beyond official proclamations of reforms in Sweden tend to reflect a rather less rationalistic and constructive picture than that promised (Brunsson and Olsen, 1993). Budgeting processes emerge very much as 'game-playing' scenarios in which the budget tends to serve principally as an external legitimating function for the organisation and has little impact on underlying operational activities. Indeed, it has been argued that budgetary reform, in itself, has had a distinctive ideological motivation – to reflect ambition and the desire for change on the part of an organisation without necessarily requiring the organisation to go through all the trauma associated with the practice of 'real' change (see Czarniawska-Joerges and Jacobsson, 1989). The shape and strength of competing political factions in Sweden have also been singled out as reducing the likelihood of dramatic change in public-service organisation and significance (for a discussion, see Premfors, 1991).

Nevertheless, there are growing indications that considerable shifts have taken place in the Swedish approach to the public sector in recent years. Several writers have spoken of the increasing emphasis on issues of financial efficiency, on the way in which moves towards decentralisation and the devolution of responsibility, without the provision of additional resources, have forced local government to make some very hard choices with respect to services provided (e.g. see Sainsbury, 1991). Clear parallels can be seen with the British situation in the work of Elander and Montin (1990) when commenting on the growing use of delegated budgets: 'the message from central to local government may be summarised like this: you are freer than before to do as you want but within a narrower financial framework' (p. 177). Further, in 1991, the Swedish Social Democratic Party was defeated at the polls (in what has been described as the 'earthquake election'). This defeat and the establishment of a right-of-centre coalition government (led by the 'Moderate' Party and its leader, Carl Bildt), whilst not producing a total change in governmental outlook towards the public sector, has influenced perspectives on welfare and the standing of public services, even amongst Social Democrats. As Carl Bildt has noted of them, 'they are the ones who are adjusting in our direction. They now talk of the market economy in a way they would not have dared a couple of years ago' (*The Financial Times*, 21 December 1993, p. V).[7] The pressure for change in Sweden is also increasingly coming from international sources, through bodies such as the OECD who continue to highlight the need for Sweden to take tougher action with respect to the reform of welfare policies and the treatment of budget deficits (see *The Financial Times*, 17 February 1994).[8] Privatisation of state-owned services has also begun to figure much more prominently on the political agenda. In the last few years, some large enterprises in the defence and pharmaceutical industries have been privatised and additional privatisations are planned in the state banking sector.

Olson and Rombach (1993), more recently, reflected on issues of public-sector reform, noting that notions of 'economy, efficiency and effectiveness' and of 'business-likeness' were increasingly influencing discourses with respect to local government, making ideas of the welfare state and welfare politics less important. A recent significant development through the promotion of notions of 'business-likeness' has been the adoption by municipalities of accrual-based systems of financial reporting, which sees them producing consolidated financial statements in a fashion virtually identical to the practices of Swedish private-sector companies.[9] Further, financial accounting systems are starting to be utilised internally as budgeting systems (with associated divisional responsibility centres), with the intention of establishing clearer relations between a municipality's central administration and its individual divisional units or companies. Such systems are bringing with them a new language, in which more traditional notions of budgetary politics and issues of equity/fairness have been replaced by talk of divisional contributions and profits and measures of input-oriented financial performance measures. According to Olson and Rombach (1993), such a language is increasingly serving to legitimate ideas concerning the privatisation of public services and the restructuring of public organisations into units of 'buyers' and 'sellers', with developments in the British National Health Service being highlighted as useful practical models to study.

Some Critical Reflections on the Continuing Resort to Accountable Management

It costs £326.10 for only 210 pages but there is no better account of the standards of public life which prevail in the Age of Avarice. It is the Commons' Public Accounts committee report on the Wessex Regional Health Authority computer scandal, during which in the name of Thatcherite thrift, at least £320 million of NHS money was poured down the drain. (P. Foot, the *Guardian*, 20 December 1993, p. 18)

Most people spend their waking hours learning the new language of incentives, cost-effectiveness, quality audits, performance indicators and the rest of the managerial newspeak, in which the crude calculus of market forces is covered over by the thin fig-leaf of systems analysis mumbo-jumbo and quack psychology. Ways of thinking, formulating strategies and defining objectives which reflect the actual practices they are engaged in have become 'lost languages', and a whole new form of institutional non-speak has been born. One institution of higher education recently, discussing the lack of adequate planning for new courses, expressed this problem as a failure 'to think with any clarity about the nature and delivery of our product portfolio'. It is just over a decade since these were referred to as 'courses' and the customers for whom they are being designed 'students' and the activity 'education'. And not a shot has yet been fired . . . (Hall, 1991, p. 14)

Whilst it may not yet be appropriate to label accountable management as a global phenomenon, its (increasingly similar) application in two countries with traditionally quite different political viewpoints on the welfare state, coupled with a growing prominence of such ideas in discussions internationally about public-sector reform, suggests that it would still be prudent to 'watch this space'. Indeed, with some historically quite vociferous opponents of accountable management (such as the British Medical Association) choosing no longer officially to oppose its utilisation, and with countries not previously noted for their promotion of accountable management beginning to develop such reforms, it could be suggested that the range of accepted modes of public-service organisation and control is noticeably narrow-ing.

Such a status for accountable management, however, is particularly intriguing, not least because the evidence that exists of its practical application is not overly convincing. The last two decades are littered with 'unintended consequences' of accountable management reforms; of examples of performance indicators being manipulated, of 'effectiveness' and quality-of-service audits focusing only on matters of costs and inputs; of 'rational' and 'objective' resource allocation models being moulded to support a desired organisational or political outcome; and of financial management information systems projects struggling to get beyond the prototype stage. One is frequently reminded of Wildavsky's (1978) observation with respect to a management-by-objectives (MBO) initiative in an American public-service organ-isation. When administrators were asked what they would recommend as improve-ments beyond MBO, they mentioned things such as management accountability, better teamwork, clearer goals and priorities and the development of management information systems – the very things that MBO was supposed to accomplish in the first place! Likewise, one can still see today accountable management initiatives struggling to relate indicators of service quality to those of the cost of service provision – the same issue that planning, programming, budgeting systems (PPBS) failed to solve three decades earlier.

Wildavsky asked despairingly, 'Why (why, why, WHY) idealize a system like PPBS that causes many more mistakes than it can correct?' (p. 83). His questioning has a continuing applicability with regard to the accountable management philosophy and technologies of today. In many ways it can be argued that the benefits of accountable management have been, and continue to be, presumed. Attempts are often made to talk up the reforms, with reviews of reforms often looking like an assessment of what some people would like to happen (or like to believe has happened). Further, no matter how many problems are experienced in practice with accountable management, the belief is maintained that such problems will disappear in time; that the promised 'glorious tomorrow' will arrive once the initial teething problems of implementation have been surmounted. And for each individual sceptic, there remain a whole lot more accountants, auditors, inspectors, management consultants, academics and public-sector managers who will tell you to be patient and to dream only of the future. As Humphrey *et al.* (1993) commented:

> Difficulties or failures can give rise to an even greater commitment to the initial aspiration. Teething troubles become the refrain of the reformer. In time it is held that collected information will become more reliable, staff resistance will be reduced, management will handle their planning tasks better, quality of service measures will be developed, resources will be allocated more accurately in relation to need, and a better value for money service will be provided. One effect of this belief is that it tends to stifle discussion on alternative processes of change. A fundamental questioning of the operation and impact of accountable management initiatives is labelled as premature and unnecessarily critical. (p. 21)

It has been argued that implementation problems can give strength to calculative technologies, enabling consultants and advisers to supplant the failings of one technology with the offer of a new and 'better' one. Likewise, Czarniawska-Joerges and Jacobsson (1989, p. 37), writing in the Swedish context, commented that in a country where gradual progress is the expectation and where confrontation is avoided, reform has served as an ideological carrier enabling those implementing (failed) budgetary reforms to promise that changes are at hand, and to claim that the future under budgetary control will be better.

The question begged by such analyses is 'when does a teething trouble become a fundamental problem?' – two years, five years, ten years ... surely not fifteen or even thirty years? If teething troubles is the undeniably correct diagnosis, why hasn't it prevented one public-sector organisation from copying the mistakes and 'teething troubles' of others? Why does there continue to be little learning across organisations, with the British Police Service, for instance, struggling with the same issues and methods which the British Health Service had struggled with five years earlier? Why has there been little learning by individual nations from the experiences of other countries? Further, why are the reforms so often centred around techniques and approaches to management which have been long rejected in the private sector as overly mechanistic and out-of-date (see Hopper, 1986)?

The continuing application of accountable management technologies in the public sector has to be seen alongside the growth in managerial ranks in public-sector organisations. However, the current reliance on, and belief in, management itself appears similarly paradoxical when consideration is given to the general nature of the management task. Deetz (1992), for instance, highlighted the questionable status of the management function:

> Managers . . . seek places to display control (even where control is not needed), and yet use their skills to cover up real problems and avoid upsets and conflicts. They spend the majority of their time praising each other, discussing the difficulties of their jobs, making endless agenda lists, inventing elaborate strategies, and trying to decide what to do, and yet they communicate in ways that inhibit resolution of key problems and they rarely say what they mean. . . . Such a routine of 'skilled incompetence' becomes systematic and creates the chaos that skilled managers appear needed to control. Created problems self-referenced in the system are far easier to manage than the intrusion of the outside environment. (p. 229)

From a different perspective, Whitley (1989) stressed that the knowledge base of managerial skills is 'less standardized, formal and general than that of medical and engineering skills' (p. 216), suggesting that the effect of recent accountable management reforms has been to put faith in something as intangible as, if not more so than, the expertise of public-service professionals. It could also be argued that the most appropriate forms of public-service management are those which encourage the self-management of work by public-service professionals – yet these are the approaches most vulnerable to the demands of more 'market-related' practices because they do not generate a readily visible management function.

If you retain any scepticism over such questioning of management concepts, a quick visit to your local bookshop can very effectively make the point – if management issues were so clear-cut and well defined you would expect to see one or two key texts on 'how to be a manager'. Today, you will be overwhelmed by the sheer number of texts promising the 'best way to manage' or 'how to be a successful manager'. Alternatively, consideration could be given to Plowden's (1985) observation that it was only as recently as the mid-1970s that British management was the poor relation of European management and yet now public-sector organisations are being required to follow such managerial techniques.[10]

Such questioning is not restricted to the British context. Guillet de Monthoux (1991), for instance, challenged the ever-extending application of managerial concepts in Swedish society (where, he noted, even doctors are being encouraged to train in business administration), commenting that it was surprising to find Sweden referred to as a 'socialist' country when the solutions to so many social problems are being attempted through 'managerial pragmatics' and when only small-scale special schooling is provided for prospective state and local government officials (with programmes of public administration heavily outnumbered by those of business).[11] Wærnes (1993) expressed a similar degree of scepticism:

> Today all agencies speak in terms of products and productivity, economic efficiency, service, operational markets, competition and marketing. Government agencies have

become preoccupied with learning new means of presentation and packaging, new terms, a new administrative style – no matter how little significance this may have for actual operations. (p. 142)

Concerns also exist with respect to the forms of performance measurement and systems of auditing being promoted in the name of accountable management. For example, the adoption by Swedish local authorities of external and internal reporting systems based on accruals accounting (required in British local authorities, from April 1994) sits uncomfortably with concerns over the world-wide manipulation of accruals accounting in the private sector and the rise of what is publicly known as 'creative accounting'. Although it is acknowledged that having accounting systems which mimic international private-sector organisations can provide a strong degree of external legitimacy, it is also feared that the adoption of such practices could in future limit the scope of functions performed by local authorities. For instance, if business magazines in Sweden are assessing the performance of local authorities in much the same way as for private-sector multinational companies (as has happened recently in the case of Gothenburg City Council), how long will it be before pressures for short-term results (which have for so long hindered long-term investment in the private sector) prevent local authorities from embarking on major, and much-needed, long-term public investment projects?

Value-for-money (VFM) audits, conducted most prominently in Britain by the Audit Commission, the National Audit Office and associated public-sector inspectorates and in Sweden by the National Audit Bureau, often make headline news in the general media (most often with respect to savings or improvements that could be achieved through organisational reform). However, VFM audits have seldom moved beyond issues of inputs into areas of service quality and effectiveness, even though persistently promising this. Little is known about the technology itself, with recent studies having started to raise questions about the construction of VFM audits and the independence of evidence-collection procedures (see Humphrey et al., 1993). More generally, the positive promotion of VFM auditing as a managerial and evaluatory technique in the public sector contrasts with concurrent concerns in the private sector over the scope and capacity of auditing and the existence of 'audit expectations gaps' (see Power, 1994).

Raising contrasts between the pursuit of accountable management and what is being achieved in the process ultimately goes very much to the heart of issues of democracy and the responsibility of government agencies to the public they are presumed to serve. Accountable management reforms have been promoted on the need for the public sector to be more accountable to those who receive, pay for or monitor public services; to provide services in a more effective, efficient and publicly responsible fashion. Yet, paradoxically, in Britain, the accountable management era is increasingly suggestive of the label of 'unaccountable management' as reference is made to a 'crisis of accountability' or a 'democratic deficit' (see the *Guardian*, 19 November 1993, pp. 18–19). In recent months much attention has been given to the increasingly fragmented nature of the public sector and the growing role of 'quangos' in processes of public regulation and service provision. The Thatcher administrations of the 1980s had stressed strongly the need to cut back on waste in government and to reduce the number of such 'quangos' in making government practices more open and transparent. Officially, it is stated that the last four Conservative administrations have reduced the numbers of such bodies – from 2,167 in 1979 to 1,444 in 1994 (see the *Guardian*, 28 January 1994, p. 1). However, they have also presided over a massive increase in the power and expenditure levels of such bodies and it has been claimed that some 73,000 individual appointments for the governing boards of 'quangos' now rest directly in the hands (and patronage) of central government ministers (see the *Independent on Sunday*, 22 May 1994, p. 9).[12] As John Stewart, professor of local government at Birmingham University, pointed out (see the *Independent on Sunday*, 28 March 1993, p. 19):

> What is new is that quango's staffed by people with a pro-Government bias now have power in the crucial areas of public life. The rules that govern local government on open meetings, the publication of information, and the declaration of members' interests are simply not there in most cases. Britain is increasingly governed locally by Westminster appointees, who can in no sense be regarded as locally accountable. Indeed, the public does not know who these people are. It is government by the unknown and the unknowable.

Such concerns have been heightened by some very critical reports on corruption and waste in government. For example, in January 1994, a damning report by the Public Accounts Committee (which has an important oversight function with respect to public expenditure issues) cited twenty-one separate cases where significant amounts of public money had been wasted. The report summed up the position by stressing that 'these failings represent a departure from the standards of public conduct which have mainly been established in the past 140 years'. The creation of executive agencies, the growth in contracting-out, the delegation of responsibilities to local offices and the encouragement of a more entrepreneurial approach by managers were all blamed for the rising tide of financial scandals (see *The Financial Times*, 5–6 February 1994, p. 7).

The Need for Alternatives to and Alternative Approaches Towards Accountable Management

Over the last few years, Prudential Insurance PLC have run an advertising campaign emphasising the way in which it can help people secure their expectations and ambitions in life. The catchphrase of the campaign has been 'I want to be . . .' and has seen, amongst others, young children and newly married couples stating that they 'want to be' a footballer, a dancer, parents, house owners, or even just 'happy'. So far, no one has admitted to wanting to be 'inefficient' or 'ineffective', or not to give 'value for money' and clearly no one is likely to express such a wish. After all, these days, how can one argue against being efficient and effective? But as Hopwood (1979) has pointed out, 'there is no such thing as effectiveness per se':

> Concepts of corporate effectiveness are socially constructed, their meanings and roles stemming from the articulation of particular social concerns, interests and demands and the specific contexts in which the concepts operate. And, as such interests and contexts vary and change over time, so do the prevailing notions of effectiveness.

Such comments have a particular appropriateness to accountable management reforms, for what has been achieved by such initiatives in the name of efficiency and effectiveness seldom has sat comfortably with what was officially promised as the likely outcome of reform. The powerful appeal of the language of accountable management, however, has facilitated its continuing application in spite of such practical problems, with one accountable management initiative merely being replaced by the latest in an apparently endless line of like-minded alternatives – from financial management information systems (FMIS) to resource management information systems (RMIS); from efficiency scrutinies to value-for-money audits; from planning, programming and budgeting systems (PPBS) to systems of delegated budgets.[13]

While recognition must be given to the semantic appeal of accountable management, it should also be understood that any such appeal depends heavily on the context in which accountable management reforms have been promoted. Their accord with governmental ideals of a regulatory state, controlling activity at a distance; the growth in the ranks of public-sector managers, inspectors and auditors; and the relative lack of investigation of the impact of accountable management initiatives have all served to maintain the apparent 'naturalness' of a resort to accountable management. In this respect, the utilisation of notions of 'teething troubles' when assessing the application of accountable management reforms has been particularly powerful in helping to maintain the reforming process, labelling any serious questioning as premature and unnecessarily critical.

The continuing pursuit of accountable management is also a reflection of the absence of, or at least the failure to promote, alternative modes of organisation and control. Such failure has been seen by some authors as going beyond issues of management to the very heart of what defines, or distinguishes, a public-service organisation. For instance, Voytek (1991) argued that reactions to moves to privatise public services have taken 'the form of defensive tactics to defeat specific proposals rather than viewing the challenge of privatisation as an opportunity to develop a comprehensive theoretical position justifying the distinctive characteristic of the public sector' (p. 165).

The problems with such a position are readily apparent. Defining public-sector organisations in a residualist mode (as little more than existing to deal with areas that cannot be, or have not been, dealt with adequately by the market system) leaves them highly vulnerable to managerial reforms which, somewhat anomalously, seek to instil quasi-market mechanisms to overcome the problems of past market failure. Likewise, operating in a purely defensive mode tends to leave the reforming agenda to be set by those promoting (accountable management) reform and proffers a potentially ever-diminishing role for public-sector organisations – a point well illustrated by the British government's recently stated desire to define 'essential' and 'non-essential' state activities as a precursor to further privatisation and the contracting-out of government services (see the *Guardian*, 8 April 1993, p. 1).

For some, the possibilities of constructing alternative agendas or justifications for (expanding) public services are limited by a variety of national and international pressures. These include, amongst other things, ageing populations and the rising costs of meeting current and future pension obligations and public health-care provision, the high burden of unemployment benefit payments, the increasingly international preference for lower rates of taxation and the growing demand for specialised private social, health and educational services that has been predicted as per capita incomes continue to expand. It has even been suggested that there may be a limited 'life-cycle' for the welfare state, determined largely by patterns of industrialisation. Further, the increasing international nature and extent of business trade and the rise of multinational corporations have been held to have reduced the scope for governments to pursue public policies which seem out of line with the dictates and interests of free-market capitalism – a pattern reinforced by the collapse of state communism in Eastern Europe, the disillusionment with traditional socialist-style economic planning in China and the Far East and by the continuing attractiveness of business schools as the education and training ground for tomorrow's, and today's, private- and public-sector managers.

Nevertheless, there is a growing number of commentators who maintain that there is considerable scope for action and predict that future government agendas will be considerably different from 'both the pro-market, anti-state emphasis of recent history and the Keynesian and welfare policies of the previous period' (Self, 1993, p. 277). As Cochrane (1993) argued, the future role and significance of budgets and the language of accountancy will not be the result of any automatic or inevitable process, but rather will be the outcome of a rather more open process of 'political infighting over accountability' (p. 48). From such perspectives, it is apparent that there is no hankering for some 'glorious', mythical, pre-1980s era. As Wilding (1992) remarked:

> We are less statist than in the past. We are all much more dubious about bureaucracy as an effective instrument. We are all more sceptical about the skills and disinterestedness of the professions. . . . Supporters of state welfare will never look to collectivist answers with quite the same simple enthusiasm as before – and that is a sea change in opinion with enduring implications. (p. 202)

But it is equally clear that the reforms of the last fifteen years cannot, and need not, be left unchallenged. For example, a number of studies in Britain have highlighted the way in which the Thatcher administrations failed to secure many of their most prominently stated aims such as rolling back the state, reducing public expenditure, improving British economic performance and enhancing citizens' rights (for a summary, see Humphrey *et al.*, 1993). Others have questioned the future effect of an ageing population, arguing that the upward pressure on welfare costs has been exaggerated or have pointed to the fact that there is no statistical basis for the frequent assertion that high welfare expenditure is inimical to economic growth and the general falsehood that private provision of welfare will be more efficient than public provision (see Self, 1993).

Increasingly, such analyses are beginning to broaden the ideological space in which public-sector accountable management reforms can be discussed. Such reflections have incorporated arguments for public-service professionals, as distinct from managers, to seek greater, local control over the focus of accountable management, to reclaim the 'politics of value' for the public services from within notions of 'value for money' and 'to recover accountability from the grip of accounting'. Increasing emphasis is being placed on the need for a greater degree of public scepticism and suspicion about accountable management techniques. For instance, speaking specifically about the (expanding) role of auditing, Power (1994) saw such scepticism as an essential first step in repositioning it as a more local and facilitative practice and one which would enable rather than inhibit public dialogue:

> External forms of audit will need to be more modestly conceived. This will require a broad shift in control philosophy: from long distance, low trust, quantitative, disciplinary and ex-post forms of verification by private experts to local, high trust, qualitative, enabling, real time forms of dialogue with peers. In this way we may eventually be in a position to devote more resources to creating quality rather than just policing it. (p. 49)

Whether such approaches will generate sufficient normative strength and support to dominate ruling depictions of accountable management remains to be seen. However, they do serve as a timely reminder that notions of public-sector control have not always depended on the existence of a dominant, centralistic government body and offer possibilities for breaking out of an apparently unceasing cycle of reform wherein audit or accounting systems 'failure' is met merely with more of the same. Accounting students and researchers can facilitate such processes of change by studying, understanding and exposing the practical operation of accountable management systems, whilst also seeking wherever possible to work with others in the construction of new public-sector agendas. The consequences of accounting practice in the public sector are too important for us to sit back and watch public services as we know them disappear while the reforming process persistently proves capable of attracting the sort of 'gobbledegook' labels received by some recent VFM initiatives in the British Health Service:

> When is a bed not a bed? The National Health Service's answer won it a gobbledegook prize in the annual Plain English awards yesterday. In a circular from the NHS's value-for-money unit a bed is described as 'a device or arrangement that may be used to permit a patient to lie down'. Beds that fail the test are those which are used for 'active intervention such as examination, diagnostic investigation, manipulative treatment, obstetric delivery or transport'. (*The Financial Times*, 7 December 1993, p. 10)

Notes

1. This sketch concerned a banker who wanted to become a lion-tamer. He visited a recruitment agency who conducted a personality profile report on him. This came to the following conclusion about him: 'You are an extremely dull person. Our experts describe you as an appallingly dull fellow, unimaginative, timid, spineless, easily dominated, no sense of humour, tedious company and irrepressibly drab and awful; and whereas in most professions these would be a considerable drawback, in accountancy they are a positive boon.'

2. For example, in Britain, it was estimated that recent changes in the provision of health and community care services would cost £200 million in their first year of operation, while annual governmental expenditure on management consultants has been estimated to be £565 million – see *The Financial Times*, 26 April 1994.

3. In an increasingly infamous investigation in Gloucester, in the Mid-South West of England, police have unearthed numerous bodies buried in houses once lived in by Frederick West and his second wife. When asked how the investigation was proceeding on an evening television news programme, a senior police representative asserted that it was going well but that the budget was going to prove a problem if the investigation continued for much longer.

4. In the last few years, the number of managers in the National Health Service has increased dramatically – from 510 in 1986/87 to 12,420 in 1991/92 (see *The Daily Telegraph*, 1 March 1994, p. 7) – a 24-fold increase in numbers, while administrative staff have increased by 18,000 in the last three years (see the *Guardian*, 17 November 1993). The percentage of NHS funds devoted to administration has risen from 4 per cent in the mid-1980s to 11 per cent in 1993 (see *The Daily Telegraph*, 11 April 1994, p. 9). At the same time, the numbers of nurses working in the Service has, strikingly, decreased by 20,000 (to 379,000).

5. Although some writers have argued that a substantial share of such expenditure savings had been achieved by nothing more than redefinitions of what amounts to government expenditure – see Premfors (1991).

6. Interestingly, given that government expenditure in Britain is approximately three times that in Sweden, this means that central government expenditure in Britain is approximately seven times larger than in Sweden, while British local government expenditure is only 30 per cent higher in absolute terms.

7. That said, it should be recognised that, to date, the coalition has done little to disturb the fundamental principles of universalism and equality of access for all to the welfare state. While there are some vociferous neo-liberals in the Moderate Party, they do not have, as yet, any major policy-making position and, as *The Financial Times* (21 December 1993, p. III) recently concluded, 'any political leader who campaigned to tear down the existing [welfare] system in the name of individual freedom would suffer severe defeat at the polls'.

8. Despite reforming efforts in the 1980s, the Swedish budget deficit, at 13 per cent of GDP, now stands as the largest in the industrialised world according to the OECD – see *The Economist*, 9 October 1993, p. 53.

9. In case the mention of consolidated financial statements in the context of a local authority sounds strange, it should be pointed out that, in Sweden, municipalities have for a long time established companies, foundations and trusts to manage the provision of certain services.

10. Interestingly, recent surveys have suggested that British management is still not well regarded in Europe – even though British managers think they are the best in Europe (see *The Financial Times*, 24 November 1993, p. 1). Further, a report by the Society of Insolvency Practitioners found that of the 1,700 businesses which collapsed in 1992 in Britain, management failure (at 34 per cent) was the largest single cause of insolvency (see *The Daily Telegraph*, 21 April 1993, p. 22).

11. A similar point was made by Self (1993, p. 279) with respect to schools of business and of public administration in English-speaking countries.

12. The report in the *Independent on Sunday* also claimed that the number of quangos – at 5,521 – is far in excess of the position in 1979.

13. One of the British government's latest attempts to raise the profile of the issue of service quality in the public sector, has been the promotion of 'Citizen's Charters'. Their impact, however, has been distinctly questionable with surveys of existing Charters highlighting the vagueness of specified obligations and the lack of independent oversight or monitoring of performance. In instances where the Charters have impacted on performance, the results have often not been those intended. For instance, it has been argued that the promise in the Patient's Charter to reduce waiting times for certain operations from two years to eighteen months has in some cases meant longer waiting times for other operations that used to have short waits (see *The Financial Times*, 14 March 1994, p. 9).

References

Bergevärn, L.E. and O. Olson (1989) 'Reforms and myths – a history of Swedish municipal accounting', *Accounting, Auditing and Accountability Journal*, vol. 2, no. 3, pp. 22–39.

Broadbent, J. and J. Guthrie (1992) 'Changes in the public sector: a review of recent "alternative" accounting research', *Accounting, Auditing and Accountability Journal*, vol. 5, no. 2, pp. 3–31.

Brunsson, N. and J. Olsen (1993) *The Reforming Organization*, London: Routledge.

Cochrane, A. (1992) 'Is there a future for local government?', *Critical Social Policy*, vol. 35, pp. 4–19.

Cochrane, A. (1993) 'From financial control to strategic management: the changing faces of accountability in British local government', *Accounting, Auditing and Accountability Journal*, vol. 6, no. 3, pp. 30–51.

Czarniawska-Joerges, B. and B. Jacobsson (1989) 'Budgeting in a cold climate', *Accounting, Organizations and Society*, vol. 14, no. 12, pp. 29–40.

Deetz, S. (1992) *Democracy in an Age of Corporate Colonization – Developments in Communication and the Politics of Everyday Life*, Albany, NY: State University Press of New York Press.

Earl, M.J. and A.G. Hopwood (1980) From management information to information management', in Lucas, H.C., jun., F.F. Land, T.J. Land and K. Supper (eds.) *The Information Systems Environment*, Amsterdam: North Holland Publishing Company.

Elander, I. and S. Montin (1990) 'Decentralisation and control: central–local government relations in Sweden', *Policy and Politics*, vol. 18, no. 3, pp. 165–80.

Fudge, C. and L. Gustafsson (1989) 'Administrative reform and public management in Sweden and the United Kingdom', *Public Money & Management*, Summer, pp. 29–34.

Gray, A., B. Jenkins and B. Segsworth (eds.) (1992) *Budgeting, Auditing and Evaluation: Functions and integration in seven governments*, London: Transaction Publishers.

Guillet de Monthoux, P. (1991) 'Modernism and the dominating firm – on the managerial mentality of the Swedish model', *Scandinavian Journal of Management Studies*, vol. 7, no. 1, pp. 3–16.

Hall, S. (1991) 'And not a shot fired', *Marxism Today*, December, pp. 10–15.

Hood, C. (1994) 'The "New" public management in the 1980's: variations on a theme', *Accounting, Organizations and Society*, forthcoming.

Hopper, T. (1986) 'Private sector problems posing as public sector solutions', *Public Finance and Accountancy*, 3 October, pp. 11–13.

Hopwood, A.G. (1979) 'Criteria of corporate effectiveness', in Brodie, M. and R. Bennet (eds.) *Managerial Effectiveness*, Oxford: Thames Valley Regional Management Centre.

Humphrey, C., P. Miller and R. Scapens (1993) 'Accountability and accountable management in the UK public sector', *Accounting, Auditing and Accountability Journal*, vol. 6, no. 3, pp. 7–29.

Miller, P. and N. Rose (1991) 'Programming the poor: poverty calculation and expertise', in Lehto, J. (ed.) *Deprivation, Social Welfare and Expertise*, Research Report No. 7, Helsinki: National Agency for Welfare and Health.

Olson, O. and B. Rombach (1993) 'The Treasurer's Department as a buffer organisation', Working Paper, Gothenburg School of Economics, November.

Plowden, W. (1985) 'What prospects for the Civil Service?' *Public Administration*, vol. 63, Winter, pp. 393–414.

Power, M. (1994) *The Audit Explosion*, London: Demos.

Premfors, R. (1991) 'The "Swedish model" and the public sector reform', *West European Politics*, vol. 14, no. 3, pp. 8–30.

Puxty, A. (1993) *The Social and Organizational Context of Management Accounting*, London: Academic Press Ltd.

Rhodes, R.A.W. (1987) 'Mrs Thatcher and local government: intentions and achievements', in Robins, L (ed.) *Political Institutions in Britain*, London: Longmans.

Rothstein, B. (1993) 'The crisis of the Swedish Social Democrats and the future of the universal welfare state', *Governance: An International Journal of Policy and Administration*, vol. 6, no. 4, pp. 492–517.

Sainsbury, D. (1991) 'Swedish social democracy in transition: the party's record in the 1980s and the challenge of the 1990s', *West European Politics*, vol. 14, no. 3, pp. 8–30.

Sandahl, R. (1992) 'Connected or separated? Budgeting, auditing and evaluation in Sweden', in Gray, A., B. Jenkins and B. Segsworth (eds.) *Budgeting, Auditing and Evaluation: Functions and integration in seven governments*, London: Transaction Publishers.

Self, P. (1993) *Government by the Market? The Politics of Public Choice*, Basingstoke: The MacMillan Press Ltd.

Thomson, P. (1992) 'Public sector management in a period of radical change: 1979–1992', *Public Money and Management*, July–September, pp. 33–41.

Voytek, K.P. (1991) 'Privatising government service delivery: theory, evidence and implications', *Environment and Planning C: Government and Policy*, vol. 9, pp. 155–71.

Wærnes, M. (1993) 'Implementation and Institutional Identity', in Brunsson, N. and J. Olson (eds.) *The Reforming Organization*, London: Routeledge, pp.127–42.

Whitley, R. (1989) 'On the nature of managerial tasks and skills: their distinguishing characteristics and organization', *Journal of Management Studies*, vol. 26, no. 3, pp. 209–24.

Wildavsky, A. (1978) 'Policy analysis is what information systems are not', *Accounting, Organizations and Society*, vol. 3, pp. 7–88.

Wilding, P. (1992) 'The British welfare state: Thatcherism's enduring legacy', *Policy and Politics*, vol. 20, no. 3, pp. 201–12.

Index

◆